# Who the hell
## is
# William Loeb?

# Who the hell is William Loeb?

## Kevin Cash

**Amoskeag Press, Inc.**
Manchester, New Hampshire

*To my mother
and to my aunt*

Grateful acknowledgment is made to David Bradley, M.D., for permission to quote from *The Journal of a Johnny-come-lately*, Copyright 1957 by Dartmouth Press, Hanover, N.H.

First edition

First Printing November 1975
Second Printing December 1975
Third Printing December 1975

Library of Congress Cataloging in Publication Data

Cash, Kevin Richard, 1926–
  Who the hell is William Loeb?

  Bibliography: p.
    1. Loeb, William, 1905–     2. Manchester union
leader.  3. Knox, Franklin, 1874–1944.  I. Title.
PN4874.L59C3      070.5'092'4 [B]      75–33630

"Remember, son, whenever you get into a fight with a skunk you're apt to lose all your dignity because you're going to stink even when you win."

—HONORABLE LAURENCE M. PICKETT
(1903–1967)
Mayor of Keene, N.H.
Minority Leader,
N.H. General Court

# Contents

# Author's Note

My reason for writing this book is quite simple: I am a newspaperman and this is a story which should be told.

As a native of Manchester, N.H., and, more particularly, one who began a newspaper career as a copy boy on the *Manchester Union Leader* while it was under prior ownership, I have long been conscious of the notoriety which has become attached to this newspaper, as well as to its present publisher. Myths, legends, fables and exaggerations abound. It is important to know that the *Union Leader* was, at one time, a highly respected journal. The reputation which it has recently earned and the curiosity it now arouses overshadow other finer points, as well as many present and past glories, of both the city and the state.

Research for this book has been as complete as my resources, time, and facilities have allowed. Although I have made no attempt to communicate with William Loeb himself for purposes of this book, my reasons for not doing so should become obvious to the reader.

It would be nearly impossible to acknowledge individually the assistance of all those who have been helpful to me in my research and writing. This in no way diminishes my gratitude to them all.

Exceptional hospitality and cooperation were extended to me at every newspaper and library which I visited, for which I am most grateful. I would like to express my thanks especially to the staffs of the Carpenter Memorial Library in Manchester, the Vermont State Law Library in Montpelier and the Edsel Ford Memorial Library at The Hotchkiss School, Lakeville, Conn.

KEVIN CASH

# Prologue

William Loeb announced on Dec. 12, 1946, in the first of his now-famous Page One signed editorials in the *Manchester, N.H., Union Leader,* that the watchword of his newspapers would be henceforth a quotation from Daniel Webster: "There is nothing so powerful as truth."

These words of Webster have been printed in the *Union Leader* each day since, incorporated into the newspaper's masthead which appears atop Page One, as well as on the editorial page and on the back page. In the columns under the masthead of the *Union Leader* on Oct. 21, 1974, the following editorial was published in all editions of these newspapers for the day. It is quoted in its entirety (the emphasis and error in syntax are as the editorial originally appeared):

### "A Working Newsman AND Publisher

" 'Loeb is not now and to our knowledge never has been a working newsman.'—Excerpt from a Concord Monitor editorial of October 9th.

"The Monitor editor's knowledge is as limited as his interest in gathering facts before he writes!

"Any employe of the Union Leader could have informed him that Publisher Loeb started his newspaper career in 1939 working for Hearst's International News Service ($15 a week), moving on to the old New York World, the Springfield Union, the Springfield Republican and the Paul Block newspapers.

"Incidentally, we have a few harried editors who wish the publisher was somewhat less of a **working** newsman!

"Doesn't the Concord Monitor **EVER** check its facts?"

Yet facts are facts. The facts are:

—William Loeb was never a staff employe of Hearst's International News Service at any salary.

—The "old" *New York World* ceased publication in 1931.

—During the summer of 1929, Loeb, while still a student, contributed certain articles to the *Springfield,* Mass., *Union* and *Republican* concerning the ninth annual session of the Institute of Politics which was held during August of that year at Williams College. He received a "by-line" and was paid "stringer" rates.

—Paul Block, Jr., board chairman of the *Toledo Blade,* says: "I would like to be able to tell you that your subject (Loeb) worked in such and such a place and was dismissed for cheating but, alas, I cannot."

During April, 1975, William Loeb appeared as a guest on the "David Susskind Show" which was telecast by the Public Broadcasting Service and, during an hour-long interview, Loeb said: "The personal life of a man tells you what kind of a man he is."

This book is largely about the personal life of William Loeb, and, as Daniel Webster said: "There is nothing so powerful as truth."

# I
# When?

As the free press develops, the paramount point is whether the journalist, like the scientist or scholar, puts truth in the first place or in the second.

—WALTER LIPPMANN

# 1

William Loeb is a newspaper publisher, most widely known for his controlling interest in the morning and evening *Manchester, N.H., Union Leader* and the *New Hampshire Sunday News;* he is also publisher of the *Vermont Sunday News* and the *St. Albans, Vt., Daily Messenger* (his first newspaper, control of which he secured in 1941). In the past three and a half decades, William Loeb has also been publisher of the *Burlington, Vt., Daily News* and of the *Connecticut Sunday Herald,* both of which are now defunct, and he was founder and publisher of the *Haverhill, Mass., Journal,* also defunct. For a very brief period, William Loeb was also publisher of the *Haverhill Liberator* and the *Lowell, Mass., Liberator.* (Both of these are also now defunct, but neither was considered, nor were they intended to be considered, as "newspapers" in the usual sense of the term.)

All of the newspapers of William Loeb display the motto, "There is nothing so powerful as truth," with the exception of the *Daily Messenger,* which proclaims itself "The only daily newspaper in the world that gives a darn about St. Albans and Franklin County." This latter boast is perhaps still valid, but it is only fair to point out that the *Daily Messenger* has given rise to a competitive semi-weekly journal which challenges the daily as the city's leading newspaper.

Daniel Webster's statement has stood the test of time and, although the newspapers of William Loeb declare this as their hallmark, this does not mean that his newspapers adhere to the precept. The truth is that they do not, and the truth is that, because they are to a large extent monopolistic in nature within the limits of New Hampshire, they powerfully reflect William Loeb's politics and philosophy—and power. In Vermont, Loeb's newspapers are innocuous because there are established competitive journals which surpass those of William Loeb. In New Hampshire, Loeb is without any serious competition and his newspapers are the most powerful in the entire state.

Besides Daniel Webster, New Hampshire has produced a President, the fourteenth, Franklin Pierce, a Democrat from Hillsborough; and the state is the birthplace of the first American in space, Alan B. Shepard, an admiral from Derry. Another of its native sons was General John Stark, the commander of significant victories at Bunker Hill and Bennington; an "adopted son" who himself was a veteran of two wars and died during his third while serving as Secretary of the Navy and, between times, was a candidate for the governorship of New Hampshire and the Vice Presidency of the United States, was Colonel Frank Knox, himself a predecessor of Loeb as publisher of the Manchester newspapers.

New Hampshire is the home of Dartmouth College, the Old Man of the Mountains and has some of the finest skiing in the East, due largely to the White Mountains which also offer magnificent foliage during the fall of the year. The state, though small in population, offers such an abundance of seacoast, lake and mountain retreats that tourism is the state's second largest industry. It was the first of the original colonies to declare its independence from Great Britain and it was the first state in modern times to introduce a state lottery

But the grandeur of New Hampshire and the deeds of Webster, Pierce, Shepard, Stark and Knox are all now challenged by a new phenomenon which has indelibly attached itself to the famous and staid Granite State. Because while it is still a fact that "There is nothing so powerful as truth," it is also a fact that in New Hampshire there is no one so powerful as William Loeb. Loeb's name now challenges the immortality of the other state heroes, and it is a fact that throughout the nation the mention of the state of New Hampshire now often evokes the response, "New Hampshire? That's where the pinwheel runs the lousy newspapers."

New Hampshire was "discovered" in 1614 by Captain

John Smith, of England and later of Virginia, who wrote back to England:

"Here should be no landlords to rack us with high rents, or extorted fines to consume us. Here every man may be a master of his own labor and land in a short time. The sea there is the strangest pond I ever saw. What sport doth yield a more pleasant content and less hurt or charge than angling with a hook, and crossing the sweet air from isle to isle over the silent streams of a calm sea?"

Persecution in England was not the reason for the founding of New Hampshire, therefore, but rather as a colonization project by King James I, who made the first land grant along the coastline of the Atlantic Ocean in 1623, at the mouth of the Piscataqua River, now Rye and Portsmouth, the grantee being Captain John Mason, an Englishman. The grant given Mason extended far inland to a river bank occupied by the Pennacook Indians. Many of the Scotch-Irish settlers pushed inland within that grant, exploring the land and establishing villages. At a stretch of the Merrimack River which contained a series of falls and rapids and which the Pennacooks called "Namoaskeag," meaning "a place of much fish," another grant was made in 1722, by the governor of the province, Samuel Shute, of Boston, and what was then Old Harry's Town is now the largest city in the state of New Hampshire—Manchester. The establishment of the community by the Presbyterians precipitated the arrival of Puritans from Massachusetts and, although feuds between these two groups were frequent, the area prospered and grew into Harrytown, later Derryfield, and finally Manchester.

When "the shot heard round the world" was fired on April 19, 1775, Ebenezer Sargent and hundreds of others laid down their plows and hastened to Massachusetts to become privates in companies of Minutemen, Sargent a private in Captain Mathias Hoyt's Company at Amesbury.* By June 17, 1775, the New Hampshiremen were so

* Private Sargent is the possessor of as fine a military record of anyone in what is now the Cash family, and it is only fair that he get in here somehow.

eager to repel the British before the Redcoats could advance onto New Hampshire soil that General Stark organized an army of several hundred New Hampshire volunteers and this group was the backbone of the Revolutionary force at the Battle of Bunker Hill and later at Bennington.

On Jan. 5, 1776, New Hampshire became the first of the original colonies to declare its independence from Great Britain, even though the Revolutionary War had spread through all 13 original colonies. Thus, it was nearly six months prior to the Declaration of Independence that New Hampshire had adopted its own Constitution. The pioneer document, only 911 words long, evolved through three subsequent Constitutional Conventions and in October of 1783 the present Constitution, which insisted upon the creation of what has become the most democratic (though not yet Democratic) legislature in the world, the largest of all state legislatures. This Constitution, in itself, was used as a model for the U.S. Constitution, and the State of New Hampshire was the ninth, and ratifying, state to grant approval to the U.S. Constitution.

Early in the 19th century a series of canals were dug in Manchester and, using the water as a source of power, sawmills and gristmills came into being. The Amoskeag Manufacturing Company was organized in 1831. This was to become the largest company in the world devoted to the manufacture of cotton cloth.

Manchester got its first newspaper in 1839 with the founding of John Caldwell's *Representative,* which in 1841 became the *Manchester Memorial,* and in 1844, the *Manchester American.* In 1850, the *Mirror* was established; it was consolidated with the *American* in 1863. Meanwhile, the *Manchester Democrat* was founded in 1841, and in 1851, the *Union Democrat,* another separate newspaper, was established as a morning journal. In 1879, these were merged into one newspaper, the *Union,* with the advent of the "paper trains" the same year. The *Union* gained statewide circulation as it was carried by the railroad up the Merrimack Valley to other New Hampshire cities and towns.

Because of the rise in the percentage of population of French-speaking Canadians, largely come to Manchester as mill workers for the Amoskeag Manufacturing Co., more than one hundred attempts were made to publish a French-language newspaper. Only one was successful. *L'Avenir National* (The Future of the Nation) brought out its first edition in 1889 and became a daily fixture shortly thereafter. *L'Avenir National* continued to be published as an afternoon daily newspaper in Manchester until 1950 when it evolved into a weekly called *L'Action* (Action), which survived until August, 1971, when it, too, was abandoned, the principle reason being the virtual disappearance of French as a spoken language among the descendents of the original French-Canadian population.

Numerous of the newspapermen of Manchester became involved with the body politic, a devotion, in itself, not far apart from the publication of a newspaper for the community, to the point that they themselves became candidates for public office. Edgar J. Knowlton, editor of the *Union* when it became a morning statewide paper, served as mayor of the City of Manchester for two terms, from 1891–94, and he was succeeded for four terms, until 1902, by Mayor William C. Clarke, who wrote a column of news and gossip interest in the *Mirror,* owned by him and his brother, Arthur E. Clarke. Colonel Knox, president and publisher of the *Morning Union* and *Evening Leader,* which he founded in 1912, was a candidate for governor in 1924 and for Vice President of the United States in 1936. Knox's partner, John A. Muehling, was a delegate to several Republican National Conventions. Josaphat T. Benoit, a Massachusetts newspaperman who came to New Hampshire in 1938, resigned his position at *L'Avenir National* to become the first full-time mayor of the City of Manchester in which office he served from 1944 until 1961. (Benoit became publisher of *L'Action* as an avocation towards the end of his term in office.)

Another New Hampshire native who gained fame and power in journalism and politics was Horace Greeley, founder of the *New York Tribune.* Born in Amherst in 1811, he went west to Vermont at the age of 14 to become a printer's apprentice and, upon reaching journeyman status, went farther west to New York where he became an editor. In 1841 he founded the *Tribune,* which was merged many years later with James Gordon Bennett's *New York Herald.* Greeley became active in the Whig party and was elected to Congress in 1848. He toured Europe and, after his return, wrote extensively. As the nominee of the dissident Liberal Republican Party for the Presidency in 1872, he was also endorsed by the Democrats and campaigned against President Ulysses S. Grant, claiming Grant's administration was riddled with scandal. As bad as his administration might have been, Grant won in a waltz. Greeley's most lasting fame, however, is still largely within the newspaper industry. In January, 1851, he organized the printers at his *Tribune* into a local union and this spread within the year to other New York printing houses. A nation-wide union, with headquarters in Cincinnati, was chartered in 1852 and by 1869 there were Canadian locals. The group which Greeley first organized is today Local 6 ("Big Six") of the International Typographical Union of North America.

William Loeb—in Vermont, in Massachusetts, in Connecticut, but mostly in New Hampshire—has taken a different approach to his involvement in politics. Fearing, perhaps, that certain facets of his personal life, if made public, would doom him to failure, Loeb early-on chose to become involved as the man-behind-the-scenes, the "kingmaker," so to speak, the man upon whose decisions of editorial support or opposition so much would depend both on the local and state level. Because of the unique political structure within New Hampshire and its unique position with regard to Presidential primaries—New Hampshire has the first in the nation each quadrennium—Loeb has been able to make his presence felt across the entire breadth of the United States, but not as a "kingmaker" as much as a "spoiler."

Loeb, who was brought up in the lap of luxury and, literally, in the lap of the President of the United States,

had virtually no practical newspaper experience or training when he first came to New Hampshire. And he has
attained his place as New Hampshire's most powerful man
by converting a once proud and dignified institution into
what it is today. There can be little doubt that the *Union
Leader* and *N.H. Sunday News* are the way they are only
because that's the way William Loeb wants it and he'll
have it no other way.

In the Sept. 2, 1972 edition of *Editor & Publisher*—
"The Encyclopedia of the Newspaper Industry" by its own
designation—appeared a three-page story entitled:

## "LOEB . . . His Strong Personality Is Imprinted on His Newspaper"

To quote from this article:

"There is but one reason for the Union Leader's profound effect. The newspaper IS publisher-dominated and
the publisher, of course, is William Loeb . . .

"William Loeb and the Manchester Union Leader are
one and the same entity—the man is as much a part of
the newspaper as if they were both alive and breathing—
as Siamese twins.

". . . The power of the man's personality and the nature
of his ideas are the driving forces behind the newspaper,
in spite of his physical absence.

"In truth, he is not really absent—he is there and
every editor on the staff is as aware of his presence as if
he were standing with him.

". . . The nerve center of William Loeb's newspaper is
the editorial department where the paper's policies are
implemented. Loeb dominates that department like a
chief surgeon in the operating room. He not only decides
who is to be cut up, but often specifies how and into how
many pieces.

"His surgical assistant is James J. Finnegan, chief editorial writer, who has learned his job well by aligning
his thought processes with those of 'The Boss.' Their
relationship has developed to the point where Loeb has
only to give a basic hint to Finnegan and the editorial

expansion which follows is almost automatic. In fact
there are so many topics that Finegan (sic) is so sure of
how Loeb feels that he can write without checking and
come up with what Loeb would have done himself.

"But when it comes to those unique front page editorials for which the paper is so well known, full credit
must go to Loeb for their conception and authorship."

It is widely known and it is an accepted fact both within
and without New Hampshire (mostly, of course, within
the newspaper industry itself), that Loeb's newspapers do
not always tell the truth. To quote again from the *Editor
& Publisher* article:

". . . The day-to-day operation of the paper's newsroom is affected by Loeb's personality and desires . . .

"The staff receives daily direction from Loeb in the
form of memos, telephone calls and letters. Cryptic com-
ments pencilled in red on various articles, columns, clip-
ping (sic) and letters convey Loeb's wishes to the editors
. . . He occasionally contributes an 'inside' editorial in
addition to the daily front page editorials which are his
hallmark.

"Much of the work done in his home office is in the
form of correspondence to people all over the world, in
addition to memos of instruction to the Union Leader
staff. Three secretaries in Manchester labor to keep up
with the voluminous flow of writing which emanates from
him . . .

"As is only natural, there are times when the opinions
of Loeb and those of his editors do not coincide. Then
there is a confrontation and the winner is invariably
Loeb . . .

"When you add all of the unique aspects of the Union
Leader together, you find a personality emerging—the
personality of William Loeb, omnipresent in the newsroom and editorial offices and ever powerful in his influence of the day-to-day operation of his newspaper, in
spite of the accusations of 'absentee publisher' flung at
him by some of his peers. Maybe one cannot see him there
in the newsroom—but believe me, he is always present!"

To quote from the footnote in *Editor & Publisher* concerning the author of this article:

"Tom Muller is assistant city editor of the Manchester (N.H.) Union Leader. An electronics engineer by training, Muller gravitated to his vocation as a newsman upon the realization that his niche in life was doing what he enjoys most. His view of William Loeb is that of an insider looking up rather than the usual caricature provided by an outsider looking in. He says Loeb told him 'to write it the way I see it' and he didn't want to see the manuscript before it was submitted for publication."

Muller was apparently following the doctrine about which he was writing and it must have pleased Loeb, the "absentee publisher," because within a matter of days after the publication of the article, Muller, who had worked at the Union Leader Corp. only a short time, was elevated to the position of city editor and the man who had held that post for 25 years was demoted to copy editor.

The article which Muller wrote also showed the personality of Loeb because it is not an "accusation" that is "flung" at Loeb to state that he is an absentee publisher, but a simple statement of fact. Muller's article itself only emphasizes that the absentee publisher is a man of many moods and complexes.

Loeb resides with his third wife, the former Nackey Scripps Gallowhur, herself a descendant of a prominent newspaper family, in Pride's Crossing, Mass., in a huge house which is located on an 80-acre tract surrounded by a tall fence and protected by electronic devices and floodlights, as well as a Doberman and a German shepherd. His legal domicile is 1750 Skyline Boulevard, Reno, Nev., a location also protected by a special fence.

Basically, the reason why William Loeb is an absentee publisher with such secluded living accommodations—the living style of the Loeb family is like that of the Borgias—is twofold: first, Loeb is reluctant to come face-to-face with the people he castigates, and, second, although he will be 70 years of age on Dec. 26, 1975, he has never "grown up" and he has been, at various times during his spotted career, in serious trouble with law enforcement authorities, usually at the urging and lawful pursuit of his own family members.

The fact of the matter is that Loeb averages little more than a monthly visit to his newspaper offices in Manchester. His visit to his offices in Burlington, Vt., during December, 1973 was the first time he had entered those premises since 1951. He never made a visit to his Connecticut newspaper office.

And this is one reason why Loeb's newspapers are so often wrong. It is impossible for a newspaperman to remain in constant touch with the facts behind such a barricade as Loeb has built.

The newspapers of William Loeb do print some of the news, but to a lessening degree with each passing year and with the addition of each new column of opinion which is printed at the sacrifice of news space. That portion of the news which does appear in the newspapers of William Loeb is not always accurate or complete. If the article agrees with and supports the opinion of William Loeb, or if written by a person who supports and agrees with William Loeb, it is given prime display. Opinion of the same order is given similar treatment, be it in the form of a letter to the editor, unsolicited manuscript or a treatise by an accredited or unaccredited columnist. Very little news and almost no opinion which does not coincide with the thinking of William Loeb is given "spread" treatment in Loeb's newspapers.

As it has stood since 1946 in New Hampshire, Loeb's *Union Leader* is the "only game in town" and, as long as it is, New Hampshire apparently will be playing by William Loeb's rules.

One of William Loeb's rules is that you never say bad things about William Loeb. Countless politicians have learned this rule to the point where most now strictly abide by it. But it works far beyond the realm of politics as well.

One such occasion was the sixth midyear commencement of the University of New Hampshire at Durham on Dec.

22, 1974, at which some 800 students received their degrees before an audience of some 2,000 persons. This event received five-column coverage in the *Union Leader* in both morning and evening editions of Dec. 23, 1974. The main speaker was Atty. Bradford E. Cook, of Manchester, a former Student Body President on the Durham campus, in which office he served during his senior undergraduate year. The title of the address delivered by Cook was, "Perspectives—four and a half years after graduation from UNH." Here are portions of the speech, as quoted in the *Union Leader* account of the event:

"J. Fred French received the honorary doctor of laws degree in recognition of his service to the school as a 12-year member of its board of trustees and 'dedicated service in a variety of roles.' The degree was presented by Philip S. Dunlap, chairman of the trustees, and conferral was conducted by UNH President Eugene S. Mills . . .

"Speaking on his perspective of New Hampshire, Cook said it is the best place to live in the United States. He also said:

" 'Here at UNH we all thought William Loeb was a bad person. But I must admit that secretly I suspected that he couldn't be as bad as people in Durham said he was: that it was merely a group prejudice which made us hate him so. I can report to you after working for two years 100 yards away from his publishing plant that his power is more perverse, his influence greater and his effect on the present and future more insidious than I even suspected.'

"Cook cited as an example the recent election saying Loeb said 'neither candidate was worth voting for.'* Cook said 'many of us agreed but it is more important to realize why decent and outstanding candidates don't run. Many of them cannot stand the villification, family insult and personal pain which William Loeb inflicts on those who try to stand for decency in this state. We cannot let this

---

* The Reference is to the 1974 contest for U.S. Senate, the result of which was so close that it was ultimately referred back for a special election in September, 1975, to decide the eventual winner.

defeat us. Loeb's power must be diluted and what he stands for must be destroyed.'

"Cook received slight applause at this section of the speech.

"The invocation was by the Rev.........."

The *Union Leader*—whether the next to last paragraph was inserted by the reporter or later by an editor—could not find it within itself to refrain from giving an untrue report. Countless eyewitnesses to the event, including the recipient of the honorary degree, J. Fred French, himself a member of William Loeb's Citizens' Advisory Board, were in total agreement that the applause which greeted this portion of Cook's speech was equal to, if not louder than, that which used to follow a game-ending double play resulting in a victory for the home team in Ebbets Field.

Of course, Attorney Cook would suffer public penance for having committed the sin of uttering against William Loeb. Politicians William Loeb usually answers very promptly so that the effect might be felt before an election. Laymen, the likes of Attorney Cook, apparently go somewhere into the computer of Loeb's mind to pop out at any given moment, and, because Cook joined a group of people who are willing to call it as they see it—the truth, in effect—they automatically become "enemies" of William Loeb.

It was not until Feb. 5, 1975, that Page One of the *Union Leader* contained the answer of William Loeb to the observation of former Student Body President Cook, which, by the way, appeared on Page Two. Loeb appropriated more than two full columns of news space, in a type size larger than the news columns, often in heavy full-face, lambasting Cook. This came as a surprise to no one, including Cook, who knew full well what he was getting into when he accepted the call to deliver the address.

Loeb's editorial was entitled, "Cook's Christmas 'Hate-In' " Loeb wrote:

"It is interesting to note that the University of New Hampshire is willing to allow itself to be used as a plat-

form for the spewing of such hate as would have done
credit to one of Hitler's 'Brown Shirt' youth goons trying to stir up fellow Nazis to hate some German publisher who didn't go along with their totalitarian views.

"When is the University of New Hampshire going to
start paying attention to serious problems and stop this
sort of childishness?

"Certainly, banker J. Fred French, who was given an
honorary degree for good reason—for his service to the
university, his community and the state—must have
thought his own degree diluted and cheapened by the
selection as commencement speaker of such a silly young
man.

"This newspaper assures its readers that neither the
publisher nor this newspaper will be deterred by this type
of smear and this weak and transparent attempt to rabble-
rouse against us.

"At any rate, we think lawyer Cook certainly illustrated
the extent of his Christmas spirit most vividly with his
speech, two days before Christmas.

"/s/ William Loeb
"William Loeb, Publisher."

Of course, not all of Loeb's lapses are intentional or the
result of oversights. Some are, at the very least, foolish and
stupid errors of which a most critical publisher, particularly Loeb, should be most careful. In 1974, as always,
Christmas fell three days after December 22. And, in itself,
this may prove an insight into one of the many reasons
why William Loeb is about the only major newspaper
publisher in America who has not received at least one
honorary degree.

But Loeb's attacks and counterattacks on persons and
issues are not confined to his editorials alone. There have
been many occasions of spurious letters to the editor of the
*Union Leader,* the most famous having been the one to
which Sen. Edmund S. Muskie (D-Me.) reacted during the
Presidential campaign of 1972 and which, for all intents
and purposes, disqualified the Maine Democrat from further consideration as a serious candidate. (See Appendix
C.) Less noticed are any number of occurrences, the re-

ports of which in the *Union Leader* are in conflict with the facts. The natural question which arises is whether or not the *Union Leader* tells lies and distorts the news just to stay in practice.

The *Concord Monitor* is the only other New Hampshire daily newspaper which provides its own full-time staff coverage of the State House and Legislature. The following news story is reprinted in its entirety from Page One of the *Concord Monitor* of March 12, 1975:

## "No Support For State Complex Bill
### "By ROGER TALBOT

"A hearing on Gov. Thomson's bill to move state government out of Concord lasted 13 minutes this morning—ending without any favorable testimony.

"Rep. Victor Joos, Sr., D-Milton, was the only witness.

"He told the House Public Works Committee House Bill 410 was 'detrimental to everything the State of New Hampshire stands for. . . . The City of Concord would lose if we built a state office complex outside the city . . . Financially it would never be feasible . . . What would we do with all the (historic) buildings we have now?'

"There was no other testimony on the bill which would authorize borrowing $1.5 million to purchase land for a state office complex at an unspecified location within a 20-mile radius of Concord.

"Not even Rep. George I. Wiggins, R-Sunapee, who sponsored the bill, showed up.

"Rep. Richard I. Ellis, R-Greenland, a member of the committee, left the hearing room to search for Wiggins or someone else to present the governor's position on the bill.

" 'This can't be too important,' said one waiting committee member.

" 'It's a stupid bill,' commented another legislator.

" 'This bill was drafted when somebody got a parking ticket on Main Street.' suggested a third.

"There was laughter.

"Ellis returned alone.

"Committee chairman Forsaith Daniels, R-Manchester,

closed the hearing at 10:13 A.M., saying HB 410 was a bill that would 'require a lot of study!'

"Daniels left open the possibility of a second hearing if proponents of the bill indicate a desire to testify."

Both majority and minority committee members who were in attendance at the hearing agree that Talbot's report in the *Monitor* was accurate, even painstakingly so. Chairman Daniels contacted the office of Gov. Meldrim Thomson, Jr., of Orford, who informed the chairman that he had instigated the drafting of the bill but there was no need for any further committee action; that the governor would deal with the matter in a portion of the capital budget. The other committee members were informed that HB 410 was a closed matter as far as the committee was concerned and it was officially reported out of committee as "Inexpedient to Legislate."

Two days later, in the March 14, 1975, editions of the *Manchester Union Leader*, the following three-column headline appeared on Page Four:

### "Barry Presents Thomson View For Land Bill"

and the story ran nine paragraphs, the first two of which are as follows:

"CONCORD—James J. Barry, Jr., of Manchester, special counsel of Gov. Meldrim Thomson, Jr., appeared Wednesday before the House Public Works Committee on behalf of the governor to testify in support of HB 410.

"The measure being considered by the House committee deals with the purchase of land for a state office complex and for making an appropriation for such land acquisition and the construction of a building."

The final seven paragraphs are quotations of Barry's alleged speech in favor of the measure. This all may sound innocent enough except for the fact that Atty. James J. Barry, Jr., is a partner in the Boston and Manchester law firm of Malloy, Sullivan & Barry, in addition to his temporary assignment as legislative, or special, counsel to the governor. The governor is incontrovertably beholden to the publisher for every inch of his political progression. The law firm of Malloy, Sullivan & Barry maintains offices in Manchester largely because it is general counsel to the Union Leader Corporation, William Loeb, president and publisher.

Back on Aug. 3, 1830, Daniel Webster, the New Hampshire native who gained such fame as a public official, a lawyer and an orator, was appearing before the Essex County term of the Massachusetts Supreme Court in Salem, Mass., in the case of the alleged murderers of Captain Joseph White. Certain testimony had been offered by a person named Leighton, of questionable mental ability and stability; Webster, in defense of this testimony, was attempting to impress the court that it was beyond the realm of possibility that someone as dim-witted as Leighton could have invented a conversation he had related as a matter of his testimony under oath. Webster said:

"How could Leighton have made up this conversation? 'When did you see Dick?' 'I saw him this morning.' 'When is he going to kill the old man?' 'I don't know.' 'Tell him if he don't do it soon, I won't pay him.' Here is a vast amount in a few words. Had he wit enough to invent this? There is nothing so powerful as truth; and often nothing so strange. It is not even suggested that the story was made for him. There is nothing so extraordinary in the whole matter, as it would have been for this ignorant country boy to invent the story."

As has been pointed out, the single quotation, "There is nothing so powerful as truth," even taken out of context, has indeed stood the test of time and is as valid today as when it was uttered by Daniel Webster in 1830.

The *Manchester Union Leader* and the *New Hampshire Sunday News* would be better newspapers, both in themselves and as a service to the community and state within which they function, and William Loeb would be a better publisher and a more worthy recipient of the guarantees offered by the First Amendment if this publisher, through these newspapers, paid more heed to the words stated by Daniel Webster during a testimonial to himself at the City Hotel in New York on March 10, 1831:

"Our government has been tried in peace, and it has been tried in war, and has proved itself fit for both. It has been assailed from without, and it has successfully resisted the shock; it has been disturbed within, and it has effectually quieted the disturbance. It can stand trial, it can stand assault, it can stand adversity, it can stand every thing, but the marring of its own beauty, and the weakening of its own strength. It can stand every thing but the effects of our own rashness and our own folly. It can stand everything but disorganization, disunion and nullification."

# 2

The word was all over town on William Loeb, Jr.; he had been a headline hunter since the day his father died. The old man was quite a guy on Wall Street and he had gotten there because he was apparently the closest man to President Theodore Roosevelt. But the kid, he was something else. His father was hardly buried when this kid was going to reorganize an auto company. That failing, he got himself mixed up with revolutionaries and weirdoes of every description and this William Loeb, Jr., was forever putting out some press release or another on how he was going to boycott Russia or reorganize the Dominican Republic or tell the Dies Committee how to conduct its business. And apparently he figured the whole world had forgotten the stories in the *Trib* and *The Times* and the *Daily News* when he walked out on the school teacher wife who had supported him for five years and he had gone running home to his mother and father.

But, nonetheless, that little "filler" was processed and it did see the light of day, for there, on Sunday, Oct. 26, 1941, down next to the "gutter" on Page 35 of *The New York Times,* there appeared the one-paragraph item:

## Loeb's Son Buys a Newspaper

ST. ALBANS, Vt., Oct. 25 (AP)-Sale of the St. Albans Messenger, oldest evening newspaper in Vermont, to William Loeb of Oyster Bay, N.Y., was announced today by Edward F. Smith, president of the company. The price was not announced. The new owner of the paper, established in 1861, is the son of William Loeb, who was executive secretary to Theodore Roosevelt. The Messenger was established as a weekly in 1837.

It must have been mostly because newspapermen care what happens to newspapers and are concerned about who directs their destinies, and only partly because it was "Loeb's son" that the item found its way into print at all on that morning because the nation had a lot of other, certainly much more important, news on its mind.

It would be only six more Sunday mornings that the United States would enjoy peace. And it was to be years of Sunday mornings until the United States would know peace again.

Franklin Delano Roosevelt was in the ninth year of his Presidency, having been elected to an unprecedented third term less than a year before, this time with Henry A. Wallace, of Iowa, as his running mate. And, at a news conference reported in *The Times* the day before, President Roosevelt showed that he was still playing politics and infuriating some of his most vocal supporters during his reelection campaign. President Roosevelt had endorsed the candidacy of New York Mayor Fiorello H. LaGuardia, the Republican incumbent who was locked in a tough reelection fight with the Tammany Hall Democratic candidate, Brooklyn District Attorney William O'Dwyer. President Roosevelt said Mayor LaGuardia had given the nation's largest city the most honest and efficient municipal government of any within his recollection.

And the "Little Flower" said: "The President knows New York City. It was indeed nice and generous of him to give me that strong endorsement."

"Boss" Flynn of the Bronx was infuriated and as chairman of the Democratic National Committee he immediately issued a statement "expressing regret that the President, not a voter in the city, had seen fit to express an opinion about its municipal elections," and he recalled how the city's Democrats had stood loyally by FDR since he was first elected governor of New York. Flynn, however, denied rumors that he would quit his national party post and said that, the President's endorsement notwithstanding, nothing anybody could say or do could defeat O'Dwyer.

*The New York Times* said editorially that it was "an event reflecting great credit upon both men; for the Mayor, the most striking tribute yet to the high character of his administration; for FDR, an act of political courage and independence." ("Boss" Flynn was to prove himself to have been a poor prophet.)

At the same news conference, President Roosevelt also announced that he would soon request of Congress funds to double the nation's tank-building program, the first of several requests to increase the U.S. armaments against the threat of war. And the President was asking John L. Lewis, president of the United Mine Workers, CIO, to prevent the strike of 53,000 coal mine workers, which was scheduled for midnight Sunday.

But the man who was apparently working hardest and on a full-time basis at minding the store—making the nation ready for war—was Secretary of the Navy Frank Knox, an erstwhile newspaper publisher from New Hampshire and Illinois who had moved into the national limelight as the losing Vice Presidential candidate in the FDR landslide of 1936. He had subsequently been read out of the ranks of the Grand Old Party for his acceptance of President Roosevelt's challenge to prepare the woefully rundown United States fleet for duty in the almost inevitable battles of World War II.

Colonel Knox, an Army veteran of the Spanish-American War and World War I, who was always referred to by his Army rank and the abbreviated version of his given name, earned, by far, the largest headlines of the day with the warning that a clash with Japan was near—that the huge Eastern power showed no signs of abandoning her expansionist policies and that a collision between the United States and Japan was virtually certain, "and could occur on very short notice."

A Russian mechanized spearhead was reported to have broken through a continuous line of attacking Germans about 65 miles from the capital city of Moscow. And Colonel Knox said that keeping the Russians fighting had to be the foremost objective of the United States at that time. Knox said that a clash with Japan would force closing the port of Vladivostok through which Russia was receiving vital military aid supplies from the United States. And, in this event, warned Knox, use of the port of Archangel would put the United States vessels in dire jeopardy of bombing by German planes as the ships proceeded slowly through the ice-clogged waters.

The Vichy Government announced that morning that French Somaliland was being attacked by British and Free French forces, but in Vichy itself, 54 more persons were executed by the Germans, bringing to 100 the total of those put to death in reprisal for the assassination of two German officers at Nantes and Bordeaux.

On the Sunday morning of that October weekend in 1941, the same intermingling of foreign and domestic developments made the headlines. John L. Lewis announced that he was defying the President's request and that he was issuing the order to go ahead with the coal strike at midnight, despite the harm the strike might do to the nation's war effort. The mines in question were all owned by the nation's steel-producing companies and the mines' output was used in the production of steel, so vital to the manufacture of arms.

The German Government announced the capture of Kharkov, the industrial center of the Ukraine, on that Sunday morning, putting most of the strategic Donets Basin in German hands.

And Colonel Knox? He was still minding the store. He had held a meeting of selected Republican senators in Washington the day before, including the senior senator from his own home state, Styles Bridges of New Hampshire. He had told this group of senators that he would back them for reelection and campaign in their behalf only if they adopted a hard and fast stand behind the foreign policy of Democratic President Roosevelt.

As Colonel Knox said, "I am an old soldier who fought in two wars, and if my Commander-in-Chief gave me a rifle and told me to start out again as a buck private, I'd do it. I am an American first, a Republican afterward."

William Franklin Knox was born in Boston on Jan. 1, 1874, but his family moved to Grand Rapids, Mich., when young Franklin was 7. He delivered newspapers after school as a youngster and later worked as a $5-a-week shipping clerk to aid his family; but he lost this job during the 1893 depression. He was persuaded by a Presbyterian minister to seek higher education and it was arranged for him to enroll at tiny Alma College in central Michigan, from which he received a degree in 1898. At this time, the 32nd Michigan Infantry was forming at Camp Eaton, Mich., to go to Tampa, Fla., and to go from there to join in fighting the Spanish-American War in Cuba. But at about the time he arrived at Camp Eaton, Knox learned of the death of the father of his Alma coed sweetheart, Annie Reid, and Knox went back to Alma for the funeral. Returning to Camp Eaton, Knox found he had missed the swearing-in of the regiment. With no official status, he was transported to Tampa, anyway. Encamped near the 32nd Michigan at Tampa was a "rag-tag" outfit called the "Rough Riders," of no official designation, commanded by a bespectacled, mustachioed cavalry officer named Lieutenant Colonel "Teddy" Roosevelt. Knox was recruited for the outfit, sworn in as a private and taken to Santiago, Cuba.

Illness forced the return of Knox to Grand Rapids before the single biggest victory of the "Rough Riders" at the

Battle of San Juan Hill in Santiago, but not before Private Knox had been wounded in action. So the young Army veteran got a job on the *Grand Rapids Herald*. He rose rapidly within the hierarchy of the newspaper's staff, becoming city editor and then circulation manager. At about this time, a friendship blossomed between Knox and John A. Muehling, a man several years Knox's senior, who was owner of a small job-printing and bookbinding shop in Grand Rapids.

New challenges were beckoning. In 1901, Knox, his bride, the former Annie Reid, and Muehling severed their connections in Grand Rapids and, with the blessings and some financial backing of the Grand Rapids publisher, went to Sault Sainte Marie on Michigan's rough and bawdy Upper Peninsula, seeking to continue in the newspaper business.

Knox and Muehling founded the *Evening Journal*. With Knox as the crusading editor and Muehling as the skillful production manager, they converted the financial backing of the Grand Rapids publisher into a going daily newspaper. Knox quickly found an outlet for his crusading talents and backed the causes in which he believed, among them the rights of the Great Lakes seamen and the Upper Michigan miners and lumberjacks. Legend has it that many of these roustabouts and migrant workers were systematically bilked of their pay when they came into town to visit some of Sault Sainte Marie's "protected" saloons. The campaign by the *Evening Journal* in their behalf became so violent at one point that the windows in the newspaper office were shot out and Knox retaliated by decking a local saloonkeeper.

It was not long before the *Evening Journal* was such a financial success that Knox and Muehling were able to obtain control of the competing *News Record,* and the surviving Knox-Muehling enterprise was called the *Evening News*.

Knox took an active part in the Michigan Republican Party, while Muehling took care of the physical production of the newspaper. Knox became campaign manager for

Chase C. Osborn, later to be elected governor of Michigan, and, through it all, he kept in close contact with his old military commandant, Theodore Roosevelt, at annual reunions of the "Rough Riders" in Washintgon, D.C., and at Sagamore Hill, Oyster Bay, Long Island. (The Veterans of Foreign Wars was founded as the natural successor organization to the "Rough Rider" reunions.)

It was after Knox had acceded to the post of Republican state chairman that President William Howard Taft asked Knox to manage the Taft reelection campaign in Michigan. When Knox asked former President Roosevelt's advice, his former commandant told him of his own plans to bolt the G.O.P. and to run for election on the Bull Moose ticket. Subsequently, Knox turned down Taft's request and he began stumping in all parts of the country gaining signatures on nominating petitions in Roosevelt's behalf. Then the ex-President decided on an even better way to utilize Knox's proven talents.

At the invitation of New Hampshire Gov. Robert P. Bass and Winston Churchill, a wealthy novelist from Cornish, N.H., Knox and Muehling liquidated their assets in Sault Sainte Marie and proceeded to Manchester, N.H., to enter the newspaper business there, the basic idea being to woo the Granite State's votes into the Bull Moose column. The price for the *Morning Union,* founded in 1851, which also published an evening edition, was prohibitive and the *Manchester Mirror,* an evening newspaper which had started as a weekly in 1841 and as a daily in 1850, was not for sale. So Knox and Muehling inaugurated publication of the *Evening Leader.* And, although the political aims of the newspaper were not successful, the venture was financially rewarding, largely because of the expertise of the Knox-Muehling combine.

"The election is over," wrote Knox in an editorial on the day after the Bull Moose Party suffered a stunning setback at the polls, "now let's settle down to business. We are here to stay." Knox meant what he wrote. It was not long before the *Morning Union* abandoned its evening edition and the *Evening Leader* took up the slack.

Then came World War I.

In New Hampshire the *Morning Union* was enjoying
great growth as a morning daily and the *Evening Leader*
and the *Manchester Mirror* were sharing a growing audience of readers in booming Manchester, where the prosperity of the Amoskeag Manufacturing Company made
the city one of the largest and most productive of the
cotton manufacturing centers of the world—the largest, in
fact, under one management.

Knox's newspaper career was interrupted when he enlisted in the 1st New Hampshire Infantry in 1917. He was
selected for officer training, was commissioned a captain
and was sent to serve with the 78th Division. He was pro-
moted to the rank of major while on foreign service and
transferred to the 153rd Artillery, with which unit he
served until he was mustered out of service in February
of 1919 with the rank of lieutenant colonel.

Muehling had more than adequately taken care of
things while Knox was gone and it was not long before
the *Evening Leader* was doing well enough to hurt the
revenues of the competing morning and evening newspapers. Yet, although Manchester, as well as other New
Hampshire cities, was on solid financial footing, things
were not so rosy in the field of agriculture, which was,
after all, New Hampshire's leading industry. New Hampshire farmers did their biggest trading, in a commercial
sense, at Boston's Faneuil Hall markets, and were being
pushed out by the bigger farmers from Massachusetts.

Recognizing this problem, Frank Knox took a brief
leave from his newspaper business in Manchester and
made a trip to Denmark to study the system of farm co-
operatives there. On his return he organized the New
Hampshire Cooperative Marketing Association. Assisting
Knox, at his invitation, were James Farmer, a Keene insurance man; Fred Rogers, head of the New Hampshire
Grange; Dr. Ralph Dorn Hetzel, president of the New
Hampshire College of Agriculture and the Mechanic Arts
(later to be the University of New Hampshire), and J. Fred
French, a young man from Manchester recently graduated

from Bentley School in Boston, who served as the cooperative's executive secretary. This organization was of im-
measurable assistance to the New Hampshire farmers and
it prospered for many years until regional farmers' ex-
changes became more profitable and popular to the
individual small landowners.

By 1924, Knox and Muehling had become so powerful
with their *Evening Leader* that they obtained the assets of
both the *Union* and the *Mirror* and they formed the
Union-Leader Publishing Co., Inc., and published two
daily newspapers, the *Manchester Union*, which circulated
throughout the state in the morning, and the *Manchester
Leader*, an evening newspaper which confined itself largely
to Manchester and its surrounding communities. The two
newspapers were immensely rewarding as advertising
media, mostly because they were packed with all the news
that Granite Staters wanted to read.

Politically, the newspapers were Republican in flavor,
but not so much so as to injure the burgeoning Democratic
tastes of metropolitan Manchester. The city, like so many
other New England "mill towns," had had for many years
a distinct French-Canadian element among its 78,384
residents. But, by now, greater numbers of these immigrants from Quebec and other Canadian provinces who
had easily found employment in the mills were learning
to speak and read and write in English, and were taking
time to register to vote. The vast majority of these new
citizens ended up in the Democratic column. For them,
the Republican Party was the voice of the millowners, the
bankers, and the other tycoons who were oppressing the
proletariat. The unwieldy New Hampshire General Court
now included some of these citizens, and their champions,
and their combined voice helped enact laws having to do
with child labor, wages and hours, right to work, labor
unions and other previously neglected subjects.

The morning newspaper, along with other state news,
included the daily market prices of farm commodities
native to New Hampshire and stories of most city and
town civic meetings. A network of correspondents and

"stringers" blossomed throughout New Hampshire and its Queen City. The *Union* and the *Leader* were popular, informative, persuasive and, above all, respected. They became the "bibles" of the state and the city.

Colonel Knox, having acquired a taste for politics, had ambitions of his own, and, in 1924, he sought the governorship of New Hampshire, but he was soundly defeated in the Republican primary by the eventual winner, John G. Winant, a teacher at St. Paul's School in Concord. Knox was the strong conservative and Winant was the closest thing to a Democrat that the G.O.P. in New Hampshire had seen.

(After serving a third, non-consecutive term as governor in the 1930's, President Roosevelt was to enlist the services of former Governor Winant as first director of the Social Security System and later as ambassador to the Court of St. James in England during the days immediately following the outbreak of World War II, after the then ambassador, Joseph P. Kennedy, and President Roosevelt had had obvious differences.)

Knox's activities in New Hampshire were attracting the attention of a far bigger, much more important and equally politically ambitious publisher, William Randolph Hearst, who was apparently having a hard time making a go of it in the fiercely competitive world of Boston journalism. In 1927, Hearst enticed Knox to take over the management of Hearst's *Boston American,* which was losing money. Hearst allowed Knox to retain his interests in Manchester, which functioned under Muehling's watchful eye. Knox took with him to Boston a young veteran of World War I, Edmund F. Jewell, who had become an advertising salesman with the *Union-Leader* after his graduation from Boston University. Soon the Hearst newspaper was on a paying basis and Knox resigned and returned to Manchester.

It was not long, though, before he was again being wooed by Hearst. The Hearst empire was spread too thin in too many cities and it was racked with internal politics. "The Chief" always did have a "fear" of letting a good man go, and he tried desperately to entice Knox back as general manager of all Hearst Newspapers. To Hearst, circulation was everything and he figured Knox was a specialist at building circulation. Knox knew, as did Hearst, that managing a newspaper and managing a chain of newspapers were two different things and, even though Hearst insisted, Knox was adamant in his refusal to rejoin "The Chief." Personal friends of Knox in Manchester told him that a gracious way to refuse Hearst's continued offers would be to name a salary figure which would be out of the question. So Knox told Hearst that he would assume the general managership of all of the Hearst newspapers at a salary of $150,000 a year. Hearst wired Knox a reply as soon as he received Knox's terms: "Be in Boston Monday morning and go to work." Knox was in Boston on Monday morning.

Knox still retained his Manchester connections and, while Muehling was minding Manchester, Jewell was advancing within the structure of the *Boston American,* becoming assistant business manager, and later assistant to the publisher. In 1928, Jewell went to Hearst's *Washington Herald* and *Times* as advertising director.

Knox spent most of his time in the general offices of the Hearst Corporation at 57th Street and Eighth Avenue in New York City but he made periodic trips to various of the branches of the sprawling Hearst domain. In late July, 1930, Knox made just such a visit to the Washington office of the *Herald* and *Times* to cope with the problem of new leadership for the morning *Herald,* which was showing more than its share of losses. He called the top men of the *Herald* together and, already having decided what he was going to do, promised them a new editor of unquestioned ability.

On the steamy morning of Aug. 1, 1930, so typical of the Washington summertime, Knox strode to the center of the city room of the *Herald* and introduced the new editor to the staff. At his side, tall and elegantly tailored, her red hair glistening like copper, stood Eleanor Medill "Cissy" Patterson, a newspaper thoroughbred with blood lines extending from the *Chicago Tribune* and into the *New York Daily News.*

"Cissy" spoke to the staff briefly in a tone of quiet command, in a voice that was throaty, like that of an actress. The men of the staff had begun to slip into their coats, but the new boss said: "And you don't have to wear your coats when I'm around, either." With that, the new editor, married and divorced, married again and widowed, turned and drifted from the city room, leaving behind her the sweet scent of heady perfume.

The Herald would never be the same again. Knox confided to those close to him that he had acted on orders from "The Chief" and it was his own opinion that "Cissy" Patterson wouldn't last six months. But, "Cissy" Patterson, as *Collier's* magazine said in 1946, was to become, "using her charm like a horsewhip, one of the most powerful women in America." Shortly thereafter, Edmund F. Jewell became general manager of the Washington Times Co.

Hearst soon began to have second thoughts about Knox's talents as head of all his newspapers. Some of the Hearst papers still didn't show a profit, and a new threat was on the horizon—radio. Hearst was never one to cut salaries; when things were going badly, he'd abolish jobs. So in 1931, with the bare announcement that Knox and Hearst had reached irreconcilable differences, Knox left the employ of the Hearst Corporation and returned to Manchester.

It was soon obvious to Muehling and several others in the Knox inner circle that Colonel Knox's ambitions could no longer be satisfied by Manchester. With the partial backing of a Worcester, Mass., industrialist and publisher, Theodore T. Ellis, Colonel Knox bought the *Chicago Daily News,* which was in deep financial trouble, together with the newspaper's new radio station, WMAQ.

The American Legion Junior Baseball Program had been principally supported by a $50,000 annual grant from the office of Baseball Commissioner Kennesaw (Mountain) Landis since its inception in 1925. But, in the aftermath of the Great Depression, in 1933–34, the commissioner's office, troubled by sagging admissions and rising expenses, was forced to withdraw its aid, placing the fledgling American Legion program in jeopardy.

Legion Americanism Director Dan Sowers of Kentucky discussed the problem with James F. O'Neil, a member of Henry J. Sweeney Post, No. 2, of Manchester, N.H., at a Legion convention; O'Neil, always an active Legionnaire, was then the police reporter for the Manchester *Leader*.\* They decided the most logical approach was to interest a large corporation in "adopting" the Legion program. O'Neil sought guidance from his boss, Colonel Knox, who had been New Hampshire's first state Legion commander and also a member of Sweeney Post, in Knox's Chicago office. Knox was dead set against the idea, saying that if such would happen the baseball program would become the public relations gimmick of the corporation and it would lose its American Legion identity. But Knox was adamant in his belief that the program should be kept going, if for no other reason than he himself had seen the program in action at the 1932 Little World Series which had been held in Manchester.

Colonel Knox proceeded to give O'Neil his personal check for $5,000—a nice round number anytime, but especially in the post-Depression years—only after O'Neil promised to keep the gift anonymous until after Knox's death. Knox then made a donation in the name of the *Chicago Daily News* and he gave O'Neil letters of introduction to other publishers. O'Neil, Sowers and Paul Griffith of Pennsylvania subsequently received donations from the *Omaha World-Tribune*, the *San Francisco Chronicle*, the *Indianapolis News*, the *New Orleans Item-Tribune* and the *Atlanta Journal*. Other monies were received from the Cities Services Oil Corp. and the A. G. Spalding Sporting Goods Corp., and the American Legion Junior Baseball Program survived.

---

\* James F. O'Neil was subsequently Manchester chief of police and in 1950 he resigned from this position and was elected National Commander of the American Legion. He is currently publisher of *The American Legion Magazine*.

Colonel Knox and Mrs. Annie Reid Knox never changed
their domicile from the comfortable home they had built
on North Union Street in Manchester, and the Colonel
made frequent trips to Manchester, even though the day-
to-day operation was left pretty much up to Muehling.
During one of his visits to Manchester, he dipped into the
pool of talent which was producing the *Union* and the
*Leader* and took one of the brightest young newsmen,
Bernard J. McQuaid, a recent Georgetown University
alumnus, and converted him into an editorial writer for
the *Daily News*.

Slowly at first, but with ever increasing vigor, through
the pages of the *Daily News* in the Midwest and the *Union*
and *Leader* in the Northeast, and in frequent speeches
throughout the nation, Knox became one of the most outspoken and vocal critics of FDR's New Deal, and he started
a move intended to gain the 1936 Republican Presidential
nomination. One of his loudest supporters was William
Randolph Hearst through the pages of his several newspapers. If his run at the Presidency were to be successful,
Knox had to be prepared to run his newspapers almost
totally in absentia. The strain of the years was beginning
to take its toll on the aging Muehling, so Knox lured
Jewell back from Washington as publisher of the *Union*
and *Leader*.

The bandwagon of Kansas Gov. Alfred M. Landon had
gained too much momentum for Knox to get the key
nominating votes at the Cleveland convention, and New
Hampshire's Knox was named instead to the ticket as the
Vice Presidential nominee.

"Off the rocks with Landon and Knox," was the battle
cry of an aggressive campaign. But although they travelled
some 20,000 miles and visited 30 states, Landon and Knox
went down to an ignominious defeat, losing every state
except two, Maine and Vermont. Even the strong backing
of the *Union* and the *Leader* wasn't enough to obtain the
electoral votes of the normally Republican stronghold of
New Hampshire, although the Manchester newspapers covered the state like a blanket.

But the backing which the Landon-Knox ticket received from the Manchester newspapers and the *Chicago Daily News* was nothing compared to the support given by William Randolph Hearst. Defeating Roosevelt and John Nance Garner was, to "the Chief," like winning a war. Every one of his newspapers treated it as such.

William Randolph Hearst, Jr., and his brother, Randolph, were at this time toiling in the "vineyards" at 57th and Eighth in New York City, learning the business. One evening in mid-November of 1936, the two brothers left the office after a day's labor, strolled down Broadway to 52nd Street, turned the corner as far as Jack White's, a popular watering hole of the era. As the two junior executives entered the bistro, the master of ceremonies seized the microphone, motioned for the music to stop, and said, "Ladies and gentlemen, here come Maine and Vermont." Everyone knew what he meant and thunderous applause and laughter erupted.

Immediately after his defeat, Colonel Knox, through the editorial columns of his Manchester and Chicago newspapers, pledged tempered support of President Roosevelt, reserving the right to oppose the New Deal on future issues.

The newspaper domain of Colonel Knox was profitable. The *Chicago Daily News* was coming out of the deep hole it had been in. The financial reward which the Union-Leader Publishing Co. was reaping as the result of publishing solid statewide monopoly newspapers were enough for Knox and Muehling to build the present Union-Leader Building on Amherst Street in Manchester. At the time of its construction in the 1930's, it was the most modern, large newspaper publishing plant in Northern New England.

In Washington, "Cissy" Patterson had made the *Herald* newsier, brighter, breezier, more gossipy and hard-hitting and, as a result, the circulation of the *Herald* had doubled. "Cissy" had found it difficult to accept the hard Hearst line on the Landon-Knox ticket and, even though she favored them slightly over the reelection of Roosevelt and Garner, she was not, as yet at least, violently opposed

to FDR and the New Deal, which had flooded her town
with its supporters. The savagery of the Hearst campaign
for Landon and Knox—especially "canned" editorials and
news stories which she felt were sometimes unfair towards
Roosevelt—was almost unbearable to Mrs. Patterson.

"The Chief" was in trouble on a grand scale during
1937–8, overextended in his operations and badly in need
of capital. It was a kind of "open secret" at the time that
Mrs. Patterson dipped into the family bankroll to aid
Hearst in his financial dilemma. So it is easily understood
why, at this same time, Hearst leased to "Cissy" the two
Washington newspapers with an option to buy. In 1939,
she purchased the two newspapers for a reported $2 mil-
lion and merged them into the *Times-Herald* which she
published round-the-clock.

After war was declared by England and France in September, 1939, it was obvious that the United States was
pitifully unprepared for any kind of war. And shortly
thereafter President Roosevelt dipped into the Republican
ranks to enlist the support of Colonel Knox as Secretary
of the Navy and Col. Henry L. Stimson as Secretary of War.
With these two as the cornerstones, Roosevelt made pre-
paredness for war his first priority. It was at this time that
Colonel Knox advised his former political comrades that
he was for "America first."

Knox took leave of absence from his publishing domain
and assumed full-time control of the Navy Department on
July 11, 1940. Although he still preferred to be addressed
by his Army rank rather than as "Mr. Secretary," and
although he was totally involved in building the nation's
seagoing might, Colonel Knox apparently never forgot for
a moment that he was a newspaperman. He religiously
conducted 9 A.M. press briefings in his Navy Department
office, which were attended by the reporters assigned to
the vital Navy press office. Any time there was an urgent
development during a business day, Colonel Knox would
either summon "the boys" from the press room or convey
word down, and it was not at all unusual for the Secretary

of the Navy to make an unannounced personal visit to the press room, never to pry, but only to bring personal word of any new development he felt was of news value.

While Knox's main job was the building of surface ships, submarines, and airplanes for the Navy, as well as recruiting the personnel to man them, he was faced with the increasingly important problem of security for the active fleet, mostly based in the Atlantic. The demands for supplies from the United States to the European and Russian fronts were becoming greater with each passing day and Nazi submarines were reported lurking—even sinking shipping—as near as the fishing banks off the New England coastline. Navy gun crews sailed aboard merchant freighters as "armed guard" escorts, but these relatively minor batteries of armament were never a match for the fire power of a Nazi submarine.

Navy and civilian shipyards all along both coasts were working night and day building ships and boats of every description, and repairing those currently in commission.

The Coast Guard was a part of the Navy in the wartime scheme of things and the U.S. had an operating base of sorts in every harbor and inlet along the entire Atlantic coast. But it was still not enough. The convoys were being sunk closer and closer to home.

The Massachusetts fishermen from Gloucester and Boston and New Bedford, and the Maine and New Hampshire lobstermen, were quietly installed as boatswain's mates, USNR, and their small plodding trawlers became U.S. Navy patrol craft and bore a small number on the bow. These boats carried a .50 caliber machine gun and a powerful radio. The high-powered yachts of the wealthy were conscripted from such ports as Bar Harbor, Me., Marblehead, Mass., and Newport, R.I. These became either patrol craft or submarine chasers, equipped with a modicum of surface armament and communications gear.

The patrols increased in size and in number but the sinkings continued. Colonel Knox needed help; he needed someone of proven ability whom he could trust implicitly. So the Secretary of the Navy made a quick trip to his home in Manchester, N.H., to rearrange elements of his news-paper organization. He put Business Manager Cornelius Dekker in full charge of the Union-Leader Publishing Co., with Arthur T. Brush as advertising director. Managing Editor Robert M. Blood was put in full charge of the news department.

The Secretary of the Navy, who was also president of the Union-Leader Publishing Co., Inc., told the then-editor and publisher about the plans for his new assignment. So while Edmund F. Jewell did not change bosses, he did change employers; he donned a blue suit with gold buttons and stripes and reported to 150 Causeway St., Boston, Mass., as director of the Office of Naval Intelligence for the First Naval District (the New England states, less Connecticut).

And so it was on that Oct. 25, 1941, a crowd estimated at 100,000 lined New York's Fifth Avenue to watch elements of the nation's military might on parade. It was Navy Day, a quasi-holiday instituted when Theodore Roosevelt, Jr., was Assistant Secretary of the Navy in 1921. The cruiser USS *Juneau* slid down the ways at the Kearny, N.J., shipyard and the new warship, after being doused with a bottle of champagne, was called by the Comman-dant of the Third Naval District "another nail in Hitler's coffin."

But it was not an all-victorious Navy Day that bright, sunny Saturday afternoon. Up in Cambridge, Mass., in a coliseum known as Soldiers' Field, 11 midshipmen of the U.S. Naval Academy at Annapolis were lined up in a death struggle to break a scoreless deadlock with Harvard by trying a field goal placement from the 42-yard line with only two minutes to play. At the snap of the ball a single Crimson jersey broke through the Navy defense, the kick was blocked and the game ended in a 0–0 tie. The Crimson jersey which figured in that crucial play was worn by guard Endicott Peabody, a likely enough sounding name for a Harvard gridiron warrior. (Peabody was to be the last of an era of All-Americans to be named from Harvard teams;

a Democratic governor of the Commonwealth of Massachusetts; a Vice Presidential candidate in the 1972 New Hampshire primary, and, in 1973, a member of the National Football Hall of Fame.)

The Army did a little better that day, downing Columbia, 13–0, at West Point. Before 39,500 in New York's Polo Grounds, Fordham got two more touchdowns after Texas Christian had tied the score in the last quarter and the Rose Hill Rams won, 28–14. The "subway alumni" were happy as Notre Dame rolled over Illinois, 49–14, at Champagne, and this was only a "warm-up" for the South Bend team because the Fighting Irish were to play the Black Knights of the Hudson for the championship of all the thrones and dominions in Yankee Stadium a week hence.

The national championship was decided at Ann Arbor, Mich., that October 25 when Minnesota, the nation's top-ranked team, scored a one-touchdown victory over the resident Wolverines, 7–0, before a record crowd of 85,753. And over in Brooklyn, Adelphi snatched a last-second come-from-behind verdict from Brooklyn Prep at Boys' High Field, 19–13. It would be just about the last game for a long spell that not one Paterno boy would be listed in the Brooklyn Prep lineup.

The "Roosevelt Thanksgiving" was coming up, with some states planning Turkey Day on the fourth Thursday, as FDR asked, and some observing the holiday on the last Thursday in November. This created a void in the schedule of Manchester, N.H., High School Central, which would therefore play its game at rival Haverhill, Mass., on the Saturday in between. Pressure was building for a Thanksgiving Day game in Manchester between once-defeated St. Joseph High School for Boys (314 students) and once-defeated Manchester Central (2,066 students), the first such renewal since 1902. Each team added to its credentials on Oct. 25, 1941. Bill Jennings scored two touchdowns and Leo Muzeroll and Babe Larkin one apiece to lead St. Joe's to a 27–0 win over Franklin, while Teddy Osiel scored three touchdowns and George Anagnostou one as Central whipped Portland, Me., 24–0. (On the fifth Thursday of November, 1941, the "grudge" match was played at Manchester's Athletic Field. The final score: St. Joseph 12, Manchester Central 12.)

The financial world was at relative ease over that October weekend in 1941, with Friday's market prices closing fractionally higher in only moderately active trading of 699,310 shares. The average price of common stock on the New York Stock Exchange was $22.66.

Five debutantes were presented on Friday evening to the Four Hundred who were in attendance at the 54th annual Tuxedo Autumn Ball at Tuxedo Park, up in suburban Orange County, New York.

All in the "horsey" set hailed Saturday's hunt meet at the Essex Fox Hounds in Far Hills, N.J., as the most outstanding in the history of the event, the barometer used for such a superlative being the large crowd at the races and the attendant house parties held at "Froh-Heim," the estate of Mr. and Mrs. Evander B. Schley in Somerset County, New Jersey.

One other sports note of the day: Fair Call, owned by the Mill River Stable, paid $75.90 for $2 in winning the $12,225 Ardsley Handicap before a crowd of 26,745 which bet a total of $1,361,090 at Empire City Track in Yonkers. Finishing a poor second, six lengths up the track—from Maine to Spain, as the railbirds say—was Bright Willie.

# 3

The Loeb from whom "Loeb's son" was descended was a remarkable man. The son of a German immigrant, he rose from the station of a part-time telegraph clerk to be executive secretary to the President of the United States, and shortly after the turn of the century the phrases "Tell it to Loeb" and "Blame it on Loeb" were commonplace in the highest corridors of government in his father's adopted land. After leaving government service and becoming somewhat of a Wall Street tycoon, William Loeb was still referred to as "one of the fifty-nine rulers of America."

If there is one thing which is consistent about the Loeb family it is in the naming of male offspring; three generations of male children have been named William. So, to take it from the top, the eldest William Loeb was a German immigrant who arrived in this country midway through the 19th century. He settled in Albany, N.Y., and conducted a business as a hairdresser or barber, and he and his wife, the former Louisa Myer, had four children, Louisa, Amelia, Lillian and William, the only son born in Albany on October 9, 1866. Loeb the elder insisted that his son receive as much formal education as he could afford for the boy, and young William attended grade school. In order to assist the family, the lad worked as a telegraph messenger in his spare time after school and he did odd jobs about the telegraph office. In this connection, he sometimes jotted down incoming messages to be transmitted by the wireless and, thus inspired, undertook the formal study of shorthand in school. In the course of his deliveries, he also came face-to-face with many of the city's leading figures, mainly because these were the people to whom young Loeb was delivering telegrams. One of these was the Episcopal bishop of Albany, who engaged young Loeb to do some shorthand work in connection with the administration of the diocese. By the time he was 22 years old, Loeb had become stenographer to the New York State Assembly and served as a law and general reporter and secretary to many public officials, notably Lieutenant Governor Saxton and Speaker of the Assembly Malby. By 1894 he was so proficient in his secretarial skills that he was a stenographer to the New York State Constitutional Convention, and to the grand jury and district attorney from 1895 until 1898.

Theodore Roosevelt, rough and ready as ever and dead set against a lot of things, among these the idea of women ever holding any position of responsibility, returned to

Albany as governor of New York in January, 1899. He had
previously served in the Assembly, as U.S. Civil Service
Commissioner, as New York City police commissioner, and
Assistant Secretary of the Navy until resigning this post to
form the "Rough Riders."

After his inauguration, Governor Roosevelt engaged the
services of William Loeb as a stenographer on a fill-in
basis when his regular secretary, William J. Youngs, became ill. Loeb was taken to Oyster Bay during the summer
of 1899 as a full-time replacement at an annual salary of
$1,200, but at the end of August, Governor Roosevelt,
praising Loeb's "excellent judgment as well as the utmost
alertness and industry," gave him a 50 per cent pay raise
to $1,800 annually and took him back to Albany as his
full-time secretary. (Youngs' illness had become so severe
that he was prevented from returning to work.) Loeb went
on the Federal payroll in that capacity when Roosevelt was
elected Vice President in 1901.

It was about six months after Inauguration Day when
an assassin's bullet cut down President William McKinley
during a visit to the Pan-American Exposition at Buffalo,
N.Y., on Sept. 8, 1901, and at 2:15 A.M. on September 14,
McKinley died. Theodore Roosevelt became President of
the United States.

George B. Cortelyou had been a stenographer and executive clerk to President Grover Cleveland. He was appointed assistant secretary to President McKinley in 1898,
and in 1900 became secretary. When President McKinley
was shot at Buffalo, Cortelyou held him, mortally wounded,
in his arms and shouted for medical aid. When doctors
arrived, Cortelyou surveyed them coolly and after being
assured by John G. Milburn, to whose house McKinley
had been taken, that the doctors were the best available,
he told them to operate immediately.

"Now?" asked the attending physicians.

"Certainly now," was Cortelyou's reply. He had been
instructed long before by surgeons at New York Hospital
that the delay of an unnecessary minute at a critical period
could prove to be fatal. Cortelyou was widely acclaimed

for his coolness in such an emergency situation at Buffalo, even though the surgery these doctors performed was not enough to save McKinley's life.

President Roosevelt retained Cortelyou as his secretary and Loeb as assistant secretary, and Roosevelt set about the awesome task of running the country. They found Roosevelt to be a demanding and exacting taskmaster.

Loeb, 36 years of age in 1902, had meanwhile fallen in love with a young Albany stenographer named Catherine Wilhelmina Dorr. Her father, Henry Dorr, was also a German immigrant and he ran a saloon in Albany. Mrs. Dorr, the former Henrietta Hans, was a native American. On Feb. 3, 1902, William Loeb married Catherine Dorr, then 26, at Albany City Hall, with City Clerk T. Garry Burns doing the honors. The couple hurried back to Washington soon after the service.

Then in July, 1902, President Roosevelt decided it was time for a rest. He packed his family and went off to the Roosevelt estate at Sagamore Hill, Oyster Bay, Long Island. This particular piece of real estate, the President figured, did not belong to the United States of America; it belonged to Theodore Roosevelt. While he was there he would enjoy it as such. Cortelyou and Loeb were permitted to bring their own families to Sagamore Hill and Loeb and his wife settled in a house on West Shore Road in adjacent Mill Neck, which Loeb used for little more than as a place to sleep. By this time, Mrs. Catherine W. D. Loeb had opted to change the spelling of her name to "Katharine."

The two secretaries handled all press relations and most other details incumbent upon the running of the nation from Oyster Bay. No newspaperman and very few visitors were allowed near Sagamore Hill. Cortelyou and Loeb rented two rooms on Audrey Avenue, over the Oyster Bay Trust Company, and then pushed into a third room which had been occupied by the local dentist who, according to reports at the time, "was not at all sure that, under the Constitution, he need have his dental apparatus moved to provide space for the two stenographers." Loeb and Cortelyou generally took the President's dictation in the library next to the front hall at Sagamore Hill and transcribed their notes and conveyed Roosevelt's messages from their offices over the bank in downtown Oyster Bay.

President Roosevelt had an understandable soft spot in his heart for Cuba and the Cuban people, their welfare and their economy. After all, he had become close to the Cubans during his wartime expedition to their island. Some of the infantry which accompanied the "Rough Riders" in their charge up San Juan Hill had taken refuge and used as fortifications some of the huge, rough, cast iron kettles which, when placed over an open, roaring fire, the Cubans used to distill the raw sugar which they had, under normal peacetime conditions, harvested in these very fields. President Roosevelt was becoming distressed over the amount of trade with Cuba, legal and illegal, and he took steps to do something about it. The President named Cortelyou Secretary of Commerce and Frank Steinhart consul-general to Havana. Loeb became chief secretary to President Roosevelt.

The trade between the United States and Cuba grew at an amazing rate. The McKinley Act, enacted in 1890, had raised duties on certain agricultural products, including tobacco, and remitted the duty on raw sugar, but this law was repealed in 1894. Tobacco and sugar were still the main products involved in the trade with the United States, but there were also vast quantities of iron ore in Cuba, particularly along the northern coast of Oriente Province. And not only did trade with the outside world mushroom, but Cuba itself began to become heavily industrialized. American investment in Cuba had averaged $30,000,000 annually in the period from 1898 until 1902, but by 1906 it totalled some $200,000,000, representing large interests in banking, railroads, electric railroads, sugar and tobacco planting and growing, telephone, fruit and fruit land, cattle, real estate and unimproved land, mining, mortgages and steamships.

There were vast quantities of money in Cuba and vast

quantities of money were made in trading when the developers had done their job. The American Cigar Company and the American Sugar Company were but two of the principal, U.S.-based firms which marked tremendous growth during those years. According to Moody's, the American Cigar Company, which was wholly-owned by the American Tobacco Company, owned $3,500,000 in bonds of the Havana Commercial Corporation, plus two-thirds of the stock of the company. The Havana organization was, in turn, a holding company for the various factories it owned, and carried securities of the latter at $41,860,000.

The amazing career of Consul-General Steinhart is also worth mention; it is an example of how enterprise was rewarded, all legal and above-board by Roosevelt lieutenants during this period. Steinhart was a German immigrant who had settled in Pennsylvania and had decided on the Army as a career. He had twice been named for officer training and twice had been bounced out, once for gambling and once for neglect of duty, but he won the favor of General "Phil" Sheridan because he was a "muleskinner" second to none. In his spare time, however, he studied law and Spanish and he became an aide to Sheridan. When the war was over, Steinhart told his superiors that he liked it in Cuba and he would just like to mosey around a bit, and he became a member of the Army of Occupation. President Roosevelt called him back for duty as a White House aide until he had served out his enlistment and was discharged with the rank of sergeant. Roosevelt immediately named him consul-general to Havana in which office he served until 1907.

It was later disclosed that Steinhart was head of the Havana Jockey Club, the Havana Electric Railway, two insurance companies, two banks and a large warehousing firm. He made periodic trips to New York, even while he was consul-general, to take part in huge manipulations of stocks and bonds, once involving a loan purchase by the Archdiocese of New York. On this particular occasion, Steinhart was badly in need of some fast money. He had attended to some official courtesies for some Catholics in

Cuba and his daughter attended a convent school in the New York archdiocese. So he approached Archbishop John Farley (later a cardinal) and proposed that the archdiocese buy a million dollars' worth of 5 per cent bonds at 85, with the guarantee that Steinhart would buy them back at 90 within a year. The archbishop went for it and Steinhart and Warren Bicknell, an experienced traction man from Cleveland, obtained control of the Havana Electric Railway. In the first five years after Steinhart took over the Havana Electric Railway and converted the old horse cars into trolley cars, the line showed a profit of $40,000 for each mile of its 60 miles of track.

There were the Dukes, the Schleys, the Wideners, the Ryans, the Bradys—to name a few—and nobody was asking anybody where they got their dough. But President Roosevelt was interested. Cortelyou resigned his Commerce post to become chairman of the Republican National Committee and to manage TR's successful reelection bid in 1904. Then Roosevelt appointed Cortelyou Secretary of the Treasury with firm instructions to keep a sharp eye on the workings of the U.S. Customs Service.

As he managed the secretarial duties for the President, Loeb became the overseer of a group of stenographers who took the dictation and typing, but he always did the most important jobs himself. This left a little more time for more intimate relations with the Roosevelts and it was not long before Loeb was being called "Uncle Bill" by the Roosevelt children. He was included in many family activities, such as the children's birthday parties, and Loeb, who loved children, enjoyed this role and even counseled the children, at the President's invitation, on educational and other personal matters. Loeb also became somewhat the master of the family exchequer, as well as TR's personal business manager.

Katharine Loeb became pregnant in the spring of 1905 and on December 26, 1905, she delivered a boy. Naturally, he, too, was called William. The Roosevelts were as happy as Loeb and when the infant was christened at an Episcopalian baptism, President and Mrs. Roosevelt acted as god-parents.

But the life of William Loeb as executive secretary to President Roosevelt was a hectic existence. He was away from his own home and family for long stretches and it was seldom he got a full day off, even on a weekend. He was not only a secretary, but a factotum who served as buffer between the impulsive President and a host of other impulsive people, impetuous office holders and office seekers, offerers and seekers of favors. Loeb was always at the elbow of the President at the White House and elsewhere. When Loeb announced to the press any one of a number of items in behalf of the President, there was always an undercurrent of speculation as to which of the decisions announced in the President's name had been made by the President and which had been made by Loeb. And there wasn't a man among the whole press corps who ever had the nerve to ask. Loeb could be very gracious, but, when need be, he could be bold and forceful.

Loeb monitored the press relations for all branches of the Roosevelt Administration and he was not above chastising a court decision when it went against one of the Roosevelt interests. He was generally helpful to the press and usually went out of his way to pacify its members when things were not going well. But he could also get pretty roiled up himself.

The *Boston Herald* had been a severe critic of many facets of the Roosevelt Administration and after Thanksgiving Day in 1904 the newspaper ran a story and an editorial which told about a Boston citizen who had donated a turkey to the White House for their Thanksgiving feast. The story had it that the turkey, instead of being immediately killed and dressed, had been let loose on the White House lawn, while the Roosevelt children engaged themselves in chasing the bird, plucking at it and teasing it. The *Herald* further said that TR himself stood by and watched this cruelty and apparently thought it was pretty entertaining.

Loeb was furious. He immediately issued a statement

that the bird donated by the Bostonian had been immediately killed and dressed and was, indeed, used at the White House Thanksgiving. Yes, there was another turkey; it had been donated by a Wisconsin company and was immediately shipped to Oyster Bay where it was living a life of tranquility. Then Loeb notified the length and breadth of the Executive Department of the government that the *Boston Herald* was to get no press releases or interviews or any other news of any government office. An immediate order was transmitted within all government departments and, as a result, the *Boston Herald* was even cut off from getting forecasts from the U.S. Weather Bureau at Boston.

Being so close to the President at all times and in practically all of his dealings, Loeb became a member of the inner circle of TR's friends and advisers. These included James R. Garfield, Secretary of the Interior; Elihu Root, Secretary of War and State; William Howard Taft, Secretary of War; Gifford Pinchot, chief of the Forest Service; Sen. Albert J. Beveridge of Indiana and Sen. Henry Cabot Lodge of Massachusetts. All these, and countless other lesser advisers, seemingly got along fairly well during the Roosevelt days. But Lodge, the wealthy Brahmin, brought with him to Washington an air of superiority which made him seem cold and distant. Even TR considered him something special.

Lodge was widely known as a scholar who enjoyed a high measure of respect on both sides of the Senate aisle. It had been Lodge who, early-on, had been sort of a "godfather" to TR in politics and it was Lodge who had secured the Civil Service Commission job for the young Theodore before the war. And he was still aggressive and ambitious through the Roosevelt days and until well after World War 1. It is interesting that in the papers of Theodore Roosevelt, in the countless letters and memos to and from Senator Lodge, the Massachusetts statesman normally referred to the President's secretary as "Loeb," with terse notes, "have Loeb do this," or the like. The President's reply would always say, "Mr. Loeb did this," etc.

If William Howard Taft owed his nomination in 1908

to anyone besides Theodore Roosevelt, it was to William
Loeb. It was Loeb who finally dissuaded TR from seeking
a "third" term and doing it in sufficient time to allow
Taft to stage the build-up necessary for him to gain the
nomination. Loeb then set to work lining up state delegations for Taft and made available to Taft his voluminous recall of the important persons in specific locales
who could be helpful.

About this time, Loeb was widely mentioned as next
chairman of the Republican National Committee and
there may have been some talk of Loeb being included in
the Taft Cabinet. It was also known that Loeb was investigating possible employment in the fields of railroads,
utilities and insurance. But when the Taft Administration
came into the White House in 1909, Loeb was named
Collector of Customs of the Port of New York, a nomination made by retiring President Roosevelt to President-
elect Taft. Loeb set about, post haste, to weed out the
graft, corruption and smuggling which had beset the New
York waterfront and which had always been administered
to by heads of that branch of the Customs Service in a
happy-go-lucky fashion.

Loeb ended the system of gentle grafting which was
everyday practice, and incurred the wrath of the inefficient
and shady customs officials. He fired many from the service
and declared open war on smugglers. Quite naturally, the
New York merchants loved him; for they were getting a
fair shake. (Some of them probably didn't realize that they
were being short-changed along the docks until the Loeb
Administration came into being.) Loeb, meanwhile, was
receiving many warnings that he was being measured for
cement swimming trunks and might be given the opportunity to try them out.

Loeb is reputed to have told a group of friends: "The
rich duty jumper is not going to get off any easier than
the poor duty jumper. A man may be a multi-millionaire,
but if he defrauds the government he is going to land in
jail. I can't see any difference between the dressmaker and
the society woman. A big clubman trying to evade duty

on jewels looks just the same to me as the immigrant trying to smuggle a cheese through in his chest." From certain sugar interests alone, Loeb exacted refunds totalling
$3,434,304.37. All duties were weighed fairly and several
customs officials were indicted and tried for past misdeeds.
And when Loeb left the job as Collector of Customs of
the Port of New York, he enjoyed the reputation of scru-
pulous honesty and fairness to all. He was known as a me-
ticulous dresser and had very neat business habits, a neat
desk, orderly notes, and he was also known as a "really
nice guy."

It was not long after Loeb stepped down as collector
that the world sugar market was moved from Hamburg,
Germany, to become part of the New York Coffee Exchange at 79 Pine Street in New York City where business
is conducted to this day.

During the conflict between Taft and Roosevelt over
the 1912 nomination for President, Loeb maintained loyalty to both and he tried to dissuade TR from seeking the
Bull Moose nomination. It was Loeb's firm opinion that
Roosevelt could have gained office in 1916 and he went
to the Republican nominating convention in Chicago in
1912 to work with Cortelyou to the end that Roosevelt
would get the nomination four years hence.

But the break came. Loeb all but vanished from the
public eye when he stepped down as collector in 1913. He
was by that time a moderately wealthy man, having been
paid well over the years and having invested wisely. Besides this, the demands President Roosevelt had placed on
his time had restricted whatever wishes Loeb might have
had to spend money on pleasures, such as vacations, lavish
homes, or other luxuries. He had gone on a few hunting
expeditions with the President, mostly as TR's guest. Loeb
and his wife and only child continued to live in Mill Neck,
and young William had been brought to play with the
Roosevelt children at Sagamore Hill, as well as at the
White House.

Loeb became manager of the Guggenheim properties
after resigning from the Customs Service and became a

vice president of American Smelting and Refining Co.
Oscar Strauss, Secretary of Commerce and Secretary of Labor, was in private life president of American Smelting.
He had urged Loeb to join the company since he left
Roosevelt's employ in 1908. American Smelting and Refining was engaged in development work on a large scale
in Western copper mining and the opening of natural resources. The corporation had vast interests in a wide variety of projects, from explorations and development in
Alaska to rubber gathering in the Congo, mining in the
United States, South Africa, Australia and the Orient.

Loeb brought to Wall Street the diligence and executive
ability—not to mention high government and political
contacts—which had distinguished his prior federal service. He maintained a close friendship with Teddy Roosevelt, and was frequently summoned to Sagamore Hill for
conferences with Senator Lodge, Colonel Knox, Senator
Beveridge and other senior advisers. Loeb twice served in
public office, both on a part-time basis, as mayor of the
"millionaire villages" of Mill Neck and Bayville, Long
Island. He became president of the Albany Society of New
York and he belonged to the Masonic Order, advancing
to its 33rd degree, and was a member of the National
Republican Club.

But all this time, Loeb was using his power, knowledge,
ability and accrued wealth to attain even more wealth and
he became a director of Pacific Tin Corp., Connecticut
Light and Power Co., Connecticut Electric Service Corp.,
Yukon Gold Co., Angola Mines, Congo Mines and the Reo
Motor Car Co. And when he went on his pleasure trips,
hunting or fishing, it was to such places as Montana, Colorado, Western Minnesota, or the Congo, thus affording
Loeb the opportunity to survey the local scene and talk
with local people, thereby gaining first-hand knowledge of
any prospects of development of new natural resources.

Loeb suffered, along with most other members of the
financial world, during the stock market crash and the Depression which followed, but he managed to keep his head
above water. In 1934, he retired from American Smelting

and Refining, the vice presidency of which he had held continuously since 1913. But he retained his many directorships and attended advisory committee meetings on a regular basis. He devoted much time during his retirement years to the National Roosevelt Memorial Association, of which he was a vice president, and the Oscar Strauss Memorial Association, of which he was president.

Within one month of his 71st birthday he became seriously ill with pneumonia and, after an illness of 12 days, he died on Sept. 19, 1937, at the North Country Community Hospital, Glen Cove, Long Island. With him when he died were his wife and only child.

Hundreds of floral tributes and telegrams were received by Mrs. Loeb, including messages from President Franklin D. Roosevelt and Former President Herbert Hoover. And when funeral services were held in Oyster Bay on September 21, Christ Episcopal Church was filled to overflowing with neighbors, employes, tradespeople, and men and women prominent in society, the financial, diplomatic and political worlds.

One of the six ushers was Capt. Archibald Roosevelt and among those in attendance were Col. and Mrs. Theodore Roosevelt, Jr., George B. Cortelyou, Former President Carlos Hevia of Cuba and Mrs. Richard Derby, the former Ethel Roosevelt.

When Loeb's will, which he had made on Jan. 5, 1932, was admitted to probate on June 2, 1938, it was shown that he left an estate valued at $256,405.05. Of this, he bequeathed the sum of $15,000 to his three sisters, Louisa Loeb Neudorf, Amelia Olive Loeb and Lillian May Loeb. The remainder was left to his widow, Mrs. Katharine W. D. Loeb, who was also named executrix.

"Loeb's son" was not his heir. As a matter of fact, he was mentioned not at all in the one-page document.

# 4

All accounts indicate that William Loeb, Sr., was not only protective and kind, but sincerely loving and solicitous towards the four children of the President, the youngest of whom was Archibald Bulloch Roosevelt, born in April, 1894. And the Loeb family was treated reciprocally during the years their only child was growing up. William Loeb, Jr., or III, as he was sometimes referred to, was given free rein on the White House lawn in his earliest years and, after TR had left Washington, young Loeb cavorted in the orchards and on the vast lawns of Sagamore Hill in Oyster Bay. He was always under a watchful eye, however; if it was not one of the Roosevelt children, it was Mrs. Loeb or a governess or maid.

It was not unusual for the President, if he were present, to fawn upon his godchild. And it was unusual when, in a note or memorandum to his secretary and friend, the President did not include regards and love to Mrs. Loeb and the boy.

William's early schooling was by tutors, and then he was sent to the Allen-Stevenson School at 50 East 57th St. in New York City, a very private, very exclusive and very expensive school indeed. William hated it. During a trip to Europe with his mother and father in the fall of 1919, when he was 13 years old, he told his parents he wanted out. So it was decided to send young William to The Hotchkiss School in Lakeville, Conn., and he took the entrance examinations in the spring of 1920 for admission to the lower middle (sophomore) class. There was a little bit of trouble here; young Loeb got 73 in Latin, 60 in French, 70 in English (if you didn't count spelling which was awful) and 18 in Algebra. Rev. Dr. Huber Gray Buehler, the headmaster of Hotchkiss, had become friendly with Mr. Loeb during the course of negotiations for William's admission, and he wrote Mr. Loeb that if the boy were reexamined in September he was sure young Bill would be admitted to the Lower Middle. Mr. Loeb wrote Rev. Dr. Buehler back, suggesting that Buehler and his wife join the Loebs on a European sojourn that summer.

Bill Loeb was admitted to The Hotchkiss School in the fall of 1920 as a member of Lower Middle. At school, Loeb was a moderately good student, even though he never did learn to spell. But, he was a member of St. Luke's and Olympian, social societies, the class football team (one year) and the Debating Union. Firearms particularly fascinated him and he was a member of the Gun Club every year at Hotchkiss, but was never proficient enough to qualify for the rifle or pistol teams.

Loeb's biggest problem at prep school was getting along. He came on pretty strong with his schoolmates and they always referred to him tauntingly as "the Jew kid," but it was his personality rather than any racial bias which set him apart from the others. The nicknames which accompany his cherubic picture in the *Misch*, the Hotchkiss yearbook, are "Snake" and "Valentino" but those are the kindest things he was called by his classmates. He was pretty much a loner; his name is conspicuous by its absence from the list of other students, with their dates and dates' chaperones, which regularly appeared in the school weekly newspaper on the occasion of any dance or prom. Also accompanying his picture in the *Misch* is the quotation, "It's my eyes that makes the girls fall for me!", indicating either that Loeb had a pretty high regard for himself as a lady-killer or that he had a pretty low regard for the rules of English grammar, or both. Loeb received only token mention in "How the Class Voted."

All this while, young Loeb was the apple of his parents' eyes. The Loebs had a lot of company at their home in Mill Neck, and a lot of these guests had a lot of credentials. The Loebs had moved into a larger home in Mill Neck, "Westerleigh," also adjacent to the Roosevelt mansion. Many of the Loebs' guests were those who would combine a visit to Theodore Roosevelt at Sagamore Hill and then a more casual and relaxed visit with Mr. Loeb and his wife. Then, too, it was not at all out of the question for the President to invite more than one person for lunch or to give more than one group an appointment for the same hour or for dinner. To assuage feelings and to prevent any unpleasantness, the Loebs bent over backwards to make these people always welcome in their home. Young William was usually brought forth to meet the visitors—ambassadors, businessmen, senators, statesmen, bishops, vicars, rabbis and even real royalty. He was taught impeccable manners, in the parlor and at the table, but he was encouraged always to display his brilliance by being allowed to enter into conversations, up to a point. He was always dressed neatly in expensive clothes.

Bill Loeb became a freshman at Williams College in Williamstown, Mass., in the fall of 1923. Zeta Psi was Loeb's choice of fraternities and his interest in firearms and forensics continued with membership in the Rifle Club and Class Debate. Outside of classroom hours, Williams men of that era had their minds on movies, football, raccoon coats, Vanity Fair, beer, "Silent Cal" Coolidge, Lucky Strikes, Hupmobiles; for female companionship, the Williams men opted for brunettes, and Vassar was the favorite women's college, a close choice over Smith, with Wellesley a distant third. It was a big lark to spend a weekend in New York, but if you couldn't get there, Northampton would do.

So it was that, far from the cloistered setting of Hotchkiss and the watchful eyes at the White House and Sagamore Hill, Loeb ventured to Northampton and Smith College in his leisure time and there he was fascinated by, and became enamoured with, typically, a brunette. The lady of Loeb's choosing, however, was not a student but a member of the Smith College faculty, eight years his senior.

Whether it was the security of an older woman or the intellectual exchange—his major was philosophy and his weekend date was an instructor in philosophy—the romance grew and blossomed. On May 29, 1926, before the end of his junior year and over the adamant objections of his parents, William Loeb, Jr., and Miss Elizabeth V. Nagy became man and wife.

*The New York Times* did not get around to reporting

the marriage until Sept. 22, 1926. The manner in which it was then reported—even that it was printed at that date at all—gives some indication of the importance of the Loeb family at the time:

## WILLIAM LOEB JR. WED
## TEACHER ON MAY 29

### Married Elizabeth V. Nagy of
### Smith College—He Is a Senior
### at Williams College.

"NORTHAMPTON, Mass., Sept. 21 (AP).—William Loeb, Jr., of Oyster Bay, N.Y., whose father was Secretary to President Roosevelt, and Elizabeth V. Nagy, daughter of Mr. and Mrs. George J. Nagy of East Haven, Conn., were married at Petersburg, N.Y., on May 29, they announced today.

"The bride is Instructor in Philosophy at Smith College. She is a graduate of Connecticut College and received a Doctor of Philosophy degree from the Yale Graduate School. Mr. Loeb is a senior at Williams College, and plans to attend the Harvard Law School after his graduation from Williams.

"At the offices of William Loeb, Sr., at 120 Broadway it was said yesterday that Mr. Loeb was out of the city inspecting plants of the American Smelting and Refining Company, of which he is head. No members of the family could be reached last night at their home in Oyster Bay. Nothing was known of the reported marriage of William Loeb, Jr., and Miss Nagy either at the home or at the office."

Elizabeth Nagy was of French-Austrian ancestry and had received her B.A. at Connecticut College for Women in New London in 1920. She returned to her native New Haven and did graduate work at Yale University, receiving her doctorate in 1923, the year Loeb was graduated from Hotchkiss, in upstate Lakeville. She maintained an apartment at 16 Arnold Avenue in Northhampton and Loeb spent all the time he could there—while he wasn't at the Zete House at Williams, that is.

But Zeta Psi, too, became a problem, because, again, Loeb couldn't seem to get along with his fraternity brothers. Indeed, he gained quite a reputation on campus for "mouthing off" about the "injustices" of the admissions policies of his fraternity, which got him nowhere but outside of the fraternity house. But Loeb's reputation spread far beyond fraternity row when, as president of Forum, he invited William Green, president of the American Federation of Labor, to give an address on campus. This excited all the conservatives among the administration and faculty, as well as those among the undergraduates. After all, the laboring class in the United States had very few real connections with any of the Williams College "family" at this point and any invitation to such a guest speaker was considered "radical," or at the very least, "liberal."

Loeb was graduated with the degree of Bachelor of Arts in June, 1927, and then his wife quit her job at Smith. Loeb had been receiving support from his parents for both himself and his wife, and she had been receiving a salary, also. Following his graduation, the Loebs resided variously at Heartwellville, Vt., Winston, Mass., and Georgetown, S.C., and in the spring of 1928, they arrived at Oyster Bay to visit Loeb's father and mother. It appears that Mr. and Mrs. Loeb were happy to have William at home; but not the daughter-in-law, who spent the night in a lodging house. Young Loeb and his wife quickly left for Cambridge, where Elizabeth Nagy Loeb again secured a teaching position and William entered Harvard Law School in the fall of 1928. His parents were still paying William's bills at least, and the couple found an apartment on 95 Prescott St. in Cambridge. Domestically, it was a mess. Loeb wasn't setting any scholastic records, either, at Harvard Law School and, before the completion of two years he packed up and returned to his parents' home at Mill Neck. He filed an annulment action and Elizabeth

Nagy Loeb filed an alienation of affection suit for $100,000 against Mr. and Mrs. Loeb. Then Mrs. Elizabeth V. Loeb filed a divorce suit. On Oct. 4, 1932, the petition was heard by Supreme Court Justice Charles J. Druhan, sitting in Mineola, Long Island, the seat of Nassau County, New York. Mrs. Loeb asked alimony of $200 monthly, in addition to counsel fees.

The case attracted the attention of *The Times,* the *Herald Tribune* and the *Daily News,* all of which reported it because of the prominence of the elder William Loeb. Justice Druhan reserved decision when Mrs. Loeb and her attorneys presented her case, and ordered William Loeb, Jr., to respond to the action by Oct. 7. Loeb, Jr., appeared on the date specified and he told Justice Druhan that he was virtually without funds, that he would default in pleading to the divorce action and allow his wife to take an inquest in the case. Loeb told Justice Druhan that Elizabeth could not make a *prima facie* case even if the action were not defended; that his mother and father had made an offer, which they deemed more than adequate, to the wife to settle this divorce, but it was withdrawn when she turned it down and threatened to bring a divorce action in Massachusetts. Besides, said Loeb, who was almost 27 years old at the time, the woman was a school teacher and was capable of earning her own living. *The Times* of Oct. 8, 1932 reported further:

"Referring to charges of extravagance and statements by Mrs. Loeb that her husband received a yearly allowance, Loeb declared that his father's salary had been cut in half, and that his income had been seriously reduced. He said that his father had been giving him only a small amount of pocket money, and that he couldn't afford a lawyer."

On October 11, 1932, Justice Druhan awarded Mrs. Loeb $30 weekly alimony and counsel fees of $350. It was later disclosed that Mr. and Mrs. Loeb paid Mrs. Elizabeth Loeb $5,000 to settle the alienation of affection suit. It was also later reported that Mr. and Mrs. Loeb paid their son's alimony until Elizabeth, who assumed the name of Laine, remarried.

She is now a widow and in poor health, living in California.

There is reason to believe that Loeb contested this decree by Justice Druhan, even though his mother and father were making the alimony payments. Listed by title in the libers of Nassau County are many documents which indicate hearings and depositions in the case as late as 1939, but, even though the documents were registered and given a case number, the notation on microfilm indicates that the records were missing when the microfilm was photographed. They exist nowhere else in the court house. No one in the Mineola office building can explain the nonexistence of the records of the case of Loeb v. Loeb, Case F-3144.

William Loeb told several friends and acquaintances that his ambition was to be a newspaper publisher, to be the "power behind the throne," and he got a job as a cub reporter on a New York newspaper and, the story goes (as repeated in *The New York Times* of Dec. 12, 1971), he was assigned to cover a round table discussion on the subject of independence for India. According to Loeb: "It was conducted by, of all people, a British civil servant who helped design colonial policies in India." Loeb became so incensed during the proceedings that he joined in the discussion and a restraining hand from a reporter from *The Times* is all that saved Loeb from being tossed out of the meeting. "He gave me hell for not keeping my mouth shut," said Loeb. So, although this was not the reason given, it appears that Loeb's journalism career, at least for the period, came to a halt.

Loeb next dabbled in politics of the international variety, working for the Nationalist Chinese and the Dominican Republic, but he still received an allowance from his father. When Loeb's father died in 1937, his mother put him in charge of managing her portfolio of securities, largely in the fields and interests in which the elder Loeb held directorships. Young Loeb's income was one-half of the net profits which the mother realized from the sale of these securities, and it was immediately profitable, because there was no way young Loeb could lose.

William Loeb, Jr., became a director of the Reo Motor Car Co. with the stock which his mother inherited. But Loeb's career as an automotive tycoon lasted only slightly longer than his career as a newspaperman. In March and April of 1938, he got himself involved in a caper which cost him the directorship.

On March 30, 1938, Loeb asked for proxies in anticipation of the regular stockholders' meeting, to be held on April 19, so that control of the company could be shifted and completely reorganized. In a letter to stockholders, Loeb said he was joined in the move by Frank A. Vanderlip and Charles G. Sinclair, fellow directors. On April 1, both Sinclair and Vanderlip denied any complicity in Loeb's announced arrangement and both immediately resigned as directors of Reo. Loeb, however, issued a public statement that the resignations of Vanderlip and Sinclair would "in no way deter me in my firm resolve to see that the stockholders of Reo Motor Car Company get a break," again according to reports in *The New York Times*. The Reo annual meeting was held in Lansing, Mich., and on April 26 the company announced the results of the meeting. Not only did Loeb's plan for reorganization fail to materialize, Loeb was not reelected a director of the company. Earl W. Goodnow of Lansing was named to replace Loeb and Ray Potter of Lansing and Carleton Higbie of Detroit were both reelected. It was announced that successors to Vanderlip and Sinclair would be named at a future meeting.

Loeb then became an expert in the fields of world trade and international relations. By January of 1939, the Committee for a Boycott Against Japanese Aggression, of which William Loeb was chairman, announced that it was changing its name to National Boycott Against Aggressor Nations and this statement was made through Chairman Loeb. Signing the manifesto supporting this change were many professors and persons who had been formerly in political office—individuals known in pre-war days as "parlor pinks."

Later that year, while the so-called Dies Committee of
the U.S. Congress was investigating Communist infiltra-
tion into the United States, J. B. Mathews, committee
research aide, released a report stating: "A great part of
the current popular and official attack upon advertising is
the direct result of Communist propaganda in the field of
consumer organizations." Chairman Loeb said that
Mathews' methods were extremely "detrimental to public
confidence in the sincerity and accuracy of the Dies Committee's work." He said that he welcomed investigation
into un-American activities and denied most emphatically
that his boycott group "was ever dominated or influenced
by Communists," according to *The Times*. And on the
very next day, Loeb's boycott group announced that it was
extending its boycott to include Russia, which had in-
vaded Finland. This statement was issued jointly by Dr.
Mary E. Woolley, president emeritus of Mt. Holyoke
College, and Chairman Loeb from the boycott group's
offices at 5 Maiden Lane in New York City.

One of the products which was foremost on the list
which this country was asked to boycott was manganese.
The prime, and only, use for the manganese imported into
this country during those pre-war years was in the making
of gun barrels and cannons, which manganese could
strengthen as could no other metal.

According to several persons who knew Loeb at this
time, it was obvious that Loeb was being used as a "dupe"
and the groups with which he was involved were interested
only in using Loeb's name, now that he was going without the "Jr.". This was a very large prestige factor on
Wall Street and fund-raising was the name of the game
for these do-gooders.

Although Loeb was a sometime member of the social set
on the Long Island North Shore, he never made it to the
inner circles. But about this time he met the woman who
would become the second Mrs. Loeb. It was at a tea dance
that Miss Eleanore McAllister and William Loeb were introduced. She remembers him as "being kind of puny" but
likable. "He looked very Jewish and he hated it," she

recalls, "and all he talked about was how he was going
to be a big newspaper publisher . . . never a newspaperman, just a publisher."

They were together frequently and grew fond of each
other. Miss McAllister was an accomplished horsewoman
and, as such, she was involved in the social whirl of Long
Island. Loeb was always pleasant company, she says, a perfect gentleman and a more than adequate conversational-
ist, although he was quite a name-dropper.

It was in late 1939 or early 1940 that Loeb became
acquainted with Charles Graham Weaver, editor of the
Oyster Bay weekly newspaper which was owned by Bronson Griscomb. Weaver had been born in Atlanta, Ga.,
attended the University of Virginia and "had gravitated
north in the newspaper business." He was five years older
than Loeb.

Charlie Weaver is most loquacious in his reminiscences
of William Loeb. In 1975, after twenty years as a member
of the staff of U.S. Sen. George Aiken (R-Vt.), he and his
wife, Dot, share a retirement home on a mountain top in
Kirby, Vt., a town with 13 miles of roads, all unpaved.

Weaver says he knew Loeb's mother, "an absolutely
sterling and wonderful woman, one of the finest women
I've ever known in my life, and I understand that Bill's
father was the same kind." He tells the story that he, as
the Oyster Bay editor, had become involved in a local high
school teacher tenure fight which attracted wide interest
and that Loeb had been quite some moral support to him
at the time.

"The political forces in the town resented the way I
championed this cause," says Weaver, "but they were taking this person and throwing the book at him, and I was
very discouraged because no matter which way I turned, I
found the establishment was crushing me. And I knew
that certain very powerful forces had gone to Bronson
Griscomb and Bronson was after me to let up.

"At just about that time, Bill Loeb walked into the
office one day and he said, 'I understand you're under a

lot of pressure.' I said, 'I certainly am.' I didn't know him
at all, never had run into Bill at all. 'Well,' he said, 'You're
doing the right thing. You're fighting for what you think
is right,' and he said, 'I'll give you support.'

"And, I believe, as I recall, he called up Bronson Griscomb and told him not to let go, and we took that case to
Albany before the commissioner of education. We won it
hands down and I would not have been able to have done
that if Bill hadn't given me the help he did. We had riots
there in Oyster Bay at the time," Weaver continued. "The
school kids were all out and I can recall the newsreel
cameramen came out from New York; this thing was in
the newsreels all the time. Cripes, I was up on a platform
there with the superintendent of schools trying to quiet a
mob. Damnedest experience I ever had in my life."

Another catalyst which brought Weaver and Loeb closer
together was the candidacy of Wendell Willkie for President. The two worked in the "Willkie for President" headquarters in Oyster Bay, as did Mrs. Marka Truesdale
Loening, who, approaching 30, had just become separated
from Grover Loening after 10 years of marriage. Mrs.
Loening and her husband, parents of three, had both
known of Loeb and knew the Loeb family; she and her
family were residents of Mill Neck. She had been married
at 19 and was 22 years her husband's junior.

Loening, son of the U.S. consul to Bremen, Germany, at
the time of his birth, had become an aviation industrialist
after his graduation from Columbia University and he had
invented the strut-braced monoplane and the Loening
amphibian airplane. It was no secret that the separation
agreement provided generous support for Mrs. Loening
and the three children. It was also very obvious that Mrs.
Loening was a most charming and very attractive lady.

"Then," says Charlie Weaver, "after that (school) thing
was over Bill walked into the office one day—that thing
stretched out over a period of months—he walked into the
office one day and he said, 'Charlie, let's go to Vermont
and put out a newspaper.' Well, that sounded great to me."

So Loeb and Weaver scouted Vermont and Northern

Massachusetts looking for newspaper properties which were available. Weaver says that he would fly up on weekends and meet Loeb, who had been in the area all week. They investigated possible purchases of dailies in Greenfield, Mass., Brattleboro and Montpelier, Vt., and a string of weeklies in Vergennes, Vt.

"But I would come up," says Weaver, "and we'd go driving all over hell and go looking for newspapers and we finally stumbled onto the St. Albans paper. Somebody told us we might be able to buy it. That's how we got it."

So with $40,000 which Loeb's mother advanced to him, Loeb purchased the *St. Albans Daily Messenger,* effective Oct. 25, 1941. He gave Charlie Weaver stock in the corporation and Weaver became second in command.

"Loeb's son" became Publisher Loeb.

# II
# Where?

Writing good editorials is chiefly
telling the people what they think,
not what you think.

—ARTHUR BRISBANE

# 5

The new ownership of Vermont's oldest evening news-paper was proclaimed in a two-column "box" on Page One of the edition of Saturday, Oct. 25, 1941:

## Announcement

We take pleasure in announcing as of today, October 25, 1941, the transfer of this property to Mr. William Loeb, of Oyster Bay, N.Y.

Mr. Loeb is the son of the late William Loeb, executive secretary to Former President Theodore Roosevelt during his term in the White House.

We believe that the Messenger will continue to give the community and county the same service that it has in the past, and we do not hesitate to commend Mr. Loeb to our subscribers and advertisers and solicit on his behalf their continued support.

ST. ALBANS MESSENGER COMPANY

Loeb and Weaver established temporary quarters at the Hotel Kelley on Main Street a short time before the sale was announced in the paper and anybody who was anybody in this one-street little city knew all about Loeb and Weaver before the date of the announcement, or they thought they did. The bellman-porter-handyman-clerk at the tiny hotel was, in fact, exaggerating the quantities of booze he said he took to their rooms.

The two were instantly recognizable figures, forever going to, or returning from, the *Messenger* offices near the depot around the corner. Well tailored, nice appearing, both had a distinct "big city" flair to them, real or imagined, Loeb a little the more so. Weaver was the taller and he gave the impression of being more congenial than the somewhat stoic, constrained and stocky Loeb.

On Monday after the takeover, if the readers of the

*Daily Messenger* were looking for anything novel or different in the newspaper, they were disappointed. The product fashioned by Editor Daniel Tobin was of the same format and the same flavor which everyone was in the habit of seeing.

But on the afternoon of Tuesday, Oct. 28, 1941, readers who expected to see the same old local news hashed over in the *Daily Messenger* were given a new angle on life. In a Page One headline, the readers were told:

## EXTRAVAGANCE OF DUCHESS DEPLORED BY WILLIAM LOEB

### Messenger Publisher Sends Wire to Former Wallis Simpson At White House

In the accompanying news story, Loeb said that he was "impelled by the rising reaction inimical to good British-American relations" and wired the Duchess of Windsor at the White House where she was lunching that day with President Roosevelt. He quoted the text of his telegram where he called her trip to America a "sad waste of ammunition money" and said her "extravagant behavior compares most unfavorably with the pitifully gallant sacrifices of the plain British people." Loeb continued, "This is especially painful to us because you are an American." He suggested the duchess cut short her trip and devote herself "unobtrusively to war work" which "would erase harm you are doing to British cause here."

Loeb continued to be quoted in the news story, outside of the text of the telegram. He called for an "honest U.S. declaration of war on the Nazis," and went on, "the duchess, showing off with her private railroad cars and her pointless social engagements, reminds us of that part of England for which we will not sacrifice and of the wit-

less parasite hangers-on of cafe society in our own country."

And on Wednesday, Oct. 29, 1941, Loeb's *Messenger*
carried on its editorial page a long paragraph to the effect
that his protest of the duchess' visit had been carried on
Associated Press wires throughout the country, had been
mentioned on four coast-to-coast broadcasts and displayed
prominently in metropolitan newspapers. "What with the
news dispatches and the broadcasts, St. Albans was definitely identified with the day's events in no uncertain
degree yesterday," the editorial concluded.

So, Loeb, in his very first outing, displayed the editorial
trait that would be the trademark of his entire journalistic
career. If he failed to take the measure of his readers be-
forehand, he was always trying to speak in their name.
The particular breed of Vermonter in the St. Albans area
wasn't altogether sure that this was the type of identification he wanted. To most people, Windsor was that town
over on the other side of the state near White River Junction. Some others remembered the Duchess of Windsor
vaguely, something about the King of England, but that
was a good five years or so before. To top it all, Edward VIII
had never been the most popular figure in northern Vermont. The Province of Quebec wasn't even a half-hour
away, and this influence was foremost among the heavily
French-Canadian population. There had been some instances, and there would be recurrences in later years, of
political candidates from the lower reaches of Vermont
actually campaigning in Canada for days without realizing
they were across the border; that's what this country was
like.

To Loeb, who had been brought up at least in part in
the White House amid household talk which involved
international and diplomatic relations at only the highest
level, the visit of the duchess to the capital was obviously
disturbing, at least to a small extent. Maybe it was
jealousy. But to the vast majority of those who knew of this
play by Loeb, it was a distasteful display of egotism.

But Loeb paid no attention to, if he knew at all, the

general attitude of Quebec, or Quebec-oriented people, towards the crown. And he most obviously didn't know that the Vermont Legislature had on Sept. 17, 1941, already declared war on Germany. War bonuses for Vermonters in the service had already begun to accrue since Sept. 11, 1941. What was especially painful to these Vermonters was not the hoity-toity stuff in Washington, it was that their sons, fathers, husbands, brothers and neighbors were going off to war every day. They had little time to relate to a duchess having lunch at the White House.

Loeb's unprecedented attack on the Duchess of Windsor, which the newspaper's readers could interpret only by reading the follow-up story, was an intrusion into affairs of the President, a side of life they had never glimpsed before, and it placed them in somewhat of a quandary; most readers were dismayed, if they followed it all.

The next day, the *Daily Messenger* carried another un-usual Page One story, this time two columns wide:

**New York Publishers
Join in Sending Best
Wishes to Messenger**

**Congratulate Loeb
On Purchase of
Historic Daily**

**Tributes Paid by Leaders
In Metropolitan Pub-
lishing Field**

What followed was a "straight" news story, more than a full column long, quoting at length the various messages received by Loeb upon taking over as publisher of the *Messenger*. The names of the senders were meaningless to most readers, and the titles of the senders were, in most cases, supported by dependent clauses identifying the publication or organization of which the sender was an officer.

The story that day in Loeb's newspaper said the announcement of his buying the *Messenger* was "prominently mentioned in the metropolitan press" and it again pointed out
in the lead paragraph that the new owner was "son of the
late executive secretary to President Theodore Roosevelt."

Notable among the senders were Archibald B. Roosevelt, who extended "my best wishes to young Bill Loeb,"
and Joseph Ridder, president of *The Journal of Commerce*
and head of the Ridder chain of newspapers.

Then, on Monday, Nov. 3, 1941, Loeb ran his first Page
One editorial, and in it he said:

> ". . . I want to call this 'home' . . . Being new it would be
> foolish to announce any local policies until I have had a
> good long look around . . . I consider a newspaper to be
> the servant of the community whose support it enjoys . . .
> Furthermore, in this great hour of decision in this nation's
> history, silence on the fundamental issues of the day would
> be cowardly . . . Therefore on today's editorial page, in a
> statement 'Vermont Stands For Victory,' I say clearly and
> simply what I believe, and set forth those principles for
> which The Messenger will fight.
>
> > "William Loeb,
> > "Publisher."

"Vermont Stands For Victory" ran almost two full columns on the editorial page over Loeb's printed name and
he outlined 12 points on which he based what he said
would be the aims of his new newspaper. "In conclusion,"
he said:

> "I feel confident that we in St. Albans will fight the good
> fight. I know THE MESSENGER will be as a sword to a
> ready hand. I know that we will win until [sic] the forces
> of evil yield in complete surrender as they did in the days
> gone by to those who fight 'in the name of the Great Je-
> hovah and the Continental Congress.' "

At about this time, the voters of St. Albans cast their
ballots at the regular November election and a referendum
in favor of a tax reduction and financial aid to a new
industry for the city. The *Daily Messenger* had jumped

on the bandwagon for the proposal at a very late date and, after the question had won the approval of the populace, the newspaper claimed credit for the passage. Soon the name of Daniel Tobin, editor, disappeared from the mast-head.

In a little over a month, it was obvious to anyone who cared to notice that William Loeb was out of his element. For someone who said he wanted to call St. Albans "home," living in the Hotel Kelley and sending the bell-boy out for booze all the time was a funny way to show it.

Another thing was obvious about the operation of the *Messenger*. With Dan Tobin gone, neither Loeb nor the other new "fella," Weaver, showed much grasp of the recent political or cultural history of the city. Circulation began to dip when subscription renewal time came on January 1 and advertising lineage slumped.

It was clear that Loeb was off on the wrong foot, and his glaring error in judgment in having assumed to be the mouthpiece for the people of St. Albans and Vermont had been compounded twice: first, by telling everyone that he had "local policies" in mind; second, by presuming to tell them about the heritage of Vermont.

When it comes to new people in town, Vermonters are unique. They accept no one's "new" ways; that's what makes Vermont Vermont. "Newcomers" either conform to Vermonters' ways or they can leave. They can visit all they want, but "we'll" decide when they can call this "home."

There is an old chestnut which has been making the rounds in Northern New England for generations which goes roughly like this:

A Vermont resident, who had lived there for more than 20 years, was complaining to one of the town fathers about how he resented being treated like a "newcomer" after living in Vermont for so long. Finally, he said to the Ver-monter, "At least my children are Vermonters. They were born here."

To which the old-timer replied: "If a pussy-cat goes into the oven to have her kittens, they don't come out muffins."

There was definitely a conflict of ideologies here and the battle lines between Loeb and the people of St. Albans were clearly drawn. Most persons who got to know Loeb found he was a charming man, possessed of all the social graces and courtesies, dignified and with a sense of humor. They found him to be a man in control of himself at all times. But they also found he had a tendency to overstate his case in print. Loeb was apparently oblivious to all this. For it was a mistake he would make in each succeeding entry into a community.

# 6

Loeb's entry into another city came soon. On the last day of February, 1942, Charles Phillips Hasbrook, who had purchased the *Burlington Daily News* from Col. H. Nelson Jackson in 1939 and who had founded Radio Station WCAX in Burlington, announced the sale of the daily newspaper to William Loeb. Hasbrook cited rapid expansion of the facilities of WCAX as the main reason for selling, but he also mentioned circulation gains on the part of the *Daily News* in the announcement of the sale, which indicated that it was a sacrifice of a going enterprise.

The actual story of the sale of the newspaper is quite different. Simply put, Hasbrook had found a "live one." Colonel Jackson had become a sometime publisher in a very competitive situation. The *Burlington Free Press,* the city's morning daily, was a regional paper of far greater resources, staff and influence. Its circulation was larger and it could, justifiably, demand higher advertising rates. Colonel Jackson had allowed his hobbies, predominantly politics and automobiles—Colonel Jackson is reputed to have been the first man to have driven coast-to-coast in an automobile—to interfere with the time required to be spent on publishing a competitive newspaper. Hasbrook had grabbed the *Daily News* when Colonel Jackson wanted to bail out, but he found it required a lot more work, capital and time to make a newspaper profitable than it did for a small radio station, especially when radio was still somewhat of a novelty. Hasbrook, in turn, wanted out.

Loeb and Weaver had gotten word that Marka Truesdale Loening had relocated to Putney, Vt., with her three children, and that she was dickering for the purchase of a weekly newspaper downstate. She had moved to Vermont to establish residence and then to inaugurate divorce proceedings against Grover Loening. At that time, the only grounds for divorce in New York State (where she had been married and where she had resided all her life) was adultery. It is doubtful that Marka Truesdale Loening was the type—and if she were the type, the Truesdales and the Loenings were not—to claim such grounds and drag such a case through the courts, and the newspapers, in New York. She has recently said that she had all but decided on buying the weekly when she was visited by Loeb and Weaver, and they urged her to invest in the *Daily News*.

The purchase price from Hasbrook is hard to determine. There are wide variances in recollections as to the amount. But on one point, Marka Loening is quite clear; she didn't realize at the time of the purchase that it was practically all her money that was being used to swing the deal. The remainder, relatively small, she says, and Charlie Weaver concurs, came from Mrs. Loeb, Sr.

On Monday, March 2, 1942, the *Daily News* carried a double column, full-face Page One editorial, "A Message to Our 10,000 Readers," which ran the length of the front page and was continued onto the editorial page, signed by "William Loeb, Publisher, *Burlington Daily News* and *St. Albans Daily Messenger*." It said, in part:

". . . THERE IS NOT GOING TO BE ANYTHING MILD OR TAME ABOUT THIS NEWSPAPER."

The editorial conveyed the tone of a tongue-lashing more than a statement of policy, and it went on:

". . . no favorites . . . special interests . . . mausoleum-like section of the Republican Party . . . domination and control by either Wall Street's J. P. Morgan or Washington's John L. Lewis . . . decadent and dying social and economic viewpoint . . . rank materialism of this age . . . sad decline in the devotion of man to God and to religion.

"We feel that in the unity of happy families and with the support of Almighty God, Vermont can yet be the greatest State in the greatest nation on earth."

Again Loeb had violated the local consciousness. One would be hard put to find a Burlingtonian who wouldn't say that Vermont was already the greatest state in the greatest nation on earth. The word had been all around town on Loeb before he made his first 30-mile trip down from St. Albans; the same as it was all over New York and Long Island when he left there. The advertising lineage in the *Free Press* showed a small pick-up with the advent of Loeb into Burlington, the only explanation being that these were ads which had always gone to the *Daily News* and *Daily Messenger* (the morning *Free Press* circulated then, and still does, in both areas). But Mayor John J. Burns officially welcomed Loeb and his staff to Burlington in a Page One story accompanying the editorial.

Loeb and his little band must have appeared to the Burlingtonians much as if they were a road company of "The Great Gatsby." Marka Loening moved herself and her three children from Putney into the Patrick Hill estate on the shores of Lake Champlain in Charlotte, just south of Burlington, and Charlie Weaver says that she helped him buy a cottage just "a mile up the road on the right hand side" for him and Dot.

Loeb? Well, in Charlie Weaver's words, "He was a barnstormer." He would check into the Hotel Kelley in St. Albans when his mother visited from Long Island. (Mrs. Loeb always stayed at the Jesse Welden House in St. Albans during her visits.) Other than that, Loeb camped anywhere he could. Sometimes he stayed with Weaver and his wife and sometimes he stayed with Marka and her three children. An awful lot of the time he would simply disappear. As Marka explains: "Loeb got to be a problem." She says that she really didn't want to see him sleep out on the lawn or in a car, which he would threaten to do. Weaver says that Marka was "in love with Bill," which is apparently what Loeb wanted everyone to think, but Marka is very, very adamant in denying this.

"Bill Loeb was always a most pathetic man," she says, "and the only emotion I ever had, and the only emotion I have now, for that pathetic man is pity. I haven't laid eyes on him since I got out of that newspaper in Burlington."

Rumors spread, however, and became wildly distorted. And Loeb did nothing to quell the popular notion that he and Marka were living as man and wife. This in no way affected the respectable mien which he displayed at all times in Burlington—when he was there—during or outside of business hours. In the Burlington City Directory, he showed up as "pres Burlington Publishing Co res St Albans Vt." and the very next entry read "LEONING [sic] MARKA T v-pres Burlington Publishing Co res Charlotte."

Marka Loening worked as a member of the news staff of the *Daily News* and she became very popular with her co-workers. Weaver was editor and general manager, and Harry Holden was business manager. Loeb, of course, was president and publisher. The weak point in the starting line-up was that of advertising manager.

Enter William J. Montague. He was an advertising salesman on the staff of the *Bridgeport Star* in Connecticut. He found himself with a wife, three children and no job when the *Bridgeport Post* bought the *Star*. He answered an ad in *Editor & Publisher*, met Loeb and moved his family north where he became advertising director of the *Daily News*. Montague was to be the one anchor to windward which Loeb would have throughout the next two decades.

Financially, the *Daily News* and the *Daily Messenger* were anything but successful. It wasn't a situation so bad that a good newspaperman couldn't get the organization on its feet, but Loeb was not that man. There was financial crisis after financial crisis. Hasbrook had not sold Loeb and his conferes anything but a name, worn-out equipment and a lot of headaches. But, there was always Marka and, in a pinch, there was Mrs. Loeb. The banks of Burlington did not see Loeb's operation as much of a credit risk.

But the people of Burlington were unhappy with Loeb's editorials which were appearing more and more frequently on Page One. Loeb always seemed to have a personal axe to grind. Editorials such as, "Aiken, Austin—Applesauce," were a little much for the tastes of the Vermonters who had elected these two U.S. senators. It wasn't just that Loeb was showing himself to be an iconoclast; simply, Loeb was showing that he didn't have due respect for local opinion.

Those who came into contact with Loeb couldn't believe that this charming, polite, well-mannered, well dressed man was the same man who would, by the tone and language of his editorials, come off as brash, arrogant and mean. Loeb was consistent in one sense in all his editorials: he would always assume the cloak of righteousness and dignity by invoking God, country, Vermont and the war effort—sometimes even the boys in the service who were fighting so gallantly.

Loeb engaged in many a running battle through his own Page One—notably with U.S. Senator Warren Austin— although he never broached one of these subjects personally or at the regular weekly meetings of the Kiwanis Club of which he was a member. But the main issue Loeb pressed was that Senator Austin was impeding the war effort; that the Unsworths, the Patricks and the Edlunds (representative of the millowners in Burlington), were conspiring with Senator Austin to keep Bell Aircraft Corp. from taking over a vacant factory near Burlington's lake front because Bell Aircraft was paying higher salaries than workers in Burlington were used to. Loeb claimed the millowners received the senior senator's patronage in this respect because of their campaign contributions. Bell Aircraft finally took over the old factory and employed hundreds of Vermonters, and William Loeb took 100 per cent of the credit, and if you didn't believe it you could read the *Daily News*. When Loeb and the *Daily News* hosted a cocktail party for city officials and the Bell Aircraft executives at the Hotel Vermont to celebrate Bell's takeover of the plant, Loeb refused to invite Senator Austin.

Loeb was not in the publisher's office every day. Weaver says that he was never quite sure where Loeb was, and Loeb never told him. "He made a lot of trips to New York; that much I do know," says Weaver. Another thing is sure: Loeb wasn't working very hard, nor was he putting in many hours as a newspaper publisher. His Page One editorials sometimes appeared, signed by Loeb, when it was known that he was out of town. And, in addition to the fact that the editorials were appearing more frequently, they were becoming more tiresome; the language they contained, their adjectives and adverbs, and accusations were more biting; they were long and poorly constructed. But Loeb always invoked God and country.

As for news content, the *Daily News* was running a poor second to the *Free Press*. Routine news of social events was spotty, at best; deaths and funerals all right; and in politics and general local news, the *Daily News* was getting to play a lot of favorites and it came as a shock to no one that the best way to get your picture or your name in the newspaper, the *Daily News*, that is, was to become friendly with Loeb, and, that failing, Charlie Weaver. Marka? Forget it, she just worked there.

Weaver could feel the pulse of the community better than could Loeb for two reasons. First, he knew a lot more about the business. Second he was working full time at it. He could see the circulation and impact of the *Daily News* beginning to decline. It was Weaver's belief that the main cause of it was that people did not want to read Loeb's editorials, that they were too harsh, too long and too boring, and that Loeb was attacking too many of the local sacred cows. Montague didn't have to be a genius to know how difficult it was to hold advertising lineage, let alone show any significant gains, and he attributed it largely to the enemies Loeb was making for the newspaper with his pen. Weaver says that he often begged Loeb to put these editorials aside overnight and reread them the next day before demanding that they be inserted in the newspaper, more often than not on Page One. He says Loeb's reply was always to the effect that the editorials were good because they made people think and that if he went over his editorials a second time he'd make so many changes the editorials would lose their effectiveness.

Yes, Weaver says he agreed, but the effect they then had was that they were killing us. And they were.

There was a young man in St. Albans at about this time who is reputed to have been the most willing hand available for any and all assignments and tasks which were given him. It had long been the ambition of this young man to become a newspaperman and he was indefatigable, but almost unobtrusive, in offering to do anything he could to help the operation of the *Daily Messenger*. This young man had a serious problem, though; he could hardly see, and his eyesight was becoming worse. It was Loeb who saw to it that he was provided the finest ophthalmological care and treatment. The treatment included eye surgery, and this, too, was arranged and paid for by Loeb.

Although there was no happy ending to the story—the young man did not regain his sight—it suggests a side of William Loeb that is seldom seen.

# 7

During the many periods when Loeb was absent from Burlington and active in Long Island, he kept the money flowing his way. He also received half of the net income which his mother's portfolio of securities realized—a real consideration in the booming wartime economy.

Eleanore McAllister, the young lady whom Loeb had squired in the Long Island "tea dance" set, had become employed as an equestrian instructor at the Foxcroft School in Middleburg, Virginia, and she had spent the summer of 1941 working at a horse training and breeding farm in Vermont. (There are quite a few such farms—so many, in fact, that the state animal of Vermont is the Morgan horse.) During at least some of the time that he had told Charlie Weaver that he was scouting newspaper properties in Vermont he had been seeing Eleanore, and the romance had blossomed, but it was a secret that Eleanore and Loeb shared alone.

In the fall of 1941, when Eleanore returned to Middleburg from the summer in Vermont, she and Loeb promised each other they would wed.

Loeb, however, delayed the date because of the uncertainty of his future, which he assured her would be in the newspaper publishing business. "He was full of promises," Eleanore remembers, "and he was very, very convincing." Out of the goodness of her heart and having every assurance that it was for their common good, Eleanore got herself into the habit of forwarding her weekly paycheck to Loeb in Vermont, cutting to the bone her personal expenses and getting by as best she could on the living allowance which was part of her contract with the Foxcroft School, a very proper school for very proper young ladies. Loeb was devoted in his correspondence to Eleanore, composing long letters (almost always poorly typewritten) and (after he became a publisher) always on the company letterhead with his name and title imprinted on the top. Loeb's correspondence always quoted the day of the month in ordinal numbers, a style which was used by the officials at the Allen-Stevenson School, with the year a line beneath. His letters prove that he never did learn to spell.

As a young man, Loeb had had some trouble with duodenal ulcers, but never so serious that he required hospitalization. At times he watched his diet for this reason. Loeb was not so bothered by the ulcers that he abstained from alcohol, however.

Once Pearl Harbor Day came and went, however, there wasn't a soul in Northern Vermont who didn't know that William Loeb was bothered by ulcers. Part of his routine was to drink milk and to order bland foods and to nibble on bland unsalted crackers, although he would take a cocktail in private. To Eleanore McAllister, he made it clear that he felt he would never serve in the armed forces of the United States, not because of the ulcers, but because it was below his station in life. KP, basic training, taking orders from sergeants, were just not part of the life which was designed for William Loeb, son of the executive secretary to former President Theodore Roosevelt. And it was another of the secrets he shared with Eleanore that he would use this medical pretext to avoid military service. Also, he told her, a lot of persons high in government had been very good, close friends of his father; he would, if forced, write them, and they would most certainly see that he was provided with an instant commission in a branch of service of his own choosing.

But Philip Stevenson, a member of Selective Service Local Board 711, Glen Cove, Long Island, New York, had a pretty good scouting report on Loeb. Stevenson dogged Loeb with draft notices and it became a battle of wits for Loeb to keep coming up with reasons for deferment of a physical. Thus began a most illuminating series of letters to Eleanore McAllister, always on newspaper letterhead stationery.

The significant letters began with one dated

> Sunday afternoon
> February 15th
> 1 9 4 2

(which gives an indication that besides being in Vermont so much in 1941 for the purpose of scouting newspaper properties and for the purpose of squiring Eleanore, there was valid reason to stay out of the sight and hearing of Philip Stevenson and Local Board 711.) In this letter Loeb said he had made it his business to cultivate the clerk of the local Selective Service Board in St. Albans and had provided him favorable publicity. Loeb told

Eleanore that he had written to the Glen Cove draft board
and asked them to transfer his records to the St. Albans
board where officials had been given copies of all the letters
Loeb's doctors had written to the Selective Service officials
on Long Island which detailed a serious and aggravated
ulcer condition. He told Eleanore that if the draft officials
asked him to take a physical he was taking no chances of
his being found suitable for military service; that he would
wire "Knox" directly and ask him for a commission on the
personal staff of the Secretary of the Navy or in the New
York office of Naval Intelligence, maybe in the new production department of the Navy Department.

Coincidentally, the procurement of personnel for the
armed forces was the first order of national business at that
time and on the day following Loeb's February 15th letter,
the Federal government called for the third registration of
United States male citizens for possible draft call, this time
including the age brackets from 18 to 21 and 37 to 44 years
of age. Loeb was 36 at the time and he had been required
to register earlier.

Stevenson at Glen Cove apparently paid no heed to
Loeb's request, because at

> 1:18 A.M.
> Thursday
> February 26th
> 1 9 4 2

Loeb wrote Eleanore that he would be required to see a
"draft" doctor in Vermont, and he told her that he had
read something in the newspapers to the effect that Draft
Director Hersey would be considering deferments for vital
newspapermen and that Hersey might be making this
recommendation to local draft boards.

On

> Wednesday morning
> March 11th, 1942

a quick letter told Eleanore that Loeb had telephoned
Glen Cove because they had been lax in sending up to
Vermont his records and the person to whom he had

spoken assured him that the complete file would be forth-coming.

The clerk of the St. Albans draft board says that, while he was cognizant of William Loeb's effort to have his records shifted to Franklin County from Glen Cove, N.Y., Loeb was the least of his problems. And Loeb's records were never shifted, he says. The clerk's job in Franklin County was a full-time occupation, even though the county was of relatively small population. Customs officials and military police would board the Montreal-bound trains at White River Junction, Vt., and begin to process passengers. By the time the trains reached St. Albans—whatever time of day or night—and made their last stop before reaching the Canada-U.S. border, the Customs men would usually deliver to the draft board at least a dozen persons who were on their way to Montreal without proper credentials.

The clerk does remember one day, though, when Loeb entered his office, very upset, and he remembers to this day the incident. Loeb was carrying a large portfolio case which contained his own stomach X-rays and he was accompanied by Dr. Byron H. Herman, of St. Albans, now deceased. Loeb told the clerk that he had been ordered by the Glen Cove board to report for induction and he showed the clerk a telegram to that effect. The clerk explained that there was nothing he could do because it was a matter under the control of the Glen Cove board. He says that Loeb repeatedly offered to produce his X-rays and have Dr. Herman read them for the clerk. However, the clerk says he again told Loeb that he was very busy and that it was not a matter for his decision, anyway. He left no doubt in Loeb's mind, he says, that he felt that Loeb was beginning to make a pest of himself and that his patience was beginning to wear thin. Loeb was an infrequent visitor to the Franklin County board offices after this.

On

Wednesday evening
March 18th
1 9 4 2

Loeb wrote Eleanore a very long letter and nine paragraphs were spent describing how the "Glen Cove gestapo" would not transfer the records to Vermont because of "Stephenson." He outlined a plan: if he volunteered immediately for the Army, he would be called for a physical in Vermont, where he had been able to make friends with many Selective Service personnel. He told Eleanore that if, by some strange chance, he passed the physical examination, he would immediately request a direct commission from either "Knox" or "Stimson" but it would be easier all around if he failed the physical and were classified 4-F. He explained that the Federal center for Vermont was in Rutland and that he would be going there for the physical, he thought. However, in paragraph 11 of the March 18 letter, he said that before he went for the X-rays involved in the physical examination, he would have had enough straight alcohol to "iritate (sic)" his ulcers.

    Loeb's letter to Eleanore on

Tuesday
April 7th
1 9 4 2

was striking. Apparently one of the persons whom Loeb had cultivated most closely was Lt. Col. Fred S. Kent, Medical Corps, U.S. Army, chief medical officer at Selective Service Headquarters in Rutland. Dr. Kent, 51 at the time, was a graduate of the University of Vermont and its Medical School and had practiced in Burlington before being called into service. He had been active in alumni affairs at UVM and was team doctor for many athletic squads. (In 1974, he was inducted into the UVM Hall of Fame for his service as team physician both before and after the war.)

    Loeb told Eleanore that he had volunteered for the Army and had had X-rays taken at UVM Medical Center in Burlington before going to Rutland for the remainder of the physical. Apparently, Dr. Kent had arranged for the X-rays to be taken by Dr. A. Bradley Soule at the Medical School. (Soule was then and is now a nationally-known figure in radiology.) It took Loeb four paragraphs to tell

Eleanore how splendid Col. Kent looked in his uniform with his medals gleaming as he stood in front of the desk of one Capt. Powers and told Capt. Powers that Loeb had ulcers and he, even though he was most willing and had volunteered for the Army, could not pass a physical examination because the X-rays showed that Loeb had ulcers. "Capt. Powers" was B.S., 1936, and M.D., 1939, from the University of Vermont where he had been acquainted with Dr. Kent as a member of athletic teams. He had been a student under Dr. Soule. (William J. Powers, MD, died in 1971.)

Capt. Powers said that if Dr. Soule had taken the X-rays, it was good enough for him and that if both Dr. Soule and Col. Kent agreed on the gravity of Loeb's ulcer condition, it was good enough for him and that he would disqualify Loeb on the two other doctors' say-so.

He enclosed for Eleanore a carbon copy of a letter which Capt. Powers sent to the local draft board in St. Albans:

WJP/pz

## HQ Third Recruiting and Induction District
## Office of the Commanding Officer
## 38½ Center Street
## Rutland, Vermont

4 April 1942

Clerk of Local Board
Franklin County
St. Albans, Vermont

Dear Sir:

I have this day examined William Loeb of St. Albans for possible enlistment into the Army of the United States. Mr. Loeb has had a duodenal ulcer for several years and recent X-rays taken and read by competent doctors prove that his ulcer is still active.

No physical required.

William J. Powers
Captain, Med. Corps
Medical Officer

Uniquely, Colonel Kent was the guest speaker before the Monday, April 6, 1942 meeting of the Montpelier Rotary Club, the day being a quasi-holiday because of a three-day observance of Army Day, proclaimed by an edict of Secretary of War Stimson. Dr. Kent told the Rotarians that he was finding that over half of the rejects from Selective Service physicals were the result of bodily neglect on the part of those being called for induction.

Stevenson and the Glen Cove board would not let go of Loeb; they kept trying to have him inducted and they constantly refused to transfer the records to Vermont. Always Loeb referred to the Long Island authority as the "Glen Cove gestapo" and he had unkind words for "Stephenson." As late as

> Sunday
> January 30th
> 1 9 4 3

Glen Cove was still corresponding with Loeb and trying to force his induction into service. In the meantime, Loeb had, in fact, written Secretary Stimson asking, in vague terms, what was the liability of his military service and what the odds were of getting a desk job. But on this date, Loeb told Eleanore that "Glen Cove gestapo" would not accept the diagnosis of the doctors in Rutland and that he would be going down there on January 31. He said he hoped the ulcer was not in one of its "ocasional [sic]" quiescent stages.

Loeb was a member of the Kiwanis Club of Burlington, and it was the custom of the Burlington Kiwanis to send a newsletter to all of the members of the club who were serving in the armed forces, including an individual message from each member of the club who was still in Burlington. The newsletter often included the sentiments of William Loeb, "If there's anything I can do for you, please let me know."

At age 36, with a history of ulcers, Loeb had a right to avoid conscription by any legitimate means open to him. And, indeed, we have no way of knowing whether Loeb did—as he stated to Eleanore that he would—deliberately attempt to exacerbate his duodenal ulcer by a bout of heavy drinking before his Army physical X-rays, or if he did, in fact, drink straight alcohol, as he told Eleanore he would do.

But there is ample reason to ask whether he did seek honestly to serve with the armed forces in World War II, as he has later claimed—or whether, in fact, he actively sought to avoid military service. The occasion to question Loeb's motives for service during World War II will arise in due course as we see Loeb's attitude towards the war records of other persons.

# 8

Eleanore McAllister again took a summer job in Vermont during the vacation period in the summer of 1942, this time on a horse farm in Londonderry. William Loeb was a frequent visitor, many times spending the night before returning to Burlington. But never once during that time did Eleanore go to northern Vermont nor did she ever visit his newspaper offices. Loeb, it turns out, had been continuing his "relationship" with Marka Loening and he had even told his mother that he had intentions of marrying Marka once her divorce from Grover Loening was final. Mrs. Loeb, of course, made no secret of this among her friends and associates on Long Island. She was under the impression that Eleanore was out of sight and out of mind.

At the close of the summer, very close to the time that Eleanore would have to return to the Foxcroft School, she and Loeb visited Clarence F. Stotts, town clerk of Colebrook, Conn., a little town in the foothills of the Berkshires high in the northwest corner of the state. On Sept. 21, 1942, they were issued a marriage license. It goes without saying, I suppose, that Loeb didn't want Eleanore to know that he was sleeping on Charlie Weaver's couch or camping with Marka Truesdale Loening. In any event he swore solemnly on his marriage application that he resided in Rochester, N.Y. Town records show that the couple returned on Sept. 26, 1942, and were joined in matrimony by Rev. Henry J. Wharton. Colebrook had a small reputation for this type of thing and witnesses to a marriage were no problem there.

Eleanore says that she immediately went to Middleburg after the ceremony without benefit of honeymoon. She says that she continued to send her pay of about $5,000 a year to Loeb in Burlington and that she continued to get by on her living allowance. She says that Loeb had $47 in the bank when she married him. She adds: "I felt sorry for him."

Marka, meanwhile, was having problems of her own; it wasn't easy to support herself, three children, a huge estate and a losing daily newspaper on the amount of money Grover Loening was sending as temporary alimony. And she was having troubles arriving at a permanent divorce agreement. But Loeb had a solution. Naturally, he wanted Marka to have a little more "mobility" when it came to dollar bills. He told Weaver and many others that the way was to threaten Grover Loening that Loeb would let it be known far and wide that Loening was a homosexual. As Loeb said, "There's no way a man can defend himself against a charge like that."

"Comes Marka T. Loening" before the honorable Probate Court of Chittenden County in Burlington asking that she be appointed guardian on a permanent basis for her three children, Louise, 11, Michael, 10, and Priscilla, 6, and that "notice of this petition be given to Grover Loening of Washington, D.C."

Postal Telegraph in Burlington delivered to the court the following reply to the notice:

                            "Washington D.C. JULY 29 1942 1144P
"JUDGE FRANCIS D FOLEY PROBATE COURT CHITTENDEN COUNTY DISTRICT BURLINGTON VT

"BEING ENGAGED IN URGENT WAR WORK HERE IT IS IMPOSSIBLE FOR ME TO ARRANGE AT-TORNEYS TO REPRESENT ME AND DETECTIVES TO INVESTIGATE EXTORTION AND BLACK-MAILING THREATS INVOLVED IN APPLICATION OF MARKA T LOENING A QUESTIONABLE PER-SON, FOR GUARDIAN OF MY CHILDREN. RE-QUEST SIXTY DAYS DELAY TO ENABLE ME TO ESTABLISH A DEFENSE AGAINST A MOST IM-PROPER ACTION WHICH HAS BEEN THRUST UPON ME UNWARES [sic] AND WITH VICIOUS INTENT. SERVICE MADE JULY 29TH REQUIRING RETURN AUGUST 4TH ENTIRELY TOO SHORT FOR FAIR CONSIDERATION. PLEASE WIRE RE-PLY SHOREHAM HOTEL WASHINGTON.

"GROVER LOENING

925A"

The Probate judges of Vermont are elected, and Judge Francis D. Foley, a Democrat (as are most elected officials of Burlington and Chittenden), was running for reelection in the fall of 1942. It goes without saying that newspaper support is always welcomed by any political figure.

Marka Loening was granted permanent custody of the children by Judge Foley in the Chittenden Probate Court but they were also made wards of the state, and Marka was ordered to report annually on the amount which Loening was ordered to place in trust for their support. By Dec. 31, 1942, Marka had $5,800 cash and $32,700 in securities for the children, but she had already converted another $35,640 into 360 shares of Burlington Publishing Co. preferred and another $6,000 more into a 6% mortgage note for Burlington Publishing Co.

So with the *Burlington Daily News* taking a new interest in the local political structure (Judge Foley was re-elected), there began to be a renewed interest in, and an aura of mystery about its publisher, William Loeb. He was "here today, gone tomorrow," living—when he was around —apparently, with that "good looking woman" at the lake-front mansion in Charlotte. Loeb always appeared well, however, reserved but friendly, healthy, well-dressed, and he always gave off an attitude of superiority. Just who is this man, people asked, who seemed to feel his station in life is to come to Burlington and St. Albans and "take over." Inevitably there was a lot of gossip about Loeb. The one piece of gossip which was the most persistent—and apparently the part of each yarn spun about him which rankled Loeb the most—was that he was a "New York Jew" and Loeb decided it was time to quash this rumor and, perhaps, do a little name-dropping at the same time.

So Loeb ran on Page One of the *Daily News* an engraving of his baptismal certificate, saying that "William (Third) Loeb was received into the congregation of Christ's flock, by Holy Baptism" by the Episcopal bishop of Washington, D.C., on March 3, 1906, and the certificate bore the signatures of Theodore Roosevelt and Edith Kermit Roosevelt as sponsors.

In retrospect, this must be viewed as one of the major blunders which Loeb had made thus far in his publishing career. The reactions were immediate, varied, and none of them was good.

"Does he think that the fact that he was baptized makes him a newspaperman?", "Is he trying to impress us with the fact that his father worked for Teddy Roosevelt?", and the most nagging of all, inasmuch as the purpose of publishing the baptismal certificate was so transparent, "What the hell is wrong with being a Jew?"—or "He's a Jew trying not to be a Jew."

These last reactions were the ones which were most important. They lasted longest (they still linger), and they did Loeb the most harm. He apparently didn't know, or didn't care, that Jews had been in Vermont since the Civil War and that the first Jewish community, Ohavi Zedek, had been founded in Burlington in 1885. At the turn of the century, more than one per cent of the population were members of the Jewish faith. By the time of Loeb's editorial, three congregations had merged into one, and, of Burlington's 27,686 residents, 1,096 were members of the congregation, and a good percentage of the retailers and manufacturers in the Greater Burlington area had some Jewish ties.

The facts of Loeb's background are simple, and most scholars of Jewish heritage knew them well. The surname Loeb is acknowledged as a Jewish name. Both of Loeb's parents had been born in Albany, both of his grandfathers had been German immigrants. Both had arrived here in the United States in the mid-1800's; this was when the second wave of Jewish immigrants arrived in this country, 200,000 of them from Germany. These people were largely tradesmen, of little formal education, who, for generations in Germany, had been forced to live in ghettoes and wear a special Jewish badge. They had been forbidden to marry, and been subjected to countless indignities. When these people came to America, they may or may not have actively practiced their religion, and temple and rabbinical records were rarely kept because these people had all been through persecution before and they weren't about to risk it again. There were three Jewish communities in Albany in the mid-1800's, but no records exist of their membership, or chronicle of their histories.

Both of Loeb's grandfathers were minor tradesmen; both married after arrival in this country. Grandmother Loeb's maiden name was Myer and Grandmother Dorr, Hans.

In addition, there was another rumor making the rounds that years before President Theodore Roosevelt had resigned from the Union League Club in New York City, a move which was prompted by the "bias" shown when the application of his secretary, William Loeb, had been refused.

At any rate, within hours after Loeb had published his baptismal certificate on Page One of the *Daily News*, it was generally and widely interpreted as a thorough repudiation of a large number of fine citizens, a slap in the face to the Jews. A lot of faces felt slapped and they were not, by a long shot, all in the Jewish community.

While the advertising lineage in the *Free Press* did not
make any significant gains, the retail lineage in the *Daily
News* took a nosedive, a nosedive from which it would
never recover.

However, apparently nothing seemed to bother Loeb. He
was gadding around so much it was hard to understand
what Loeb was thinking, or even if he cared what was
going on. When he was around, though, everybody knew it.

"You see, our feeling was," says Miss Irene Allen, a longtime employe, a copy editor, "we got the paper out, so
help us. Loeb was just every now and then coming along
with his editorials and rocking the boat . . . and we would
set to work and patiently get the thing put together again.
That was the way we saw ourselves."

Loeb and Weaver and the *Daily News* took the side of
the Textile Workers Union of America in a showdown
with the American Woolen Company, and Burlington
Mayor Burns fought the union, and His Honor was joined,
at least for a while, by a spokesman of the Roman Catholic Diocese of Burlington. The church quickly divorced
itself from this tussle when Most Rev. Matthew F. Brady,
D.D., bishop of Burlington, named a new vicar general.

The Textile Workers Union won the showdown election and Loeb and the *Daily News* became the self-ap-
pointed champions of labor. It was not long after that,
however, that the printers at St. Albans tried to organize
into the International Typographical Union and Loeb
showed what a friend of labor he was. He closed the printing facilities at St. Albans and consolidated all production
for the two newspapers in one plant in Burlington, trucking the *Daily Messenger* the 30-odd miles to another city.
Several jobs were lost, but Loeb's remained a non-union
newspaper. He billed the closing as an economy move,
and, God knows, it was obvious to everyone that an economy move had to come with the income down so low.
Loeb was undaunted in his own public posture, through
the medium of his editorials, as the working man's best
friend.

About this time there occurred what Loeb called in the
Aug. 30, 1943, *Daily News,* "the annual meeting of the
*Burlington Daily News* and the *Daily Messenger* staffs at
the home of Mrs. Marka T. Loening." If that August 29
Sunday afternoon affair was, indeed, an annual meeting,
then such "annual meetings" had been held for two sum-
mers on at least a semi-monthly basis with varying degrees
of attendance.

However, the newspapers' staffs gathered with their
families and many invited, and some uninvited, guests at
the Charlotte estate, and among those in attendance was a
prominent Burlington radio personality named Reginald
H. J. Nash. He was a man in his early 50's, of theatrical
ability, known throughout the area for his radio shows on
various local stations over the years, particularly for his
role as Santa Claus, which he carried on both on the radio
and in person. Nash, legally separated from his second
wife, Helen, who was then in her early 20's, also derived
considerable income from advertising sales of commercials
which he would air in the course of his radio broadcasts.
It was not at all unusual to see Nash having coffee, or
having lunch, with Marka Loening in Burlington, many
of those who served on Loeb's staff recall. Marka says she
had no particular fascination for Nash, other than the fact
that he was an entertaining person. However, most of the
*Daily News* employes seem to feel that seeing Nash and
Mrs. Loening together rankled Loeb more than a little bit.
It was, in fact, bad for his image.

At some point during a bibulous afternoon "annual
meeting" on that August 29, Loeb, Weaver, Montague,
Mrs. Loening and Nash repaired to the house and discussed a new advertising program—which would be implemented, with Nash acting as an advertising salesman
for the *Daily News* and *Daily Messenger*—a program that
would be in conjunction with radio tie-in advertising during Nash's own radio broadcasts. To hear Weaver tell it,
it was a unique plan and one which would have been
most lucrative for all involved.

At the close of the discussion, the quintet returned to

the lawn for more merriment and more refreshments, even dancing. Loeb rarely drank, except on social occasions (he had ulcers, remember?) and never to the point where there was a hint he was losing his self-control or his poise. But it soon became obvious to most everyone in attendance that Loeb seemed anxious to have Nash leave shortly after dark because, they say, Nash seemed to be paying too much attention to Marka Loening to suit Loeb, and, what is more, Marka seemed to be enjoying herself. The character at center stage definitely was not William Loeb and he was becoming very annoyed, even though he was trying to hide his provocation, and not doing too well at that.

Weaver recalls that Loeb asked him to ride back to his home with Nash, but Weaver says he declined because he could see that Nash was knee-walking drunk. Weaver says he chose instead to ride a little later with Judge Willsie Brisbin. According to the *Daily News* of Aug. 30, 1943, the last person to speak with Nash at the party was Loeb.

(Some 32 years later, in 1975, it can safely be said that in all of Loeb's years as a newspaper publisher, his "favorite" target has been the Kennedy family. Since 1969, Sen. Edward M. Kennedy [D-Mass], the sole surviving male member of the family, has been the subject of Loeb's particular criticism, mainly as a result of an event which occurred in the aftermath of a party during the summer of 1969 on the Massachusetts island of Chappaquiddick, off Martha's Vineyard.)

On Monday morning, Aug. 30, 1943, the captain of the early morning Essex, N.Y.–Charlotte, Vt., Lake Champlain ferry guided his boat into the slip in McNeill's Bay on the Charlotte side. But he could not make the landing. He went astern and came forward repeatedly. Failing in each attempt, he could only assume that a submerged object was blocking the ship. Divers were sent down to investigate. What they found was the automobile belonging to Reginald H. J. Nash under 10 feet of water, with the body of Reginald H. J. Nash behind the wheel.

Mrs. Gert Langlais, society editor of *Daily News,* was the first to contact her friend, Mrs. Helen Nash, who in

1974 conducted a boutique on Church Street in Burlington. "Gert told me that Mr. Loeb would take care of everything," Mrs. Nash recalls. "Reg and I weren't married too long; he was like a father to me. But there was never any unpleasantness, we were very good friends. We just should never have gotten married."

Loeb wrote a Page One editorial which appeared Aug. 31, eulogizing Nash. The editorial was titled "There'll Always Be a Santa Claus," and the facts of the drowning were carried in both the *Daily News* and the *Free Press,* topped by eight-column streamers on Page One in the *Daily News* and included with local news in the *Free Press.* (In that day, it can only be assumed that if Christ were to have reappeared on this earth and such an advent were to have taken place in Burlington, Vermont, it would have been included with the local news on Page Three.) Extensive eulogies by public figures were carried in all area newspapers. The City of Burlington flew flags at half-mast during the services on Sept. 1, 1943, which were conducted by Rev. Oliver H. Sisson, pastor of the First Baptist Church, at the James P. Dower Funeral Home. There was a small platoon of bearers, of whom Loeb was one and Judge Brisbin another. Charlie Weaver was an active bearer.

State's Attorney Clarke Gravel ordered an autopsy performed and Dr. C. F. Whitney, state pathologist, called it "simple drowning." The vehicle ramp at the ferry slip showed skid marks, and there were signs that Nash had clawed at the interior in an effort to free himself from his underwater tomb. Mrs. Nash says she was furnished a copy of the autopsy report which showed an alcohol blood content, as she remembers it, of .27. She, in turn, gave the autopsy report to her attorney.

About a week after the funeral, Mrs. Nash recalls, Gert Langlais telephoned her and asked her to come to the *Daily News* office to see William Loeb, the publisher. Mrs. Nash remembers that Loeb told her that he thought it would be best if she "got out of town." She says she was puzzled by this and asked Loeb why, and he said that he thought it would be best all around, or words to that effect. Nothing specific. Mrs. Nash says she stalked out of Loeb's office.

She says she subsequently received another telephone call from Gert Langlais informing her that the "word" was around the *Daily News* office, "Don't let Loeb see you with Helen Nash." Mrs. Nash says she got a call from the Dower Funeral Home about two months later, asking when the funeral expenses would be taken care of. She promptly paid the bill, she says.

A year later the *Burlington Free Press* in its "A Year Ago Today" column on its editorial page said:

> "The body of Reg Nash, popular radio entertainer, was found in his car on the lake bottom at the end of the ferry dock, McNeill's Bay, Charlotte. Autopsy disclosed death from drowning—also showed high alcoholic blood content. No inquest."

A thorough search of the records of Chittenden County in Burlington, the Vermont Medical Center and the state pathologists's office at the University of Vermont Medical School in Burlington, and the state archives in Montpelier fail to yield a copy of the autopsy performed by Dr. Whitney. (The Vermont State Police did not come into being until 1947.) However, there is a file card showing that an autopsy had been performed, with Dr. Whitney's signature. In the archives there are reports of autopsies before that date and after that date. No autopsy report on the body of Reginald H. J. Nash is available. There is nothing official to show Nash's high alcoholic blood content when the accident occurred. (The attorney general of the State of Vermont in 1974 said he did not know why this information is not available.)

State's Attorney Gravel was a young Republican who was the first to break the Democratic barrier for major elective office in the Burlington area for some time. In the fall of 1944, he decided to run for the office of judge of probate against Judge Francis D. Foley. Foley, the longtime Democratic officeholder, seemed to be complacent in his incumbency and, too, he now enjoyed the solid support of the *Daily News*. It was by no means a spectacular campaign; campaigns for judgeships rarely were. But while Foley was just going through the motions, the younger and more aggressive Gravel was out shaking hands and knocking on doors and making new friends every day. It was looked upon as a major upset when Gravel won the probate court seat, a plum for any young attorney on the rise, in the election of 1944.

If the death of Reginald H. J. Nash did nothing else in the Burlington community, it made Judge Gravel a little more interested in the affairs of the *Daily News,* which had endorsed his opponent, and those persons who made it tick.

Marka T. Loening had neglected to file an annual report on the disposition of funds for her children on Dec. 31, 1943, as was required, and, apparently, Judge Foley had not called this to her attention. And when a report was not forthcoming for Dec. 31, 1944, Judge Gravel asked for an accounting. It was then disclosed that during this two-year period, Marka had sold the securities which were being held in trust for the children and given the money to Loeb; she had sold stocks of International Paper, Freeport Sulphur, International Nickel Canada, Great Western Sugar and Archer Daniels Midland. Where was the money? Burlington Publishing Co. 4% mortgage notes, $17,200; Burlington Publishing Co. demand notes, $2,200; Burlington Publishing Co. preferred stock, $1,980; Burlington Publishing Co. common stock, $4,520, and $3,000 for a promissory note which Burlington Publishing Co. had given her father, Joseph R. Truesdale. (The company was in default, so Marka had paid it off and she was holding the "paper.")

Judge Gravel admonished the lady and told her that the money was for her children, not for the conduct of Loeb's newspaper. He instructed her to divest herself of these local investments before the next accounting.

Marka says: "Loeb was a pretty convincing guy."

# 9

Personnel problems were as common to Weaver at the *Daily News* and to General Manager Ike Merry at the *Daily Messenger* as they were to the proprietor of any other business during this time, especially when you consider the fact that the biggest single personnel problem to both newspapers was the publisher, William Loeb, any way you look at it.

Most male employes were, at best, transient, because of the demands of the Selective Service System. As permanent employes, Loeb's two newspapers relied on a news staff the hardcore of which was formed by Charlie Weaver—by all reckoning the most experienced newspaperman of the lot—as editor and general manager; Harry Holden, business manager who doubled as city hall and court reporter; Gert Langlais, who tried to confine her activities to being social editor; Barbara York, Marka Loening, Charlotte LaFleur and Irene Allen, the latter a Westford, Vt., native who had worked in the extension service of the University of Vermont which prepared a newsletter on agricultural topics, among other functions.

The original idea behind luring Miss Allen to the staff was to build a farm page in the *Daily News,* but the idea never materialized, mainly because Miss Allen was kept so busy with other tasks. Irene was usually the first one in in the morning and the last to leave at night and she soon became one of the most professional newshens in the office—able and, more than that, willing to tackle any difficult and new project.

Typical of her problems was one which concerned a story about the ladies of the Burlington Country Club who had reached an impasse at their luncheon meeting. The *Daily News* headline read:

## BURLINGTON CC LADIES LAID ON TABLE

Irene Allen was such a proficient newspaperperson that she was able to make over the page in minutes, and it's probably a good thing she was able to do so, because there was no one else around. A few copies got out, though.

Although Loeb tried for a long time to keep his first marriage under wraps—in any of countless interviews for newspapers, magazines or television, he has made no effort to correct the misconception that he had been married only twice—Irene Allen knew about it. As she tells the story, Carl Sandburg, the famed poet and biographer, was giving a lecture at Ira Allen Chapel at the University of Vermont and she was assigned to cover it. Loeb told her, "Say something nice to him for me."

So, at the close of the lecture, Miss Allen approached the guest of honor to convey the best wishes of William Loeb, her publisher, to which the august poet, after a long, studious pause, said, "Yes, I knew him and his wife in college." Asked if she ever mentioned this to Loeb, Irene Allen said, "Oh, no, not me. Do you think I'd want to get shot in the head?"

On the subject of keeping the staff together, Irene Allen says, "Well, Marka was a very nice person and full of good deeds. Other than that, it's kind of hard to explain. We were working hard, but we weren't suffering. I enjoyed the crazy, mixed-up business. We'd get things going good and then Mr. Loeb would come along and rock the boat. When you look back you can't decide whether you were being made a sucker of, or if Loeb was, because here's the thing. . . .

"About the first, oh, I'd been there a year, let's say, it was at some kind of water carnival out there at North Beach—the *Daily News* was sponsoring it—and Loeb gave me a ride back and I was full of, well, but I said, 'Mr. Loeb, I've, things like, I've enjoyed this year,' you know, all buggy-eyed. And he said, 'Well, I'm sorry I can't pay you more.' I wasn't asking for a raise, for crying out loud, I was just being a big-eyed . . . I started not believing in him from that minute on."

As to salary, Irene Allen says the "working man's best friend" started her at $25 a week in 1943 and that, by the time she left in 1957 and returned to work at the University of Vermont, she was making $30-something. "I never did get as high as $40," she says.

At one point, Gert Langlais, the social editor, was in charge of promoting and staging the Golden Gloves, which was run under the auspices of the *Daily News*. Irene Allen says, "Apparently we were out of sports editors at the time."

There had been some correspondence between "Loeb's son" and Colonel Knox because personnel of the Union-Leader Publishing Co. had been most helpful to Loeb's people, in an advisory capacity, during his years in Burlington and St. Albans. Cornelius Dekker, general manager of the *Union-Leader*, had provided counsel to Loeb from the time he first became a publisher. "If he [Loeb] hadn't been a good friend of Knox, we never would have had the help that we had from Neil Dekker during the days when we were setting up this operation over here in Vermont," says Charlie Weaver. "Neil used to come over here and we'd go over the whole business end together. I worked with him hour after hour."

Weaver also tells the story of how Loeb's *Burlington Daily News* won the National Headliners' Award for public service. He says that one day while Loeb was out of town he decided to write an editorial about juvenile delinquency and the need for counseling facilities so those adjudged delinquent might be rehabilitated to reenter society. This prompted a visit by a nice-appearing young man who had been a "pupil" at the Weeks School in Vergennes, Vt., a reformatory for teen-agers, and he described to Weaver the conditions there, "a tale of horror that shocked the hell out of me," says Weaver. He investigated the charges which the young man alleged, found other former "students" and obtained their statements, also. He prepared a complete dossier and forwarded a copy to the probation officer and another to Governor Wills at Montpelier. After the chief executive had had enough time to have received the information, Weaver called him and asked him what he was going to do about the conditions at the Weeks School, with the clear implication that if the governor were not to announce any direct action, he would print the stories in the *Daily News*.

Weaver says the governor told him, "You and Bill Loeb are two dirty, yellow journalists and you're just trying to make something sensational that will reflect on the good name of Vermont."

Weaver broke the series of stories, complete with pictures of the boys who had told them. After the series had begun to appear in print, Loeb reappeared on the scene and, says Weaver, "He was all for it, my golly, he was really pushing on this one. But we ran the stories and things began to happen. All of the respectable people in Burlington were shocked to death at these lies the *Daily News* was telling . . . all hell began to pop. There was whitewash from one end of the state to the other. But the net result was that they had to bring in an outside expert, a man named McLaughlin, from Connecticut—he was a penologist of real reputation—and he studied the whole situation down there and completely confirmed everything we had written. And we won the National Headliners' Award for that year for outstanding service on that thing."

But this did not help Loeb's local image. The award to Loeb's newspaper didn't get much space, if any at all, in newspapers other than his own. Most persons who read it didn't think it was that much of an achievement and you couldn't really say that the *Daily News* series on the Weeks School was ever one of the top items of conversation in and around Burlington. Advertising lineage and circulation continued a steady downward trend.

Both Weaver and Montague pleaded constantly with Loeb to tone down his editorials, his harangues; (to put them in a desk drawer overnight and read them again in the morning)—after all, these were the two men who had to live with the results which these editorials caused; Loeb was never around to back them up—but Loeb persisted in doing things his way, always saying he was "telling it like it is." Montague said that he finally gave up reading Loeb's editorials, or any of the newspaper's editorials, for that matter, a custom he continued through his later days at Manchester. This did nothing to enhance his friendship with Weaver, the guy who wrote what editorials Loeb did not write. Montague always said that, as advertising salesman or as advertising director, when he made a call on a prospective advertiser and found that instead of getting an order for an advertisement he became sidetracked onto a defense of Loeb, it was much, much easier in the long run to simply say, "I didn't read the editorial and I don't know what the hell you're talking about," chalk the call off as a lost cause, and proceed to the next prospect.

Loeb did have a coterie which supported him, however, even in his most outlandish editorials. These people were generally favor seekers, "yes men" who would say "okay" to anything so long as, by currying Loeb's favor, they would get support for their own pet projects, usually political. Usually, they were successful. They were also the type who would take the time to write letters to the editor supporting Loeb's positions. Loeb would point to such mail and say, "Look at all the support I'm getting." Weaver and Montague soon found that it was a losing battle trying to tell Loeb that he was wrong about anything.

William Loeb did nothing to enhance his personal image. For all the years he had been around, he still didn't acknowledge many people. He made no obvious effort to be publicly friendly or to conform to other local ways. The fact that he kept a loaded gun in his desk, and very often on his person, did little to invoke friendliness. After all, Burlington was the kind of small New England city where people would think nothing of leaving their houses wide open, and most everyone greeted other persons in passing on the street. And, all the time there were more wild stories about carryings-on at the estate in Charlotte, and there were continuing echoes about Reginald H. J. Nash.

Everyone knew who Loeb was, though. The persons who ate lunch with him—the elected officials, some of the business and academic community—usually came away from these meetings amazed at his charm. They found it hard to square this Loeb with the man who mounted such gutter attacks in the newspaper.

Rumors flew and legends grew, mostly about Loeb himself. One story from this time that is still talked about by many of the people involved with the *Daily News,* concerns the office cat at the newspaper office. It is the type of story that not even the *Daily News* would print.

Most Vermont homes in the rural areas—and there are few urban areas in the Green Mountain State—have cats around, mostly as necessary pets. And it is the exception, rather than the rule, when a business property in downtown Burlington does not have a cat as a permanent resident of the building. Perhaps the reason is the proximity of the shore of Lake Champlain. At any rate, Vermonters know cats' habits.

One afternoon as most of the *Daily News* staff was leaving or had already left (Irene Allen was always there, it seems), Loeb entered the building and, without speaking a word to anyone (which was not unusual), walked through the outer offices, down the passageway on the ground floor to the publisher's office, which was located near the rear of the building at 123 College Street. There was no denying it was a pistol shot which the employes heard shortly after Loeb entered his office. Everyone knew of the financial difficulties the company was having (their paychecks reflected it), and everyone, to a man, looked at each other in utter horror. After the initial shock wore off, two or three employes rushed back to investigate. Seated at his desk with a still-smoking pistol in his hand was William Loeb. Lying on the floor, spurting blood, was the office cat. Loeb is reputed to have barked at no one in particular, "I thought I told you to get that goddam cat out of here."

The next morning, the business manager was summoned to Loeb's office and when he returned to the combination news room and business office, he called for attention and he told his fellow employes, "Mr. Loeb told me to tell you that yesterday afternoon the office cat was having a convulsion in his office and he did the only proper thing by putting it out of its misery."

The "annual meetings" at the estate in Charlotte never received the publicity of the one in the aftermath of which Reg Nash died, mainly because that was a tough act to follow. But Marka Loening did have some noteworthy guests at her home, besides her plenipotentiary transient, William Loeb. She acted as hostess and Loeb acted as host when Mr. and Mrs. George W. Gallowhur, residents of Reading, Vt., came calling.

Gallowhur had attended The Hotchkiss School as a member of the class behind Loeb, then Princeton University. Early in World War II, on a special assignment from the government, he had developed a solar still for the conversion of salt water to fresh water. He was a pharmaceutical chemist and was by this time developing for marketing his later successful "Skol" suntan lotion and "Skat" insect repellent.

Mrs. Gallowhur was the former Nackey Scripps, a member of the founding family of the Scripps-Howard newspapers and the United Press.

Over in Manchester, N.H., meanwhile, Bernard J. Mc-Quaid was back in town. He had hardly been seen since Colonel Knox took him to the *Chicago Daily News* as an editorial writer more than a decade earlier, but he had certainly been heard from. He had been among the first U.S. foreign correspondents to be assigned to a war zone, filing from Europe (and from Alaska during the threatened invasion there) daily reports for the Chicago Daily News Syndicate, one of the earliest and one of the best independent news feature services. McQuaid had stayed in Europe until 1943, where one of his traveling companions was William Randolph Hearst, Jr., a foreign correspondent for the Hearst-owned International News Service. Together the two men packed a powerful clout. Columns by one or the other, or both, appeared in nearly every major metropolitan market in the United States.

The Manchester newspapers regularly carried McQuaid's dispatches topped by an eight-column streamer on the back page.

McQuaid had gone from the European Theatre of Operations to the Pacific when the war was about one-half over and he continued to file magnificent, first-hand reports of the action there. If there is one thing which can be said about McQuaid at this time it was that he had the guts to be on the scene to see what he was describing, and another thing is that McQuaid was a consistently excellent writer. He often, against all advice of ranking Naval officers, would jump into a landing craft so as to be with the first assault wave when it hit the beach. He included many of these exploits in the brilliant daily stories he filed from combat zones.

McQuaid, one of four sons of a well-known and respected Boston newspaperman, Elias McQuaid, was regarded much the same as a war hero, especially around the Union-Leader, when he arrived home. He rarely appeared in public, but one affair, however, at which he kept all listeners on the edges of their chairs was at the annual dinner meeting of Local 167 of the American Newspaper Guild, AFL-CIO, almost 100 per cent of the membership of which were Union-Leader editorial employes, at the Rice Varick Hotel in Manchester in late February, 1944.

# 10

John A. Muehling had retired from active participation in the affairs of the Union-Leader Publishing Co., Inc., in the late 1930's, not long after he served as a delegate from New Hampshire to the 1936 Republican National Convention in Cleveland where he played a part in trying to get the Presidential nomination for his partner, Knox. He had become very feeble and he only rarely ventured from his Elm Street home even as far as Webster Street to visit his grandchildren.

Muehling spent more and more time in the warm climate of St. Petersburg, Fla., where he died April 19, 1944. The funeral services were conducted on Sunday afternoon, April 23, at the First Congregational Church on Hanover Street in Manchester. Executives and department heads of the Union-Leader acted as bearers and as ushers at the church, and more than 100 other employes of the paper assembled outside the newspaper building on Amherst Street and marched in a body to the church. At the door they were met by the president of the publishing company, the Secretary of the Navy, who had come from Washington to pay tribute to his partner of more than 40 years, and all Union-Leader employes entered the church in a body. The publisher, Capt. Edmund F. Jewell, USNR, was serving at the time as U.S. Naval attaché to the governments-in-exile in London. (What most persons at the funeral did not know, except Colonel Knox, was that D-Day was little over a month away and Captain Jewell was unavoidably detained from attending the funeral.) A large floral piece, donated by the Union-Leader employes, dominated the altar. The flowers spelled "(30)."

Knox, for the first time in anyone's memory, had prepared a three-column Page One editorial eulogizing John A. Muehling, for publication in the Monday, April 24, editions of the *Union* and *Leader*.

During the service, Knox did not feel well, but he passed this off—it was indigestion, he said. He traveled as far as New York City that evening and suffered another attack which he again dismissed as indigestion. Doctors later diagnosed the ailment as a coronary occlusion. He continued on to the capital by railroad on Monday morning and said he felt much better. (Knox had been somewhat of a physical fitness zealot. He often stayed overnight aboard the yacht *Sequoia* which was moored at the Naval Gun Factory, and he could be seen during his morning "jogs" through Southeast Washington.)

Colonel Knox went to his Navy Department office Tuesday morning, but omitted his usual press briefing and soon returned to his home at Linnaean Avenue NW. His situation worsened during the next few days and, a week after the passing of his old friend, Muehling, Colonel Knox succumbed to a succession of heart attacks on April 28, 1944.

Mrs. Knox was at her husband's side when he died and, among others, were Assistant Secretary of the Treasury John L. Sullivan, a Manchester attorney who was a North Union Street neighbor of Knox and who was later to succeed James Forrestal as Secretary of the Navy, and Rev. Dr. Fred Buschmeyer, pastor of the Mount Pleasant Congregation Church in suburban Washington and former pastor of the First Congregational Church in Manchester.

President Franklin D. Roosevelt said that Knox could be termed a war casualty and that "his death was a very real loss to the conduct of the war." Navy Undersecretary James Forrestal, as acting secretary, told the men and women of the fleets that their chief was dead. He dispensed with the firing of salutes and the wearing of mourning badges because of wartime conditions, but directed flags on all ships and stations to fly at half mast until the Monday funeral. Tributes poured in from all corners of the world, U.S. Navy commanders sent messages which indicated that they considered Colonel Knox a friend as well as their boss. The message from Admiral Ernest J. King, Chief of Naval Operations, was in true Navy tradition:

"Well done, Frank Knox. The nation has lost a great patriot; the Navy, a great leader. We dedicate ourselves, one and all, to what would have surely been his last order: Carry on."

Colonel Knox was given a hero's burial at Arlington National Cemetery.

He had written a will a short time before his death in which he specified that his widow, Annie Reid Knox, would be a trustee of his estate and individually she would inherit the Union-Leader Publishing Co., Inc. Upon his wife's death, the income would be paid to her sister, Adelia Reid, and, upon her death, the property would pass to Edmund F. Jewell. He specifically gave Mrs. Knox power, as trustee, to sell the Union-Leader. As far as the Chicago Daily News, Inc., was concerned, he directed the executors

of his estate to make such disposition of his interests to insure "continuation of a management preserving the character and traditions of the newspaper which it publishes."

The Union-Leader Publishing Co. not only remained
on an even keel from D-Day and Roosevelt's death through
V-E Day, Hiroshima and the ultimate end of World War
II on V-J Day, it did better than that; it made money,
largely due to the leadership of the two old veterans at its
helm, Dekker, the general manager, and Blood, the managing editor.

The Union-Leader had seen 61 employees go to war.
The newspapers had published, despite all the shortages
of newsprint, a special letter-sized edition of the newspaper
which was sent periodically to all employes in the service
and which relayed the doings of their fellow employes
who were in the service, and, as a public service, published
the weekly *Grenier Field Beacon* for the benefit of the
U.S. Army Air Corps personnel who were stationed at
the converted Manchester airport, which had been re-
named to honor the memory of Jacques Grenier, a pioneer
air mail pilot from Manchester, when the field was made
into an Army Air Corps base.

Sixty-one names went onto the large World War II me-
morial tablet which was erected in the main lobby of the
Union-Leader Building to honor those who had defended
America's freedoms, including freedom of the press. Fifty-
seven of those whose names went onto the plaque returned.
Four did not.

There were many then who felt that somewhere on that
plaque Managing Editor Bob Blood should have received
some sort of special mention. A truly fine man, in addition
to being the most capable of editors with the highest of
ethical standards, Blood had received two notable messages during World War II; one from the War Department that his older son, 1st Lt. Nickerson Blood, USAAC,
had been killed when his training plane crashed in Texas;
second, from the Navy Department that his other son, 2nd
Lt. Rogers Blood, USMC, had been killed in action lead-

ing the first wave of Marines onto the beach at Eniwetok, for which he was awarded a posthumous Silver Star medal for gallantry. It was at this point that the only other child of Mr. and Mrs. Blood, Elizabeth, a recent Smith College graduate, enlisted in the Navy as a Wave and quickly rose to officer status.

During all of this, Robert M. Blood never missed a day's work at the Union-Leader, reporting early and staying late, putting in seemingly endless hours, always in his green eyeshade, barking commands to, and seeing that they were carried out by, a woefully undermanned news staff. However, by his example alone, he demanded and received a level of editorial excellence which very few could equal.

Along with the other veterans of World War II, Captain "Ned" Jewell returned to Manchester. The G.I. Bill of Rights, which, incidentally, had been authored by a prominent Manchester attorney, Maurice F. Devine, himself a pillar of the community, guaranteed that all veterans, even "Ned" Jewell, would get their pre-war jobs on their return. But things had changed; Colonel Knox wasn't around anymore.

"Cissy" Patterson was sniffing some post-war prosperity in Washington with her *Times-Herald*. Ten years before, when she took over the *Times* and *Herald,* the newspapers had a combined deficit of $1,363,000. In 1943, the *Times-Herald* made a profit, before taxes, of $44,700; in 1944 the profit was $639,000; in 1945 it was in excess of $1,000,000, of which $110,500 was funneled back to 26 executives and department heads in bonus money. The *Times-Herald* had come a long way since Hearst lost money on it. It was a bigger organization, a better newspaper, readable, credible and popular. "Cissy" Patterson offered "Ned" Jewell his old job back as advertising director, naturally at more money with a bonus arrangement.

Jewell, although he wanted to accept the offer, felt he had some equity in the Union-Leader Publishing Co., if not under the terms and in the spirit of Knox's will, surely on the grounds of longevity and faithful service in Knox's

employ in Manchester, Boston, Washington, as well as in
the U.S. Navy. Annie Reid Knox felt otherwise. These
two old Yankee traders would have made the merchants
on New York's Orchard Street blush as their haggling and
negotiations went on and on, between Manchester and
Hillsborough County, New Hampshire, and Chicago—
Knox's will had been made, executed and probated in
Cook County, Illinois, where Knox had maintained a residence at The Chicago Club, even though he voted in
Manchester.

Finally a settlement was arrived at which provided something in the neighborhood of $100,000 in cash for Jewell.
He accepted Mrs. Patterson's offer and became once again
advertising director of the *Washington Times-Herald*.
This would prove to be a most fortuitous move on the
part of "Ned" Jewell. When "Cissy" Patterson died in
1949 she willed her newspaper property to eight of her
executives, seven of whom survived her: William C. Shel-
ton, general manager; Frank C. Waldrop, editor-in-chief;
Edmund F. Jewell, advertising director; Michael W. Flynn,
supervising managing editor; Harry Robinson, circulation
director; John Irving Bolt, mechanical superintendent,
and Mason S. Peters, III, night managing editor. Col. Robert McCormick, owner of the *Chicago Tribune,* bought
the *Times-Herald* for a reported $4,500,000. The Wash-
ington Post Co. bought the *Times-Herald* from Colonel
McCormick in March, 1954.

Just about the last thing Annie Reid Knox ever sought
to be was an active newspaper publisher. She was a housewife from the Bible Belt, seldom seen in Manchester outside of her own neighborhood, and was only rarely seen
there. She was not the figure some might think the wife
of such a prominent man as Colonel Knox to be. She came
back to live on Heather Street with her sister, Adelia, a
spinster, after the Colonel's death, and she was hardly what
anyone would call one of Manchester's more public-
spirited citizens.

She had control of two newspapers, the likes of which
are seldom equalled. It was a monopoly business structure,

solidly founded and well-supported. It was of such a staunch foundation that it might even be regarded on the same plane as the U.S. Mint; it was said then, and has been said much more often since, "Mickey Mouse could run the Union-Leader and make money."

It was also of such broad base and so solidly founded, even protected by the topography of the region it served, that, to this day, most businessmen realize that it would be financial suicide to try to found a competing daily, statewide morning newspaper, or even a Manchester evening newspaper.

The number and frequency of inquiries as to whether her New Hampshire publishing properties might be for sale convinced Annie Reid Knox that she was near the pot of gold at the end of her rainbow. She was comfortably fixed, anyway, but she had made very few close friends in Manchester during all the years she had lived there, she had no ties other than her luxurious home, and she could see no reason to stick around. So Annie Reid Knox finally decided to liquidate her assets and go to Florida where she and her sister, Adelia, could bask in the sun in their declining years.

Marshall Field of Chicago wanted the Union-Leader; the Gannett chain wanted the Union-Leader; and these were but two of the large newspaper operators who wanted this money-maker to add to their stables. But Annie Reid Knox declined all offers of this type. It finally came down to a battle between two parties as to who was to succeed the Knox family as owner.

On the one hand was John McLane Clark, a New Hampshire native. Clark, a graduate of St. Paul's School and Dartmouth College, was a protégé of Former Governor Winant from his prep school days (a fact which may have worked against him, since Winant was the one who defeated Knox in the gubernatorial primary in 1924). He was a scion of one of the state's best-known and widely respected families, whose grandfather was a former governor, and a former newsman for the *Washington Post* before wartime service with the Office of Strategic Services.

Clark had cash in hand and a bank loan to cover the one million dollar offer he made Mrs. Knox for the purchase. (A bank loan to a McLane in New Hampshire is not a hard thing for any Granite Stater to understand.)

On the other hand was William Loeb, publisher of the *Burlington Daily News* and the *St. Albans Daily Messenger,* son of the secretary to Colonel Knox's old military commander, who had upped his offer to a million-and-a-quarter. Besides, Mrs. Loeb (the one everyone knew about, not William's secret wife who was sending him her pay) and Mrs. Knox were old friends from the days of the "Rough Riders" reunions.

The sale is most aptly described in Chapter VII of *Journal of a Johnny-Come-Lately,* the biography of John McLane Clark, written by David Bradley, M.D., a longtime friend, after Clark's untimely death in a canoeing accident in 1957, published by Dartmouth Publications, Hanover, N.H.:

> "The *Manchester Union* fell to William Loeb. The sale was consummated under Sophoclean forebodings: Loeb arrived by private plane from New York just twenty minutes before the midnight expiration of his option. Funds for the higher bid had been secretly guaranteed by the Ridders, owner of a Teutonic empire of newspapers in this country. Mrs. Knox did not know the money was Ridder money (she had specifically forbidden John and his friends to seek help from them), nor did she think to ask where the money had come from until after signing the papers. Worse still, she had not bothered to examine the two newspapers that young Loeb already operated in Vermont. She signed and it was John's "Uncle Judge" (Atty. John W. McLane, Sr., of Manchester) who, as attorney for her partners (trustees of the will), had to complete the formalities."

Clark, in private correspondence, had described Loeb's newspapers in Vermont as follows, again from Dr. Bradley's book:

> "We wouldn't mind so much except that the guy runs a lousy newspaper. Awkwardly New Dealish, violently

anti-Russian, almost isolationist, it is a strident pamphle-
teering sort of thing, crammed with 'We learned today
from an exclusive source which cannot be disclosed . . .
etc.' "

In the *Manchester Union* of Saturday morning, Nov. 2,
1946, there was an announcement, two columns wide, in
full-face type. It stated that William Loeb had purchased,
along with his associates, all of the stock of the Union-
Leader Publishing Co., Inc. He identified the associates as
being Bernard H. Ridder, Victor F. Ridder and Joseph E.
Ridder, "who will give me the benefit of their wisdom and
experience, and make available the resources of their large
and expert organization." Loeb said further:

> "I intend to identify myself with Manchester and be-
> come a part of New Hampshire and pledge to do every-
> thing in my power to earn your friendship and coopera-
> tion."

Loeb closed his six-paragraph "announcement" by reprinting the words of Frank Knox and John A. Muehling
which had for many, many years dominated the upper
lines of the editorial page masthead of "New Hampshire's
Family Paper":

> "This paper will be the organ of no man, or set of
> men. As an institution, it will belong to New Hampshire
> and will attempt, to the full extent of its power and
> ability, to serve solely the highest traditions of the state."

William Loeb had both feet in the door—and as it later
turned out he didn't have much other than his feet in the
door—of a relatively small, but strategically powerful and
lucrative newspaper domain. He would, within 30 years,
convert this to a despotism and become the most powerful
and most feared man in the state of New Hampshire. Because of the unique position, politically, of this small state,
he would also become one of the most powerful men in
the United States.

# 11

Eric Ridder, publisher of *The Journal of Commerce*, recalls vividly the negotiations with William Loeb in 1946; he says he attended all sessions with his father, Joseph E. Ridder. Eric Ridder sits in his 17th floor office at 99 Wall Street which looks out over part of the shipping which his newspaper reports daily, and he is moderately talkative about his family's dealings with William Loeb in the purchase of the Union-Leader Publishing Co., Inc. But Eric Ridder is not smiling when he is moderately talkative about his family's dealings with William Loeb. As a matter of fact, it is May, 1974, and it takes his mind off the forthcoming Newport-to-Bermuda race. Eric Ridder and his general manager, Adelric Benziger, both knew William Loeb; they knew Eleanore McAllister, and they knew Marka Truesdale Loening from the "tea dance" days on the North Shore.

The Ridder interests, in 1946, included, besides *The Journal of Commerce* (the commodity-trading and shipping daily), the *St. Paul*, Minn., *Dispatch* and *Pioneer Press*, the *Grand Forks*, N.D., *Herald*, *Aberdeen*, S.D., *American News*, *Duluth*, Minn., *Herald* and *News Tribune*, and a large part of the *Seattle*, Wash., *Times*. He says he did not know, nor did any of his family know, about any feelings which Mrs. Annie Reid Knox may have had about the Ridder family being involved in the purchase of the Union-Leader. (There are some reports that Mrs. Knox's feelings were based on the fact that the Ridders were of German descent, and others to the effect that it was because they were all ardent Catholics.)

Ridder says that all meetings were held in New York City and that Loeb had as his attorney Herbert Brownell of New York, later U.S. Attorney General under Eisenhower, and that Brownell was with Loeb at all of these sessions.

"I arranged the next morning after our last meeting

with Loeb prior to the expiration of his option, for The Bank of New York to lend us $1,100,000 as our 50 per cent of the deal," says Eric Ridder, "which we gave to Loeb and he used this to complete the transaction." He gives the impression that borrowing one million dollars was a routine and simple matter for the Ridder family. Apparently, Loeb did not tell the Ridders the purchase price of the newspaper.

"But the fact of the matter was that Loeb had only the 'up front' money, and that was all he had invested. We found out about this after the deal was closed and we knew we were in trouble with this guy from the start.

"We had made an agreement that two Ridders would serve on the board of directors with Loeb and another of Loeb's choosing, [Loeb chose John N. Eustis of New York City], and it was thoroughly agreeable to us to have Brownell as the fifth member. After all, Brownell was a lawyer not unfamiliar to us and we felt we were safe with a man of his unquestioned ability and reputation. So, my father and Uncle Victor were named our representatives."

The Ridders also had as part of the basic agreement that they would have one of "their" people as a sort of watchdog at the Manchester operation, and Edwin C. Hedekin thus became business manager of the Union-Leader. The Union-Leader Publishing Co., Inc., was disbanded and the Union Leader Corporation was chartered as a New Hampshire corporation, recorded in Hillsborough County on Nov. 21, 1946.

"Well," says Eric Ridder, "you can imagine that this relationship was stormy, to say the least. It boiled down to the fact that the Union Leader was doing business with 90 per cent of our money and we had 50 per cent control. Something had to give."

Charlie Weaver was summoned by Loeb to Manchester to attend the early sessions of the new partnership where mechanics of the Loeb-Ridder control were worked out. Weaver (with Montague) would pretty much take care of the Vermont newspapers. It is obvious that Loeb let Weaver know just what he wanted to let him know.

Weaver's loyalty is obvious and he talks about the matter most sincerely, as follows:

"Let me tell you that that was the damnedest set of negotiations I ever saw in my life. One of those Ridders, I don't remember which one, I'm sure he didn't have a drop of blood in his veins, I know he would have cut his mother's heart out for a quarter. Hard, tough, absolutely unfeeling, and I sat for several days of negotiations down there.

"What impressed me about those Ridder brothers, they were something. I can't imagine anything worse than working for one of those Ridders, from what I saw of them in these negotiations and they were very, very hard on their points. And I was amazed. Bill gave in on this point, on that point, and the other point. And finally we had everything worked out to a final thing, the lawyers were going to work out the details, you see, in writing, for us, and all we'd agreed on.

"Bill took me down to the railroad station that evening —I was coming back up to Vermont—and we stopped on the platform and he said, 'Well, what do you think of it?' I said, 'Frankly, Bill, I'm scared to death. Why the hell did you give in to them the way you did?'

"And he looked at me and he smiled, a characteristic Bill Loeb smile, showing me there was something else going on in that mind of his. I think he had a 30- or a 60-day clause in there during which he was given management of the paper, you see, and they thought they were going to, at the end of 60 days, cut him up into little pieces and throw him away, you see, and I was afraid that was going to happen. But Bill got his hold on that paper."

As to how much money Loeb had invested, Weaver says, "I don't remember the details, the financial end of it. I was concerned with the operating end."

As to whether it had been Mrs. Loeb who had advanced her son the money, Charlie Weaver says, "Yeah, sure, oh yeah. But the result of the whole damned thing, was simply this. At the end of 60 days he had taken the Ridder brothers and had torn them into such little shreds that they were damned glad to get out and leave Bill with it. He was a brilliant negotiator, absolutely brilliant. He handled that thing masterfully. I was scared to death for him. He brought (Leonard V.) Finder in and he kicked the Ridders out. And I don't think the Ridders have ever been kicked out of anything before or since. God, what operators they were. They were terrific.

"Bill Loeb wanted power," adds Weaver, "that's what he wanted. He wanted power and he knew that in that paper he would get it and he knew the paper well because he had been a friend of Knox."

So William Loeb had obtained for himself a new and much bigger and broader power base in New Hampshire, and the Granite State was a new and wonderful place to him. Loeb had given the distinct impression to all concerned—and this was one of his biggest problems—that he was never really interested in the affairs of St. Albans, Burlington, or Vermont, for that matter. Businessmen, as well as most employes, had the idea that Loeb felt he was doing them all a favor by being involved at all and that he was just a little bit "above it."

New Hampshire is a beautiful state; the "Switzerland of North America," it's called. Its scenic wonders are endless. The White Mountains, the highest in the Northeast, get their name from their snow cover in the winter and the rugged beauty of the granite, of which they are formed, in the summer. The seacoast of New Hampshire, while only 18 miles in length, has a flavor and beauty all its own with wide, sandy beaches and some rocky, rugged points. There are the Isles of Shoals, about 10 miles offshore. Seemingly everywhere between the mountains and the seacoast, there are lakes, wide lakes, narrow lakes, big lakes, small lakes, deep lakes, shallow lakes, all of them beautiful, the largest and most scenic of which is Lake Winnepesaukee in the central part of the state.

These mountains and lakes and the streams and rivers which feed them and run out of them are some of the Manchester newspapers' greatest natural assets. Because of the terrain, transportation can be rough going in New Hampshire. There is only one city, Manchester, which is anywhere near large enough to support a statewide newspaper organization and, at that, Manchester is not centrally located. The thought of bringing a competition newspaper in from out of state is beyond the realm of practicality. As it now stands, there are some parts of New Hampshire which don't receive the morning paper except by U.S. Mail and, if that is delayed or a connection missed, the newspaper arrives a day late.

New Hampshire has another distinction. It is about the only place in the whole world where everyone, almost without exception, has a friend highly placed in the government. The bicameral legislature of New Hampshire is the third largest law-making body in the English-speaking world, ranking behind the British Parliament and the U.S. Congress. As a matter of fact, the only law-making bodies in the entire Free World, besides the United States and Great Britain, which are larger, are the national governments of Italy, Germany, France, Japan and India.

New Hampshire has 400 members in its House of Representatives and 24 in its Senate. The state retains the Governor and Council system, the governor being the "supreme executive magistrate" and empowered only to nominate to the five-member Council, whose members may accept or reject the governor's proposals, and these councillors are elected from geographical districts. There is in the whole state not nearly one million people; New Hampshire ranked 41st in the nation in the 1970 census and yet it is the only state of the 50 with neither a sales nor income tax. So the question naturally arises, how does the state maintain its economy, being so topheavy with lawmakers?

And the answer is simple; they don't get paid, unless you want to call $200 per biennium pay. The governor is the only one who receives a salary, or living wage.

The New Hampshire General Court—and not just because of its size—is one of a kind. Because Court members are paid only $200 a biennium, plus a mileage allowance on days the Legislature is in session and which sessions they attend, the job attracts only special kinds of persons. Historically, as with most law-making bodies which stem from Colonial times, the General Court, particularly the Senate, was the province of the landed gentry. However, the passage of more equal rights legislation ultimately eliminated all preliminary qualifications for membership (for example, to own so many acres of land to be eligible to run for the Senate). Because of the low measure of remuneration, though, only those who were able to adequately support themselves could think of running for the Legislature. This made it a logical retreat of the rich man, and laws evolved favoring this class. But then, seeing this, groups with special interests took it upon themselves to "sponsor" certain members and this, of course, made these members "captive" of the sponsoring group.

There was always some honor attached to being a member of the Legislature, especially from the smaller communities. To this day, the legislator who represents a single community, which is itself a district, is a much bigger "wheel" than his colleague who is one of five legislators elected from a Manchester ward, let us say. It has always been more difficult to be elected from a small town as a one-man delegation than from the more populous city wards.

The Republican Protestant town representatives have historically held the controlling hand in the General Court because there have always been more of them, but, what may even be more important, practically 100 per cent of these representatives have gone to the Legislature to work. Among the delegates from the city have been many ward heeler types, some of whom got themselves elected to the Legislature as a status symbol, or for something to do, or as a place where the free drinks were usually abundant; some, even, have gone there to sleep, and many have gone to sleep there.

Growing up in my era in Manchester, Patsy Sweeney was a living legend; Patsy was one of the last of the old-time prize fighters. He was usually to be found plying his trade in the Ritz Ballroom on Lowell Street at least one night a week, and sometimes Patsy would climb into the squared circle in one of the surrounding towns, if the price was right. Over the years the punch of the glove, and the punch of the grape, had taken their toll on poor Patsy, and he would shuffle along Elm Street, or set up camp on a bench in Merrimack Common, accepting gratuities from friends and admirers. Patsy was by this time on a fast downhill express. Trolley conductors, kind men like Tom Sullivan and Pat Winston, made no secret of the fact that they'd keep a weather eye out for Patsy as they came down Elm Street. They were very careful indeed with the bell for fear Patsy would clean off the sidewalk on signal.

"Bricks" Healy (the old Irish always pronounced this Hay-ly) was major-domo of the Knights of Columbus home on Hanover Street where he and a number of confreres could usually be found day or night discussing the weightier subjects of the day, such as Sharkey's potential ability to knock out Dempsey, whether or not Rabbit Maranville was the greatest shortstop of all time, or if Venske, Hornbostel, Cunningham or San Romani would win the K. of C. mile at the Boston Garden, or if any of them could have beaten Bonthron. The matter of the welfare of Patsy Sweeney came into their purview one election year, and Bricks and the boys decided it would be a simple matter for them to get Patsy elected to the General Court from Ward 5 in Manchester. Patsy could sure use the $200, if that's what it was in those days, and he could collect the mileage allowance even if he rode up to Concord with someone else—Patsy could still sign his name—and Bricks and the boys were sure they could arrange a six-month car pool for Patsy.

It is important to know that one of the provincialisms of the area was, and is, to call an institution by the name of the locality in which it located: e.g., "Durham," the University of New Hampshire; in this case, "Grasmere," the Hillsborough County Farm, and "Concord," the State House (if you were a reasonably upstanding member of the community) or the New Hampshire State Hospital (if you were not).

Bricks became ex-officio campaign manager for Patsy Sweeney and he and his friends dispersed themselves to different parts of Ward 5 to conduct a small fund-raising campaign; after all, they had to pay the filing fee to get Patsy on the ballot, and then they at least had to have a clean shirt and jacket for Patsy so he would look presentable standing in front of the Lake Avenue Engine House, the polling place, on Election Day.

Bricks Healy had assigned himself to the three-deckers on the lower part of Lake Avenue, near Chestnut Street, and he was conducting his door-to-door canvass when he knocked on the door of the Murphy home. Mrs. Murphy, lovely lady that she was, answered.

"Mrs. Murphy, and a good day to you. We're going among our friends to get together a little money so that we can send Patsy Sweeney to Concord," said Bricks.

"Why, God bless you, Bricks. Let me go to me bag," said Mrs. Murphy. Returning, she said, "Here you go, Bricks, and God help us, but don't you think poor Patsy would be better off in Grasmere?"

History tells us that having received 1,744 votes, Hon. Patrick J. Sweeney, Democrat, Ward 5, Manchester, won election as a member of the 1937–38 term of the New Hampshire General Court.

In the present day, the Legislature has adopted a much more serious mien. That is not to say, however, that there are not those who combine six months every two years in the Legislature with a few months a year working at a race track. And it is a simple matter to see where lie the sympathies of these lawmakers. Conflicts of interest are common in Concord.

There are many retired persons in the N.H. General Court and the average age, which used to be well over 60, is now down to the mid-50's, largely because there are many members under 25, some even under 21 and the persons whom these younger persons have replaced were, in many cases, over 80. The office is attracting more and more the educated housewives who, years ago, were an unknown quantity in New Hampshire politics. Electronic voting has also made the avocation more attractive; those countless 400-member roll call votes near the end of the session when the days were hot discouraged many from attendance. The private interests are still represented in the Legislature and, in most cases, represented well.

However, the members of the New Hampshire General Court as a group have never been, nor are they now, "old bums," as William Loeb called them in the *Manchester Union Leader* of Oct. 6, 1974.

The New Hampshire General Court, even though it is the largest, is the only state legislature which still meets in the original chambers which were designed for its use.

It had early been the custom and later became the law in New Hampshire that during the time of the year when the worst of the winter weather was over and the spring planting had not yet begun the "folks" would get together to hold Town Meeting, decide on the town budget, the business of the schools, the roads and the library (if the town had a library), and the cemetery. These town meetings got to be almost social events. For some people, living only a few miles apart, it was the only time of the year they would see one another. When it was decided that New Hampshire would be a "primary" state rather than a "convention" state for the purposes of naming delegates to the national conventions of the respective political parties, it made sense to have these delegates chosen statewide on Town Meeting Day, because the "folks was meetin'" anyway. The towns have always been able to control the Legislature on any given vote in New Hampshire, there being today only 13 cities.

From this chance beginning, the New Hampshire first-in-the-nation Presidential primary came into being. The New Hampshire people always loved the notoriety it afforded them, but there were two larger reasons why this primary has blossomed into a major event: New Hampshire's second largest industry (after agriculture) is tourism and the primary boiled down to free advertising and publicity; New Hampshiremen, all of whom personally know their representative in Concord, really got to feel that if a man wanted to be President, the New Hampshire primary was so early that there should be nothing to prevent a candidate from coming a little early so the Granite Staters could have a chance to "look him over." Besides, if he got elected, that might be the last chance they'd ever have to see him.

On Dec. 12, 1946, William Loeb introduced himself to his readers in New Hampshire with the first of his Page One editorials. In it, he gave his new readers a lesson in the true heritage of Daniel Webster. "There is nothing so powerful as truth," Loeb quoted the statesman, whose birthplace was in New Hampshire but who gained fame as a senator from Massachusetts.* "We shall endeavor to continue to produce a newspaper of which Daniel Webster would have been proud," said Loeb. "It will be independent and fearless. It will serve no man or group of men, but only New Hampshire. God grant it the wisdom to see and do the right always. /s/ William Loeb, Publisher."

Loeb also announced on that December day that the names of the newspapers would be changed, no more *Manchester Union* and *Manchester Leader*. Henceforth the newspapers would be known as the *New Hampshire Morning Union* and the *Manchester Evening Leader*. (To this day, despite Loeb's changing the newspapers' names, the morning newspaper is still widely referred to as the *Manchester Union*. There are references to the newspaper

---

* In many parts of New Hampshire there is, to this day, quite some resentment towards those who would refer to Daniel Webster as a "New Hampshireman." As a matter of fact, the Legislature refused to have the statue of Daniel Webster erected in the State House plaza at public expense and, as a result, the only way the memorial could be erected was as a gift to the state by Benjamin Pierce Cheney, Esq., of Hillsborough, a fellow townsman of President Pierce and one of the founders of the American Express Company. The Legislature specified that up to "two rods square in some convenient part of the state-house yard in Concord" could be used by Mr. Cheney for his gift. The joint resolution, approved Aug. 8, 1883, further specified that "the custody and future protective care of said monument shall be assumed and forever hereafter remain and be vested in the governor and council."

by this name included in the House Journal quoting some legislators who were not born when the names of the *Union* and *Leader* were changed.)

The new publisher also announced that the newspapers would have separate staffs, each with a managing editor of its own, including separate editorial writers and policies, but that Robert M. Blood would remain in general supervision of the news and editorial departments of both newspapers. Loeb was thereby telling the whole staff that he was very limited in experience in the day-to-day operation of a newspaper, because such a scheme rarely works in newspapers of this size.

Maybe Loeb should have asked Bob Blood first, because, even though he retained the title of executive editor and Loeb kept his name in the masthead, Blood had had enough. He had been there since the early 20's, having worked for a couple of other New England dailies after receiving his degree from Dartmouth College. It was a rare event when Blood had ever taken one day off. He even went in on Sundays and during this time he used to read the Boston newspapers (there were four Boston Sundays then) and *The New York Times* from cover to cover and what he didn't read in the office he took home to finish. In very bad weather, or if Blood were sick (which was seldom and, at that, always happened on Sunday), the Sunday copy boy's first task was to get those out-of-town newspapers to Mr. Blood's house.

Blood had gotten to know Loeb and had seen the *modus operandi* and he decided he had seen all he wanted to see with this new "competing against ourselves" concept. He retired and spent the rest of his days with his "bride" at their home on East High Street in Manchester. Their only surviving child had married a Navy man while she was in the service and, although he never said a word about his grief, the Blood household was never the same when his own two sons did not return from the war.

Robert M. Blood died in 1950 and the obituary which appeared in the *Morning Union* and *Evening Leader* was the one which Blood, himself, had written many years

before and he had left strict orders that that only was to
be used. The funeral services at the Goodwin Funeral
Home were attended by just about every Union Leader
employe, of that time or in the past, within whose power
it was to be present, as well as practically all of Manchester's dignitaries. Each person was greeted smilingly,
and by name, by Mrs. Blood and her daughter. Manchester
had lost one of its true pillars.

The "cogniscenti" of the Manchester business community viewed Loeb's pontifical pronouncements and Blood's
retirement with jaundiced eyes. The State House reporter
for the *Union* and *Leader* had been making the rounds
quietly before the Knox-Loeb-Clark negotiations telling
the "smart money" in Manchester that if they wanted to
save the Union-Leader, better "get it up." Edmund T.
King, who had replaced another McQuaid, David, in the
State House billet when David went to war, said that he
had received many "scouting reports" on Loeb and they
were all bad. King's plan would have been for the employes to run the newspaper themselves with local capital.

There isn't much communication, as a practical matter,
between Burlington and Manchester; these cities are at
opposite ends of the "Twin" states. To Manchester residents, by and large, Burlington is the place where, on
driving to Montreal if you stop for gas, you look for
"hommes" and "dames" instead of "men" and "women."
To Burlingtonians, driving to Boston, Manchester is the
place with the endless wall of red mills along the river.

But too many things were happening at the local newspaper to suit the local gentry, who had for long years taken
for granted the sedate and ethical management of the
Union-Leader. Dekker retired. Dave McQuaid never came
back to his old job. Ed King, when he couldn't raise
enough interest in his plan, quit and accepted an offer
from Senator Styles Bridges to be the senior senator's press
relations man. Jim Mooney, the copy editor who was the
foundation of the place, left when Blood did. Loeb replaced Arthur Brush, one of Jewell's boys, as advertising
director with Walter McLaughlin, but McLaughlin was no

dummy; he said he'd take the job only if Loeb gave him a written contract and Loeb did. Many others were returning from the service and staying at the Union-Leader only briefly, if at all. The story of Loeb's publishing his Baptismal Certificate in his Vermont newspaper drifted into town and, as rumors will, became magnified from the facts of the case.

So, a group of the "boys" were discussing the matter of the new publisher of the local newspaper during a post-luncheon bull session one day at the Derryfield Club, the downtown businessmen's preserve, and Eddie Campbell, a local stockbroker, volunteered:

"Archie Roosevelt and I had the next bunk to each other when we were both first lieutenants and we've stayed pretty friendly. I'll give him a call and check out this guy Loeb." And when Campbell returned from the phone booth, he said, "Archie Roosevelt says to watch this guy. He's a phony. I also asked him if Loeb was Jewish and Archie said, 'I don't know if Loeb is a Jew, but his mother and father were.' "

New Hampshire and Manchester had had enough of this "hate" business; ethnic and religious strife was a thing of the past, or so everyone hoped.

The past merits telling. Catholics did not have civil rights in New Hampshire until 1877 and, because of this, the state was part of the diocese of Portland, Maine, until shortly before the turn of the century. In the years immediately preceding World War II, there had been numerous incidents involving racial and religious bigotry, all involving Catholics. This was due largely to the smoldering bigotry which remains—to some extent even to this day—in the smaller towns in New Hampshire, which, as was pointed out before, maintain control of the Legislature.

The first occasion of polarization on this issue came in the 1932 Presidential primary when every Smith delegate to the Democratic national convention was defeated and every Roosevelt delegate elected, and this, in itself, evoked memories of local incidents during the 1928 Presidential election when New York Gov. Al Smith ran against Herbert Hoover.

Shortly after the 1932 election, and not directly connected, of course, a revolution, of sorts, almost occurred
within the ranks of the Catholic diocese of Manchester.
Some prominent Franco-Americans insisted that the
French-Canadian language (which is, indeed, very different
from Parisian French) be taught, not as a foreign language,
but to be the basic language of their parish schools, with
English to be taught as a foreign language. This cancer
had spread from Rhode Island (the only state which is a
complete diocese with a higher percentage of Catholic
population than New Hampshire), where there had been
public excommunications. The bishop of Manchester, himself of French-Canadian extraction, stopped it before it
got to this stage. Many pastors, however, were replaced
and the memory lingered on.

During the gubernatorial campaign of 1934, it began to
look as if the Democrats had an even-money chance of
electing a Manchester man to that office, Atty. John L.
Sullivan, who had been nominated to run against a Concord man, a Republican, H. Styles Bridges, a member of
the State Public Service Commission and a native of
"down" in Maine. Bridges was fighting a battle of recognition, as much as anything else, within the state, but the
country, as a whole, was thinking Democrat at the time;
there was the NRA of President Franklin D. Roosevelt
and it was the time of getting it all together after the
Great Depression.

Sullivan was the namesake not only of a famous prize-
fighter of an era gone by, but he was also the namesake
of a famous New Hampshire Revolutionary War hero who
led many battles in the seacoast region. He was gaining
strong support, particularly in the cities, and the Franco-
American vote seemed to be securely in Sullivan's corner,
if for no other reason than because Sullivan was a Roman
Catholic. In the waning days of the campaign there became attached to the Sullivan candidacy a slur against the
Franco-American population which would have made the
"Canuck" incident involving Sen. Edmund S. Muskie in
1972 look like a compliment.

One of the bridges across the Merrimack River linking

the downtown part of Manchester to McGregorville, a heavily French neighborhood, was being rebuilt and was not usable. This was the era of the political "rally" and at one such "rally" at a French social club, a "snowshoe club," a spokesman for Sullivan was asked, "What's John L. going to do about the bridge?"

There are, to this day, persons in Manchester who swear that they were there and they themselves heard the answer. Now, if this, in itself, is so, Madison Square Garden couldn't hold all the witnesses to the event. And there are those who say that on the night of the full moon, you can hear the voice as clear as a bell coming out of the trees over St. Joseph's old cemetery. At any rate, Tom Jennings, one of the Jennings from 'Squog, the Irish section, is reputed to have loudly answered:

"Let the frogs swim across the river."

H. Styles Bridges was elected governor of New Hampshire by a little over 2,400 votes. If you trace the vote closely enough it is easy to see that, while Sullivan did win the Manchester West Side wards, he didn't win them by much and he even lost wards in cities such as Berlin, Laconia and Nashua which could have made the difference. This was the beginning of a long political career for H. (for Hiram) Styles Bridges, who sometime later dropped the H.

When the issue of whether or not parochial school pupils would ride on public school buses came before the N.H. Legislature, it seemed sure that the attitude "let the bishop buy his own school buses" would prevail. The Roman Catholic bishop attended the last public hearing of the bill, but only as a spectator. Before adjourning the hearing, the perplexed committee chairman asked the bishop if he would like to be heard, at which point His Excellency told that legislator he had come to listen, not to talk, but, inasmuch as the chairman had called on him, the only thought he would like to leave was that on the day after this bill became law, all parochial schools in the state would be closed. When the solons added up the enrollments of the Catholic schools and got an idea of the education costs the diocese was assuming, the minuscule expense of extra school buses suddenly became paltry, and the bill was reported "Inexpedient to Legislate," and was never again heard of.

Manchester and New Hampshire, by 1946, was over this unpleasantness, and those who remembered it well wanted no more. In Manchester alone, there were many racial and ethnic backgrounds, an unusual number, as a matter of fact. In the Roman Catholic churches in the city, there were "national" churches which conducted services in English, French, Polish, Syrian, Ukrainian and Lithuanian. One of the city's larger parishes, St. Raphael, was, and is today, staffed and ministered to by the monks of the Order of St. Benedict of St. Anselm's abbey because that branch of the Benedictine order was an offshoot from the Bavarian abbey at Metten and these priests were strategically placed at St. Raphael to cater to the distinct German and Belgian cultures of the parishioners in this part of town. There were three Greek Orthodox churches of slightly divergent denomination. There were Polish Roman Catholics and Polish Catholics. There was a Russian Orthodox church. There were two synagogues, orthodox and reform. There was just about every Protestant denomination.

In Manchester everyone had had enough of racism and bigotry. No one was needed to come in and upset this applecart, because the apples bruised too easily.

But the Manchester community had heard about Loeb and his baptismal certificate and they heard about it because they were naturally curious about this new publisher who had come into the community and started up with outspoken front page editorials. The baptismal certificate story was the highlight of any conversation about Loeb, and there were many conversations about Loeb, for he appeared to be a person who had maligned and slandered a particular group of citizens.

In his first public appearances in Manchester, Loeb did very well: was dignified, gracious, and accommodating. But those who had long been accustomed to the *Leader*, sedate as it was, viewed him with reserve and mistrust. Nonetheless, Loeb had his fingers on the Union Leader, some of them anyway, and he wouldn't let go.

The Loeb-Ridder relationship was a hectic one, to put it mildly. The Ridders were specialists. One member of the family or another had become an expert in one particular facet of producing a newspaper, whether it be stereotyping, printing, composition, advertising sales and promotion, bookkeeping methods. Whatever the situation, there was a Ridder who had the training to handle it. Some of the Ridder team made periodic trips to Manchester and made recommendations for streamlining, and making more profitable, the operation of the Union Leader Corp. Loeb assumed the role of the "small guy" who was interested in his trusted employes and they were all being pushed around by these big-city newspapermen "who had forced their way into the operation."

The Ridders felt that since 90 per cent of the money being used to finance the operation was theirs, they should have had at least 50 per cent of the say in how things were run. But there was disagreement after disagreement and Loeb made no secret of the difficulties he was having with his partners. Some even viewed Loeb's turning for public sympathy as being ethically questionable. But Loeb usually won these squabbles by procrastination. The Ridders had too many enterprises to take too much time in solving minor problems in Manchester.

Leonard V. Finder had been born in Chicago in 1907, had been educated at the University of Illinois and its law school and had come east where he married a Boston girl, then had gone into public relations in New York. During a vacation trip to Vermont in early 1946, Finder became interested in Loeb's Burlington operation merely by reading the newspaper. Apparently sensing that the newspapers were in financial trouble because of the poor quality of the printed product, Finder, on his return to Manhattan, wrote Loeb a letter "cold," expressing an interest in purchasing the properties if they became for sale. Loeb replied that they were not for sale, but he thanked him for the inquiry and told Finder he would keep it in mind.

After Loeb had gotten control of the Union Leader in partnership with the Ridders, he must have figured a way out as soon as he figured his way in. Finder and his wife were invited to dinner at the Republican Club in New York City with Loeb and his mother. It was a long meeting and it was at this time that Finder decided to enter a partnership with Loeb in Manchester. Finder knew only that Loeb and the Ridders were partners and he accepted Loeb's version of the conflict then apparent in their Manchester association. After the dinner meeting at the Republican Club, Finder convinced his father, Meyer N. Finder, and his brother, Dr. Jerome G. Finder, to help with the necessary financing. Finder's wife, Anne, had also received an inheritance, part of which was used. Mr. and Mrs. Finder immediately moved to Manchester, buying a house on Chestnut Street, with their children, Michael, 7, and Beth Jane, 4, and they did all they could to blend in with the Manchester community.

"Finally," says Eric Ridder, "we had a meeting in New York to decide what we were going to do about this situation. Herb Brownell came up with the idea that Loeb be given the opportunity, since it was considered his 'find,' to buy the Ridder interests at the Ridders' price, inasmuch as it was almost all Ridder money used in the first place.

"And that's the way it ended," said Eric Ridder, "that's when Loeb got Finder to buy us out." He will not discuss the "Ridder price," but it is a fair assumption that the Ridders didn't lose money, nor did they work six months for nothing.

Manchester and New Hampshire people were getting more and more opportunities to read Loeb's pontifications, and in a Page One editorial on May 27, 1947, he called Leonard V. Finder his "esteemed and good friend." Said Loeb further:

"A change in ownership of the Union Leader Corporation forever assures that there will be a *New Hamp-*

*shire Morning Union,* and that it will always live up to
the immortal words of Daniel Webster which appear
each day at our masthead. For that reason, this seems to
this writer to be an especially grand and glorious morning."

It took William Loeb slightly less than three columns to
say that Leonard V. Finder was his new partner. Loeb was
to be president and publisher of the *Morning Union* and
Finder vice president and publisher of the *Evening Leader.*

But there was a new act in town. Manchester and New
Hampshire had another statewide newspaper, the *New
Hampshire Sunday News.* Bernard J. McQuaid had hatched
the plan, after leaving the employ of the *Chicago Daily
News,* to publish a Sunday newspaper. He had gotten his
friend, Blair Clark, who had worked for the *St. Louis Post-
Dispatch* before going into the Navy, to be the publisher
and heaviest investor in the new enterprise. Arthur Brush,
who had been dismissed by Loeb as advertising director,
was in charge of that department at the new newspaper.
Others on the staff included Benjamin C. Bradlee (in 1975
executive editor of the *Washington Post*), who had been
recently released from duty as a Naval officer after having
completed his studies at Harvard, and Elias McQuaid,
brother of Bernard, both of whom were reporters. Bernard
McQuaid was associate publisher and chief editorial writer.
The newspaper, complete with color comics, was being
printed at the Haverhill, Mass., *Gazette* and trucked the
26 miles to Manchester, from there trans-shipped and sold
on newsstands and in front of churches on Sunday mornings throughout the state.

The *Haverhill Gazette* was printing the newspaper as a
"job shop" proposition. The regular *Gazette* printers,
stereotypers, pressmen and mailers did the actual work
and were paid overtime rates. The *Gazette* charged the
*Sunday News* on a cost-plus basis.

# 12

Eleanore McAllister Loeb had had quite enough of the Foxcroft School by 1946, especially when she never got to enjoy her paycheck, sending it faithfully to her husband, Loeb, in Burlington, so she quit her job and came north to Vermont. She and Loeb settled in a small house in Middlebury, Vt., where Loeb at least spent the nights when he was not in New Hampshire trying to arrange for the purchase of the Union-Leader Publishing Co. It is awfully confusing at this point to determine who knew what about whom, but apparently, Mrs. Loeb, the publisher's mother, still didn't know that her son was married and was still of the opinion that he and Marka Truesdale Loening were headed in that direction.

Whether or not having Eleanore on the scene was the final argument in that direction, Marka decided in early 1947 that she was going to give up the huge estate in Charlotte and buy a smaller house of her own for herself and the children. But since she was going to use the children's support money heavily for such an investment—her job at the *Daily News* still wasn't very lucrative—she had to petition the Probate Court for permission because this was an unusual expediture. Before granting its license, the court wished to know the attitude of Grover Loening towards this venture, and Loening was contacted by mail by Marka. In replying at length, Loening disapproved of the idea and made the court an information addressee of the letter so that his reply thus became a public record.

According to Loening's reckoning, Marka had gone through $120,000 in six years, "which is about $20,000 a year—or $7,000 a year apiece," the letter said, for the three children. He said he felt that the Vermont Probate Court had been very lax "in their approval of your acts—particularly when you were allowed to appropriate funds (that I had given my children primarily for education) for the financial support of a risky personal aggrandizement

enterprise on behalf of Mr. Loeb's promotions." The long
and the short of it all was that the court, Judge Gravel
presiding, denied Marka's application for a license to buy
the new house out of the children's funds.

Loeb was even less on the scene than ever before, which
was little enough. Weaver and Montague were doing the
best they could, but the bills were piling up at the Burlington Publishing Co., Inc., the Loeb corporation which
owned the *Daily News* and *Daily Messenger*. There were
many former employes who had gotten out of the service,
but none of them really wanted to have much to do with
the *Daily News* and the word was all over town that the
operation was going bad. Just to let the local gentry know
he was still alive and active, however, Loeb would kick a
little in a periodic Page One editorial.

In Manchester, when Loeb editorially introduced his
readers to his "esteemed and good friend," Leonard V.
Finder, he devoted a long paragraph to the fact that he
would assign more space in his newspaper to editorials and
news coverage, but newsprint was short. The truth of the
matter was that Loeb's credit with the paper companies
was short—it had been for years—and his reputation in
Vermont had followed him to Manchester, and the Union
Leader Corp. was suffering for it. In fact, Loeb's reputation was not confined to the upper reaches of the Northeast United States, by any means.

In Burlington, the old *Daily News* had lost a little of
its charm and Marka apparently wanted out. She had kept
up contact with one of her childhood "beaux," Alexis
Felix duPont, Jr., with whom she kept company as a teen-
ager. Marka says she met him at dances at St. Paul's School
in Concord, N.H., where he was a member of the Class of
1925. He had married about two years after Marka had
married Grover Loening, but divorced his wife in 1945,
about the time he was discharged from the Army Air Corps
as a lieutenant colonel. On Aug. 2, 1947, Marka and Felix
were married; she packed up her children and left the
estate in Charlotte and laid eyes for the last time on William Loeb. She went to live where all of "the" duPonts

live, in Wilmington, Del., where her husband, she says, "used to work in the paint department."

This wedding had the effect of a minor earthquake in a certain part of Mill Neck, N.Y., where the elder Mrs. Loeb lived. She was almost 71 at the time and she had thought that Marka and her son, Bill, would be marrying very soon. She had given her son the "loan" of $250,000 in 1946, believing that this was enough to buy half of the Union Leader. She got the word back that Marka Truesdale duPont had gotten quite a sum of money from Loeb to bail out at Burlington and Mrs. Loeb was mildly inquisitive as to where her son had gotten the money.

But she was just sitting down to contemplate this shock when William arrived home with Eleanore to whom he had been secretly married for almost five years. Mrs. Loeb was gracious enough and accepted Eleanore but no public announcement was made of this marriage until Christmastime.

Loeb still wanted to keep Eleanore away from Burlington, so they bought a small farmhouse which she says was in a sad state of disrepair in Windham, Vt., halfway between Manchester and Burlington. On Christmas Day, 1947, *The New York Times* said that the couple had been married in Colebrook, Conn., on December 7 of that year.

The *New Hampshire Sunday News* was going along pretty well. Ben Bradlee and Elias McQuaid, the reporters, had come up with quite a few significant New Hampshire stories which had never before seen the light of day. The circulation was steady, even though it was still a newsstand newspaper, little or no home delivery. Brush, long familiar with the local advertisers through his long association with the Union-Leader, was picking up lineage. And the newspaper had quite a focus on sports news, under the guidance of Deak Morse, abetted by a peppery columnist, Jack Kane, who lived up to the name of his regular column, "Raisin' Kane."

The *New Hampshire Sunday News* had even won a Heywood Broun Award from the American Newspaper Guild for the so-called "Story-Cote Case," which disclosed that the state comptroller was in the habit of awarding state contracts to a favored Manchester contractor without bothering to offer the jobs out to bid. Of course, the state comptroller, and certain others in state government, could ponder giving out these jobs while they relaxed beside their private swimming pools which the contractor took care to install. Each of these two men got a little more time to ponder in the New Hampshire State Prison before it was all over.

The *New Hampshire Sunday News* did have one big problem, however, and it was Associate Publisher Bernard J. McQuaid. He was "intractable as hell," says Publisher Blair Clark. He couldn't seem to get along with anyone on the staff, including his brother, Elias, and so, by mutual consent in late 1947, Bernie McQuaid "took a walk," but he didn't walk far. He walked over to the Union Leader. Maybe he even saved a few steps by going up the back street, Seneca Lane—who knows?—he spoke to Loeb and Finder and became associate publisher of the Union Leader Corporation. McQuaid wasn't seen around the Union Leader too much, even though he was provided an office—executive-type, for the Union Leader—and came in to work every day.

Leonard Finder had become what Manchester, or any other city, for that matter, was looking for in a newspaper publisher. He was an active community leader and took part in many civic endeavors. The *Evening Leader,* after all, was the city paper and this fitted right in, all around. Under Finder's tutelage, the Union-Leader Fund, Inc., was started and it sponsored concert series at the high school auditorium, forum and lecture series at the Carpenter Memorial Library auditorium and, when the audience expanded beyond its limits, these were moved to the gymnasium of the Jewish Community Center.

A Sunday newspaper had always been McQuaid's baby and he was secretly working out plans to have the Union Leader Corp. bring out a Sunday edition. Bernie McQuaid never did know very much about the financing of the original *Sunday News,* never having been an investor him-

self, although Clark did give him a severance payment
(perhaps more to get rid of him than anything else). Mc-
Quaid was having trouble, however, putting together the
formula required for what he considered a successful Sunday paper. He would have to have certain feature sections
which would at least rival those in the other Sunday newspaper, and it seemed that some of those in the existing
Sunday newspaper had caught on pretty well; the comics
were popular and apparently a good mix the kiddies liked;
"Raisin' Kane" had its following; and Elias McQuaid and
Ben Bradlee were always coming up with pieces that kept
the management of the Union Leader on edge. Ben Bradlee was known, at this time, to drop in at the Manchester
Press Club and, over a glass or two of beer, was able to
pick up more "leads" on the stories which the Union
Leader reporters had been working on, and use them in
the next Sunday edition of his own newspaper. It got to
be a habit for some of the printers and pressmen at the
Union Leader to go out of their way to act as "spies" for
Bradlee, voluntarily, just to annoy Union Leader reporters. Bradlee was a likable guy.

Loeb, of course, continued his balancing act. (It appeared
that what he was balancing was eggs.) He was in Burlington, Manchester, Windham, and all over. But never in one
place long enough to be effectual. When in Manchester, he
would stay at the Manchester Country Club, and some
there got to know him as "Finder's partner" which galled
Loeb immensely. But people in Manchester seldom read the
*Morning Union;* they usually read the *Evening Leader*
which was, in most cases, home delivered. In the morning
they read a Boston or New York newspaper. (These reading habits are still true in 1975.)

Under constant pressure from McQuaid to the effect
that the Union Leader should go into the Sunday newspaper business—after all, that was what McQuaid was doing there—Loeb and Finder apparently made up their
minds that it was the thing to do; they also gave a solid
indication that, in fact, "Mickey Mouse" was indeed running the Union Leader.

Blair Clark was just about out of money. He had gotten
his relatives, friends, and even some relatives of Ben Bradlee to get together a few bucks to keep the *Sunday News*
going. The big thing was, of course, the printing bill every
week at the *Haverhill Gazette,* and, as the newspaper got
larger, so did the printing bill; the newspaper would have
to take a chance on the advertisers' credit. They also took
a big risk in Sunday sales. On rainy or snowy Sundays, lots
of newspapers got wet and people will not buy wet newspapers. On exceptionally bright, sunny Sundays, people
would buy only the New York or Boston or Portland Sunday newspapers, and refuse to buy the *New Hampshire
Sunday News,* because they were going to the lake or sea-
shore with their families, or they were going skiing. The
*Sunday News* circulation had apparently reached a plateau.
As a matter of fact, it became very much touch-and-go at
the *Sunday News* whether or not the next Sunday morning would come with no newspaper.

But Clark, Elias McQuaid and Bradlee played their
cards very close to their vests and so, Loeb and Finder and
Bernie McQuaid invited Clark to discuss negotiations about
selling out. Clark did sell the corporation, its name and
good-will, not to mention its subscription list and physical
assets, to the Union Leader Corp. for about $100,000, or a
little more. Loeb and Finder were up tight for cash at the
time, so Clark got enough money immediately to pay off
his relatives, Bradlee's relatives, and the rest of some $80,-
000 he borrowed over a period of 10 years. But written
into the sales agreement was a non-compete agreement, on
the sides of both parties.

Bernard J. McQuaid went into the Page One editorial
field on Sept. 5, 1948, and announced that the Sunday
News was then a part of the Union Leader Corporation
and "will continue in all vigor and staunchness to maintain its own independent editorial viewpoint." McQuaid
said:

> "The opportunity to serve the public well and faith-
> fully is always the highest privilege that can come to any
> newspaperman."

Bernard McQuaid also began that Sunday his custom of writing all editorials for the *New Hampshire Sunday News*. The Page One editorial by McQuaid on Sept. 5, 1948, is the last one to appear in this position over his name, and only on rare occasions has Loeb had a Page One editorial in the *Sunday News* since. However, early-on, it became apparent that Bernard J. McQuaid was an alchemist. He could put his ideas into a typewriter and come up with acetylene.

It was only a matter of days before Loeb put both feet on the ground in Manchester long enough to count up the score on the purchase of the original *Sunday News*. He ran into the same difficulties in selling the paper to the public and, actually, he lost some circulation because many felt the new Sunday sheet was just a rehash of the daily *Union* and *Leader*. Some advertisers backed off because they figured they would be buying duplicate advertising. Loeb was paying a little bit less for his actual printing costs than the Clark management had been paying the *Haverhill Gazette,* but he really wasn't saving that much because his printers, engravers, stereotypers, pressmen, mailers and the reporters were all unionized and this was an overtime day for most and they were getting time-and-a-half for their Saturday night efforts. The *Sunday News* staff with which McQuaid had to work all week was really only about four people, who did the Sunday morning features. The rest came from the bench of the *Union* and *Leader*. And Loeb, with a bad credit rating with the newsprint companies hanging over his head had to pay these people cash United States or they wouldn't do business. Without newsprint, what can a newspaper publish on?

Then Loeb and Finder had to send the payments to Clark, and this nagged at Loeb. The physical assets he got were two used typewriters, a broken filing cabinet, a mailing list of about 80 names and that's about all. Loeb was apoplectic. He became enraged at everyone who had anything to do with the original *Sunday News,* and this rubbed off to a degree on McQuaid, who certainly must have known something of the bad shape the Clark group was in. McQuaid had a solid contract with the Union Leader Corporation, but it would make himself look a lot better if he let the public image remain that Clark and Elias and Bradlee and Brush had given them a snow job.

Loeb was a dinner guest at the Finder home very frequently, and, according to Finder's wife, the children grew to think most fondly of him, mainly because Loeb would many times bring them thoughtful, little gifts. They called him "Uncle Bill" and an apparently warm friendship developed.

Mrs. Finder herself also became involved in the community. She became a member of the League of Women Voters, the P.T.A., the Red Feather campaign (Red Feather was the predecessor of the United Fund), Hadassah, and the Elliot Hospital Associates (Manchester's version of the Junior League, or whatever).

Loeb was also accepting dinner invitations to other homes in the Manchester area. He was a charming guest. At certain of these engagements, he arrived in company with Mrs. Nackey Scripps Gallowhur, even though it was known all over the city and state that Loeb was a married man and that his wife, the former Eleanore McAllister, was pregnant. The relationship (which was by now quite obvious) between Loeb and Mrs. Gallowhur could not fail to be recognized and many of those who had invited Loeb failed to invite him again. The nagging question was simple: how could a man who preached on Page One of a newspaper on such subjects as immorality and divorce in the "modern" society, himself be conducting an open, obvious affair with another woman, who herself was married and a mother? No one could quite understand this, and eyebrows were up all over town.

Finder didn't really like having Loeb bring Nackey to his home. When the announcement was made that a daughter, Katharine Penelope, was born to Mr. and Mrs. William Loeb on Oct. 29, 1948, at the Mary Hitchcock Memorial Hospital in Hanover, N.H., Loeb graciously accepted congratulations all around. But that didn't stop him

from showing up with Nackey. On many occasions he took
her to the Manchester Country Club, and only the naïve
failed to see Loeb disappear with Nackey up the stairway
off the main lobby for the night. Loeb was introducing
Nackey as "Mrs. Loeb" and he must have thought the
people in Manchester were dreadfully stupid, particularly
those around the Manchester Country Club; because the
woman he was introducing as "Mrs. Loeb," was not always
Nackey Scripps Gallowhur, and not always the same
woman he introduced to them the night before as "Mrs.
Loeb" in the club dining room and with whom he had
apparently spent the previous night.

And what galled many members of the Manchester
Country Club most of all was the fact that Loeb would,
when sitting down at the table for dinner, take his gun
from its holster and place it at an empty place setting,
careful to cover it with a napkin from the place setting.

Loeb had been known as a tough negotiator with the
labor unions which he inherited when he bought the
Union Leader. Many of the negotiators who usually came
from Boston or New York to do the actual bargaining at
contract-renewal time, had various versions of their difficulties with Loeb; but they were almost unanimous in reporting that he had a habit of placing his gun on the desk
between them and then dramatically saying, "Let's talk."
This turned their stomachs and they usually wanted to
leave the room, and not because they were afraid.

Loeb then instituted a new wrinkle—profit sharing.
Half of the profits from the Union-Leader would go back
to the employes which they would get in quarterly incre-
ments. Such a feature was written into all contracts at the
Union Leader. This was a bonanza for the employes. It
was money they would otherwise not save and it came in
large amounts every quarter, so they were more than
pleased. Loeb became a national figure within the strata
of the National Council of Profit Sharing Industries and
he flew all over the U.S. and Canada making speeches and
attending seminars and, finally, he became vice chairman

in 1947–8 and chairman in 1949. Within these circles, William Loeb, of Manchester and Burlington, was a very big man. He put his Burlington operation, which was largely nonunion, on the same basis. Naturally, there was considerable internal strife up there because they had heard of the Manchester employes receiving large chunks of money while they, in Burlington, were all working for peanuts. Loeb told them if they could put the newspaper on a paying basis, they would get profits, too.

Loeb was apparently upset at being shut off socially in certain Manchester homes, and one of these was, of course, the home of Mr. and Mrs. Leonard V. Finder. Besides, Finder was becoming ever more what a newspaper publisher should be in the community and he was becoming immensely popular with his employes. Finder mingled with the employes, sat at their desks, talked to them about their families, and other personal issues. Loeb soon became very bitter towards Finder and everything he did. It soon became apparent that one or the other would have to go.

Finder wanted very much to buy the Union Leader Corporation, and he was successful in raising the necessary capital to buy Loeb out. But, Loeb had written into the original agreement that he would have first option at buying the other partner's share and he was adamant about doing just that. His mother had gone to the limit she was willing to go, and she still had the $250,000, she thought, in New York, guaranteeing the first part of Loeb's purchase. No bank would look at William Loeb because of the record in his earlier days in Burlington—and a full report on his haughty attitude always accompanied the actual credit report.

Senator Styles Bridges had been tipped off post haste by Eddie King about Loeb as soon as King had joined the senator's staff. Time was running out on Loeb to get up the capital to buy Finder out, and Senator Bridges finally interceded and sent his administrative assistant, a young lawyer from Hampton Falls, N.H., Wesley Powell, to do what he could to help Loeb. Loeb had had some dealings with the Bank of New York. Records show that he received a $600,000 loan from the bank acting as trustee in October, 1946. Part of this was guaranteed by Mrs. Loeb's $250,000, and part by the Connecticut Mutual Life Insurance Company, Hartford, Conn. Where all that money went to at the time, only Loeb knows, but the loan was upped again to $673,000 in 1948.

Anyway, Wesley Powell has made no secret since that time of the fact that he was instrumental in putting a lot of loose ends together for Loeb and making it possible for him to buy Finder's share of the Union Leader Corporation, which he did in May, 1949.

Finder, after leaving the Union Leader Corporation on May 23, 1949, began to structure a newspaper in Dover, N.H., but it never got off the ground. There is reason to believe that Loeb assisted *Foster's Daily Democrat,* the existing Dover newspaper, in withstanding the competition of a new newspaper in town. There was also a very damaging fire in Finder's plant which was quite a setback. Not long thereafter, much as he wanted to stay in New Hampshire, there really was not much opportunity for Leonard V. Finder. He accepted an offer from the Universal Match Co. to become vice president in charge of its armaments subsidiaries and he moved to St. Louis, Mo.

Leonard V. Finder died on July 3, 1969. At the time of his death, Loeb wrote a letter of condolence to his father, Meyer N. Finder, expressing sympathy. Loeb did not contact the widow, who had had him as a guest in her home on so many occasions, even to the extent of a simple card. She has since remarried.

About the only significant change in Burlington while all this was going on was that the *Burlington Daily News* had discontinued its Saturday edition and begun publication of the *Vermont Sunday News,* containing much of the same feature material as was included in the *New Hampshire Sunday News.*

# 13

Whatever political focus had been brought to bear on the *Morning Union* and *Evening Leader* during the 1948 Presidential primary could be laid to Leonard V. Finder.

In late 1947, Finder wrote to General of the Army Dwight D. Eisenhower, then in Paris as commander of SHAPE, urging the hero to run for President in 1948 on the Democratic ticket. Eisenhower, according to his papers, had told President Truman that he would not oppose him and he politely declined Finder's offer of support in the New Hampshire primary.

Many months later, on his triumphal return to the United States and a hero's welcome, it was Leonard Finder who was in the back seat of the convertible with Ike during the ticker tape parade.

In New Hampshire there was some support for Harold Stassen, Eisenhower, Sen. Robert Taft (R-Ohio) and New York Gov. Thomas E. Dewey among the Republicans, and President Truman was the champion on the Democratic side. Truman captured every delegate of the New Hampshire Democratic contingent in the March primary. Two Republican district delegates were pledged to the New Yorker, but the other six G.O.P. convention delegates were elected declared to no specific candidate.

And thus started a long, unbroken tradition that the nominee who wins the November election must have been first a winner in the New Hampshire first-in-the-nation Presidential primary.

Alone at the helm of three New Hampshire newspapers, plus three more in Vermont, William Loeb began to cut quite a figure. His Page One editorials in both locations—in Burlington and in Manchester—began to appear more frequently and the language in them became more vitriolic and the accusations stronger, often within an eyelash of being libelous. They were almost all insulting. McQuaid, the alchemist, showed more than ever that he had never in his entire life been wrong about anything. Loeb generally kept hands off the *Sunday News* in New Hampshire, but, at times, the Sunday newspaper and the daily *Union* and *Leader* put on a disgusting "Alphonse and Gaston" act. Loeb was developing a whole set of pets in New Hampshire and his campaigns in their behalf began almost to approach the limits of vendettas. Generally, the readers weren't too happy; Loeb's editorials usually had the air of talking down to the reader, and, in case after case, the story Loeb told the thousands of readers in the *Union* and *Leader* every day was something different from the full, actual truth.

It fast was becoming obvious that the "truth" as practiced and preached by William Loeb in New Hampshire and Vermont was at variance—by omission, commission and superimposition—with that which the people of the United States had come to accept; that is, "the truth, the whole truth, and nothing but the truth."

And it was for this reason, far more than for any other reason of his own personal conduct, that there came to grow a greater resentment towards Loeb and the tactics he implemented in the *Morning Union* and *Evening Leader*, not to mention the *Daily News* and *Daily Messenger*. As far as Loeb himself was concerned, the Vermont newspapers were fast approaching orphan status.

Loeb and his advertising director in Manchester, Walter McLaughlin, had the difficulties which McLaughlin had anticipated when he demanded and received a written contract from Loeb. Loeb was forced to buy up the unused portion of McLaughlin's contract, not without a little urging in court, and he brought Montague from Burlington to be advertising director. It was very shortly after he arrived, however, that Montague became general manager of the Union Leader Corp.

Loeb's "loud" voice was heard on a variety of subjects, and he apparently never outgrew the childish idea that he who shouts last and shouts loudest wins the argument. He was always preaching "honesty, decency, morality and

truth" and there was seemingly nothing which could escape his scrutiny when he desired to make it his business.
To make matters worse, Loeb neither lived nor voted in
any community where he published a newspaper.

Many Granite Staters and many Vermonters were becoming blindly opposed to Loeb and Loeb's ideas, on the
ideological grounds that they resented being pushed around
by an outsider. Thus sprung up a stubborn and blind "If-
Loeb-is-for-it-we're-against-it" clique. But it was becoming
more and more difficult to ignore the man. Whenever
Loeb started telling the "truth," Loeb was "telling it like
it is" and those who didn't agree with him were simply
afraid of the "truth." It became the "truth" when Loeb
said it was the "truth" and this is always a bitter pill.

There were many, however, who supported Loeb and
Loeb's ideas. There are always those who will believe anything as long as it's in black-and-white. And there are always those who are advocates of the particular person or
cause which Loeb is "pushing" at a given time. There are
the opportunists who would support anything Loeb was
for, if it meant that they would receive his support for
their idea or project in return. And to many persons, particularly those in politics, there may be nothing so powerful as truth, unless it's getting your name in the newspaper
and mentioned favorably.

But really, people had no choice other than to read the
Loeb newspapers in Manchester and in New Hampshire;
that is, they had no choice if they wanted to read the news
of New Hampshire politics, New Hampshire sports news,
town and city news, deaths, weddings, department and
food store advertising and legal notices, to name but a few
features which any local newspaper prints. The Boston
newspapers would give national and world news and some
New Hampshire news, but they could never hope to publish a New Hampshire edition. Besides, Boston has a City
Hall and a State House of its own and it has never been
accused of being a dull place, from a newsman's point of
view.

A lot of radio stations were springing up in New Hampshire, but there was (and is today) no single powerful voice which blanketed the state. The mountains prevent it. Television faced the same natural obstacle, but it was coming along and a station blossomed from the top of Mt. Washington; its studios were in Maine, however, and the station's programming had a distinct Down East flavor. But the preponderence of New Hampshire's population is in the southern part of the state, more than 100 miles from Mt. Washington. Negotiations began to open a Manchester television station, and Loeb became a factor in these. He even went to the extent of again raising his loan with the Bank of New York and Connecticut Mutual Life Insurance Company. Loeb's stiffest competitor in getting the Manchester television rights was Former Gov. Francis P. Murphy. Guess who won the rights to WMUR-TV?

Loeb had said that his newspapers would be "fair" and they were "fair" because the "truth" was that William Loeb said they were "fair." Loeb became more and more despotic in his editorials. His critics began looking for flaws in the man, grounds upon which they could discredit him, flaws in his person, flaws in his dress, anything. The nitpicking against Loeb grew more and more outrageous— but there was really little pity for Loeb because the man had put himself in this position. Indeed, he adopted the role of the stalwart hero of the oppressed and he let it be known that most people were against him only because he was so courageous.

There was little fault to find in Loeb's person or manner. He was always well dressed and his charm only increased with years. He had, of course, the finest upbringing and attended the finest schools and traveled in the best circles. Loeb had said his newspapers would be "fair" and would "publish the truth" regardless of whom it concerned, including himself. He claimed he always published announcements of his financial dealings with various backers and partners, prominently in the newspapers he controlled. But there was strong reason to believe that he did not always publish, or even tell, the truth about his full acquisition of the Burlington Publishing Co., Inc., in Vermont or of the Union Leader Corporation in New Hampshire. Senator Bridges had a far larger group of acquaintances in New Hampshire than did Loeb, and there were many people who had had little conversations with Wesley Powell, too, not to mention the fact that Eddie King would never visit the state of New Hampshire without dropping into the Union Leader city room and spending a couple of hours with his old friends. And these sessions invariably ended in the wee hours at the Manchester Press Club.

Soon it became public knowledge that the prime factor in Loeb being granted the final approval for the loan which had been granted to him to buy out Finder and getting full control of the corporation had been Senator Bridges, and people also knew far and wide that Wesley Powell had figured in the deal somewhere, or they didn't know Wesley Powell. And they did know Wesley Powell.

The question of Loeb's personal morality became an issue in private conversation. But it can be said that this was largely because of Loeb's own conduct. For one who was so vitriolic and vocal, so concerned with "decency" and "public morality" and "conscience," Loeb showed a strange lack of good sense personally, and professionally.

The membership of the Manchester Country Club decided that the club would function much better without Loeb, big publisher though he was, and he was discontinued as a member.

Loeb commuted back and forth to Burlington from Manchester, ostensibly spending the night with his wife and child in Windham, Vt., or visiting his mother who had bought a retreat in Reading, Vt., where she could be near her daughter-in-law and grandchild. Mrs. Loeb never disguised her delight that her only grandchild was named after her. But Loeb did not always arrive in Burlington after he had left Manchester and efforts to raise him on the telephone from the Manchester office were often fruitless. Naturally, when Loeb reappeared no one asked the publisher where he had been. Loeb always gave the appearance of stern superiority and command during his in-

frequent strolls through the Manchester plant, and there
was little question in the minds of the employes that these
strolls were taken to establish the fact that Loeb was
around.

Nackey Scripps was becoming more and more of a familiar figure in Burlington as she had been in Manchester.
Charlie Weaver's got a pretty good memory about this:

"He brought Nackey in and Nackey came up there [to
the Daily News Building] and she began to poke around. I
remember the morning of the Soap Box Derby—it was in
July [of 1949]. Bill dropped into the city room there. It
was a Saturday and he said, 'Beautiful day out,' and I said,
'Yeah,' and he said, 'Let's go out and look at the sky.' Bill
would do this, you know, so we went out and sat on the
front stoop and looked at the sky and as he was looking
at the sky he said, 'Well, Charlie,' he said, 'Nackey and
I are going to get married.'

"However, Bill and his women was one thing and I
never got too wrapped up in that," says Weaver.

One man who was getting wrapped up in the matter of
Loeb and his women was George W. Gallowhur of Read-
ing, Vt., and the reason was that Nackey Scripps was
George Gallowhur's wife.

After John McLane Clark lost out in his attempt to purchase the Union-Leader Publishing Co., Inc., in 1946, he
took a job at the *Springfield Republican,* and subsequently
bought the *Claremont,* N.H., *Daily Eagle,* a small, but respected, journal in a small city halfway up the western
border of the state. As its publisher, he was also its editor,
editorial writer and columnist, his outpourings being
grouped for the purposes of his column under the heading,
"Journal of a Johnny-come-lately," from whence Dr. Bradley took the title of his biography of Clark. The only
serious competition for the *Daily Eagle* was the *Morning
Union,* if that could be called competition, and the weekly
*Argus-Champion* of neighboring Newport. However, it
could not be disputed that the *Daily Eagle* was the most
influential newspaper in largely rural Sullivan County.

And so it happened that on Thursday, Aug. 4, 1949, the lead editorial in the *Daily Eagle* attracted considerable attention. It bore the headline:

## "BRIDGES SHOULD RESIGN
## ... as UMW Trustee"

The editorial was long, covering well over a quarter page, and well written. It said, in part:

"The people of New Hampshire lack full confidence in their political leaders. This comes about largely as a result of the discovery a year ago (by the original *N.H. Sunday News*) that the state comptroller had been handing out loose cost-plus building contracts to a single firm headed by a man with political connections that ran as high as the governor's office. The firm, moreover, proved to have done private construction work for a number of political figures, state as well as national . . .

"Now comes one more blow to public confidence in its political leaders. A witness at a hearing in Washington has disclosed that the three trustees of the United Mine Workers welfare fund—which provides the pensions that provoked last year's coal strike and Judge Goldsborough's heavy fines—are paid $35,000 a year . . . However, the secret is now out and may well have profound political repercussions in New Hampshire.

"For one of the three trustees is Senator Styles Bridges. He was named in April, 1948, to be so-called 'public' member of the three-man board controlling the $100,000,000 accumulated by assessing twenty cents on each ton of bituminous mined. A man named Van Horn represents the mine owners on the board, while John L. Lewis himself, as might be expected, sits for the miners. Incidentally, Mr. Lewis does not draw his $35,000, doubtless finding his $50,000 salary from the UMW adequate for keeping body and soul together.

"Senator Bridges, on the other hand, presumably can count on nothing like a $50,000-a-year income. He receives $12,500 as a senator plus a $2,500 tax-free expense allowance. Considering the social and other demands on a man in his position, it is understandable that an extra

$35,000 might be welcomed by him. And, so far as the letter of the law is concerned, there is nothing to prevent him from accepting money from outside sources. But, from the standpoint of public morality, he will have disappointed many friends and supporters for having accepted the UMW's checks ...

". . . If he had gone on the payroll of a business concern, that would have been bad enough. But it is almost beyond the pale to learn that he has, in effect, gone on the payroll of John L. Lewis and the UMW ...

"For the good of the body politic generally and in New Hampshire in particular we hope Senator Bridges takes advantage of the fact that his appointment as a welfare fund trustee was temporary and resigns his office forthwith.

"J. McL. C."

Loeb-watchers in Vermont and New Hampshire, and by this time they were legion, remembered that Loeb had singled out John L. Lewis as one of his prime targets whenever he got a chance. On the day after Clark's editorial, the *Morning Union* was strangely silent on the matter of the *Daily Eagle* and Senator Bridges. And the *Morning Union* had nothing to say on Saturday, either. Usually Loeb sprung to the defense of Bridges like a lioness protecting her cubs; it was abnormal that Loeb would not launch his usual outrageous and irrelevant counter-attack.

Dr. Bradley, in his book, reports John McLane Clark's end of a telephone conversation with Senator Bridges who was in his Washington office:

"Yes, Senator . . . Good morning, sir . . . Yes, that is right. I wrote the editorial . . . Yes, I simply reported what was carried in *The New York Times* . . . Oh, I'm sure you don't mean all that . . . No . . . What? Libelous? Is there anything wrong with my facts? . . . Then, I don't really see that there is anything you can do . . ."

The nagging questions persisted: Where was Loeb? Why didn't he react with a blast at Clark and the *Daily Eagle?* Loeb's answer to Clark's editorial was most conspicuous by its absence, and Loeb was always loudest when he was in defense of his "secret" financial arranger, Senator Bridges, especially against an attack by a smaller newspaper in the state which Loeb could always bully by referring to it as the "pipsqueak press."

Then the truth came out. Loeb was pretty much obliged to explain where he had been and there was no escaping it; had it not been for Clark's attack on Bridges at that particular time, Loeb might not have been missed, but it didn't happen that way.

In the *Morning Union* of Monday, Aug. 8, 1949, the following news story began on Page One and was continued to an inside page and it is quoted in its entirety:

## PUBLISHER SUED
## FOR ALIENATION

### Loeb Jailed Under Old
### Vermont Law Until
### High Bail Raised

"WOODSTOCK, Vt.—William Loeb, publisher of the New Hampshire Morning Union and Manchester Evening Leader and other papers, was released from Windsor County jail Saturday afternoon after providing bail in the amount of $150,000 in an alienation of affections suit.

"The publisher was jailed late Friday night under an old Vermont statute permitting the issuance of a body writ in a civil action. The law is the same under which three Vermont veterans were imprisoned for indefinite periods for failures to satisfy judgments in debt cases.

"Ironically, Loeb's two papers in Vermont had vigorously opposed the jailing of the veterans and editorially condemned the law itself. The cases attracted nationwide attention.

#### "At Home of Mother

"Chief of Police Wesley Krupinsky of Woodstock served the writ on Loeb at the summer home of his mother, Mrs. Katharine W. D. Loeb, at nearby Reading just before midnight Friday. The necessary papers were issued on the insistency of Harold O'Brien, Rutland attorney, on behalf of his client, George Gallowhur of Reading.

"The suit charges Loeb with alienating the affections of Mrs. George Gallowhur.

"Chief Krupinsky also endeavored to serve divorce papers on Mrs. Gallowhur. She was not present, although she had been there earlier for dinner with Loeb and his mother. Chief Krupinsky insisted that Loeb knew Mrs. Gallowhur's whereabouts and demanded the right to search the premises. He was reminded that he did not possess a search warrant. The chief nevertheless insisted on this procedure although the house was occupied only by the 73-year old mother of the publisher and her two elderly maid-servants.

"When the search failed to produce Mrs. Gallowhur, Loeb was told if he would reveal Mrs. Gallowhur's whereabouts he would not have to go to jail. Loeb said he 'would not if he could, and could not if he would.' The officer jailed Loeb at approximately 2 A.M.

"Bail was set in the full amount of the suit. A. Luke Crispe, Gov. Ernest Gibson's law partner and the newly elected commander of the Vermont American Legion, was awakened to protect Loeb's interests.

"Efforts to win leniency from O'Brien Friday evening failed and the publisher was taken to jail until bail could be arranged Saturday. C. Prescott Hoffman of Brattleboro furnished bail and Judge Henry Black ordered the release.

"The divorce writ was served on Mrs. Gallowhur Saturday morning.

"It was learned that a Gallowhur divorce has been contemplated for some time. Active negotiations had been in progress between Gallowhur and his wife's attorneys during the last three weeks.

"Main points in the dispute had been the custody of their three-year old daughter and the repayment of approximately $278,000 which the Scripps family and Mrs. Gallowhur claimed was secured from them by Mr. Gallowhur during the last three years."

Loeb really had no alternative other than to tell that he had been in jail. But, at that, he obviously couldn't help embroidering the facts of the case and adding misleading and wholly irrelevant statements and references to the news item.

The word travels fast in New Hampshire and Vermont. Word was out to the N.H. State Police as soon as Krupinsky went after Loeb, and the night editor of Loeb's Manchester newspapers immediately dispatched a reporter-photographer to the scene, apparently taking Loeb at his word that all the news should be covered fairly in the Manchester newspapers, regardless of whom it concerns. The night editor knew that if Loeb were in the can, it was a news story and he had better be protected. But none of the facts which the reporter sent back or the photographs he took were used in the *Morning Union* or the *Sunday News*. The editors sat on the story until Monday morning, hoping that they could keep it quiet. Then, by Sunday, it became apparent that the arrest, which was, after all, a public matter, had gotten out and the *Morning Union* had better carry it. However, the story which the *Morning Union* carried was written by Loeb himself, assisted by George E. Connell, an editorial writer, who, in 1975, is general manager of the Union Leader Corp. The reporter's version was discarded as were all his pictures.

The real story was that Nackey Scripps Gallowhur had for some time been taking overnight excursions from the home she shared with her daughter and her husband. Many of these coincided with Gallowhur's business trips and many of them she could disguise. But then during that summer, Gallowhur found some letters written by Loeb to Nackey and, from their contents, there could be no denying that Loeb and Nackey had been having an affair.

The letters were written on Union Leader stationery, typed crudely. Who, but the copy boy, would type letters on the publisher's stationery? And, if the copy boy did it, would he spell gesture "jesture" and judgment "judgement?" No, these letters were the real thing. Loeb talked of "true mating" and all that. Loeb even pinpointed the places where he and Nackey had spent nights together, particularly one inn in Vermont where the owner opened the hostelry a few days early for the publisher of the *Daily News*.

George Gallowhur was convinced that Nackey and Loeb were conducting an adulterous affair and he wanted to di-

vorce Nackey because of it. So Gallowhur went to the clerk
of court in Windsor County in Woodstock, just a few
miles from his home in Reading, and swore out a divorce
complaint against his wife and a "body writ" in an alienation of affections suit against Loeb. The "body writ" employed by Gallowhur and his attorney is a form of the
law commonly called "country justice," but it boils down
to this: the plaintiff launches a civil action based on a
criminal act seeking damages and he usually places the
damages so high that the defendant is unlikely to be able
to raise that amount of bail. The defendant is consequently incarcerated until he either raises bail in the
amount of the damages claimed or until a hearing is held
and an injunction issued by a judge, if he so decides.

The case referred to in the article in Loeb's newspapers
concerned two Vermont men who had refused to pay the
judgment of the court in a civil suit and they had been
jailed when they did not pay the amount the court told
them to pay. At that time, Loeb's Vermont newspapers
said the law was outmoded.

Gallowhur's alternative avenues of recourse would have
been (a) to seek an injunction against Loeb seeing Nackey,
which would have been impractical because it would have
tipped his hand, or (b) smash Loeb in the face, which
would have been impractical because Loeb always carried
a loaded gun.

As a practical matter, in most cases of adulterous behavior such as this, a little more discretion is normally
exercised because lewd and lascivious and illegal conduct
usually enters into the matter of the divorce settlement
and alimony judgment when the case finally is heard in
divorce court. But in this case, both Mr. and Mrs. Gallowhur were of adequate means and, consequently, the matter
of alimony and support was not the prime consideration.
Another circumstance which makes the case notable is that
newspaper publishers and mothers of infant daughters,
who are incidentally millionaire heiresses, well educated
and well bred, usually do not act like sailors on shore leave.

Eleanore McAllister Loeb says she knew that Loeb and
Nackey were carrying on at the time, and she says that the

main lure for Loeb was that "Loeb knew of all the Scripps money and the Scripps power." She says that she was just as happy to "finally be rid of him" as long as he provided for Katharine Penelope. She also says that on the night when Loeb was arrested, he had taken Nackey to his mother's home to introduce her to his mother and break the news that he was thinking of divorcing Eleanore, news to which Mrs. Loeb did not take kindly.

When Loeb visited his mother at her home in Reading on Friday, Aug. 5, 1949, Gallowhur knew from the letters that such a move had been planned, and Krupinsky was waiting for Loeb and Nackey to be in the house so that he could serve the necessary papers, the body writ on Loeb and the divorce complaint on Nackey; but Loeb stalled Krupinsky, and Nackey took off out through a back window of the house into the Vermont night air.

The writ served on Loeb said, in part:

"State of Vermont, Windsor County, ss: To any sheriff, or constable in the state, or to an indifferent person, greeting:

"By the authority of the State of Vermont, you are hereby commanded to attach the goods, chattels, or estate of William Loeb, of Manchester, in the County of Hillsborough, and State of New Hampshire to the value of one hundred and fifty thousand dollars and him notify thereof according to law; and for want thereof his body take if to be found within your precinct and him safely keep so that you have him appear and also notify him to appear......

"In an action of tort, for that:

"Nackey Scripps Gallowhur is, and at all times material was, the wife of the plaintiff and for the period from November 27, 1944, until about the 19th day of May, 1949, the plaintiff lived, cohabited with and supported the said Nackey Scripps Gallowhur and they lived together happily as man and wife;.....

"And in a further action of tort . . . that the defendant well-knowing the said Nackey Scripps Gallowhur to be the wife of the plaintiff, did, on or about the 19th day of May, 1949, and at diverse times and places prior to and since said date, which times and places are unknown to the plaintiff, have sexual intercourse with the plaintiff's said wife; that the said Nackey Scripps Gallowhur is, and at all times material was, the wife of the plaintiff; that by reason of the defendant's said wrongful acts, the plaintiff has been deprived of the comfort, society, aid and services of his said wife, her affection had been alienated and destroyed and the plaintiff has suffered great distress of body and mind and has been otherwise damaged.

"To the damage of the plaintiff, as he says, One Hundred and Fifty Thousand Dollars, for the recovery of which, with just costs, the plaintiff brings this action. . . . . ."

Loeb, of course, didn't have 150 big ones lying around and his mother—well, she was livid. Loeb had no other choice than to go with Krupinsky and spend the night in jail.

Loeb was let out on that Saturday afternoon when Hoffman went bail, at the invitation of Attorney Crispe. On the next Tuesday, Aug. 9, 1949, Loeb petitioned Judge Henry Black in the Superior Court at Woodstock to reduce the bail because the professional bond fee would be $3,000 if it were required any longer. There is on file in the Woodstock court house building certain correspondence between O'Brien and Crispe in which Crispe says, in effect, "Don't worry, I'll have him here," for a hearing on the case which was scheduled for Aug. 23, 1949.

It is hard to imagine what the purpose was in including in the news story in Loeb's newspaper that Crispe was Governor Gibson's law partner or that Crispe was the newly elected commander of the Vermont American Legion, other than to mislead the reader or blow a little smoke Crispe's way. By all reasonable standards, it could hardly be expected that Loeb would win leniency from O'Brien when O'Brien was the attorney for the plaintiff in the case, Gallowhur. The divorce suit by Gallowhur against his wife was an entirely different matter from the issue which involved Loeb.

However, the hearing in the case was postponed, and on Sept. 14, 1949, George Gallowhur, plaintiff, and William Loeb, defendant, filed a stipulation with the county court at Woodstock that the action of *Gallowhur v. Loeb* would be discontinued, without prejudice, and the complaint withdrawn; that the defendant be released from arrest and the bail bond be cancelled and annulled; neither party be entitled to any reimbursement, and the plaintiff authorized the defendant to submit for approval by the court an order in accordance with these provisions.

Eleanore McAllister provides the most accurate answer as to why the action was dropped. She remembers it vividly. She says that Loeb told her he had threatened Gallowhur that, if he did not drop these charges against him, he would run stories in his newspapers to the effect that Gallowhur had been kicked out of The Hotchkiss School because he was a homosexual.

Mrs. Eleanore McAllister Loeb says she asked Loeb, "Is it true?"

She says Loeb said to her, "Aw, all boys who go to prep school do these things. So what?"

The records of The Hotchkiss School show that the behavioral record of George Gallowhur, who was still a student there after Loeb had been graduated, was perfect. He did, however, have academic problems in his senior year, and was entitled to honorable dismissal midway through the academic year 1923–4, so that he might make up work in which he was failing so that he could be considered for admission to Yale or Princeton.

The matter of Loeb being arrested and thrown into jail in Woodstock, and the attendant publicity in all the newspapers in Vermont and New Hampshire, had a serious and lasting effect on the lives of all concerned. Nackey left Gallowhur and she took an apartment in Burlington at 37B University Heights. Loeb took immediate notice of the fact that his mother, a millionaire, was furious. He told his mother and his wife, Eleanore, that he was renouncing Nackey and he asked their forgiveness.

But Loeb continued to see Nackey Scripps Gallowhur. And Eleanore McAllister Loeb knew it and his mother, Mrs. William Loeb, knew it.

# 14

Business with Loeb's newspapers in Vermont was bad and getting worse, while business in Manchester was just as good as ever, the profit-sharing continuing to keep all the Union Leader employes happy.

Loeb was stepping up his role as chairman of the Council of Profit Sharing Industries, making speeches all over in favor of the plan, saying it was the key to increased productivity, a method of checking the rise of inflation. Loeb even saw profit-sharing as a key to the battle against Socialism. What Loeb was overlooking was that for a company to have profit-sharing it must have profits.

And the employes of the Burlington Publishing Co., Inc., were less than enthusiastic about their profit-sharing plan for the reason that there were never any profits. Loeb was getting a pretty good salary in Manchester. What did he care, they thought? Instead of profits at Burlington, there was a mounting deficit. No one was getting paid that much and the *Daily News* and *Daily Messenger* were in a tough fight, getting tougher all the time, with the *Free Press*. The biggest factor in favor of the *Free Press* was that its publisher knew what he was doing, and was running a pretty good newspaper.

The International Typographical Union had something of a local at the Burlington Publishing Co., but it was a loosely-knit group, by no means a union shop and the normal rules observed and enforced in other newspapers (touching of type and other equipment in the composing room) were never strictly adhered to. Then in the fall of 1949, the membership banded together and asked for a raise. Loeb was spending a little more time in Burlington then, mainly because Nackey was there, and Loeb smelled labor trouble.

So on Oct. 11, 1949, Loeb came to the Daily News Building at 123 College Street and fired every one of the union printers in the composing room. He said that their wages "averaging $4,200 a year, with new demands for a 50-cent-an-hour raise" were too much and that he would "replace the printers with girls trained in operating special keyboards attached to ordinary Linotypes" and further, Loeb said, he would run his Vermont newspapers "without printers, pretty permanently." The automated equipment was already in Burlington, together with the instructors who would put out the editions while the local help learned the new method. The two newspapers came off the presses without printers, and the quality of the product showed it.

Nackey Scripps Gallowhur was one of the new employes of the Burlington Publishing Co., Inc., and she "worked" in the composing room, if, as her associates at that time say, "you want to call it working." She would show up in blue jeans and a sport shirt or blouse and, with pony-tails wagging, go to the composing room where she supposedly set type. Her fellow workers say there was no doubt that everyone got the message—that this cute little rich girl was from a famous newspaper family and that it wasn't beneath her dignity to dirty her hands. Many persons who were *Daily News* employes at that time say that, although she had a pleasant enough disposition, she was hardly an asset to the day's output.

To hear Charlie Weaver tell it, "She was in and out, but she really wasn't working there. I wouldn't say that. You knew who she was, of course, we could tell you about the Scripps background."

Others say it was not at all uncommon for Loeb to enter the newspaper building, disappear into his office, emerge in white shorts and a shirt and come to the composing room and say, "Time for tennis, Nackey." It would be an understatement to say that this had an adverse effect on morale, which was low enough, anyway. Profit-sharing, anyone?

Eleanore McAllister Loeb and Katharine Penelope were still living in Windham and there had been no legal moves by either Eleanore or Loeb to terminate the marriage. Very often he would spend the night at Windham, but usually he was at Burlington or in Manchester. Eleanore says Loeb must have thought she and his mother believed his line that Nackey was out of his life. Indeed, Loeb must have thought so because he continued to insist that such was the case. Yet, at about the same time, Nackey Scripps Gallowhur began being listed in the City Directory for Burlington.

John W. Riley, vice president and assistant treasurer of Miles & Riley, his father's haberdashery on Church Street in Burlington, lived at that time with his wife, Joanne, at 32A University Heights. He says that he used to make it a point to watch through the kitchen windows so that he would get to the street to his automobile at about the same time Loeb would be getting into his expensive sports car which, most usually, had been parked in front of Nackey's all night, and Riley says he would make it a point to engage Loeb in conversation.

Riley says that he would usually twit Loeb about the fact that, if Loeb were in town, he would go to a different church every Sunday. And Riley says that the particular church Loeb chose to attend on a given Sunday depended on which prominent, wealthy family was visiting the area and which church they attended. Riley says the conversations went pretty much according to ritual:

"How are you?"

"Fine. Yourself?"

"Good. Things going okay?"

"Yeah, swell. How about you?"

"Good, thanks. Say, Bill, the Methodist church would be a good bet for this Sunday. So-and-so was in the store yesterday for a couple of golf shirts."

At this point, Riley says, Loeb would flush, purse his lips, gun the motor on the sports car and roar away, showing his N.H. "vanity" license plate "WL."

Meanwhile, back in New Hampshire, Senator Bridges' administrative assistant, Wesley Powell, the young Hampton Falls lawyer who had taken such an active part in securing the financing for Loeb, was feeling his own po-

litical oats and he had decided to run for the U.S. Senate.
Charles W. Tobey, the state's junior senator, in his 70's,
was coming up for reelection to his third term. Tobey, a
former governor, was from Temple, a small town in the
Monadnock region of Southern New Hampshire. Temple
had, at that time, a population of 327 persons and, by the
way, boasted as many veterans of the War of 1812 as of
World War II and four times that number of veterans
from this town served in the American Revolution. Tobey,
who also maintained a Manchester residence on North
Union Street, had barely edged a young Manchester Democrat, Joseph J. Betley, by 4,000 votes out of a total of
229,000 ballots cast, in 1944. Powell figured Tobey could
be had in a Republican primary.

The junior senator had received quite some notoriety
when, during the first nationally televised Congressional
hearings, those of the Kefauver Commission on Organized
Crime, Tobey expressed such shock and horror at the admissions of the notorious underworld figures, such as
Frank Costello, all the while wearing a green eyeshade to
avoid the glare of the TV lights. Tobey quoted from the
Bible and gave every appearance of being a "Yankee
farmer," which, of course, he was.

It has long been the American way that, at some point
during a political campaign, a newspaper will editorially
comment to the effect that one or another candidate is
favored by that newspaper for election to a given office;
the newspaper will then outline the reasons for having
reached its decision. And, until 1950, Manchester, New
Hampshire, U.S.A., had been quite in step with the rest
of the nation in this regard.

During the primary campaign of 1950, however, the
readers of the *Union Leader* were given their first taste of
what it is like when William Loeb backs a candidate. It
was Powell, Powell, Powell throughout the newspaper, no
matter what day, no matter what edition. The news stories
and editorials lionizing Powell, his wife, his family, everything about him, got to the point where the *Union Leader*
could be considered the daily Powell campaign newspaper.

The primary of 1950, particularly in the Republican

contest for U.S. Senate, was a filthy campaign by any standards, and the tone was set by the Loeb newspapers and Loeb himself. At the campaign's close, on the night of Sept. 12, 1950, the votes were counted:

| | |
|---|---|
| Charles W. Tobey, Temple, r | 39,203 |
| Wesley Powell, Hampton Falls, r | 37,893 |
| Total vote, r | 77,096 |

Loeb showed by the tenor of his editorials after Primary Day that he was the poorest of losers. In a Page One "beauty" on Sept. 14, 1950, entitled "How Do You Like It REPUBLICANS?", Loeb said that a group of "bunglers and appeasers" staged an "organized invasion" to vote for Tobey, against the wishes of the "reasoned and considered judgment of those who have always been considered the backbone of Granite State voters," the people who voted for Powell. In subsequent days, he used his newspapers to call for a new election, a recount of the primary vote and a write-in campaign for Powell in the General Election.

On Sept. 20, 1950, there appeared in the "Reader's Opinions" column on the editorial page of the *Union* and *Leader* the following letter:

"Loeb, Publisher, Manchester Union Sir: You are a God damn fool and a rotten sorehead loser.

"Tobey won mainly because your paper sponsored him. I and five members of my family would have voted for the younger man but your false vitriolic attack on Tobey changed our minds, as they did thousands of others.

"New Hampshire will not stomach New York Kikes trying to inject boss rule in New Hampshire.

"No man is more despised than a poor sport or a poor loser.

"If my sons should show such spleen as you did, I'd send them to the woodshed.

"For you, get the hell out of New Hampshire back to New York and your brand of stinkers.
                                    "SID GOLDBERG

"I am proud to be a Jew, not stinking kike like you.

"Ascotou Inn

"North East Harbor, Me."

Powell's supporters immediately said the letter was a "Tobey trick" and they only attracted more attention to it than it would have otherwise received. Senator Tobey countered that Loeb was a "flagrantly offensive and partisan carpetbagger" and denied flatly that he, or any of his supporters, had had anything whatsoever to do with the letter.

So Loeb dusted off his "Baptismal Certificate Act" and once again reminded his readers what a big man his godfather was and the New Hampshire people were supposed to go for this routine.

On Oct. 18, 1950, Page One of the *Union* and *Leader* became collector's items. A skyline—eight columns wide across the top of Page One was a slam story at Senator Tobey and, on the left, even with the masthead, was a headline, "Intolerance Is Not in New Hampshire's Tradition," and immediately underneath was the engraving of the baptismal certificate: "William (Third) Loeb was received into the congregation of Christ's flock, by Holy Baptism, etc.," with the signatures of Edith Kermit Roosevelt and Theodore Roosevelt.

There were not many who had not heard about Loeb's earlier "Baptismal Certificate Act" in Vermont, but seeing is believing, and the whole newspaper for that day received far higher readership than was average. The readership of Loeb's harangues, actually, had diminished to a low level, mainly because they were always so boring and so poorly written. It was hard for most people to believe that Loeb could be so naïve as to repeat an obviously stupid play. There were many who did not, until that day, really believe that someone could be foolish enough to pull it in the first place, but there it was again and the reception was one of general disgust.

The over-all reaction to Loeb's acknowledgment of the supposed rumors that he was Jewish, and the outrage and horror he expressed, carried with it much the same response which it got in Vermont. It clearly showed the weakest side of Loeb's nature. The saving grace for Loeb in this case, as it was to be for well over 20 years to come, was that advertisers and subscribers had "no place to go." There was no competition newspaper in Manchester as there was in Burlington, no other newspaper the advertisers could use.

Wesley Powell, at Loeb's consistent urging, entered the general election for the U.S. Senate seat, running as an independent. Loeb's newspapers vehemently, even violently, urged support for the Hampton Falls man and did everything to put Tobey in the worst possible light. At times, it was hard to see whether the newspapers were for Powell or against Tobey, and the over-all performance has to be rated as somewhere between "grammar school" and "bush league." But it was a test of strength for Loeb.

The result:

| Charles W. Tobey, Temple, r | 106,142 |
| Emmet J. Kelley, Berlin, d | 72,473 |
| Wesley Powell, Hampton Falls, ind | 11,958 |
| Total vote | 190,573 |

The result showed, in no uncertain terms, the regard the New Hampshire people had for Loeb and his opinions, because he had made himself and his newspapers the key issue, almost to exclusion of all others.

Arnold Forster and Benjamin R. Epstein, co-authors of *The Trouble-Makers,* a book dealing with anti-Semitic practices, published by Doubleday & Co., in 1952, reported that a thorough search had been made for Sidney Goldberg. He had never been heard of in Northeast Harbor, Maine, and the assumption was drawn that the letter to "Loeb, Publisher, Manchester Union," had been a complete fabrication.

It is alarming to note how little time William Loeb spent in scouting his opposition, in this case Tobey; how little his editorials portrayed the true picture, but rather the scene as Loeb said it was or as Loeb said it should be, without investigating, without any footwork to really know what Tobey was like or what he did, or the people in whose behalf he worked. The way Loeb had represented the situation in his newspapers, Tobey was a staid old

Yankee who represented only their interests and he received the backing of only the old Yankees. There is no way that Loeb could have been more wrong in presuming that Senator Tobey was Yankee to the point that he was anti-Semitic.

The following story is quoted in its entirety from *The New York Times* of March 16, 1953:

## "AID FOR *JEWISH* REFUGEES
## "Society Adopts $1,930,000 Budget
## —Senator Tobey Honored

"The Hebrew Immigration Aid Society, whose efforts for the last sixty-eight years have been devoted to the aid of immigrants in foreign lands and their care in this country, adopted yesterday a budget of $1,930,000 to carry out its programs this year. More than 1,500 delegates representing Jewish religious, labor and fraternal organizations attended the annual meeting at the Astor Hotel.

"Ben Touster, president of the organization, announced that its annual award of honor had been given to Senator Charles W. Tobey of New Hampshire in recognition of his 'sympathetic interest and efforts in behalf of oppressed and unfortunate human beings.'

"Murray I. Gurfein, vice president of the society, reported that the society has assisted 3,500 refugees to immigrate from Europe last year, and was helping 25,000 other refugees in Europe."

# 15

During Christmastime in 1950, Mrs. Loeb came to her home in Vermont to visit her son and daughter-in-law and her granddaughter, Penelope, and it was no great surprise to her to find adequate proof that her son had been deceiving her in his statements about his extramarital affairs. On returning to her home in Long Island early in 1951, she decided to change her will, eliminating her son in favor of his daughter, Penelope. She notified her son of these intentions, by mail. In anticipation of entering Roosevelt Hospital in New York City for a medical examination in 1951, she wrote a holographic will at home. When the examination disclosed that she was faced with a serious operation, several friends suggested she retain Atty. Alexander C. Dick, of New York City, who visited her in the hospital. He drew a will according to Mrs. Loeb's wishes and she executed the will in the hospital on June 12, 1951.

Meanwhile, the *Burlington Daily News* and the *St. Albans Daily Messenger* were, more and more, being run by their own staff members. Nackey left town and Loeb's appearances once again became more and more infrequent; many in Burlington feel that Loeb didn't have the "guts" to come face-to-face with many of the persons who were affected when he fired all his printers. Montague was in Manchester on a full-time basis and he only rarely came to Burlington. Charlie Weaver, who was being held at the same salary for many years, couldn't see much future and when the opportunity presented itself, he resigned and joined the State Department as a press aide. Left in charge of the Burlington operation were Robert Cronin, editor, and Wesley A. Cilley, business manager.

It is difficult to pinpoint exactly the date of Loeb's departure from Burlington but the best estimate is early 1951. It would be the last time William Loeb would be seen in the city of Burlington, until December, 1973— more than 22 years later.

Cilley, who now conducts his own business as an accountant on Williston Road in South Burlington, says that Loeb's Burlington corporation was "always in trouble. The credit was bad and we would stay afloat with checks of $1,500, $1,875, sometimes as much as $2,000 monthly . . . sometimes even more often than that . . . from Manchester and they were Manchester Union Leader checks."

(The New Hampshire and Vermont newspapers were published by separate corporations. Money from the New Hampshire corporation which might have figured in the profit-sharing plan, was being used in the Vermont operation.)

"We were getting everything C.O.D.," continues Cilley, "the paper (newsprint) from Canada was loaded only on a 'sight draft' from the bank; ink, features, everything else, even comics, came C.O.D. and the bank was always on my back for overdrafts. Loeb was living with Nackey at University Heights when I first got to the paper in 1950, but then it got so we'd only see him maybe once a week, if that. He'd have a meeting with department heads, but he never told us anything. Our circulation manager was padding the figures to make himself look good and the advertising manager was including 'house ads' in the total lineage figure. Loeb never knew the difference.

"And Loeb's editorials aggravated everybody. I wouldn't even read the editorials myself. Advertising was dropping off all the time. I had the U.S. Department of Labor on my back because a guy named Rosenthal who had worked in circulation had complained to them that he never got paid overtime."

Cilley further said that any Loeb emissary who drove from Manchester brought to Burlington as many lead ingots as his car's springs would allow, all from the Union Leader.

It was at about this time, June 26, 1951, to be exact, that U.S. Ambassador to the United Nations and Mrs. Warren R. Austin were planning to come home to Williams Street in Burlington to host a mammoth open house celebration on the occasion of their fiftieth wedding anniversary, to which were invited the leaders of the diplomatic and political spheres of the United States and the whole world.

Unofficially, the editors of area newspapers telephoned each other and agreed among themselves it would be a nice idea if every newspaper carry one special editorial saluting the Austins on the occasion and no newspaper would try to outdo the other. Austin had served the people of Vermont well, they all seemed to feel, as their senior senator until President Truman, a Democrat, had honored the Vermonter, a Republican, by naming him the first U.S. ambassador to the U.N., a move which had been hailed across the country at the time.

Loeb was not personally involved with the decision to have a special editorial on that day, but he was furnished a memorandum on the subject in plenty of time. The *Daily News* staff members were aware of the long-standing feud between Loeb and Austin—calling it a feud is probably a misnomer because Austin usually ignored Loeb, which only infuriated the publisher that much more—and they figured that Loeb's wounds had been healed. Then, too, it was known that Loeb had not seen Austin personally, if, in fact, he had ever met the man, and they figured Loeb would certainly be gracious enough to contribute good wishes to Ambassador and Mrs. Austin on this occasion. After all, dignitaries from the whole world would be in Burlington and how could Loeb possibly object to a thought such as this at a time like this?

No editorial was forthcoming from Loeb (wherever he was) for that day, so, at the last moment, one was prepared by Cronin, and as the *Daily News* came off the presses, Page One included the following, two columns wide:

## EDITORIAL
## HAPPY ANNIVERSARY

Although Ambassador and Mrs. Warren Austin are as much at home in the far-flung capitals of the world, it is peculiarly fitting that they should spend their happy 50th wedding anniversary among their friends and neighbors in Burlington.

And it is for this very reason that the city is happy to extend to them the best wishes of all its citizens on one of the most joyful occasions that any married couple can celebrate.

For it is proof that despite the famed position the ambassador holds in the tense world of today his roots are firmly bound to the solid, homey, and substantial realities that are our particular way of life.

Ambassador and Mrs. Austin are noting their golden wedding anniversary in much the same manner as others in the community with friends and relatives joining quietly to felicitate them on their good fortune in finding such contentment in long and loving association.

Their observation has world overtones because of the position he holds, but that thought is subordinated among Burlingtonians. Today, we think of them only as fellow citizens who have shared happily with us an experience in community living which draws us close.

It is no exaggeration to say they are our first citizens. We share in their happiness and wish them well in the uncounted years ahead.

The editorial was unsigned.

On the day following, June 27, Page Three of the *Daily News* carried a three-column group photograph of the Austins and some of their guests at the open house, as well as a lengthy news story about the affair, listing many dignitaries who attended, including many fellow United Nations persons of embassy rank and numerous Federal and elected officials from Washington, most of whom had been colleagues of Austin in the U.S. Senate for many years.

It may have been that Loeb was miffed because he wasn't invited to the Austin affair, or it may have been that he ignored it intentionally, or it could have been that it just escaped his consuming gaze, but Loeb certainly reacted. On Friday, June 29, 1951, a two-column editorial ran on Page One of the *Daily News;* it had arrived that morning in the newspaper office by telegraph with specific instructions from Loeb to run it on Page One and sign his name. It was very long, but parts of it are quoted herewith:

### EDITORIAL
### After the Ball Is Over

There appeared on the front page of this newspaper on Tuesday an editorial congratulating the Austins on their 50th anniversary, a happy occasion in the lives of all people. However, that editorial did not in any way express approval of the official acts of Warren Austin as U.S. representative of (sic) the U.N.

As U.N. representative, Austin has been the fatuous representative of a fatuous policy which has brought this nation to the very brink of ruin. . . .

The editorial went on to denounce the Austins because Jacob Malik, the Russian U.N. ambassador, had been invited to the Austins' open house; that Austin did what Secretary Acheson, "the friend of Alger Hiss, tells him to do"; it denounced Yalta and Potsdam, and further said that Burlingtonians should remember it was Austin who tried to "prevent Bell Aircraft from locating in Burlington."

Last, but not least, we remember the story a reputable Burlingtonian told us the other night of the dark days of the depression when he worked all afternoon on the Austin place for 75 cents. When the man asked for his money at the end of the day, the Senator found he had no change. Rather than give the man a dollar, he drove all the way down town to get change.

It is one thing to congratulate a couple for a golden wedding anniversary, but this newspaper has no intention of endorsing Senator (sic) Austin's activities, thus breaking faith with the boys who have died in Korea as a result of this policy, or with those who fought to bring Bell Aircraft to Burlington, or with the little man who got 75 cents instead of a dollar.

Austin and the U.N. may believe in appeasement, but this newspaper intends to stand for what is right, no matter what the cost.

/s/ William Loeb
Publisher

Larry Vanbenthuysen, in 1975 public relations director for the University of Vermont, was working part-time in June, 1951, at the *Daily News* in the circulation department, while a student at UVM. He says that the busiest day of the week was usually Thursday afternoon because, as he explains it, "We had to go to every store and newsstand in the area and collect for the newspapers they had sold and get the money to the bank so that the *Daily News* paychecks wouldn't bounce."

But, Vanbenthuysen says, Friday afternoon of that week was, by far, the busiest day the circulation department had had yet. He says that after the 3,500 press run of the *Daily News* was over and the newspaper had hit the street, there had been 361 cancellations of subscriptions before the end of that business day alone.

Cronin immediately resigned as editor of the *Daily News*. Advertising and circulation began dropping, each drop creating a new record low. Even the legal advertising stopped coming to the *Daily News* (which usually had the bulk because of a lower rate than the competition) and it began to appear in the *Free Press*.

Only massive transfusions of money from Manchester kept the *Daily News* alive, and then barely, until 1959.

William Loeb, publisher, had cut the jugular vein of the *Burlington Daily News* and he took a long step backward and watched it bleed to death.

# III

# What?

I fear three newspapers more than
a hundred thousand bayonets.

—NAPOLEON

# 16

The most basic of all animal instincts is to go away and hide when trouble is brewing. That is exactly what William Loeb did for about six years in the 1950's. The orchestra was clearly playing Loeb's number and he clearly had no desire to face the music. Loeb's troubles were many and varied, both professional and personal. Practically all of them he had brought upon himself.

Loeb had made countless enemies in Vermont. He was making as many enemies in New Hampshire. It was the manner of Loeb to unveil a grandiose scheme in a Page One editorial. If Loeb's editoral fell upon deaf ears, Loeb would, in subsequent editorials, berate, demean, insult, even libel, those who did not follow his beckoning. And Loeb's wrath knew no limits. Following the defeat of Wesley Powell by Senator Tobey in the 1950 primary, Loeb had this to say:

> "This newspaper takes back nothing we have said about Senator Tobey in this campaign. WE REAFFIRM EVERYTHING WE HAVE SAID ABOUT HIM. We hope that some way yet may be found to undo what was accomplished Tuesday by a minority of Republicans combined with a group of Socialistic outsiders who deprived the Republican party of their [sic] right to select their [sic] own candidate.
>
> "It is quite clear that Wesley Powell was the choice of the REPUBLICAN party."

Well, in the first place, it was not quite clear that Powell was the choice; entirely to the contrary, Powell had been defeated. Then when he bolted the party to run as an independent, as Loeb's candidate, it became very evident that Powell was no one's candidate, except Loeb's. Yet Loeb was far from an "established citizen" of New Hampshire.

This was the first salvo, however, in a 25-year war declared by William Loeb on the Republican Party of the State of New Hampshire with the firm and unmistakable intention of making the Republican Party the Loeb Party. Any and all attempts to make Loeb answerable for this or any other of the charges contained in his editorials, most of which were of a far more personal nature, went for naught, because pretty soon Loeb could not be found anywhere.

The woes, many and varied, of Loeb's personal life are best told in an affadavit filed in connection with the probating of his mother's will many years later; that part of the narrative of Atty. Alexander C. Dick, of New York City, to the Surrogate's Court, County of Nassau, State of New York, which covers this period in the life of William Loeb is quoted:

"Meanwhile, after getting out of the hospital, Mrs. Loeb asked affiant to consult with Eleanore, whom William wished to divorce. Eleanore had no lawyer. Affiant recommended a lawyer in Brattleboro, Vermont, and participated to an extent in negotiations for a separation agreement. These failed, and William, after deserting his wife and child without adequately providing for their support, went to Reno, obtained a divorce in the summer of 1952 and married Mrs. Gallowhur. Blaming affiant for the stand taken by the Brattleboro attorney in his negotiations under way, and for being disinherited by his mother, William became so violent in his abuse of affiant and so threatening as to the will that it was decided to call in a new lawyer to consult with Mrs. Loeb about the will. On recommendation of The Chase Manhattan Bank, she engaged Mr. Clarence C. Meleney, who prepared a new will for her, executed May 28, 1952. Affiant later became a partner in Mr. Meleney's firm but Mr. Meleney continued as Mrs. Loeb's only advisor on testamentary matters. Affiant represented Mrs. Loeb in all other matters until her death. He prepared her income tax returns, supervised the sale of her home and purchase of another, and gave legal advice on various miscellaneous matters, including a running battle with her son over his controversy

with Penelope's mother concerning Penelope's custody
and maintenance, the burden of which, in large part, had
been assumed by Mrs. Loeb. This controversy continued
until a few months before his mother's death. Mrs. Loeb
appeared at least four times in Vermont to give testimony
in favor of Eleanore. Affiant accompanied her on such
occasions.

"Mr. Meleney drew several wills and codicils for Mrs.
Loeb, including the will and codicil admitted to probate.
Mr. Meleney early came under William's severe condemnation, however, by reason of a case his firm, Meleney &
Halliday, brought in August, 1952, for Mrs. Loeb in the
Supreme Court, County of New York, to recover posses-
sion of securities which William had deposited with his
mother to secure a loan of $250,000 which she made him
in 1946 as aforementioned (Mrs. Loeb had loaned her
son $250,000 for the original purchase of the Union-
Leader in 1946). He had caused the securities to be removed from her safe deposit box, and had pledged them
with a New York bank to secure a loan with which he
purchased the remaining half of the Manchester Union-
Leader. The securities were restored to a collateral status
securing Mrs. Loeb subject to the unpaid balance of the
bank loan. In the course of his investigation Mr. Meleney
discovered that William owed his mother $28,313.70 on
stock transactions he had handled for her. He had
'dumped' securities to get funds for the $250,000 loan.
These were sold at a loss of over $56,000. The New York
action was settled on the eve of trial entirely in Mrs.
Loeb's favor by a written agreement dated May 1, 1953.
The settlement included Mr. Loeb's giving his mother a
promissory note for $28,368.70."

When William Loeb decided to make good on his intentions to marry Nackey Scripps Gallowhur, whom everyone
knew to be heiress to a considerable fortune, he unceremo-
niously up and left. He made no provision for the support
of his wife—who had sent him her pay for several years
while they were secretly married—or for his infant daughter. According to Mrs. Eleanore McAllister Loeb, the house
in which they lived in Windham was sadly in need of re-
pairs. Both Mrs. Loeb, the wife, and Mrs. Loeb, the mother,

saw William's departure and filing for divorce as more or
less inevitable, but it was the furthest thought from their
minds that he would walk out and leave his wife and child
with no means of support, especially since Loeb was then
receiving a very healthy salary, plus his own share of the
profit-sharing plan from the Manchester operation. It was
estimated that Loeb's annual income was well in excess
of $50,000 at this time. So Mrs. Loeb, the mother, jumped
into the breach created by her son's departure and provided for Eleanore and Penelope while they continued to
live in Vermont.

Yet Eleanore was still naïve enough to believe that there
was such a thing as honor left within her husband. She was
perplexed. It was only a matter of months after Loeb had
departed that a deputy sheriff visited her at her Windham
farm for the purpose of serving her a writ from the Nevada
court informing her that her husband was seeking a divorce. Still without counsel, she apparently thought that to
avoid service of the writ was to inhibit the divorce proceeding in Reno, and the sheriff left the writ inside the screen
door of her little home. (It was later ruled that she had
been properly served.) In Reno, Loeb's divorce went off
without a hitch and he and Nackey Scripps Gallowhur
were married and settled in a home at 1750 Skyline Boulevard, Reno. Loeb wrapped himself in a cloak of dignity by
joining the Federated Church of Reno, the Reno Chamber
of Commerce and he and Nackey became president and
vice president, respectively, of Associated Newspaper, Inc.,
a corporation the function of which is quite difficult to determine, (to engage in any lawful activity, says its Nevada
charter).

Atty. James L. Oakes, of Brattleboro, was the attorney
who was engaged to represent Eleanore and Penelope.
(He is, in 1975, a justice on the U.S. Second Circuit Court
of Appeals in New York City.) Oakes immediately moved
in Vermont Superior Court that Eleanore be granted
custody of her daughter and that Loeb be ordered to pay
support for both the wife and daughter. Loeb retained
A. Luke Crispe, his attorney from his arrest in 1949, who

told the court that Loeb had become a pillar of the community in Reno, intended to reside there permanently and he wanted custody of Penelope because she'd be better off there; better schools, better community, and, besides, Penelope could play with Nackey's daughter, Naxie, Loeb's plea said.

It was just about this time that Mrs. Loeb, Sr., was informed by the Internal Revenue Service that they would like a closer look at her returns, so, with counsel, she went to audit the contents of her safe deposit box at The Chase Manhattan Bank in Manhattan. It was then that it was discovered that the $250,000 in securities was missing. Mrs. Loeb was angry. The more Mrs. Loeb thought about it, the more angry she got. The more angry she got, the more support she lent to Eleanore and her grandchild, Penelope.

Mrs. Katharine W. D. Loeb, through her attorneys, also initiated action on another front and an account of this appeared as follows in *Newsday*, Long Island's daily newspaper published in Garden City:

## North Shore Widow
## Sues Publisher Son

"New York—Nassau's North Shore is buzzing today as it has since last Tuesday with the news that the widow of Theodore Roosevelt's confidential secretary has filed a $1,000,000 suit against her son, the publisher of the Manchester (NH) Union Leader.

"In an action brought in Supreme Court by Mrs. Katharine W. Dorr Loeb of Westerleigh, Oyster Bay, the co-defendants are oft-married William Loeb and the New York Trust Company.

"The action involves the transfer of stock in Loeb's powerful conservative newspaper, and is the latest round in a series of bizaare episodes in which the publisher has been involved since 1949.

"The wealthy matron is suing for the $1,000,000 of the paper's stock that she claims her son put up as collateral for a $3,000,000 loan from the New York Trust Company.

"According to court sources, Mrs. Loeb maintains that

her son first bought a share in the Union-Leader with $250,000 borrowed from her. That was in 1946. In 1949, it is reported, he purchased controlling interest of the paper for $300,000. To do this he used the stock with the borrowed money as collateral.

"Mrs. Loeb is reportedly basing her action on the premise that her son could not have done anything with the Union-Leader without her $250,000 loan.

"In Supreme Court Tuesday, Loeb sought in vain to have the suit dismissed. The case was postponed to April 2. Reached at her Shore Road estate, Mrs. Loeb would not comment on the case.

"Loeb, first hit the headlines in 1949, when he cooled his heels in a Woodstock, Vt., jail for 12 hours before $150,000 bail could be raised. He was accused of trifling with the affections of the very-married granddaughter of E. W. Scripps, one of the founders of the Scripps-Howard newspaper chain.

"He was accused by the young lady's husband, George Gallowhur. Three years and several juicy tidbits of gossip later, Loeb divorced the former Eleanore McAllister to marry his Vermont flame, Nackey Scripps Gallowhur.

"Last August, the publisher made political news by joining Col. Robert R. McCormick, publisher of the Chicago Tribune, in calling for the creation of a new 'American Party.' In so doing he blasted many Republican leaders, singling out former County Executive Sprague and the then New Hampshire Governor Sherman Adams."

Loeb was out of the swim in Nevada. He had to be closer to the base of his newspaper operations to get the feel of the political developments. He knew, or, at the very least, he had reason to believe, that sheriffs were looking high and low for him in Vermont and New Hampshire so it was obvious that the newlyweds didn't want anything to do with any real estate in those states. They did find a "castle" in Pride's Crossing, Massachusetts, a small satellite of the Town of Beverly, in Essex County, a posh, North Shore community, a little over 20 miles northeast of Boston.

Why Pride's Crossing? This question has puzzled Loeb-watchers for years. However, there is plenty of reason to believe that Loeb had a suppressed envy, or even hatred, for U.S. Sen. Henry Cabot Lodge, Jr., a resident of Beverly, and that Loeb, in his own mind, had to have a home the equal of, or better than, that of Lodge. It had been Lodge's father who was the Boston Brahmin who was always so superior in his dealings with Loeb's father (and others). This theory gained further weight when, during Lodge's run at the Vice Presidency in 1960 and a campaign in Lodge's behalf for the Presidency in 1964 in New Hampshire, Loeb bent over backwards in his Manchester newspapers to assault and belittle Lodge.

If Loeb had no desire to see his mother or her attorneys, he wanted even less to see a judge in New York Supreme Court relative to the matter of the missing securities, and so he settled the matter, per Mr. Dick's affidavit. It cannot be otherwise interpreted than that his mother let her son off the hook. He eluded service on the matter of support for his wife and daughter and this case dragged on, with Mrs. Loeb supporting Eleanore and Penelope, until it reached the Vermont Supreme Court in 1955.

This was the first time that a Vermont court had considered the particular legal problem which this case presented: the Nevada divorce had been granted in one of the first states to grant "no-fault" divorces, and it was held to be legal; but could an ex-wife in Vermont be entitled to support for herself and her daughter while her ex-husband was living out of state? The long and short of it was that the Vermont Supreme Court held that Loeb would have to pay $700 a month support for his daughter, but Eleanore was not entitled to support payments. The court's ruling was that Eleanore had sought support as a wife, while she was no longer a wife but an ex-wife, having been duly divorced in a valid proceeding in Nevada, *Loeb v. Loeb*, 118 Vermont 472, February term, 1955.

But no matter what the Vermont Supreme Court said, William Loeb apparently figured that they had no jurisdiction, moral or legal, over him and he never did make the payment of one cent for the care and upbringing of Katharine Penelope Loeb, according to Eleanore.

Meanwhile, back in New Hampshire, there was plenty of political action and, for all his difficulties and preoccupations, William Loeb was not too busy to partake in it; of course, he took no personal part, whether or not it was that he didn't want to enter the state; it was just Loeb's style to criticize and villify all who did not cater to his whim and fancy on his own Page One, most often in capital letters.

On Jan. 9, 1951, Loeb again changed the name of his daily newspapers in New Hampshire. The morning newspaper became the "State Edition" and the evening newspaper, the "City Edition" of the *Manchester Union Leader*. Shortly thereafter, the editorial page was rearranged in the newspaper's makeup so that it became the first page of the second section. The two newspapers were subsequently published by a staff which included only one managing editor and one staff of editorial writers.

Gov. Sherman Adams had been reelected as New Hampshire's chief executive in 1950, and as the 1952 Presidential primary approached, it was Adams who led the forces of those in the Granite State who supported Gen. Dwight D. Eisenhower for the Republican Presidential nomination. Loeb, via his newspapers, was carrying the banner of Ohio Sen. Robert A. Taft. Whatever the reason, Eisenhower took every delegate vote from New Hampshire to the Chicago convention; on the Democratic side of the ledger, Tennessee Senator Estes Kefauver had stumped the state of New Hampshire in the winter snow and he had most of the support of the New Hampshire delegation at the party's Chicago fiesta, but there were still some loyalists who were elected as delegates "favorable to Truman."

Illinois Governor Adlai Stevenson won the Democratic nomination and General Eisenhower, the winner in the New Hampshire primary in March, prevailed in the November election. One of his first moves as President-elect was to name Sherman Adams, who was retiring as governor of New Hampshire, as Special Assistant to the President. Loeb had given Eisenhower qualified support after the nomination, but made it clear that he would have preferred Taft. It wasn't long after Inauguration Day that

Loeb nicknamed the President "Dopey Dwight" and his assistant, "Shermy Wormy."

Hugh Gregg, of Nashua, succeeded Adams in the State House in January, 1953, and it was apparent from the outset that he and Loeb were on a collision course. Gregg, after all, was a true son of the G.O.P. "Old Guard." He had been Wesley Powell's campaign manager in Powell's primary contest with Senator Tobey, but he disaffiliated himself from the Powell organization when Powell bolted the party to run as an independent in the 1950 General Election against Tobey.

Being absent, Loeb wasn't really up to form with editorials as frequently as before. There was definitely a time lag in keeping Loeb informed of the day-to-day situation in New Hampshire; at the same time Loeb had seemingly forgotten that Vermont and the *Daily News* and the *Daily Messenger* even existed.

However, lest the politicians in the good old Granite State feel neglected, the void left by Loeb was very capably filled by the associate publisher, Bernard J. McQuaid, whose Sunday morning acetylene, at times, approached white heat. His rhetoric was much smoother than was Loeb's and his mastery of the language was so far ahead of Loeb's that there was no contest. Indeed, McQuaid was apparently trying to outdo Loeb, and in this he was, at times, successful. The word which trickled back from Loeb, wherever he was, was that Loeb had said that his basic contract with McQuaid was that McQuaid would have his own editorial say on Sunday morning and there was nothing he, Loeb, could do to soften McQuaid's blows. (McQuaid had his own vanishing act, too. He was seldom seen outside the Union Leader. He minimized his strolls to the Puritan on Elm Street to one a day. When he appeared at the Manchester Country Club for his twice weekly round of golf, he would disappear almost as soon as he came off the course.)

Gregg got to be McQuaid's prime target. There was nothing the young governor could do to escape McQuaid's severe censure and ridicule.

Then, on July 23, 1953, Senator Charles W. Tobey died

of coronary thrombosis at Bethesda Naval Hospital at age
73, thus creating a vacancy in the U.S. Senate to be filled
at the discretion of Governor Gregg. (The death and
funeral of Senator Tobey were given adequate news
coverage in the Manchester newspapers. But Tobey's
death received nowhere near the news space allotted to
the death, a very few days later, of Ohio Senator Taft.)

Speculation was rampant over whom Gregg would dub
to fill Tobey's shoes and the governor had many consulting
sessions and a week's vacation, before naming, on August
14, Atty. Robert W. Upton, of Concord, to the Senate seat.

Loeb immediately reacted. On Aug. 15, 1953, Page One
of the *Union Leader* contained some praise for Upton in
Loeb's editorial; the publisher pointed out that Senator
Upton had been counsel to the management of the Union-
Leader before Loeb bought the corporation, and that he
had continued as Loeb's counsel for a while. But Loeb did
generally find fault with the Gregg appointment, because,
as Loeb put it, Gregg had been Powell's campaign manager
before Powell had bolted the party to run as an independent against Tobey:

> "There is no denying the fact that Powell was morally
> entitled to the appointment."

Well, that was some logic, but it was also a pretty good
assessment of where Loeb stood and would continue to
stand with regard to the affairs of the Republican Party
in the state of New Hampshire. In 1954 elections, Senator
Styles Bridges waltzed to another full term and in the
primary for the short-term seat, the Congressman from the
Second District, Norris Cotton, of Lebanon, opposed the
incumbent, Senator Upton, in the primary, as well as
Wesley Powell of Hampton Falls. Cotton won it hands-
down, with Upton a poor second and Powell, a gasping
third, and, in the election, Cotton won in a cake walk.

Lane Dwinell, a businessman and townsman of Cotton
from Lebanon, won the governorship to succeed Gregg,
who chose not to seek reelection. Loeb was largely mute
in this contest, but McQuaid and his *Sunday News* backed

the Democrat, Mayor John Shaw of Rochester. A Peterborough attorney, Perkins Bass, won election to Cotton's vacated Congressional seat; it had been Gov. Robert Bass, the new Congressman's father, who had been instrumental in urging Frank Knox and John Muehling to establish the Union-Leader in 1912.

Governor Dwinell fared no better than had Gregg at the hands of McQuaid, except that he was a more elusive target. Loeb took an occasional "sucker shot" at someone, including President Eisenhower and Special Assistant Adams, but "sucker shots" were getting to be Loeb's style.

Eisenhower had no trouble at all during the 1956 Presidential primary in New Hampshire, but his Vice President, Richard M. Nixon, did. There was a considerable "Dump Nixon" move afoot. Loeb hit hard for the Vice President, urging his support in the March primary. New Hampshire had, by this time, added a new feature to its Presidential primary which is now known as the "beauty contest." In addition to voting for delegates to the respective party conventions, voters signify their preferences for the offices of President and Vice President, but the result is nothing more than a statewide, state-sanctioned popularity contest, with no strings attached. As a result of Loeb's drive, Nixon scored a heavy write-in vote for Vice President. Kefauver again captured the Democrats' strength for the Presidency.

In the direct primary, Governor Dwinell ran for another term, and he did it without the support of the Manchester newspapers who put their full weight behind Dwinell's primary opponent, Wesley Powell (yes, Wesley Powell once again). Dwinell won by five thousand and change, and in November Dwinell easily outdistanced the candidate of the *N.H. Sunday News,* John Shaw, Cotton winning a full term in the Senate. Bass repeated in the Second District. Eisenhower had little trouble with Adlai Stevenson and again it held true that the winner of the New Hampshire Presidential primary, who was the nominee, was elected the President of the United States.

Over the years, William Loeb has always told his readers about "forces" which cause this and "forces" which cause that. In the early 1950's, William Loeb had some "forces" up there in Burlington, Vermont, who were not thinking too kindly of his operation. When strung out, these forces included the United Press International, the King Features Syndicate, the Newspaper Enterprise Association, the U.S. Department of Labor, the U.S. Internal Revenue Service and the U.S. Social Security System. These "forces" had one thing in common—they all said that William Loeb was not as fiscally responsible as they would like him to be and they would all be placated, these "forces," by the payment of cash money for balances due.

The Burlington Publishing Co., Inc., had gone in arrears to nearly everyone and it was only by the grace of some fast collections that the payroll was being met. Wesley Cilley, the business manager, figured that this was no place for him to be, so he resigned, and his place was taken by Frank Bent, a very businesslike sort who received training in accounting, as well as cavalry, at Norwich University, Vermont's military academy. He no sooner took the job than he could see ahead of him the monumental job of getting out from under. The newspaper firm owed UPI for its teletype and news service; King Features for comics and other features such as the crossword puzzle; NEA for still other features; the Labor Department for back overtime and salary to former employes who had filed complaints, and to the IRS and Social Security for large amounts of money which had been withheld from employe paychecks but had not been paid to the Government, quarterly, as was the law.

Bent says the Burlington Publishing Co., Inc., operated at a loss of $80,000 in 1952, this while the employes were on a profit-sharing basis. But Bent set up a schedule of paying the bills. With healthy transfusions of money from the Manchester Union Leader Corporation, these bills were reduced to a deficit of between $11,000 and $10,000 in 1953, according to Bent. Most suppliers to the newspaper were still performing C.O.D., but at least they were still supplying and without them the newspaper wouldn't have been able to publish.

Bent says that Loeb would send periodic memoranda to be posted on the bulletin board, urging the employes to pull harder to make the operation successful. But, Bent says, no sooner would the staff get up a head of steam and the paper would be going well than Loeb would order a "silly" Page One editorial and throw all the good work for naught. Of course, the competing *Free Press* loved this and profited by it. To get an idea of how reliant the Evening *Daily News* was on the rival morning *Free Press*, oldtimers in Burlington can tell yarn after yarn about how they would write a morning news story in such a way that when it was paraphrased in the *Daily News* in the evening, it would bear no semblance to the original happening. But Loeb began more and more to skimp on actual news coverage, preferring to print as news what was easiest acquired. This hallmark of his Burlington operation would show up in the Manchester newspapers several years later.

Bent tells the story of how he finally paid off the U.S. Department of Labor to the best advantage of the publishing company, and escaped paying an added penalty in so doing. He then called in the representatives of the Social Security System and the Internal Revenue Service to discuss the problem of the firm's arrears with them. It was Bent's contention that if they demanded immediate payment the newspaper would certainly go out of business and that it would be to the government's advantage to accept partial payments on a schedule which he, Bent, would strictly adhere to, thus liquidating the obligation. The government men agreed and Bent did as he said he would; he faithfully paid the government an increment each month and the balance was coming down. He had pleaded the same case with the United Press International and the balance with the news service was also coming down.

Then, as Bent tells the story, one day two government men entered the newspaper office on College Street and began to address him as "Mr. Bent" and asked for immediate payment of the entire balance owed to both the SSS and the IRS. It occurred shortly after the opening of business for the day and Bent says that he was perplexed; the men had been friendly with Bent over the months and they were on a first-name basis. Further, Bent had kept up his end of the bargain and had paid every time a payment was due. The government men would give no reason for their demands other than to say all right when Bent asked a delay of several hours on the same day when he would meet the payment. The balance at the time was relatively small, Bent says, compared to the original balance. But this demand would throw off his whole scheme for getting the firm out of debt. What bothered Bent most of all was that he could not, for the life of him, figure what motivated the sudden change of attitude on the part of the SSS and the IRS.

Bent says he asked around the office and no one could come up with an answer. He says he then telephoned Montague in Manchester to ask his advice, thinking that there might have been some dealings of the Manchester organization with the government and the Burlington organization was paying for its sins. Montague said this was not the case, but, Bent says, he was amazingly calm about it and advised Bent to stay cool, that things like this had happened in the past and the easiest way to find out the answer was to read his own newspaper. Montague said to pay the government accounts and he would make sure the Burlington firm got an extra transfusion of money from the Union Leader Corporation.

So Bent, who had followed Montague's lead in never reading the newspaper's editorials, started checking back. Eh . . . voila! Two days before, Bent discovered, his own newspaper, the *Burlington Daily News,* contained an editorial, the authorship of which is to this day anonymous, which went as follows: Uncle Sam is being played as a "sucker," the editorial said, by those business firms which are in arrears in payments of monies withheld from payrolls and not paid to the government. Uncle Sam is letting these firms continue to operate while they pay off their arrears bit-by-bit and thus they are, in effect, operating on taxpayers' money. The only decent and fair thing to do, the editorial said, is to immediately close down these firms even if it meant throwing them into bankruptcy. There should be no excuse for operating a private business while using Uncle Sam's money.

Bent promptly telephoned the government men and told them they could pick up their check at anytime.

According to Bent, there were many normal business practices which were not being adhered to in Burlington. There was never a credit check for a potential advertiser, and current advertisers were never assessed for their arrears. He says he corrected these, and slowly, but surely, the newspaper was coming out of the hole. He tells of several meetings of the Burlington department heads with Loeb, one in Philadelphia, another at the Hotel Taft in New York, and others at the Hotel Somerset and the Parker House in Boston. Bent says that all these meetings were held at hotels which had "due bill" advertising accounts with one of the Loeb newspapers.

Bent says that at the meeting held in December of 1954 at the Hotel Somerset in Boston, he was happy to report to Loeb that the Burlington Publishing Co., Inc., had indeed gone into the "black" and that he could show a profit of $8,000 for the year. He says he asked Loeb if he could then give everyone a 10 per cent raise or a $10 raise, offering high words of commendation for members of the staff who had worked long and hard to bring about the show of profit.

Bent says Loeb told him that Bent should make the check in the amount of the profits payable to Loeb, and that, further, there would be no pay increases in any form in Burlington. At the time, Bent says, Loeb was secretly dickering for the purchase of the *Toronto Star* and that even though Loeb was high bidder, the sellers refused to sell the property to Loeb.

The meeting at the Hotel Somerset was just before

Christmas, Bent says, and when he saw Loeb and Nackey leave the meeting, he knew why the Loebs had no friends with whom to spend Christmas.

Bent resigned from the Burlington Publishing Co., Inc., as soon as he could find suitable employment.

# 17

The clerk of the New Hampshire Senate read the resolution offered by the Senator from the Sixth District, Hon. James P. Rogers, of Laconia:

> "Whereas, the publisher of the Manchester Union Leader has on many occasions referred to the President of the United States in terms which are not consistent with good ethics or common decency; and
>
> "Whereas, the right of free speech and free press does not grant the privilege of degrading the highest elective office in the nation; and
>
> "Whereas, the repeated and malicious abuse of the President is an unhealthy influence, akin to subversion, and
>
> "Where, on page 3 of the Union-Leader of Friday, May 3, the said publisher, William Loeb, has referred to the Chief Executive in a manner which is repulsive to all good citizens; now therefore
>
> "Be It Resolved, that the New Hampshire Senate condemns the unbridled use of such vicious and irresponsible language in the public press; and
>
> "Be It Further Resolved, that a copy of this resolution be mailed forthwith to the editor of each daily and weekly newspaper published within the State of New Hampshire."

What had so incensed Senator Rogers to introduce this resolution on May 7, 1957, had been an editorial which William Loeb had carried, beginning on Page One, of course, in the May 3 *Union Leader*. The news story which led the paper that day told of how Sen. Joseph R.

McCarthy (R–Wis.) had died the day before at Bethesda Naval Medical Center, cause of death being given as hepatitis. William Loeb said, in an editorial edged in black and entitled:

## "MURDERED!"

"Joe McCarthy was murdered by the Communists as surely as if he had been put up before a wall and shot."

In the continuation of his Page One editorial on Page 3, again bordered in black and covering almost two full columns, Loeb said, in part:

"THAT IS HOW THE COMMUNISTS MURDERED M'CARTHY. AND DID THESE MURDERERS HAVE SOME PRETTY GOOD ASSISTANCE! THERE WAS SENATOR FLANDERS TO WHOM LEFT WING ORGANIZATIONS FED POISON AND THEN BLATTED IT ON THE FLOOR OF THE SENATE. FLANDERS PRACTICALLY ACCUSED M'CARTHY OF BEING A HOMOSEXUAL ON THE FLOOR OF THE SENATE.

"That was the line of the moment. The unspeakable ex-criminal Greenspan from Las Vegas boldly printed in his newspaper that McCarthy was a homosexual. Nothing too low, nothing too vile for these lice.

"Then of course the piously hypocritical newspapers, such as the New York Times, the Providence Journal and many others, ran slanted reports against McCarthy and heaped abuse and lies on his head through their editorial columns.

"FINALLY WE COME TO THAT STINKING HYPOCRITE IN THE WHITE HOUSE, WHO RECENTLY BECAME SO SMALL THAT HE ASKED EVERY OTHER SENATOR AND REPRESENTATIVE TO HIS RECEPTION EXCEPT JOE M'CARTHY. . . ."

The people of New Hampshire were sickened by Loeb and his newspapers for carrying such statements; the highly irregular talk by Loeb had been reported in other daily newspapers across the country. Senator Rogers' resolution was one of the first orders of business in the Senate on the first business day after the editorial appeared.

The Journal of the Senate continues:

> "Question being on the motion of Senator Rogers.
>
> "The President recognized Senator Lamontagne:
>
> " 'Mr. President, I would like to have my remarks recorded and this is why—I have nothing against the President of the United States. Neither do I care that he is of the opposite party from what I am. But I certainly believe that this matter here is only between the person and not the Senate of New Hampshire. I am going to be against the resolution because I believe in freedom of the press.'
>
> "Senator Cleveland stated that he would vote in favor of the motion of Senator Rogers.
>
> "Question being on the adoption of the motion of Senator Rogers.
>
> "On this question, Senator Lamontagne demanded a roll call.
>
> "The Clerk proceeded to call the roll.
>
> "Fifteen Senators having voted in the affirmative, and eight Senators having voted in the negative, the affirmative prevailed, and the motion carried."

Paraphrased, the situation was something like this. Senator Rogers, a Republican of the "Old Guard" variety, was against Loeb on most issues and Loeb had not been especially friendly to Rogers, or to his faction of the G.O.P. Rogers was truly incensed at Loeb's strong language in a newspaper which came into the hands of schoolchildren, among others.

Senator Lamontagne, a Democrat from the city of Berlin, in the upper reaches of New Hampshire beyond the White Mountains, was a trucker in private industry and he had spent several terms in the Senate with a near perfect attendance record. During Lamontagne's tenure, very, very few measures which had anything at all to do with the regulation of the trucking industry ever even reached a vote with Senator Lamontagne in attendance, and he was always in attendance. Senator Lamontagne was a Democrat, but his political affiliation could be more aptly described as Trucker. It was very important to Senator Lamontagne not to incur the wrath of William Loeb, publisher, because William Loeb would be very helpful to Senator Lamontagne when another of these trucking or highway use bills—they were always coming in —became an issue.

Senator Cleveland was a Republican from New London with political ambitions of his own. He had been raked over by William Loeb before and he would be raked over again and he saw this as a chance to put a little heat on Loeb.

Of the eight who voted against the motion, Lamontagne was joined by three Manchester Democrats who valued Loeb's support in their home city very highly, a Somersworth and a Nashua Democrat, obviously for the same reason, and two Republicans who were outspoken supporters of Wesley Powell (who would certainly be heard from again).

The third reading of Senator Rogers' resolution came before the Senate as a Special Order of Business for 11:01 on May 14, 1957, and the members debated whether the resolution would constitute censorship or abridgement of the freedom of the press. Senator Lamontagne moved that the resolution be laid on the table. A few cooler heads prevailed at this time, a full 10 days after Loeb's original editorial, and the frightened Democrats were joined by eight more Senators who apparently thought that political expediency superseded moral judgments, and Cleveland and the "Old Guard" lost a 16-to-7 count and the bill was laid to rest forever.

It was getting so that William Loeb, with his two editions a day, could play the bicameral New Hampshire General Court like a calliope.

Life was anything but easy for Mrs. Eleanore McAllister (who had reverted to the full-time use of her maiden name) and her daughter, Katharine Penelope Loeb, on the small country farm in Vermont. So at the urging of Mrs. Loeb, Mrs. McAllister and Penelope moved away from the house, sold it and temporarily moved in with Mrs. Loeb in Oyster Bay, Long Island. Their entire support was derived from Mrs. Loeb. Mrs. McAllister says that Loeb did, however, send Penelope a birthday card and a Christmas card every year.

Loeb, although not a familiar figure again in Manchester, did make a rare visit to Amherst Street beginning late in 1957. His Manchester newspapers were still profitable, although the *N.H. Sunday News* was nowhere near the revenue-producer the *Union Leader* was. The Manchester employes were happy, however. The corporation continued profit-sharing payments, and as long as this was the case, personnel problems were at a minimum and the opening of contracts for the American Newspaper Guild and the several craft unions at the Union Leader Corporation became more or less a routine matter.

In Vermont, on the other hand, it was strictly a hand-to-mouth operation. The *Daily News* was going so badly, it was considered a near miracle if the day's issue reached the street each afternoon. The *Daily Messenger* was a little better off because St. Albans had no other news medium which devoted itself entirely to that city's affairs. The *Daily News* had had several editors, and each of these was ex officio editor, or so it seemed, of the *Vermont Sunday News,* which never did seem to get off the ground. The rival *Burlington Free Press* operated as if it finally had the largest city in Vermont all to itself and, for all intents and purposes, this was the case.

Loeb was proving to be a man who never forgave and never forgot. And somewhere in that unique mind he always bore a grudge against the publisher and staff of the original *N.H. Sunday News.* He made no secret to his intimates that he was convinced that this group was part of the "forces" which were out to get him. These same people who had some meetings and conversations with Loeb always reported that no matter how much they told Loeb that it had been a matter of his having made a bad business judgment, he always felt that they had taken unfair advantage of him. And, besides Blair Clark, Elias

McQuaid, Arthur Brush and Ben Bradlee, Loeb always nourished a spot of hate for the owner of the *Haverhill Gazette*. This may have become more of an open wound since Loeb's Pride's Crossing home is in Essex County, Massachusetts, as is Haverhill, and the route from Loeb's home to his Manchester office could actually go through the Massachusetts city of 47,280 people. Haverhill was much the same sort of city as Manchester, only smaller, located on the same Merrimack River, and the industries in the two cities were similar.

During the fall of 1957, the *Gazette* was having labor troubles; members of the International Typographical Union were seeking improvements in their new contract, which was under consideration, and both sides were at an impasse. Newspaper strikes are a very uncommon thing in New England's smaller cities, mainly because those who are employed in the newspaper business in these communities are usually a little better off than the run-of-the-mill guy in the same town. The business is not seasonal; the economy of the city isn't reflected in any layoffs because these newspapers are never overstaffed; and usually newspaper employes finally settle for what they can get and are happy until contract time comes around again.

But, the *Gazette* printers finally decided to strike, and strike they did. Now, another consideration in any strike of this nature is that the union usually tries to time these events so they coincide with the absolute maximum retail shopping season, the time of year when newspaper retail advertising is vital to the commerce of the community and when the newspapers reach their top revenue of the year —that is, the Christmas shopping season. Christmas strikes put the most pressure on newspaper management; the merchants want a medium to advertise their goods and, in fact, they must have it. So here was the City of Haverhill facing Christmas shopping season with no newspaper. There was the *Lawrence Eagle-Tribune*, and the Boston dailies, but none of these could possibly fill the void if there were no *Gazette*.

William Loeb alleges that at this point he was "invited

into Haverhill to start an independent newspaper that would be devoted only to the best interests of all the citizens of Haverhill without fear or favor to anyone." The *Haverhill Journal* came into being; it was a daily newspaper, published every evening except Sunday by the Union Leader Corporation in Manchester, N.H., at the Union Leader plant in Manchester and trucked the 26 miles to its distribution points in Haverhill and environs. It bore a striking resemblance to the *Union Leader* itself, even to the Page One editorials by the newspaper's publisher, William Loeb, who, before long, had all sorts of ideas on how the City of Haverhill and the Commonwealth of Massachusetts should be run. On subjects such as the United States Government, it was not uncommon for similar Loeb editorials to appear in the *Journal,* which had long been Loeb's custom with his newspapers in New Hampshire and Vermont.

Profit-sharing immediately became a thing of the past at the Union Leader, but there was a new, instant get-rich-quick game in town—overtime. Loeb was so intent that the *Journal* be crammed full of everything, newsmen were snapped up on sight; the facilities of the Union Leader Building became crowded to accommodate the production of the *Journal,* but it worked out. In fairness, it might be said that the *Union Leader* itself took a back seat to the *Journal* in many respects within the building, but the newspapers appeared each day and anyone who wanted to work overtime could get all he wanted.

The *Gazette* tried to produce a newspaper with strikebreakers which effort wasn't too successful, but it was not long before the regular printers settled their grievances and went back to work. There were some persons who did not return to the *Gazette;* there were a few people who had joined the *Journal* and Loeb was more than happy to accept them on face value, mainly because this meant fewer *Gazette* employes would return when the strike was over.

The Union Leader Corp. employes didn't miss the profit-sharing and the cry, "Wait till we win in Haverhill" was the watchword around the Union Leader plant. Loeb must have figured it would be a short battle because his operating expenses in Manchester skyrocketed and the revenue showed nowhere near a commensurate figure. When the *Gazette* reappeared, the *Journal's* advertising was cut in half, at least, and circulation sank to a little over half. The top press run of the *Journal* when it was unopposed never exceeded 15,000. After the *Gazette* resumed operation, the standard press run of the *Journal* rarely exceeded 11,000 and nowhere near this number was paid circulation—the circulation staff of the new newspaper was constantly "sampling" areas in Haverhill or its surrounding towns.

The employes who were apparently profiting most from the dual operation at the Union Leader Building were the members of Local 267 of the Pressmen's Union. It was only a few months after the inauguration of the *Journal,* just about when the weather began to get warm, the pressmen were coming to work in new Cadillacs and Thunderbirds. These men were coining money. There were only about 16 members of the local and their contract stated that the printing of each newspaper was one day's work: the morning *Union Leader* was one day, the evening *Union Leader* of the same date another day, the *Journal* of that date, a third day. So, with the *Sunday News,* the presses at the Union Leader were producing 19 newspapers a week; that is, 19 days' work. The formula contained in the contract called for a certain number of pressmen to be on duty for a given number of pages; so most of the Union Leader Corp. pressmen were getting paid overtime starting about Tuesday afternoon each week and it was taking about two hours to run off a *Union Leader* and a little more than one hour to run off the *Journal.*

Montague and McQuaid always maintained that they tried in every way they knew to prevent Loeb from beginning the Haverhill operation and that he really had no business in the Massachusetts city at all. And Montague and McQuaid were not the only persons who felt that Loeb had no business in Haverhill. There were many,

many publishers in one-newspaper cities in New England who viewed the situation as potentially dangerous to themselves, if only as a precedent, and wholly unethical on the part of Loeb. So there came into being a corporation known as Newspapers of New England, Inc., and some of its members were the *Lowell*, Mass., *Sun*, the *Lawrence Eagle-Tribune*, the *Gazette*, of course, the *Brockton*, Mass., *Enterprise*, the *Concord*, N.H., *Monitor*, the *Springfield Republican-Union*, the *Holyoke Transcript*, the *Rutland*, Vt., *Herald*, the *Burlington*, Vt., *Free Press*, the *Worcester*, Mass., *Telegram*, to name a few.

The toll of the extra load started to make itself felt before long at the Union Leader plant. There had not been any significant investment in new machinery or equipment since before World War II. The plant of the Union Leader was tired; breakdowns were frequent, and costly. Then, too, just a few months after Loeb got his Haverhill brainstorm, the accountants gave Loeb what had to be a pretty dismal picture of extreme overexpenditure. So, immediately, there were cutbacks in everything. Overtime was pared to the bone, in every department but the press room. The *Journal* continued, however, to receive special treatment internally, much to the chagrin of the *Union Leader* oldtimers. The one avenue where no expense was spared, however, was in promotion of the *Journal* in Haverhill. By this time the *Journal* had offices of its own in Haverhill for news, advertising and circulation staff, and every gimmick was being used. In addition, the *Journal* became the public-spirited sponsor of any number of ventures; water skiing shows, baseball dinners, and the like.

A new face appeared on the Union Leader Corp. premises. He was Alexander Cymrot, an "adviser" to "Mr. Loeb" and Cymrot spent a lot of time going over financial figures. He did the same at the offices of the Burlington Publishing Co., Inc.

In Burlington, by the way, Loeb had found a new way to do business. He had had a new editor of the *Daily News* just about every other pay day for the past few years. The

latest editor of the *Daily News* was a young man, a native
of Essex Junction, Vt., a Burlington suburb, who had
barely been graduated from the University of Vermont—
George M. Rood, a member of a well-known family. It was
unusual for a man so young to have such heavy responsibilities, but that was probably Loeb's idea all along; pay
him peanuts and let the editor get so carried away with
his own importance and title that the pay was secondary
to him.

While Loeb's consuming interest was in the Haverhill
operation, the concern of Hugh Roe O'Neil, editor of the
*Union Leader* was mostly personnel; O'Neil had never
been a "heavy" when it came to editorial policy. Thomas
A. Dearborn, chief of the editorial page for years and
years, was in failing health, and a young idealist, fresh
from Boston University, James Finnegan, came to work
at the Union Leader Corporation as an editorial writer.
It was the young man's first real newspaper job. He began
serving an apprenticeship under Dearborn. However, it
was B. J. McQuaid who was calling most of the shots in
Manchester, and he was getting a chance to show Loeb
what an asset a Sunday newspaper could be.

A typical assignment from McQuaid would be to instruct
a reporter to go see that "idiot governor" and find out how
many letters "he got blasting him after our story last
Sunday."

Reporter: "Well, Bernie, what if the governor did get
a reaction and it was favorable?"

McQuaid: "Get the hell out of here and do what I told
you to do. You know we only print the news."

It was election year again and the *Union Leader* and
*N.H. Sunday News* had published many statements from
Wesley Powell over the past two years, keeping the Powell
name in the voters' eye. There was no U.S. Senate contest
in New Hampshire in 1958, so Powell decided he'd run
for governor this time. The Old Guard saw this as a threat
by the "Loeb Party" and former Gov. Hugh Gregg jumped
in, but his effectiveness was blunted when Senate Presi-

dent Eralsey Ferguson and House Speaker W. Douglas Scammon also entered the primary, making it three old-line Republicans against Powell. Then, too, there was a character named Elmer Bussey, of Salem, who filed every two years anyway, but he got only 200 votes or so.

On the Democratic side, there was a little more activity than usual. A group had formed the Young Democrats of New Hampshire in the early 1950's and they had accumulated a small campaign fund through fund-raising and organizational dinners; it had not been unusual for the speaker at these affairs to have been either of two U.S. Senators from neighboring states, Edmund S. Muskie of Maine or John F. Kennedy of Massachusetts, who were more than happy to assist the Young Democrats of New Hampshire by their appearances. The former mayor of Laconia, Bernard Boutin, entered the Democratic primary, and McQuaid trotted out his tired old war-horse, John Shaw, of Rochester.

On the occasion of a visit by Senator John Kennedy, Loeb ran a Page One editorial entitled "Modern Paul Revere" in which he lauded Senator Kennedy for his stand on national defense: "If Senator Kennedy would keep talking on THAT theme, we would support him for President any day," said Loeb.

Boutin coasted to victory over Shaw by 4,000 in the Democratic primary even though the *N.H. Sunday News,* in support of their perennial candidate Shaw, hit Boutin with just about everything but the ring post. Powell took a firm stand against any new tax of any form and, as Loeb put it in one Page One, "He'd let light and air into the places that need housecleaning in Concord."

It was a squeaker, but in his fourth try at elective office, Powell had finally won a primary:

| | |
|---|---|
| Elmer E. Bussey, Salem, r | 256 |
| Eralsey C. Ferguson, Concord, r | 1,162 |
| Hugh Gregg, Nashua, r | 39,365 |
| Wesley Powell, Hampton Falls, r | 39,761 |
| W. Douglas Scammon, Stratham, r | 3,096 |

Loeb treated the Powell victory as if he himself had won, and, in fact, many firmly believe to this day that that was exactly the case. On Sept. 11, two days after the primary, Loeb offered this thought on Page One:

"We urge, therefore, that all Republicans and all other friends of Powell supporters (sic) rejoice with us at the winning of a battle which has taken eight years to accomplish."

What Loeb was saying was that in the 12 years that he had owned the Union Leader Corporation, in whole or in part, this had been the very first time that he had come up with a winner. Powell had a little trouble with Boutin, for a Republican nominee, that is, but easily won the November election:

| | |
|---|---|
| Bernard L. Boutin, Laconia, d | 99,955 |
| Wesley Powell, Hampton Falls, r | 106,790 |

The result of this election ran a little deeper than what first meets the eye, because with Wesley Powell in the State House and with Styles Bridges one of the ranking Republicans in the United States Senate, William Loeb, with direct ties to both and in complete control of New Hampshire's only statewide newspaper, became as powerful, almost, as Powell and Bridges together.

The year 1958 was significant in other respects for William Loeb; while he was winning his first election, he was losing one and winning one in the courts.

Mrs. Eleanore McAllister had sold the home in Windham, Vt., for $21,800 and she and Penelope had moved in with Mrs. Loeb in Oyster Bay, but this, at best, was a temporary measure. Mrs. Loeb subsesquently assisted Eleanore by paying a $20,000 mortgage on a $35,000 farm home in Amenia, Dutchess County, New York, where Eleanore and Penelope moved in 1955. Mrs. McAllister used the property as a horse training and breeding farm of modest proportion. Penelope was enrolled in the local schools.

She had brought suit in the New York courts against
Loeb, seeking divorce and separation, and asking for
alimony and counsel fees. In the N.Y. Court of Appeals
in a decision handed down on June 25, 1958, the court
held that Mrs. McAllister was never a "New York wife"
and that the *ex parte* divorce granted Loeb in Nevada
in 1952 was, in fact, legal, and further:

> "While we are not unmindful of the fact that, so far as
> this record shows, defendant's conduct toward his wife
> left much to be desired, the wife has not placed herself
> in a situation helpful to her in the State of New York . . .
> Under the circumstances presented by this record, it seems
> abundantly clear that plaintiff has had no contact with
> New York at any time during the period of their marriage,
> may in no sense be regarded as a New York wife, and
> accordingly is not entitled to relief under section 1170-b,
> of the Civil Practice Act."
>
> —*Loeb v. Loeb* 4 N.Y. 2nd 542

So the net result was that the only state in which Loeb
could be held liable for payment of support was still
Vermont; it can only be assumed that the authorities of
the State of Vermont had a lot of things on their minds
besides chasing William Loeb, so it appeared that as long
as he stayed outside of the state boundaries, he was safe
from prosecution arising from being in arrears on any
support payments.

Loeb meanwhile had appealed the original judgment
of the Vermont Supreme Court which had granted custody
of Penelope to her mother and ordered Loeb to pay
counsel fees.

In an opinion filed Sept. 2, 1958, the Vermont Supreme
Court held:

> "There was no evidence but that the petitionee and
> his present wife maintain a cordial, hospitable household
> with adequate physical facilities, both in Reno, Nevada,
> and Pride's Crossing, Massachusetts, attend church regu-
> larly, conduct themselves with decency and respectability,
> and are raising the children, Naxie, Petitionee's step-

daughter, and Elizabeth, his own daughter, properly and happily.*

". . . . Their marital estrangement has deprived this child of a home shared by both parents. Without attempting to attribute fault to either parent, the findings report the need for restoring to the child paternal association and guidance. To accomplish this result, the court resorted to the only implement available, that of reasonable visitation at such place as the child may have her home with her mother. The provision, thus far, is entirely reasonable and consistent with the facts stated in the findings.

"To these visits, other conditions are attached. The defendant's visitation is restricted to the presence of the plaintiff or a person of the plaintiff's selection. No reason appears from the court's findings to justify the additional restriction upon the defendant's access to his association with the child to occasions when the plaintiff is standing by...

"By the terms of this order, should the plaintiff elect to remove her presence from the visit, the accomplishment of the reunion between the child and her father is left to the plaintiff's right of selecting a delegate to stand watch in the plaintiff's place."

—*Loeb v. Loeb*, 120 Vermont 489

Mrs. Eleanore McAllister says that Loeb never took advantage of coming to visit Penelope and never did see her except during two visits to his mother's home in Oyster Bay.

The Vermont Supreme Court did amend the prior order relating to counsel fees.

It is interesting to note that attorney for Loeb in this pleading, succeeding A. Luke Crispe, Esq., was Harold C.

* The court was in error in its reference to the names of the Loeb children. Naxie was the daughter of Mr. and Mrs. George Gallowhur, and she was adopted by William Loeb after his marriage to Nackey Scripps Gallowhur Loeb. However, at the time of the adoption, or soon thereafter, the mother and stepfather caused the child's name to be changed from Naxie to Elizabeth. Nackey's wealthy aunt, who lived near them in Reno, Nev., was named Elizabeth. Nackey Scripps Gallowhur Loeb and William Loeb later became parents of another daughter, Edith.

O'Brien, Esq., of Rutland. It might be remembered that
O'Brien was the attorney for George Gallowhur at the
time of Loeb's arrest in Woodstock in 1949 and it was, at
that time, O'Brien who had failed to show leniency to
Loeb, according to the *Union Leader*.

Needless to say, some unions were not altogether happy
with Loeb's management. One result of the Haverhill decision was to have put a halt to profit sharing and some
unions were talking in terms of a raise in pay scale, this
subject not having come up while profit sharing was paying such dividends. And Loeb was keeping a sharp eye
focused on the horizon for any potential investors.

Thus, it later came out that a meeting between William
Loeb and Ambassador Joseph P. Kennedy had been arranged, such meeting coming as an aftermath of a confab
between Loeb and four leaders of the Manchester local of
the International Typographical Union at the Hotel Braemore in Boston. (The Braemore was chosen as the location
of this meeting for two reasons: 1. The hotel was indebted
to the Union Leader Corp. for a due-bill advertising arrangement; 2. As host, Loeb would clearly have the upper
hand in the affairs of the day.)

Loeb pleaded poverty during the early part of the meeting with the Manchester ITU chapel members, but then
announced that he had been thinking of a way to inject
new capital into the Union Leader Corporation. He made
no secret of the fact that it was Richard Cardinal Cushing,
archbishop of Boston, to whom he was speaking during a
telephone conversation, Loeb's end of which was purposely
within the hearing of his four guests; he asked the prelate
to arrange for him a meeting with Ambassador Kennedy
at Hyannisport; that he, Loeb, would like to discuss some
backing he might give to the political aspirations of the
ambassador's sons.

Loeb made no secret of the fact that he was going to
meet with Kennedy the Elder before the date of the meeting arrived; as a matter of fact, it was with an air of brag-
gadocio that he told those at the Union Leader Building

who were in the know that the meeting had, in fact, been arranged by Cardinal Cushing.

During the weeks following the date of the meeting, no answer had been volunteered by Loeb as to the outcome of his meeting with Ambassador Kennedy, whether or not he had been successful in securing the needed financing to meet the wage request of the ITU. The persons who had been at the meeting—two of whom, in 1975, are deceased —just assumed that such arrangements would take time. They felt that they had been taken into Loeb's confidence, as indeed they had been, and they passed on their patience —but not all of their knowledge—to the rank-and-file.

Then one day Loeb came into the composing room in Manchester and took aside at least two of those who had been at the meeting and explained the outcome. He told them that Ambassador Kennedy—he referred to the elder Kennedy in different terms—had indeed been willing to look into the matter of Loeb's needed-financing. However, according to the story which Loeb related that day, Kennedy would be interested only if he could invest not the amount Loeb was seeking, but a larger amount, in return for which he would expect 51 per cent control of the Manchester newspapers. Loeb characterized the suggestion by Kennedy as being entirely out of line. He further explained that he naturally declined the offer because he, Loeb, did, after all, have the best interests of the Union Leader Corp. employes at heart and he would never let that (expletive deleted) Kennedy get hold of the *Union Leader* because of the effect it would have on the employes and their futures.

Of course, the four ITU members knew also that Kennedy did not amass the money he had by being stupid. It is only fair to assume, travelling in the circles he travelled in, that Joseph P. Kennedy had heard the full story of Loeb's former partners, the Ridders and Finder, and he must certainly have heard of the mother's safe deposit box at the Chase Manhattan Bank.

It goes without saying that, having failed at his offer of editorial prostitution, the scorned Loeb then executed a

180-degree turn in his editorial position towards the Kennedy family and thus began Loeb's policy wherein the vitriol and venom which he would unleash upon all members of the Kennedy family would know no bounds.

# 18

It used to be that the real salvoes of the New Hampshire first-in-the-nation Presidential preference primary would never be heard until after the first of a particular primary year. But with the advent of the 1960 campaign, it appeared that this quadrennial effort was beginning earlier and earlier. This could, at least in part, be blamed on William Loeb and his *Union Leader*. If there is one thing which can never be said for Loeb it is that he was one to shy away from any national publicity. As a consequence, the *Union Leader* apparently sought to magnify any "happening" to include political implications, all the while drawing national attention to itself and its publisher. Typical of this was the last weekend in September, 1959.

It had long been the custom at Dartmouth College to have the five-year reunion classes get together on the occasion of the homecoming football game, for class meetings, luncheons and a class dinner at Hanover. And so, on Sept. 26, 1959, the 30-year class, that of 1930, attended the Holy Cross-Dartmouth game at Memorial Field in Hanover as well as the luncheon and dinner for their own group. One member of the class of 1930 is Nelson Aldrich Rockefeller, at that time governor of the State of New York. Loeb spent the better part of a week trying to get the message across that, while Rockefeller was indeed a member of the class of 1930 at Dartmouth, he wasn't really coming to a class reunion; he was coming to "sound out"

New Hampshire's political climate in anticipation of the 1960 Presidential primary. Loeb said all but that right out; Loeb's reporters said it right out.

On the Friday before Rockefeller's reunion, Loeb adorned Page One of both the morning and evening *Union Leader* with a make-up "masterpiece." He had a three-column headline over a three-column picture over a two-column editorial. The photograph showed a smiling Governor Rockefeller with a smiling Soviet Premier Nikita Khrushchev and the occasion was the official greeting of the New York governor to the Russian leader on the latter's official visit to the United Nations in New York City. The Friday and Saturday editions of the newspapers were sprinkled with news stories and a State House column about a "Draft Rocky" movement which was underway.

On the day of the game, Governor Rockefeller landed at Concord and made a brief official visit to his fellow Republican, Gov. Wesley Powell, at the State House; then went by automobile to Hanover. For most of the afternoon, any Dartmouth cheering you could hear was for "Rocky" and it was from Dartmouth students who were reacting to the emphasis put on the matter of a Presidential candidacy by Rockefeller in Loeb's newspapers. They surely didn't have much to cheer about on the field, as the Crusaders scored in every period to stomp the Indians. (The only bright spot for Dartmouth was a 58-yard pass play from Quarterback Seth Moger to Halfback Jake Crouthamel; final score, Holy Cross, 31–8.) The students beseiged Rockefeller after the game and he held an informal meeting with them at which time he disavowed any Presidential plans "at that time." He dined with his classmates and went back to the Empire State.

On the weekend following, the New Hampshire air was again full of political talk and the occasion was a visit to Concord by Vice President and Mrs. Richard M. Nixon. Nixon would officiate at the dedication of a $30 million federal flood control dam at Hopkinton, just a few miles west of the capital. The Vice President's airplane landed at Concord airport and he was met by Governor Powell,

Sen. Styles Bridges and Sen. Norris Cotton, and multitudes of the press who were eager to ask the Vice President about his 1960 plans. There was a motorcade from the airport to the dam site, some eight miles away, and just so that no one would get the wrong impression about who was the chief executive in this state, Governor and Mrs. Powell rode in the first car of the motorcade and Vice President and Mrs. Nixon were relegated to the second car.

The *Union Leader* maintained its speculation on the upcoming Presidential primary until after the first of the year, then both Kennedy and Nixon made it official; each would seek election of New Hampshire delegates pledged in their behalf. And there was another act in town. Strolling along the streets of New Hampshire, usually wearing only a business suit and not even a topcoat, despite the severity of the Granite State winter, was an athletic-looking gentleman named Paul Fisher, who told people he was a ball-point pen manufacturer from Chicago and was seeking the Democratic nomination for President. Fisher's platform, he said, was simple: abolish the income tax. "That's nice," was the general reaction and most people immediately got the impression that Fisher was playing with half a deck.

But not so Bernard J. McQuaid, associate publisher of the Union Leader Corp. Although hardly anyone took seriously the candidacy of Democrat Fisher, least of all the senator from Massachusetts, John Fitzgerald Kennedy, McQuaid kept hammering away every Sunday morning.

The Manchester newspapers had done anything they could to embarrass officials at the University of New Hampshire at Durham for well over 10 years and another opportunity presented itself when Senator Kennedy was invited to address the student body in New Hampshire Hall. Fisher, at McQuaid's heavy urging, demanded equal time with Senator Kennedy. The university said he could have his own gathering with students, but Fisher, again seconded in the press by McQuaid, said that was no good; it was a state-supported institution operated with taxpayers' money and Fisher should be on the dias alongside Kennedy. If there had been any doubts about the whole Fisher campaign before, they were verified when the confrontation came. The students loudly booed Fisher. Fisher seemed powerless to still the boos. And Kennedy's reception was all the more warm, since Kennedy sat by and played the role of the perfect gentleman.

It soon became obvious that Governor Powell felt left out. Shortly before Primary Day in March, Powell assumed a Manchester soapbox to announce that Senator Kennedy was "soft on Communism." Now, consistency was never William Loeb's strong suit—less than two years before he had called Kennedy a "Modern Paul Revere" because Kennedy had said that the United States should not place problems of financial stability or the economy ahead of that of national defense, particularly in regard to the Russian threat—and he put Powell's statement all over his newspapers and he all but accused Kennedy of being a Russian spy. Kennedy finally felt that if he failed to respond, it would hurt his image, so he simply stated that he was running for the Presidency, not for the office of governor of New Hampshire and he suggested that Governor Powell might, if he felt so inclined, ask the only announced candidate of his own party, Vice President Nixon, if he had anything to say about how he, Senator Kennedy, felt about Communism. That ended that.

Both Kennedy and Nixon were virtually unopposed on Town Meeting Day in New Hampshire—Fisher was never taken seriously and Rockefeller had long since publicly stated that he had no Presidential ambitions at that time —and both unanimously won their party's delegations. It was a significant win for Kennedy because his 43,372 votes in the Democratic "beauty contest" were double the previous support ever given any Democratic candidate. Fisher got 6,853 Democratic votes, which spoke well for the influence of the *N.H. Sunday News* (or was it as a result of the thousands of ball-point pens he had handed out?) and Kennedy got more than 2,000 Republican write-in votes. Nixon, of course, topped the field in the heavily Republican registered state with 65,204 G.O.P votes and 164 Democratic write-ins.

It is possible that some people will believe anything they read in a newspaper, and it is possible that there are some people who have strong faith in William Loeb. It is possible that there were some people in the Democratic Party in New Hampshire in 1960 who would go out of their way to vote against Sen. John F. Kennedy and the Kennedy family. But there is no denying the fact that a guy named Paul Fisher had waltzed into the Granite State, had been seen in very few communities there, had done no advertising to speak of and had made only a small number of public appearances. And there is no denying that Fisher was able to capture a total of 12.7% of the Democratic vote cast in the 1960 Presidential preference primary while Senator Kennedy—and there is hardly anyone who could say that Kennedy was not a popular figure—received 80.8%.

If there is any lingering doubt that the backing of the Manchester newspapers was a strong factor and that this was all anti-Kennedy vote, then this myth is destroyed by the fact that 2.93% of the Republicans who voted in the 1960 primary went so far as to write in Fisher's name on their ballots. Add to this the scattering of write-ins Fisher received as Vice Presidential candidate on both parties and the inescapable conclusion is that the *Union Leader* and *Sunday News* had a hard core of readers who would follow the newspapers' lead at election time, even if it meant voting for Snow White and the Seven Dwarfs. Analyzing the Fisher vote one may only conclude that the hard core which followed the *Union Leader* line could amount to as much as 15% of the electorate.

For the better part of two years, William Loeb bent every effort to make Gov. Wesley Powell look good as the state's chief executive, but the "Old Guard" Republicans were far from happy that Loeb's man occupied the corner office. There was never a question in anybody's mind but that Powell would go for a second term; but, as it turned out, he had to work for it. Former Gov. Hugh Gregg again threw his hat into the ring and, after Powell declared, Hillsborough County Commissioner Wayne Crosby followed suit. Very few thought that Crosby was serious, but enough apparently did to make the difference:

| | |
|---|---|
| Wayne Crosby, Hillsborough, r | 1,286 |
| Hugh Gregg, Nashua, r | 48,108 |
| Wesley Powell, Hampton Falls, r | 49,119 |

It was no great showing for an incumbent, certainly not one to write home about, but it was nonetheless a win. Democrat Boutin won the Democratic primary going away. McQuaid had trotted the tired John Shaw out of the locker room for another race, but it was no contest. Some guy named Watson, also from Rochester, even got 2,000 votes.

Senator Bridges had clear sailing through the primary, as usual, and in a three-way fight on the Democratic side, the *N.H. Sunday News* gave moderate backing to a Manchester man who, at the moment, was incarcerated in the Hillsborough County House of Correction at Grasmere for having imbibed too heavily.

Loeb went to work on Senator Kennedy; he could think of nothing bad enough to say about JFK or any other Kennedy who happened to be in Loeb's mind. And, on Nov. 2, six days before the primary, Loeb completely reversed his previously stated position on his "Modern Paul Revere":

> "It is just plain nonsense to say that Senator Kennedy whose father has a half a billion dollars and whose family has $40,000 weddings can understand the problems that face the average citizen in the United States."

John F. Kennedy, Robert F. Kennedy, Edward M. Kennedy, Ambassador and Mrs. Joseph P. Kennedy and the three girls had all taken below-the-belt shots from Loeb for just about a year and, apparently, John Fitzgerald

Kennedy had had all he was willing to take without getting one last shot back.

November 7, the last day of the tiring campaign which had taken Senator Kennedy to 40 states, JFK detoured his campaign caravan en route to Boston for one last speech in Manchester, New Hampshire. A platform was erected out of doors across Victory Park from the offices of the *Manchester Union Leader* and one of the largest crowds in the city's history gathered in the chilling early evening to hear the twang of the tired Kennedy, who mounted the crude stage with his three sisters, Mrs. Jean Smith, Mrs. Eunice Shriver and Mrs. Patricia Lawford. He told the crowd that he felt that inasmuch as his campaign had begun in Manchester, it would be only fitting that it end there.

Then:

> "I would like to have the *Union Leader* print in a headline that we carried New Hampshire."

Kennedy received a deafening roar of applause for an answer. Apparently pleased with that trial balloon, Kennedy continued:

> "I believe there is probably a more irresponsible newspaper than that one right over there somewhere in the United States but I've been through 40 states and I haven't found it yet."

The crowd's roar seemed to echo off the Union Leader Building itself and lasted for what seemed almost a minute. Kennedy continued:

> "I believe that there is a publisher who has less regard for the truth than William Loeb but I can't think of his name."

And the applause this time put the previous two outbursts to shame.

The next morning the event was reported on Page One of the *Union Leader,* but the news space given Loeb's reply measured twice as long as the space allotted to Kennedy for his entire day's activity, including the local appearance. Loeb's reaction was what could be expected, a long, disjointed litany of abuses against all of the Kennedy family. (Among other things he called Kennedy a "liar" and a "spoiled brat.")

Yet this must be regarded as a coup for Kennedy; he had hit Loeb on his home ground with the greatest mass appeal at his command and he apparently hit Loeb so late in the game that Loeb didn't know how to react. It was too late for a Page One editorial, because by the time Loeb got the word in Pride's Crossing and composed himself, not to mention his reply, the deadline for the morning newspaper was almost at hand.

Slightly over twenty-four hours later, John Fitzgerald Kennedy was President-elect of the United States; he had not won New Hampshire's electoral votes—he lost the state by 20,000 votes—but the 137,772 votes which Kennedy received in the state represented the highest total that a Democrat had yet received in New Hampshire for any elective office. One doubts that the presence of Lyndon B. Johnson as Kennedy's running mate had anything at all to do with the total Democratic vote.

This has been the only incidence where both winners of their respective party primaries in New Hampshire ultimately became the nominees of the two parties for the November election. The Kennedy–Nixon election battle of 1960 will be remembered also as the closest Presidential election in the nation's history until that time. But it nonetheless held true that the President-elect had been the man of his party who had won the New Hampshire first-in-the-nation Presidential primary.

Loeb waited until after President Kennedy was inaugurated and then saluted his commander-in-chief with a Page One broadside, entitled:

### "The No. 1 Liar in the United States"

The year 1961 cannot be called a good year for William Loeb. The Haverhill operation was becoming so costly that something had to give. In May, 1959, Loeb had borrowed $300,000 from his "adviser" Cymrot; in September, 1959, $100,000 more; and in June, 1960, Cymrot gave him another $100,000, all at 10% interest—a high rate at the time. This still wasn't enough money to make ends meet; the Burlington Publishing Co., Inc., had been changed to the Vermont Publishing Co., Inc., with Loeb as president and his wife as vice president. The third incorporator was William T. Montague, son of the Manchester general manager, who had been working as an advertising salesman in Haverhill since his graduation from Boston University. Young Montague was general manager, George Rood was still editor.

The *Burlington Daily News* which had been under Loeb's control for almost 20 years, was fighting a losing battle. Advertising was way off, none of the courts were placing their legal ads in the paper anymore, and circulation was the lowest ever.

So, on May 19, 1961, William Loeb announced in a Page One "Notice To Our Readers" that that was the last issue of the *Daily News;* that the "Vermont Publishing Company . . . will, from tomorrow on, concentrate on its profitable publications, the *Vermont Sunday News* and the *St. Albans Messenger.*" Editor Rood came out with a fighting column on Sunday morning, ". . . Tell You What We're Going to Do." But the fact of the matter was that they weren't really going to do anything. The *Daily News* was dead, and a daily newspaper which began publication some 67 years before breathed its last. The readers of Burlington had had a choice and it had been clear. The *Free Press* immediately showed a jump in advertising lineage and a small circulation gain; the two-newspaper families of Burlington became one-newspaper families.

Meanwhile, in Haverhill, Mass., the long-established *Gazette* was doing as well as it had ever done. It was a better newspaper than it had ever been and the backing it had received had also included some key personnel in the editorial and business ends of the operation. Loeb's *Journal* was floundering and, as usual when things were not going his way, Loeb was ranting and raving in his editorials. And finally he decided he'd do something about it. He and his attorneys went into Federal Court in Boston and filed an anti-trust suit, claiming that these "forces" were combining to deprive him of his free enterprise.

Newspapers of New England, Inc., publishers of the *Gazette,* countersued the Loeb management, making their own claims of violation of anti-trust laws. Judge Charles E. Wyzanski, Jr., began hearing evidence in the litigation which would, before it was to be settled, have covered a six-year period.

Governor Powell of New Hampshire had not had an opportunity to name an attorney general since the incumbent, Louis C. Wyman, had almost two years to serve on his term when Powell had been inaugurated. But in the fall of 1961, Powell was moving in that direction. His choice, Atty. Maurice J. Murphy, of Dover, was not the most popular selection Powell would make, but for the better part of three years Powell had been doing largely unpopular things, only to have his judgment applauded by Loeb in his Manchester newspapers. So, on Nov. 4, 1961, Powell nominated Murphy to the attorney general's job and convened a special session of the Executive Council to approve the nomination on a Saturday.

Three weeks later, Senator Bridges, visiting at his East Concord home, was stricken with a heart attack early in the morning of November 26, a Sunday. He died almost instantly. Alone with the senior senator at the time was his third wife, Doloris, whom the senator had married in 1944. Mrs. Bridges was from St. Paul, Minn., and had been a government employe in Washington when she met Bridges.

Loeb's editorial on Bridges' death was edged in black and it was terribly long—more than four columns—and it was touched off by the tender sentiment that Bridges' death was "as if the top of Mount Washington had been blown off."

On the same Page One, Nov. 27, 1961, Loeb's newspapers carried a news story in which the publisher expounded at length on whom Loeb felt Powell should appoint to the unexpired term. "If Governor Powell can put aside his own personal ambitions," Loeb said, "it would be a magnificent act for him to name Mrs. Bridges."

The senior senator's funeral was held in the Hall of Flags of the New Hampshire State House, the first funeral ever conducted there, and it was attended by a large delegation of United States Senators and other government dignitaries, as well as state and local authorities.

On December 6, Governor Powell unexpectedly summoned newsmen to a State House news conference and announced that he would not seek Bridges' seat, nor would he run for the seat Senator Bridges formerly held in the 1962 election. He added that he would not appoint Mrs. Bridges, as Loeb had nearly demanded. There was some reason for Powell not to resign and have himself appointed to Bridges' seat. The Senate President at that time would be the interim governor who would be sworn in and serve until the next regular election and the Senate President at that time was Sen. Sam Green (R-Manchester), a lawyer who was also Jewish. For Powell to have resigned would have meant that he would have named the first Jewish governor in the history of the state.

The very next day, Governor Powell announced that he was appointing Attorney General Murphy, 34 years old, to the seat. Loeb exploded into Page One rhetoric calling Powell "vindictive" and "egotistical" and "an ingrate." He went on for almost four columns of space continued to an inside page. In this same issue was an announcement that a movement had been organized to "draft" Mrs. Bridges to run for the seat in the next regular election.

The Loeb-Powell honeymoon was over, and the divorce became final in the last five paragraphs of Loeb's editorial:

"As everyone knows we have devoted, over the years, much effort to Governor Powell's career. We have risked unpopularity with many people in the state through our support of him.

"IN RETURN, WE HAVE NEVER ASKED ANYTHING FROM GOVERNOR POWELL THAT COULD

BE OF THE SLIGHTEST POSSIBLE GAIN TO THIS
NEWSPAPER OR TO THIS WRITER.

"Our request on behalf of Mrs. Bridges was because we
thought Governor Powell's appointment of Mrs. Bridges
would be the best possible tribute to the late senator, to
whom New Hampshire owes so much.

"IT IS NOT EASY TO CONFESS A MISTAKE OR
TO SAY THAT ONE IS WRONG, BUT THIS NEWS-
PAPER FRANKLY SAYS THIS MORNING THAT WE
HAVE WASTED 11 YEARS OF EFFORT ON BEHALF
OF GOVERNOR POWELL.

"FOR A BRILLIANT MIND, A GOLDEN TONGUE
OR A GREAT AMBITION AVAILS A MAN NOTH-
ING, AND SERVES NEITHER THE STATE NOR
THE NATION, IF IT IS NOT WEDDED TO GREAT-
NESS OF CHARACTER AND HUMILITY OF SPIRIT.
AGAIN WE QUOTE FROM ST. MATTHEW: 'WHAT
DOTH IT PROFIT A MAN IF HE SHALL GAIN
THE WHOLE WORLD, AND LOSE HIS SOUL?'

"William Loeb,
"Publisher"

Truly, "the top of Mt. Washington had been blown off."

# 19

The eight-column streamer across Page One of the April
15, 1963 *N.H. Sunday News* announced:

## 'TOUGH' HOFFA DUE HERE

It announced the advent of the famous international president of the International Brotherhood of Teamsters, Ware-
housemen, Chauffeurs and Helpers, James R. Hoffa, of
Detroit, Mich. The *Sunday News* lead paragraph was a
little more colorful:

"New Hampshire truck drivers are rolling their 'Big Wheel' into the state tonight for reported 'get tough' negotiations with truck line owners."

The gist of the matter was this: as the service on the Boston and Maine Railroad declined in New Hampshire, the use of trucks had been on the upswing. (Or maybe it was because of the wider use of trucks for hauling that the Boston and Maine Railroad was on the decline.) In any event, the mills and factories in state, such as those in Manchester and Nashua, were shipping practically all of their finished merchandise to the metropolitan markets of New York and Boston by truck and these same trucks were bringing back materials for manufacture. With the network of highways which had sprung up, Manchester was only a few hours from New York and a trucker could make a round trip in one night. The 1,600 members of the Teamsters Union made it by far the state's largest single labor organization and the union contracts with the 45 leading trucking firms was expiring at midnight. The drivers were seeking a 40-hour week (a reduction from their current 45-hour work period) and a wage increase. The truck line operators were balking, but it was most obvious that the owners had no place to go. The bringing of the "tough" Hoffa to add to the negotiating team was a bit like adding another pitcher to the roster of the Taiwan Little League team.

William Loeb had twice, since the election of President Kennedy, gone out of his way to take swipes at Hoffa. On Dec. 12, 1960, Loeb said that Hoffa was "trying his darndest to smooth over his relations with President-elect Kennedy but it seems to us that his actions speak so loud it is difficult to hear what he says." And Loeb went on to allude to hypocrisy on the part of Hoffa for being indicted again, this time for using union pension funds in a land development scheme.

Since it was no secret that Loeb was hurting for funds, there are many who say that Loeb was at that time trying to butter up Joseph P. Kennedy again when the following editorial appeared in the Dec. 18, 1960, *Union Leader:*

"Having suggested earlier Joseph P. Kennedy—Jack's Old Man—for a high role in federal government, we are happy to applaud the elevation of another member of the clan, Brother Robert, to the Attorney Generalship.

"From what we saw of Robert during the campaign, and earlier in his role of counsel to the Senate labor rackets investigation, he may well be the ablest of all the younger Kennedys."

It was also the subject of much discussion among certain members of the news staff of the Union Leader Corp. when certain of these received from McQuaid memoranda which practically instructed them to "lean on" Hoffa in their news stories.

And Hoffa did come to Manchester and he was part of the strike talks at the Carpenter Motor Hotel. When he took his dinner hour, the labor chief caused quite a stir in the hotel's main dining room. The strike itself was delayed a week and Hoffa departed the city after a 24-hour visit. The teamsters went on strike the next Saturday night and within four days, Hoffa was back in town for talks aimed at settling the dispute. By Friday, April 28, both sides had agreed to terms and the five-day strike ended and Hoffa again left town.

It is significant that certain members of the news staff received memoranda from William Loeb at about this time informing them that James Riddle Hoffa was one of America's premier patriots and that he would be treated as such in the pages of those newspapers. What hardly anyone knew was that Loeb's advisor Alexander Cymrot had wanted to retire from his active business swirl and, from his New York headquarters, had "sold" the notes which he held on the Union Leader Corp. for a total of $500,000 to the Central States, Southwest, Southeast Area Pension Fund of the Teamsters Union.

The year 1962 was a year to think politics again in New Hampshire and it would be an unusual year because the voters would elect a full slate of everything—two U.S. Senators, two Congressmen and a governor. Loeb's tiresome and endlessly critical editorials had had the effect of splintering the Republican Party and creating, for want of a better description, the Loeb Party. There was the "Old Guard" G.O.P., and the Powell Republicans and there were those from both Republican and Democratic ranks who always figured that seeing nice things printed about themselves in the pages of the Manchester newspapers was far more important than a show of loyalty to any political organization. Then, too, there were the ultra-conservative Republicans, of whom Loeb claimed to be the standard bearer.

By mid-1962, William Loeb, publisher of the *Union Leader,* was sharing with the people of New Hampshire his thoughts in a Page One editorial every day of the week, except Sunday, and it was standard that a Manchester newspaper have a Loeb editorial, always biting, often scathing, adversely critical and in the harshest of terms.

Loeb had carried out his end of the divorce settlement which he had dictated to Governor Powell. He rapped Powell from every angle on every issue. In the Spring of 1962, Powell suffered a heart attack. Loeb observed the occasion by producing a news story quoting former Governor Robert O. Blood, a medical doctor, as saying that Powell should relax completely, but of course, Doctor Blood had not examined the patient. On another instance, on June 6, 1962, the *Union Leader* dutifully reported on Page One a heated dispute between Governor Powell and Former Attorney General Louis C. Wyman which allegedly took place in the men's locker room of the Manchester Country Club in which Powell is said to have threatened Wyman's bid for the Congressional seat from the First District.

The teams were choosing up sides early for the September primary: Powell would go for an unprecedented third consecutive term as governor and his principal opposition would be provided by John Pillsbury, of Manchester, vice president of the Public Service Company of New Hampshire, the state's largest electric utility, for which he earned the nickname, "Johnny Kilowatt"; a member of the Legislature where his record showed that he was never un-friendly towards the Public Service Company of New Hampshire; also an ordained minister who, after leaving the pulpit, had worked as a reporter for the *Union Leader;* he had, in addition, advocated a sales tax on occasion.

Sen. Norris Cotton would have only token opposition in his reelection bid for the full-term Senate seat, but the field for Bridges' former billet—that occupied temporarily by Sen. Maurice Murphy—was a wide-open affair. The state's two Congressmen, Perkins Bass, of Peterborough, of the Second District, and Chester E. Merrow, of Ossipee, one of the best Republicans the Democrats in Congress ever had, from the First District; Senator Murphy himself; and the candidate for whom Loeb was trying to move heaven and earth, Mrs. Doloris Bridges, the widow of the late senator.

This left the Congressional seats vacant and the field for each of them closely resembled the start of the Boston Marathon.

For fifteen years, Loeb had levelled his artillery at the Republican Party and he had scarcely bothered with the Democrats. After a full ten years of trying, he had won one with Powell in 1958, and after almost four years of Powell rule, the G.O.P. was a shattered mess. The Democrats, who had not elected a candidate to any major office since 1934—and this only in a contested Congressional race, the fight over which lasted two years—were quietly slipping in with a full slate of what appeared to be well-qualified candidates. In addition, the Democrats were filling out the ticket on the local level in all parts of the state, even for contests in which they had no hope of winning. For governor, Atty. John W. King, of Manchester, minority leader of the House; for full-term Senate, Atty. Alfred Catalfo, Jr., of Dover, former state chairman and Strafford County Attorney; for short-term Senate, Atty. Thomas J. McIntyre, former Laconia mayor and twice state campaign manager for Senator Kefauver; for Congress, Oliva Huot, of Laconia, in the First District; Mrs. Helen Bliss, of Rindge, and Eugene S. Daniell, of Franklin, in the Second District—and this represented the only primary fight on the Democratic slate.

Atty. James C. Cleveland, of New London, the state senator who had announced that he would support and lead the floor fight for the measure of censure against Loeb in the State Senate in 1957, announced for the Second District seat and he immediately moved to the head of the Loeb "hit" parade. In mid-June, Loeb called him a "One Worlder" with "left-wing economic inclinations," but Loeb had time to smash both Merrow and Bass a couple of weeks later for their Congressional votes in favor of the Kennedy trade bill.

He turned his fire towards Cleveland for the remainder of the month, harping on the fact that, as an attorney, Cleveland had defended a man who had a record of membership in the Communist Party and that Cleveland had defended the Supreme Court decision on prayer in the schools. Loeb went so far as to say it would be an "everlasting shame" to elect the New London man. McQuaid joined in and assailed Cleveland as an "inveterate egghead and liberal" on July 29 in the *Sunday News*. Cleveland responded in a Keene speech that Loeb was a "malignant growth" on the New Hampshire scene and a "cancer" among New Hampshire newspapers, to which Loeb replied that Cleveland had libelled him on Aug. 2.

By August 6, Cleveland had had enough and, in a speech at Colby Junior College in his home town, Cleveland said:

> "Mr. Loeb, I did not crawl out of a foxhole in the Pacific Theatre to come back home and crawl on my belly before a junior grade Goebbels whose combat experience has been chiefly confined to lawsuits and character assassinations . . . Far too long, New Hampshire has suffered the blighting, corroding and malignant influence of the Loeb papers. . . . Mr. Loeb implies that a lawyer who represents a Communist is a Communist. The logic has devastating implications. The Constitution of the United States emphatically guarantees the right to counsel and it is my position that Mr. Loeb is taking a position which undermines the right. More bluntly stated, Mr.

Loeb's position is dangerously subversive of important and hard-won Constitutional rights.

"Again, Mr. Loeb has not only implied that I am an atheist for simply stating that I thought the Supreme Court of the United States' decision was correct, he has openly accused the Court itself of being atheistic by referring to its recent decision as an atheistic one. This unbelievable attack on the Supreme Court is also subversive.

"In addition, I am also campaigning for an end to the reign of terror with which Mr. Loeb seeks to dominate our state by desecrating those who differ with his opinions."

The newsmen who covered the Cleveland outburst must have informed Loeb in Pride's Crossing because, in larger type, alongside the story of Cleveland's attack on Loeb, was Loeb's two-column answer titled: "Not a Communist, Not an Atheist—Just Confused." He said Cleveland had "very, very bad judgment" and, "We suggest that you take it easy or you will have to be checking with your doctor on your blood pressure every other day."

The readers had scarcely caught their breath before Loeb was blasting Powell two days later for announcing for a third term. There were many who wondered openly if Loeb were talking about Powell or of himself when he said in a Page One editorial:

"GOVERNOR POWELL, BY HIS ACTIONS IN RECENT MONTHS, HAS EVIDENCED THE TRUTH OF THE OLD SAYING THAT POWER FREQUENTLY CORRUPTS AND MAKES ARROGANT THOSE WHO HOLD IT."

McQuaid joined in Loeb's assault on Cleveland, and McQuaid got into a regular Sunday habit of also unleashing a blast at Congressman Bass. The Manchester newspapers, largely ignoring the Democrats, called for the nomination of a former Cotton aide, Chester Wiggin, in the First District, and Stacey Cole, a part-time *Union Leader* columnist, in the Second. The pontification in be-

half of Doloris Bridges reached its highest point when the
*Sunday News* announced September 9:

> "Her voice in the U.S. Senate, if she gets there, will
> be lifted on the side of U.S. security, solvency and strength
> —moral as well as physical—in both domestic and ex-
> ternal affairs."

The *Sunday News* also seconded Loeb's choice of Pillsbury
over Powell for the governor's chair.

During the voting on September 11, Pillsbury handily
defeated Powell; Louis Wyman ran away and hid from
the rest of the field in the First District G.O.P. race, and
Cleveland was a 700-vote winner in a field of six in the
Second District. For the short-term Senate seat, Perkins
Bass edged Mrs. Bridges by close to 1,700 votes, with Murphy a poor third and Merrow a badly trailing fourth.

Loeb's reaction was immediate. On September 13 he
soundly blasted Cleveland and Bass, but it was mostly Bass
whom Loeb tongue-lashed:

> "THE FACT THAT PERKINS BASS IS TO FILL
> OUT THE UNEXPIRED TERM OF STYLES BRIDGES
> IS, OF COURSE, NOTHING LESS THAN AN IN-
> SULT TO THE MEMORY OF STYLES BRIDGES
> AND TO EVERYTHING FOR WHICH THE
> BRIDGES' (sic) NAME STOOD.
>
> "Bass belongs to the group of World Federalist, interna-
> tional-minded Republicans, who together with their
> counterparts in the Democratic Party, have brought this
> nation to its present deadly peril in the field of interna-
> tional affairs.
>
> "The millionaire Bass, born with a gold spoon in his
> mouth, no more represents the hard-working people of the
> 2nd District than President Kennedy would."

Loeb, for all his interest in the New Hampshire campaign, had not been too busy during the month preceding
the primary to level two gratuitous blasts at President
Kennedy's wife, Jacqueline Kennedy, for taking a vacation
on the Italian Riviera. On August 30, Loeb said that it
was "in bad taste" for the First Lady to "spend the evening

dancing with an Italian count." Loeb queried, "Was this trip necessary?"

Apparently, the more Loeb pondered on Mrs. Bridges' defeat the more severe his aggravation became. He began calling for a run-off election. He reasoned that Bass, if he won the November election, would have been nominated with less than a majority vote; this was a fact, many pointed out, that never seemed to bother Loeb when his man Powell was twice elected to the governorship in the same manner. Mrs. Bridges, at Loeb's open urging, requested a recount, and she got it, but that was pretty sad; Bass lost 22 votes in the recount, Mrs. Bridges lost 32, for a net gain for Bass of 10 votes.

Time was running out and the Secretary of State was in the process of having the November ballots printed when Mrs. Bridges took her next step, again at Loeb's open urging. An advertisement had appeared in daily newspapers in Portsmouth, Keene, Concord, Laconia, Claremont and Lebanon on the day before the primary election, well over a quarter-page in size, signed by the "N.H. Committee for an Informed Electorate." The advertisement was headlined:

**"When a Loeb Newspaper Runs a Political Campaign, B E W A R E ! "**

The ad went on to state that Mrs. Bridges' campaign was clearly run by Loeb and his newspapers. The ad listed numerous public figures and the names Loeb had called them in print and it closed with the thought:

**"A VOTE FOR BRIDGES IS A VOTE FOR LOEB."**

Mrs. Bridges petitioned the N.H. Supreme Court, asking that Bass be ruled out as a candidate at the November election because, she claimed, the advertisement had really been one of his own and in placing the advertisement in nearly every New Hampshire newspaper (except those owned by Loeb) the cost would have put the campaign of Congressman Bass over the spending limit as set by law.

One witness summoned testified that she contributed to the cost of the ad because she was a McIntrye supporter and believed there was a connection between Mrs. Bridges and Loeb. Another witness testified that he "felt it was high time that the readers of the *Manchester Union* appreciated the tactics employed by the publisher of the *Union* in attacking people generally regarded as having good character." Still another said he thought "it was good that the electorate should be informed about that kind of journalism." And yet another said:

"My primary purpose in contributing to the ad was I felt it gave me a very slight but tangible way of expressing a conviction that I have long held, that the *Manchester Union Leader* does a great disservice to the state."

The hearing had its humorous aspects. But clearly, Mrs. Bridges was grasping at straws. The Supreme Court said:

"It would take more political naïveté than any member of this bipartisan court can muster to rule that this advertisement was not detrimental to the candidate Bridges and indirectly beneficial to the candidate Bass. However, it is clear on the evidence that many of the people who contributed to the cost of this advertisement did so as a protest against the editorial policies and what they consider to be the excesses of the newspaper [the *Manchester Union Leader*] which was supporting the candidate Bridges. This advertisement was prepared and caused to be published by a committee which assumed responsibility for it. RSA 70:8 [supp.] . . . Petition dismissed. All concurred."

## "She Was Robbed"

William Loeb said in his Page One editorial on Oct. 12, 1962, in the *Union Leader:*

". . . . It is quite clear to this newspaper that Mrs. Bridges was overwhelmed by a minority of eggheads and left wingers in the state, supported by the Bass fortune.

This confirmation was determined that Mrs. Bridges' conservative and patriotic ideas should not be heard in Washington. Because Mrs. Bridges played the game according to the rules and in the spirit of those rules, she lost out by a very small vote.

"NEW HAMPSHIRE WILL BE THE POORER WITHOUT THE BRIDGES REPRESENTATION IN WASHINGTON."

On the eve of the election, Loeb, as well as countless thousands of others, could sense that the Grand Old Party was in trouble, and he called for Republican support at the polls. He said he wasn't "taking back a single thing" he had ever said about Cleveland or Bass, and the only candidates "about whom we are enthusiastic are Senator Cotton, a great and distinguished public servant, and John Pillsbury." To quote Loeb:

"THE STATE'S MOTTO IS 'LIVE FREE OR DIE.' IF YOU WANT TO LIVE FREE, THEN DON'T LET THE KENNEDYS GET THEIR HANDS ON NEW HAMPSHIRE. VOTE FOR AS MANY DEMOCRATS FOR THE LEGISLATURE OR OTHER OFFICES IF YOU WANT BUT REMEMBER THAT A VOTE FOR A DEMOCRATIC GOVERNOR OR A VOTE FOR A DEMOCRAT FOR A NATIONAL OFFICE IN WASHINGTON WILL DESTROY THE INDEPENDENCE AND FREEDOM OF NEW HAMPSHIRE AND TURN IT OVER TO THE KENNEDYS."

Apparently not too many people were listening to William Loeb that season because when the smoke had cleared, John King had bombed "Johnny Kilowatt" Pillsbury and New Hampshire had a Democratic governor, the first since Fred H. Brown, of Somersworth, was elected for a single term in 1922; and the Granite State had a Democratic senator in Washington, Thomas McIntyre, who edged Bass by 4,500, the difference most assuredly having been the constant attack which Loeb had levelled at Bass, the Peterborough man, for many months. It was the first time since the same Former Governor Brown was elected in 1932 that New Hampshire had had a Democrat in the U.S. Senate.

It was the first time ever that two of the state's leading officials were of the Roman Catholic faith.

Senator Cotton was reelected by a large majority and Louis Wyman and James Cleveland gained the state's Congressional seats, Wyman in the first District, and Cleveland in the Second.

Meanwhile, Loeb was in serious trouble in Haverhill. The entire *Journal* operation was taking a serious toll of Loeb's finances, and he was raising money wherever he could get it. He got another half million dollars from the Teamsters in April, 1963, and he paid one installment of that debt with an editorial which covered almost three full columns in the *Union Leader* on June 7, 1963, in which he accused the Kennedys of engineering Hoffa's indictment in Chicago for wrongful use of his union's pension fund money. Apparently, the editorial stood Loeb in good stead with the labor leader.

Loeb's credit was good with Connecticut Mutual Life Insurance Company. In May, 1963, he got hold of another half-million of their dollars on a note for $673,000 from The Bank of New York, of which $173,000 was outstanding.

The noose fashioned by Newspapers of New England, Inc., was tightening. The *Journal* was fighting a losing battle.

The assassination of President John F. Kennedy in November, 1963, caused a brief hiatus in the political activity in the upcoming New Hampshire first-in-the-nation primary. Of course, the activity had been all on the Republican side, and the objective had been the defeat of the Democrat incumbent President, but now the object was a different person, President Lyndon B. Johnson.

The Republican Party in the State of New Hampshire, at this stage of the game, bore a strong resemblance to the *Titanic*. It was pretty much a foregone conclusion that Loeb would be a strong supporter of Sen. Barry Goldwater (R-Ariz.) for his part in the New Hampshire primary and it was just as strongly expected that Loeb would aim at least some of his blasts at New York Governor Rockefeller, who was making a serious move towards New Hampshire.

Just a few days after the New Year, Rockefeller arrived in New Hampshire for a campaign swing and Loeb met him with one of the most distasteful blasts of Loeb's career. The New York governor and his wife of many years, Mary Todhunter Clark, had been divorced and Rockefeller had remarried a divorced woman, Mrs. Margueretta Fitler Murphy, whose husband retained custody of their children as part of the divorce settlement.

Loeb greeted Rockefeller with a Page One job in which he called the New York governor a "wife-swapper" and he deplored "those Murphy children who were left without a mother." Given the many people in New Hampshire who remembered the story of Loeb in jail in Vermont and the many rumors and wild stories that had flown around about Loeb, the editorial probably didn't make too much of an impression on people throughout New Hampshire. The most that can be said for Loeb's display of meanness is that it didn't help.

When Goldwater arrived in January, the pages of the *Union Leader* greeted the Arizonian as if he had won both the World Series and World War II. But a mishap occurred, after one of Goldwater's first speeches in Concord, which would polarize the issues for Goldwater so extremely that he would spend the next months of his campaign explaining exactly what he meant. It also illustrates the extent to which the *Manchester Union Leader* can "shape" the news even when it doesn't want to.

Senator Goldwater, in a speech at the Eagle Hotel in Concord, said that, if elected, he would attempt to make Social Security voluntary. The city editor of the *Concord Monitor* handled the story himself, mainly because the speech was very close to deadline for the day, and the thrust of the headline and story was that Goldwater had called for the abolition of Social Security. That's what the headline said! Well, that wasn't too far from the practical truth of the matter. Most older people are interested in

Social Security and these people knew that if Social Security were put on a voluntary basis the whole system would crumble. In other words, persons would elect not to pay into the system when in their younger years, but would regret the decision at a later date. The *Union Leader*, whether or not intentionally, accepted the thrust of the *Monitor*'s version of Goldwater's speech and used it in later editorials. Because of the much wider circulation of the *Union Leader*, this idea was accepted in some cities across the country as having been the subject of a Goldwater speech in New Hampshire and he was called upon to explain his way out of this one until November of that year.

And one other "funny" thing happened to Goldwater on the way to the airport at the close of his New Hampshire visit. At that time the Cuban Government was threatening to shut down the water supply to the U.S. Navy Base at Guantanamo Bay and Goldwater was asked what he would do about this. He answered, "Send in the Marines." And the Arizona Senator had the same kind of explaining to do for the rest of his campaign.

Well, it didn't take New Hampshire people long to see that Rockefeller would never go over. He had Loeb on his back every inch of the way. He was a very, very liberal Republican, for another thing, and, as a matter of cold, hard fact, Rockefeller's recent marital developments didn't sit too well—and it wasn't only Loeb's "wife swapper" remark which pointed this out.

However, Goldwater proved to be somewhat of an intractable campaigner and at one point, after Rockefeller's supporters had continued to harp on Goldwater's alleged call for the abolition of Social Security, Goldwater reacted by saying that the Rockefeller people were misrepresenting his stand on Social Security and they were doing this because Jimmy Hoffa was running the Rockefeller campaign.

This was like spitting in Loeb's face. Even to mention the name of James Riddle Hoffa without bowing your head was, to Loeb at least, a mortal sin. So Loeb took to

Page One again and this time blasted his champion, Gold-water, with a honey which ran well over two columns:

## "A Lesson in Conservatism
## for Candidate Goldwater"

".... Conservatism does not consist, Sen. Goldwater, of fighting with labor unions or blaming the confusion about your views on Social Security on the head of the Teamsters' Union, James Riddle Hoffa. . . . The difficulty is that for years you have been speaking to a sympathetic audience of conservatives. NOW you are in the big time, trying to convince the uncommitted. . . . IF WE TOOK ALL YOUR OPPONENTS IN THE REPUBLICAN RANKS AND ADDED THEM TOGETHER, WE WOULD NOT HAVE ENOUGH BRAINS TO MAKE A SUCCESS OUT OF RUNNING A GOOD-SIZED PEANUT STAND. . . . THE DEMOCRATS OFFER US 'SNAKE-OIL LYNDON,' THE SMOOTHEST SALESMAN FOR SOCIALISM IN THE 20TH CENTURY.

".... Such statements as you made Wednesday morning—blaming your problems over Social Security on Mr. Hoffa—are so unfortunate. They're stupid, too, because one of the reasons why you have the support of this newspaper is thanks to Mr. Hoffa. When a group of 'liberal' Kennedy publishers ganged up on this newspaper, who saved it? Not a conservative but a loan from the Central States Southeast Southwest Pension Fund of the Teamsters. Mr. Hoffa and his fellow trustees realized a good loan when they saw it and, secondly, while we might not agree on many issues, he understood the basic goal of Americans, which, especially is to be free of tyranny by any one man or family . . ."

Loeb, of course, was confusing his readers, and there was no mistaking the fact that it was deliberate. The prior Teamsters' loans, either those made directly, or the "paper" which Cymrot had sold the pension fund, were not made to "save" the *Union Leader*. The *Union Leader* had proved to everyone's satisfaction that it could function without any guidance and that it could even make money in spite of Loeb. But the money was being used to rescue Loeb's folly, the *Haverhill Journal,* because while all this political activity was going on in New Hampshire, Loeb was taking a terrific pasting in Haverhill. The readers had been flocking back to the *Gazette,* as had the advertisers, and the *Journal* was beginning to look woeful. And, to boot, the federal courts were not taking kindly to Loeb's case in the anti-trust matters before it.

A groundswell had begun a few weeks earlier for the then-ambassador to Saigon, Henry Cabot Lodge, Jr., of Massachusetts, and what had been casually dismissed at the time was now assuming very real proportions. Lodge's name wasn't even on the ballot, which was another reason the Lodge cause was brushed aside, but even with the prospect of it being a write-in campaign, the Lodge candidacy was now assuming very real proportions. And it was at about this time that Loeb let Lodge have a blast which, if it proved nothing else, showed the long, long smoldering jealousy which Loeb had been harboring for his Beverly, Mass., neighbor, the grandson of the man who had treated the secretary to President Theodore Roosevelt as a servant.

He resurrected an issue which occurred in 1954 when Lodge was ambassador to the United Nations and a mixup had occurred for a meeting between the mothers of GI's missing in Korea, and Lodge, in New York City. Loeb's presentation was a three-column file picture (supposedly) and a letter from some Army captain in Colorado whose version of the event suited Loeb's taste.

Over-all it was a weak show for Loeb. He had blasted Rockefeller, Goldwater and Lodge, and Loeb must have realized he had painted himself into a corner, because he immediately began pushing Goldwater in a way no readers of the *Union Leader* had ever seen before. He even reproduced a routine thank-you telegram from the Goldwater organization that amounted to a four-column wide advertisement for Goldwater in the middle of Page One above the fold—an advertisement which no money could buy.

But the Lodge forces had done a good job with a very

popular candidate and even with a write-in campaign, the
results were nothing less than phenomenal·

| | |
|---|---|
| Lodge | 33,007 |
| Goldwater | 20,692 |
| Rockefeller | 19,504 |

Former Vice President Nixon, who had told the American public that he wouldn't be around for the press to
"kick around anymore" got 15,587 votes, although he was
not a candidate officially.

As had been noted earlier, the Republican Party in the
State of New Hampshire was a shambles, anyway, and the
disunity of the 1964 Presidential primary did nothing to
strengthen the ranks. In September, with the Democrats
already in the State House and one U.S. Senate seat, the
infighting began again.

Now, naturally, Wesley Powell announced that he'd like
to be governor again, and so did "Johnny Kilowatt" Pillsbury, and so did five other Republicans. Democratic Governor King was unopposed for renomination.

In the Congressional Districts, Congressmen Wyman, in
the First, and Cleveland, in the Second, both announced
for reelection; Wyman drew one primary opponent, Cleveland two. The defeated Democrat, Huot, of Laconia, was
faced with the prospect of a primary fight against Charles
F. Whittemore, of Pembroke, the scion of one of New
Hampshire's most respected Democratic families, while a
Claremonter, Charles B. Officer, was unopposed in the Second District. Pillsbury, Wyman and Cleveland were all
renominated and their respective opponents would be Governor King, Huot and Officer.

It is hard to believe that anyone knew exactly how
badly off the Republican Party in New Hampshire was in
1964. Goldwater, of course, had won the G.O.P. nomination for President, even though he had not won the New
Hampshire primary, and this did not augur well. It hadn't
happened yet that you could win the Presidency without
winning in New Hampshire, and the odds were weighing

heavily in favor of the man Loeb called "Snake Oil Lyndon" on the national scene, and then, too, Johnson had been a big winner in the New Hampshire primary.

When the smoke had cleared, it was a disaster. If the New Hampshire G.O.P. had looked like the *Titanic* before, it now looked like the *Hesperus*. Governor King was reelected by better than 2-to-1; Huot stole Wyman's House seat by close to 5,000 votes, and Cleveland, running in the gerrymandered Second District (where nomination by the Republicans had always been tantamount to election), wore out the skin of his teeth in edging by Officer, 62,680-to-62,382. This wasn't bad enough. The maximum representation which the Democrats had ever had on the five-man Executive Council had been two members, and this only rarely. In 1964, the people of New Hampshire elected four Democratic candidates to the Council. On the morning after Election Day, some people in New Hampshire were even looking towards the west to see the sun come up.

Excuses, excuses, excuses . . . everybody had his theory. But a part of everybody's theory was that if Loeb had kept his mouth shut, it never would have happened.

Loeb had other things on his mind, however. He was running out of appeals in the case of *Newspapers of New England, Inc., vs. Haverhill Journal*. The courts had ruled in favor of Newspapers of New England on appeal and against Loeb, mainly because they found that Loeb had certain advertisers on a salary from his *Journal* as members of an advisory board. The Union Leader Corp. suit (in behalf of the *Journal*) had been for $4.5 million and the countersuit had been for $3 million.

Derek Bok, then dean of Harvard Law School, had been appointed a master in the case to assess damages and had set the figure at $80,000, which was low, even by the layman's estimate. Atty. Robert Hunneman was then appointed master when Judge Wyzanski expressed displeasure at Bok's determination, and the *Gazette* management, which was actually Newspapers of New England, Inc., accepted on April 30 an assessment of $1,250,000.

Loeb claimed the fight had cost him more than $5,000,-
000, and the lead story on Page One of the June 1, 1965
*Haverhill Journal* was headlined, "City's Newspaper Competition Ends Today." The story began, "Haverhill's leading citizen died today. . . ." Loeb, of course, had his closing Page One editorial, which also announced the closing
of the weekly *Liberator*, in reality a weekly "shopper,"
the very obvious function of which was to practically give
away advertising to retailers so they would not use the
*Gazette*.

Richard Becker, general manager of the *Journal*, became
assistant general manager of the *Union Leader*. William
T. Montague, son of Loeb's longtime general manager in
Vermont and New Hampshire, who died in 1960, had been
sent years earlier as general manager of Loeb's Vermont
newspapers. When Loeb ceased publication in Haverhill
he had in his employ an 18-year-old boy, Clifton Noyes,
who was a dropout from Boston University after only a
few weeks of school. Loeb sent the 18-year-old Noyes to
Burlington as editor-in-chief of the *Vermont Sunday News*
and the *St. Albans Daily Messenger*.

To this day, Loeb has never gotten over the pasting he
got in Haverhill, mainly because he's still paying for it.
The Federal courts weren't kidding when they told Loeb
to get up $1,250,000, and he knew it, and he had to get
his hands on that money fast. So, with no place else to go,
Loeb went back to his friend Jimmy Hoffa, who by this
time was in serious trouble about irregularities in his pension funds—so much trouble that he was being tried in
Federal Court in Chattanooga. Loeb was able to get a loan
from the Central States, Southwest, Southeast Area Pension Fund in the amount of $2,002,656, using the Union
Leader Corp. as security once again.

Loeb tried to hassle the Boston newspapers as a display
of his anger. They had brief strikes on their hands in Boston during the 1960's and on each occasion, Loeb expanded
the press run of the *Union Leader* and trucked the newspapers to try to flood the Boston market. But it was a

poorly executed move. Loeb didn't have enough newsprint on hand, nor did he have the press capacity to undertake such a venture, again showing that Loeb's moves were rarely well thought out. Either that, or Loeb was woefully lacking in newspaper expertise, even after all these years.

A strange thing happened, though, when Loeb's staff was trying to go "big city." He had given orders to include in the *Union Leader* whatever features the Boston reading public had been used to; this included more race results and expanded sports news, including the "number" on which was predicated winners in the daily "pool."

There is an old adage in journalism which dictates that if you don't know what you're doing, don't do it; and another adage of experienced journalists is that it is okay to make a mistake in a stock table, an advertisement, but don't make one in a birth or death notice, or in a sports result; e.g., don't say Ted Williams was batting .350 when he was batting .351 because you'd get a call from every barroom in town.

The Boston "number" is based on a complicated subtotal and total of pari-mutuel payoffs at whatever major New England throughbred track is operating. (In New York, the "number" is much simpler; it is the last three digits before the decimal point in the total handle for the day.) The "number" is derived from the last digit before the decimal in a vertical line of numbers. At any rate, whoever was supposed to be figuring out the "number" at the *Union Leader* had no idea what he was doing. No sooner had the newspaper hit the streets in Boston than the Union Leader switchboard lit up like a Christmas tree. The sports department was put on stern, but anonymous, notice by the callers that if they couldn't carry the correct "number," don't carry any. If the sports department of the *Union Leader* did not heed this advice, they were further informed, it would be entirely possible that the present newspaper-publishing building could very well vanish from the earth and the premises be converted into a parking lot.

The *Union Leader* does not carry the "number" anymore.

# 20

The *Bridgeport Sunday Herald* had been a victim of the times, there was no doubt about it; it survived in 1965 only as a relic in a world which had grown beyond it. In its day, the *Herald* had had a healthy circulation in the southwestern reaches of Connecticut as a "second" Sunday newspaper, and it was eagerly looked to for ideas by many newspapers in the Northeast, because of its unique format. No one took the *Herald* particularly seriously; it was light reading; "No fear, no favor. The people's paper" was its motto. It had some good stories in it and it had most of the sports news and the social events of elite Fairfield County. The county, of course, is one of the wealthiest in the entire United States and most prep and high school athletes there had some college or university destination. The weekend doings of these athletes never were allotted much space in the metropolitan New York Sunday sports sections, but the *Herald* could be looked to for information as to who scored for Darien against New Canaan, and a little more than the line-score data on the doings of Taft versus Choate, and the like. In years gone by, there had been healthy competition to get featured position on New York's society pages and, naturally, not every bride made it, but the *Herald* was usually happy to give featured billing to a young lady whose father was *only* a vice president of a bank or major corporation, such factors having been the gauge used by society editors at *The Times* and *Herald Tribune,* although they would never admit it. These society page editors of the New York papers were some of the toughest guys in the whole city to do business with, to "plant" a story. In the *Herald,* it was entirely possible for the janitor's daughter to get some sort of featured billing on the occasion of her wedding or engagement.

The *Herald* had a flavor that was unique, to say the least. Headline writers could have a heyday; most of these

were New York newspapermen who "moonlighted" one
day a week in Bridgeport. A sports headline saying:

**Bowl Treat:**
**'Dogs Eat**
**Bear Meat**

would mean that the football team of Yale University had
defeated the varsity eleven of Brown University at the Yale
Bowl in New Haven the day before. And this type of
headline was not confined to the sports pages:

**Mary to Live**
**With William**

might mean that Miss Mary Whatsername of Cos Cob had
become the bride of William Whatchamacallit of Greenwich and the couple would reside in Greenwich. The
*Herald* was liberally sprinkled with cheesecake: Betty Gra-
ble, Rita Hayworth, and even "The Undisputed Queen of
Burlesque," Rose LaRose. It was light reading, all right,
but the *Herald* could never be counted upon to provide
the world and national picture in any depth. The circulation was quite high in areas such as Yale University
where, if word got around that the *Herald* had an intri-
guing interview with an outstanding national figure who
had been on the campus for an appearance or lecture, or
even an interview with a stripteaser, you could be assured
that the interview would have a new angle.

Of course, Sunday newspapers then cost 15 cents. During the 1950's, however, along came television and, on
Sunday afternoon, professional football became a Sunday
afternoon habit. Then, too, there were publications appearing, such as *Playboy,* which could more than match
the *Herald*'s cheesecake, and the *National Enquirer* which
could outdo the *Herald* in any one of a dozen directions
in feature-reading content.

So the *Bridgeport Herald* was on a long downhill slide
by the mid-1960's; its circulation was down to little more

than 32,000, and it appeared that there was little hope at all for the newspaper; 32,000 was not enough, not nearly.

The *Herald* was owned by Leigh Dannenberg, publisher, and a consortium of area businessmen, and, even though the Sunday newspaper for which the corporation was most widely known was losing money, the printing facilities were making money because they were busy all week long in the production of such journals as *The Irish Echo*, various "shopper" tabloids for large area stores, an alcoholic beverage trade newspaper and price list, and the like. The printing plant was profitable and the *Herald* was not. But the management was most reluctant to cease publication, mainly because the newspaper was an institution.

Donald I. Rogers had been financial editor of the *New York Herald Tribune* in the early '60's, but had accepted an offer from Dannenberg to rearrange the *Herald* and see if anything could be done to save it; Rogers was made editor and associate publisher. His first move was to temper the paper's politics. The *Herald* had been the only consistently Democratic newspaper in Connecticut and it had gone down the line on liberal causes for years and it was for this reason, if no other, that there were many homes in Fairfield County where the newspaper was not allowed. The type faces in the *Herald* were changed by Rogers to give it a fresher, more airy appearance, and its name was changed, to the *Connecticut Sunday Herald,* to give it a little wider currency outside the city of Bridgeport. But all of these efforts really didn't amount to much. There was apparently nothing that could save the *Herald,* and to continue to pump money into it was ridiculous; it was just one of those things.

In the mid-1960's, the New York City daily newspapers began to be plagued with strikes, and, seemingly, the picture would be more desperate for one or another of the city's newspapers at the end of each strike. The *Daily Mirror* had folded as a result of the 141-day strike during late 1962 and early 1963; it was known all over that the *Herald Tribune* was being held together through the good graces of John Hay Whitney, and the *Journal-American, World-Telegram* and the *Post* were just about making it, if they were, in fact, making it.

Another of these strikes occurred during the fall of 1965, and New York faced another period of no newspapers, this time during the height of the Christmas shopping season, potentially a severe blow to the economy of the city. The unions planned these strikes to occur at the most crucial times, but anytime a city is left without a daily press, it is a disaster which affects people in every walk of life, and New York had gone through it too many times.

Rogers got the idea to publish a tabloid newspaper on the presses of the *Herald* in Bridgeport and put it on trains into the city, where it would be distributed by drivers who were idled by the strike, using whatever transportation they could provide, to newsstands and stores which were devoid of any daily newspapers to sell. There were plenty of advertising salesmen available to visit their usual accounts and provide them with some advertising medium. The credit risk was borne by the *Herald,* but only the most legitimate stores were solicited.

Rogers needed a news staff and this was quickly assembled by a telephone call to the financial copy chief of the *Herald Trib,* who, in turn, visited Newspaper Guild headquarters and recruited some of his associates from the *Trib* who were on their way to, or returning from, picket line duty—most of that having been done in Ryan's Bar and Grill. The deal was simple: you'd work in Bridgeport and put out a daily tabloid for expenses every day, and when the bills were paid at the end, the profits would be split. It was a lot better than carrying a sign for one hour and watching the picket line for another hour from Ryan's; the $31 weekly strike benefits didn't go far in Ryan's and the day-old Horn and Hardart sandwiches at Guild headquarters were a delicacy which, although welcome, could easily be passed up.

Rogers had a couple of full-time editors at Bridgeport and these men became the make-up editors in the composing room. The journeymen visitors from the *Herald Trib* were the entire news staff. A couple of them monitored the New York radio stations which had gone to expanded news broadcasts during the strike and these men would track down the major stories that were breaking, using their own contacts at the New York Police or Fire Departments, on the telephone. A financial writer from the *Trib* who regularly covered Wall Street wrote a daily summary of financial activity, including the Big Board, the Amex and bond trading. A couple others rewrote the United Press International dispatches which were being received constantly on teletypes (the *Herald,* being a Sunday newspaper, could use the UPI dispatches only after noontime Saturday, but the teletypes repeated the same copy received by other newspapers on a seven-day-a-week basis). One man was assigned to rewrite UPI sports, mostly features from the UPI wire, the decision having been made to stay clear of race results and the like because a mistake could bring an invasion of the "contractors" who construct parking lots out of buildings.

The *Herald** was the name chosen for the strike tabloid and it was certainly no work of art. But, it was instantly popular and the press run was upped each day; it gave the subway riders something—anything—to read. At the close of each day, between the time the copy deadline had passed in the city room and the newspaper itself had rolled off the presses, a staff conference was held in Rogers' office, usually lubricated with a quart of Ballantine's Scotch. After *The Herald* had been checked for only the most glaring of errors, members of the "staff" would wend their way back

---

* There is very little question but that the naming of this newspaper *The Herald* was a deliberate attempt to "needle" the editors of *The New York Times,* whose propensity it has always been to capitalize the article in reference to their own newspaper. It must be realized that the rivalry between the staff members of the *Herald Tribune* and *The Times* was akin to that of Army and Navy, Harvard and Yale, etc. However, everyone who was anyone knew that the gentlemen and ladies of the *Trib* were more intelligent, better educated, more knowledgeable, more talented, better looking, better dressed, more articulate, wittier, more charming, and that the *Trib* had a hell of a good managing editor.

to New York City, or wherever, to return the next day, if the New York strike had not been settled.

The printers, stereotypers, pressmen and mailers on *The Herald* were regular employes of the corporation, who worked their normal hours on the publications in the "shop" and put out *The Herald* after normal working hours, at overtime pay.

At the close of one business day as the "staff" assembled in Rogers' office for a "conference," there were three quarts of Ballantine's Scotch on Rogers' desk, and, naturally, the question: What's the occasion?

Rogers explained that it was a momentous occasion indeed and a day worth remembering, so he had dug deep so that his co-workers could celebrate. For, he explained, he had received a telephone call from William Loeb, the New Hampshire publisher, and Mr. Loeb had called to congratulate Rogers and his staff on the "fine job" they were doing in publishing the strike newspaper. Rogers said Loeb was high in his praise of the content of the newspaper, and its make-up, and Rogers said that Loeb had said *The Herald* was something which would "make those New York publishers think twice." Besides, Rogers said Loeb told him that if Rogers were ever of a mind to sell his fine newspaper would Rogers please put Loeb at the head of the list of those who would like to purchase such a thriving enterprise.

It goes without saying that hardly a newsman in America had not heard of William Loeb. But it was still hard to credit Rogers' announcement that Loeb might seriously want to buy the *Bridgeport Herald*.

Was Loeb actually as foolish as he appeared? Was Rogers putting the staff on? How could anyone who had been in the publishing business for more than 20 years know so little about the business? Did this explain why he took such a pasting in Haverhill? Was it true that Loeb had been sued by his own mother and was this why he didn't live in New Hampshire? Was it true that Loeb got arrested and spent a night in jail for adultery with the Scripps heiress? All the normal questions came up which always pop up among newsmen at the mention of the name of William Loeb.

The theory was advanced that perhaps the reason for Loeb's continued survival in the Granite State was because of the intelligence level of those who live there, and this thought was quickly put down with the reminder that New Yorkers were known to fill arenas to capacity and beyond wherein there are demonstrations of professional wrestling and the Roller Derby, and the like; so there should be no more talk about the sophistication of Granite Staters. But rather wouldn't it be a better simile if a thought were given to the intelligence level of the Russian people or the Chinese, even, who were given one chain of thought in their press and, consequently, their politics.

Somewhere towards the end of the second quart of Ballantine's the real fun began. If Loeb was obviously so stupid as to buy this disaster, did anyone think he might be sold the Brooklyn Bridge? Well, not really, but there were several alternate proposals dished up. There was a hint that Loeb was operating, at least to some extent, with Scripps money and the rest coming from New Hampshire's own gold mine, the *Union Leader*. Why not make Loeb a decent offer, and forget about the Brooklyn Bridge? Maybe he could get Hoffa to bail him out again, and there was never too much pity lying around within a group of newspapermen for Jimmy Hoffa.

The final proposal which was arrived at during the middle of the third quart of Scotch, was that the *Bridgeport Herald* (now the *Connecticut Sunday Herald,* but newsmen usually refer to newspapers by their maiden names), the westbound subway shuttle between Grand Central Station and Times Square and the still-uncompleted Verrazano Bridge be offered to Loeb. Loeb would be permitted to buy as a present for his third (or was it his fourth?) wife, the *Brooklyn Daily Eagle* (defunct since World War II) and the Myrtle Avenue El, also in Brooklyn. If Loeb really wanted to dicker, or if he balked at the terms on the gifts for his wife, the offerers would throw in the Gowanus Canal and the Brooklyn-to-Staten Island ferry,

which would go out of service when the Verrazano Bridge
was completed.

It was a lot of fun, but no one really took Rogers seriously that Loeb had offered to buy—really *buy*—the *Herald*. It was incredible that anyone would actually pay real
U.S. money for the newspaper, least of all an established
publisher of more than 20 years experience. It had to be a
joke on Rogers' part. But Rogers had stuck to his story
and those who knew him best didn't really know whether
to believe him or not.

It was back to work in Bridgeport the next day, and
another edition of *The Herald* came off the presses. The
advertising continued to build and so did the circulation;
*The Herald* was filling a very large void. But publication
ceased abruptly the following Saturday when one of the
newsmen who was monitoring the New York radio stations
yelled that the New York strike was over. So were the days
of *The Herald*. Within a few days the "staff" of *The
Herald* had gotten its pay and no one seemed to have any
fault to find with his share of the proceeds.

But Rogers had been serious; he hadn't been kidding at
all. He quietly arranged for Loeb to be in contact with
Dannenberg. Within days, Loeb did give Dannenberg real
United States American money for the *Connecticut Sunday Herald*. Better than that—he bought only the Sunday
newspaper name and good will and existing contracts. He
wanted nothing to do with the printing plant itself and
even went so far as to agree with Dannenberg that he,
Loeb, would continue to have the newspaper printed at
Dannenberg's printing plant and would pay Dannenberg
for the printing costs.

Dannenberg, to this day, will not divulge how much
Loeb paid him. He is indeed reticent to discuss the matter
at all. His wife who retired—at the time of Loeb's purchase—as society editor of the *Herald,* confirms, however,
the facts of the matter.

It very, very soon became obvious to Loeb that he had
been had, but he couldn't blame anyone but himself. The
entire impetus of the transaction came from Manchester,

or was it Pride's Crossing? He had retained Rogers with a contract as editor and associate publisher, but within a year, he decided that Rogers was overqualified and, at Loeb's urging, Rogers undertook to its completion the authorship of *The Trials of Jimmy Hoffa: An Autobiography of James R. Hoffa—As told to Donald I. Rogers.* He was paid a good sum by Loeb for this effort.

Loeb later broke his contract with Dannenberg to have the *Herald* printed in the Bridgeport plant and to have the editorial and advertising offices located there. The office space drifted from Bridgeport to Stamford and finally to South Norwalk. The printing was done at the *Patent Trader,* another large printing plant, even larger and more modern than Dannenberg's, in Mt. Kisco, N.Y., which published many weekly newspapers in Westchester and Dutchess Counties, N.Y., and Fairfield County, Conn., as well as the *New York Amsterdam News,* consistently one of the nation's largest black newspapers, the *Gasoline Retailer* and other trade journals. The Mt. Kisco printing bill was no less expensive than the printing bill in Bridgeport.

No one on the staff of the *Connecticut Sunday Herald* ever saw Loeb, except the general manager who had been imported by him. Loeb existed only as a myth to the personnel, who were legion because the turnover was very, very high. The circulation of the *Herald* went even more on the down side of the roller coaster because it was simply impossible to sell his zany editorials to this articulate reading audience. Soon the weekly circulation of the newspaper went below the 30,000 level and was heading for 20,000. Loeb published his own circulation figures for this newspaper, as he did for some of his other newspapers, because by this time he had a running battle going with the Audit Bureau of Circulation, the largest and most widely recognized authority on circulation of all legitimate periodicals. It was Loeb's claim that the ABC was not "giving him a fair count."

The old Herald Printing Company on Lafayette Street in Bridgeport is no more. The printing equipment which was all of vintage year was sold to whoever wanted to buy, and the building itself was sold to the University of Bridge-port for use as a warehouse.

Mr. and Mrs. Dannenberg are retired and they live in one of those lovely houses on the quiet, private lanes south of the Penn Central Railroad Station in Westport, not far from Long Island Sound. There are some people in the area who will tell you that Dannenberg is a man with renewed faith after selling the Sunday newspaper to Loeb They say that it is not at all unusual to see Dannenberg take the short stroll to the shore of Long Island Sound in Westport and gaze dreamily at the opposite shore of Long Island itself. These same people say that Dannenberg firmly believes that one of these days the waters will part and he'll take a walk over to Sagamore Hill in Oyster Bay and take a look around.

# 21

It is rare to find a native of New Hampshire who has not been on skis at least once. And Bernard J. McQuaid is no exception. As a matter of fact, during the late 1950's, Mc-Quaid would regularly spend Wednesday afternoons ski-ing at New Hampshire ski areas. McQuaid and his party were always accorded the usual press accommodations— free use of the ski lifts and other area facilities. But then McQuaid gave up skiing, and during the King Administra-tion, one of McQuaid's pet crusades became the abolition of press passes to the state-owned ski areas at Cannon Mountain in Franconia Notch and Mount Sunapee in the Dartmouth-Lake Sunapee Region. This put the two state-owned areas at a severe disadvantage competitively with the many, many other privately owned ski areas. The skiing and recreation writers from the metropolitan newspapers who publicized skiing as a New Hampshire attraction naturally went to the areas where the press was customarily received. The *Sunday News* even went so far as to say that the free press passes would not be accepted anymore by members of the newspaper's own staff. (It would later be determined that staff members of the Manchester newspapers receiving a press pass and staff members of the Manchester newspapers using state-owned ski lifts free were two different things.)

But when it came to the junkets run by the U.S. Department of Defense for newspaper people, it was a different story and Bernard J. McQuaid was first in line to go on the latest sight-seeing tour of the nation's military might, be it a cruise on an aircraft carrier or a flight to inspect a new foreign installation. If McQuaid's diabetes was kicking up so badly he couldn't enjoy skiing any more, he could, at least, enjoy mixing with the "gold braid."

With the elections of 1966 coming up fast, the Manchester newspapers, both the *Sunday News* and the *Union Leader,* were in trouble, and the main trouble was that the "Loeb Party" had no candidates. They were okay as long as they could run Wesley Powell or Doloris Bridges, but Powell's divorce from Loeb was apparently still in effect, and Mrs. Bridges had lost any effectiveness she had ever had as a viable candidate. For McQuaid to dip into his stable and come up with Mayor John Shaw of Rochester again was getting to be a tired act. And, really, now there was the Republican Party, the "Loeb Party" and the "Powell Party," all splintered off the same core, against the Democratic Party which was holding all the cards with the governorship, four Council seats, one each in the U.S. Senate and in the U.S. House.

But 1966 would be important. McIntyre's short term would be over in the Senate and the Republicans of all three factions felt they had to win that one back. John King's second term was up in the State House and the Republicans wanted that back, too. And, according to the G.O.P. philosophy, Louis Wyman had to go back to Congress.

On one of his Department of Defense junkets to Goose Bay, Labrador, Bernard J. McQuaid stumbled across Brigadier General Harrison R. Thyng, of Barnstead, N.H., a small community (population 1960: 850) about 20 miles northeast of Concord, the capital. General Thyng was being retired from the U.S. Air Force in the near future and his plans were to return to his home in Barnstead to take up residence. McQuaid had found his man, or, at the very least, he had found one of his men.

It was not long before the readers of McQuaid's newspaper—and to some extent, the daily *Union Leader*, also —were introduced to General Thyng. According to McQuaid's version, Thyng was a combination of the Wright Brothers, Billy Mitchell, Eddie Rickenbacker, Alvin York and Rocky Marciano: an authentic U.S. American hero, who was willing to sacrifice the solitude and recreation of his retirement years to serve honorably as the junior U.S. Senator from the State of New Hampshire.

A Manchester man who was serving as head of the State Department of Welfare, James J. Barry, was having his troubles all around; the members of the Welfare Department were unhappy with Barry and Governor King was unhappy with Barry. It is only fair to say that Barry was also unhappy with members of the Welfare Department and Barry was also unhappy with Governor King, even though they had been boyhood buddies. Loeb spotted a viable candidate, by Loeb's standards, in James J. Barry, and it soon became evident to readers of the Loeb press that Mr. Barry could be relied upon to honorably serve as governor of his native state for the next two years—that is, after William Loeb got him elected on the Republican ticket.

As for the rest of the slate, well, the *Union Leader* and *N.H. Sunday News* could always support Louis Wyman, the one-term Congressman who was displaced. In the Second District, Cleveland, despite his narrow escape the last trip, was looming as strong as any Republican incumbent had ever loomed in the western part of the state, mainly because Cleveland was doing his homework, and, besides,

it became Loeb policy to stay out of that one. Loeb had
found out that Congressman Cleveland could and would
fight back and Loeb found Cleveland's remarks about him
being 4-F mighty embarrassing. So the McQuaid-Loeb
board of directors apparently decided to let well enough
alone. Thyng-for-Senate and Barry-for-Governor was the
entire "Loeb Party" ticket.

But the Old Guard of the Republican Party had another
candidate in mind as their standard bearer: former Governor Gregg. There was also a new faction to consider,
younger party members who were getting established in
their professional and family lives and who were ready to
strike out in politics, and who were willing and able to
come up with a dollar or two to help their cause. There
were quite a few people who figured that it was well and
good for New Hampshire to be the only state without a
sales or income tax, but the state services were suffering
so badly that it was unrealistic not to have a broad-based
tax, and Rep. Alexander M. Taft, of Greenville, who had
lost a tough fight for the speakership of the N.H. House,
jumped in the G.O.P. gubernatorial primary advocating
new taxes.

For the seat occupied by Senator McIntyre, the Republicans did not want to be restricted to General Thyng,
whoever he was. Mrs. Doloris Bridges had diligently appeared before women's clubs and any group who'd listen
for four years, merely keeping her hopes alive. She announced as a candidate. Former State Chairman William
Johnson was talking about running and so was Former
Governor Dwinell. Even though Johnson and Dwinell
were from neighboring towns, they got their signals crossed
and they both became candidates. Some fellow named
Ayer, from Bradford, became a candidate. And who else?
Why, Wesley Powell!

Loeb outdid himself. It was becoming more and more
amazing how those Manchester newspapers could take a
straight news story and make campaign literature out of
it, but they did, with Barry and Thyng, whoever he was,
the chief beneficiaries. To say that Loeb was unkind to

the man he called "King John" King (who secretly liked it because he has always been a Shakespeare buff) while he was praising Barry to the skies, and to say that the treatment received by Senator McIntyre was pejorative while General Thyng was being made to look like Nathan Hale, would be to say that the Johnstown Flood caused wet grounds.

The final score:

> For Governor:
>> James J. Barry, Manchester, r        20,791
>> Hugh Gregg, Nashua, r        33,946
>> Alexander M, Taft, Greenville, r        14,845
>
> For U. S. Senate:
>> Doloris Bridges, Concord, r        7,613
>> Lane Dwinell, Lebanon, r        10,781
>> William R. Johnson, Hanover, r        17,410
>> Wesley Powell, Hampton Falls, r        18,145
>> Harrison R. Thyng, Barnstead, r        22,741

(The fellow Ayer in the Senate race and three others in the gubernatiorial contest drew the solid support of their neighbors, relatives and good friends.)

Governor King and Senator McIntyre, Democrats, were unopposed in their primary nomination and Congressman Huot had only token opposition in the First District. In the Second District, the Democrats had gone back to their old "why bother?" routine. Louis Wyman, seeking to regain his Congressional seat in the First District for the G.O.P., won the nomination in a cakewalk.

Loeb and McQuaid once again exceeded all expectations in regaling the virtues of General Thyng, and still no one knew who he was. Senator McIntyre, on the other hand, campaigned almost exclusively against Loeb. He would always have an empty chair on the podium alongside him at public appearances and he would address his remarks to the "man from Pride's Crossing" and other appellatives which were hardly as genteel. McIntyre worked hard, appearing night and day all over the state in his efforts to retain control of the Senate seat. When he couldn't be in two places at one time, his wife, Myrtle, who had herself been very active during the Kefauver campaigns and was thus well known, appeared on behalf of her husband.

William Loeb was never one to sit at the sidelines of any political contest; apparently it was his mission in life to "guide" his readers. And there was absolutely no way in hell he could "guide" his readers behind Hugh Gregg. Finally Loeb came out in favor of a third term for the man he called "King John." Loeb's move was as clear as a cold winter's day. There wasn't a soul in New Hampshire with an I.Q. of 10 or above who would bet counterfeit money on Gregg. After the election Loeb could always say he supported "King John." Within weeks, it would come out somehow that Loeb, in fact, got him reelected. (They weren't disappointed.)

After the smoke of battle had subsided, "King John" had done it. He was the first New Hampshire governor seated for three consecutive terms, a Democrat at that, and Senator McIntyre got a full term in the United States Senate, both by comfortable 18,000-vote margins. Otherwise, things were normal in the Granite State. Louis Wyman went back to Congress where he could lock forces with Congressman Cleveland, and the Republicans got back four seats on the five-member Council.

As far as the reading public was concerned, more particularly the reading public who relied on the *Union Leader* for all the news, New Hampshire as of that day began to have only one U.S. Senator because it has been a rare day indeed since that Election Day when the name of Thomas J. McIntyre has appeared in print in Loeb's journals.

On November 24, 1966, Mrs. Katherine W. D. Loeb, mother of the publisher, died at her home at Oyster Bay Cove, Long Island, at age 90.

It was no secret to her close friends that she had long since disowned her only child and that he would have no part at all in her estate, which was considerable. William Loeb did show up in Oyster Bay with his wife, Nackey, and they were the proper grieving couple. However, according to Mrs. Eleanore McAllister and Penelope Loeb, who were closest to Mrs. Loeb, a very strange tableau unfolded at the conclusion of the funeral services. There were many persons in attendance whom Loeb did not want to see, least of all with whom to discuss his late mother. At the conclusion of the service, Loeb and his wife went into the vestry of Christ Church of Oyster Bay with the rector and waited until the rest of the mourners left the church. Then, according to Mrs. McAllister, Loeb went to the door to greet the executives of his newspapers who were just then arriving and the rector came onto the altar and conducted a second and identical funeral service.

Mrs. Loeb had named Atty. Alexander C. Dick and Chase Manhattan Bank as executors and trustees. Both parties retained Atty. Clarence C. Meleney to represent them and when he filed the will for probate in the Surrogate's Court in Mineola within a few days, a long and drawn-out dispute over the will began. Loeb claimed that "by fraudulent representations, coercion and undue influence" mainly on the part of Attorney Dick and Loeb's second wife, Eleanore McAllister, he was excluded from the will, even though his mother had notified him repeatedly that she had taken that course at the time she rewrote her will in the early 50's. Loeb's letters to his mother confirm that he knew he was excluded, and they confirm he knew he was excluded because of Nackey.

Loeb engaged the prestigious New York law firm of Royall, Koegel, Rogers and Wells. Both Attorney Dick and Mrs. McAllister knew that Loeb was a die-hard litigator and they also knew he'd spend any money at his disposal to fight the will. Mrs. Loeb had left the bulk of her assets to Katharine Penelope Loeb and had said in Article Eighth of her will:

> "In making the foregoing disposition of my property and estate I am mindful of the fact that I have made provision for my son, WILLIAM LOEB, only upon the contingencies specifically set forth in 'ARTICLE SIXTH' above. During my life time I have assisted him financially in several business ventures and have made him several substantial gifts."

Article Sixth specified that, should Penelope survive Mrs. Loeb, but die before age 30 leaving no issue, her son, William Loeb, would get some revenue from a trust estate.

Mrs. Loeb's estate was valued at close to $1,000,000.

Attorney Dick and Mrs. McAllister saw a major battle looming with Loeb and they hired Atty. Philip Handelman to conduct the proceedings of the will contest. Attorney Handelman took numerous depositions in preparation of his case for the court fight which would come up for a hearing in 1968.

The Spring of 1967 was not a happy time for William Loeb. James Riddle Hoffa was going to jail. Hoffa had been convicted of jury tampering and mail fraud in connection with a trial on misuse of pension funds, and on March 7, 1967, he began a term in Lewisburg, Pa., penitentiary.

And on his own particular labor front, Loeb was not having much better news. The unions at the Union Leader Corporation hadn't been very heavy in their demands for many, many years, since the time profit-sharing had begun in the late 1940's. When Loeb had stopped paying profits and gone into Haverhill in the fall of 1957, the unions and their members went along with Loeb, hoping for a victory, and resultant greater benefits, from Haverhill. But when Loeb had to borrow money to pay the judgment in Federal court over Haverhill and then turned right around and bought a newspaper in Connecticut which wasn't worth peanuts, or even their shells, the unions in Manchester rebelled. The Manchester employes felt that it was okay for Loeb to do what he wanted with his own money, but, as for them, they'd take an annual wage increase and whatever benefits they could get written into a contract and forget about profit-sharing.

Meanwhile, Penelope Loeb was a very good student at Webutuck High School, the regional school serving Amenia and surrounding towns—so good a student, in fact, that she was awarded a New York Board of Regents scholarship worth about $1,000 over a four-year period, if she were to

use the scholarship money at a college or university within
New York State and operated under the Board of Regents.
Penelope had her eye on Vassar College in Poughkeepsie,
not far from Amenia. Her acceptance of the scholarship
included Penelope's submission of a form countersigned
by her parents. Mrs. McAllister signed the form and it was
mailed to William Loeb so that he could sign in order
that his daughter might accept the scholarship.

The scholarship form was returned unsigned.

# 22

The accuracy of the New Hampshire first-in-the-nation
Presidential primary as a political barometer had won considerable national respect by 1968. And it was sometime
during the middle of 1967 that the trial balloons began
to hover over the Granite State. Lyndon B. Johnson would
finish out his first full term at the end of 1968 and would
be eligible for reelection, and most New Hampshire Democrats assumed he would achieve just that. However, President Johnson had his hands full with the Vietnamese
situation and he was doing nothing to heat up the luke-
warm support he was getting.

But if LBJ was not paying a lot of attention to New
Hampshire, there were an awful lot of people who were:
Michigan Gov. George Romney, New York Gov. Nelson
Rockefeller, California Gov. Ronald Reagan, Minnesota
Sen. Eugene McCarthy and a character named the "new"
Richard Nixon.

It was also a primary, in 1968, which saw a new level of
fun, frivolity and facetiousness which did, in fact, have
touches of humor at first but which wore thin as the campaigning wore on and the American public, if not the
foolish candidates themselves, realized that "playing games"
in a real live election was really no joke, after all.

First of the major candidates on the scene was Governor Romney who, many months earlier, had been a "hawk" on the matter of Vietnam, but who had changed his tune to the extent that he was saying, "We have relied too heavily on search and destroy rather than clear and hold." Romney, a Mormon who would not campaign on the Sabbath, was clearly established as a "dove" with further pronouncements such as, "We must fight harder for peace," and, "Morality and patriotism is waning in America."

The man who was moving with the most force was Senator McCarthy who had a campaign organization which was clearly operating on high blower. Advocating an immediate end to the Vietnam hostilities, McCarthy had attracted the avid support of college kids from all over the United States who were flocking to New Hampshire to be "part" of the McCarthy effort. They were well-trained, earnest, and effective, and they conducted door-to-door canvasses in every part of the state in support of the Minnesota Senator. Most of these visitors were "camping out," sleeping in gymnasiums in sleeping bags which they had brought with them, or making the best of any other makeshift facilities, at which college students excel. McCarthy's bandwagon was really getting up steam, and noticeably so when the colleges broke for Christmas and semester's end. The Democratic "strong men," particularly Governor King and Senator McIntyre, were staying away from this action, obviously awaiting the call from the Commander-in-Chief.

It was a relatively simple matter to become a candidate for the office of President of the United States in New Hampshire. Until 1952, voting had been only for delegates to the respective major party political conventions, which was still the case in 1968. But, beginning in 1952 came the Presidential preference primary, which as noted earlier became known as the "beauty contest," and it was a simple matter to become a candidate. The filing period was from 60 to 46 days before the primary and nearly anyone could walk into the office of the Secretary of State, present some sort of petition with the signatures of 50 persons from each of the two Congressional Districts and the person was a candidate and his name would appear on the ballot, with the person's own approval.

[The 1971 Legislature changed all this. Henceforth, in order to be on the Presidential preference ballot, a candidate must have 500 signatures from each Congressional District—the signatures are checked very carefully—and pay a filing fee of $500. It was still possible for a person to file in absentia, but in this case, he would have to confirm to the Secretary of State that it was done with his approval.]

On Jan. 12, 1968, among the first to file for the office of President was George Romney and on hand to greet him at the office of the Secretary of State were the usual large number of newsmen who gather in New Hampshire every four years, and a character named "Princess St. Swanee Running Water" who, in Indian garb, was "hootin' and hollerin'" and telling the television network film crews that she was going to give "old George a big smacker" when he arrived, saying to the nearest film crew, "That should make a good picture for you, honey."

Let the record show that George Romney was able to avoid Princess St. Swanee Running Water but he was not able to avoid the coterie of newsmen who asked, how come you are now a dove and you used to be a hawk, and the Michigan governor said, "I was brainwashed by the generals when I was in Vietnam." He had recently returned from an official tour. George Romney might have saved himself the trouble of having gone inside the office of the Secretary of State to file because as soon as he said, "I was brainwashed," he was dead, politically, that is.

By this time there were many "Romney Is Right" signs blossoming out in New Hampshire and it was only a matter of days after the brainwashing remark by Romney that there became almost as many "Nelse, No One Else" signs going up, urging the yet-undeclared candidacy of New York Governor Rockefeller.

William Loeb, like most other political observers in New Hampshire, hadn't taken Senator McCarthy seriously at first, but now was beginning to do so. The state's Democratic bigwigs became more vocal in behalf of President Johnson, although the chief executive said that he would not be an official candidate in the state. Loeb began to blister both the President and McCarthy. He had already identified the President as "Snake Oil Lyndon" and he harped on this theme, while for the Minnesota Senator, he chose the appellative, "Skunk's Skunk's Skunk." Loeb also started circling and jabbing towards Rockefeller, but there would be a lot of time left. He had already indelibly hung Rockefeller with the "Wife Swapper" tag.

Loeb concentrated most of his efforts in pushing Richard Nixon who had been filed as a candidate with the Secretary of State. McCarthy, of course, filed, and then who should appear on the scene but Harold Stassen, for the fourth time, this time wearing a new reddish-brown toupee. The former Minnesota governor said that it reduced the glare of the television lights and helped keep him warm. The ball point pen manufacturer, Paul Fisher, of Chicago, was back with a new supply of gift pens and the old idea of abolishing taxes. And there were a lot of other newer faces:

Elmer Coy, a Toledo, Ohio, insurance executive who campaigned on the platform that he would serve only one term because that's as long as it would take him to get the job done that had to be done;

Don Dumont, a Chicago man who billed himself as the "good-humored square" and who generously stated that Nixon would make a good Vice Presidential candidate for himself;

Bill Evans, Jr., of Wyckoff, N.J., the first active campaigner on the scene, who arrived in mid-1967 plugging away on a "disengagement" plan for Vietnam;

Herbert Hoover, of Oskaloosa, Ia., whose candidacy was based on his claim that he was a fourth cousin of the late President;

Willis Stone, the "Liberty Amendment" candidate from California, who opposed the unification of the armed forces;

David Watamull, the first native Hawaiian to run for

the Presidency, who imported a troupe of hula dancers to perform throughout snowy New Hampshire;

John G. Crommelin, the retired admiral who led the "revolt of the admirals" during the Truman Administration;

Richard E. Lee, who told New Hampshire voters they should vote for him because he was related to Gen. Robert E. Lee;

Lar Daly, of Chicago, who toured the state of New Hampshire dressed in an Uncle Sam suit;

Chief Burning Wood, alias Austin Burton, of Greenwich Village in New York City where he sold "psychedelic posters and all that jazz" who decided after a while he'd like to run for Vice President.

Princess St. Swanee Running Water came back to the State House again after her encounter—or would-be encounter—with George Romney. The Princess had decided that she'd like to be President and she told Secretary of State Robert Stark just that and he told her she'd have to use her real name which was Faye Carpenter Swain. The Princess came back again and waved some signatures under Mr. Stark's nose and the secretary all but disqualified her on the spot. (Disputing her signatures, he told the Princess to go back to the tepee.)

On February 24, Rockefeller released a statement that he would indeed make a run at the Presidency if he were drafted. That only put new fire into the efforts in New Hampshire on his behalf. It also put new fire into William Loeb who used what was now his everyday Page One pulpit to preach:

> ". . . We have always thought that Rockefeller had all the arrogance that goes with great wealth, and very little sense of responsibility. Past performance has not convinced us of the validity of Rockefeller's vows, even when given under oath."

The McCarthy campaign had gained a lot of momentum, and Governor King and Senator McIntyre headed a late charge for the President, even though it would have to be a write-in campaign, since the President had not become an official candidate during the filing period. They bought big newspaper ads to put their point across. And Rockefeller's forces, also faced with the prospect of a write-in effort stepped up their efforts, both in media advertising and with a huge direct mail campaign. Loeb reacted this way:

"Nelse the Knife . . . is a man who has used the political corpses of his fellow Republicans as stepping stones to power."

Loeb's newspapers had been making more and more mention of the name of a man named Meldrim Thomson, Jr., of Orford, in one connection or another. Then one day, late in the game, Thomson was featured on Page One of the *Union Leader* as the sponsor of a drive to nominate Gov. Claude Kirk of Florida as Vice President, and Thomson announced that he had sent out a large quantity of letters to that effect. Two questions occurred to most Granite Staters: Who was Meldrim Thomson, Jr.? And who was Claude Kirk?

B. J. McQuaid of the *N.H. Sunday News* got into the act by calling a "vote for McCarthy a vote for Ho Chi Minh." McQuaid also said that as far as Romney and Rockefeller both were concerned, "for unbridled hypocrisy there has never been anything like it."

Richard Nixon had made two lengthy campaign swings through the Granite State and the election eve polls showed him a 7-to-1 choice over Romney, the only other serious contender on the long, complicated ballot. In the final days of the campaign, the largest political ads were in behalf of Nixon and President Johnson, respectively.

And when it was all over, Nixon was an overwhelming victor on the Republican side, piling up a total of 80,666 votes to 11,241 write-ins for Rockefeller, the only other candidate to reach five figures.

On the Democratic side of the ledger, President Johnson got 27,520 write-ins and McCarthy got 23,263 votes. McCarthy, in fact, finished third in the Republican voting with 5,511 write-ins.

It was a resounding victory for Nixon. And although, on

paper, Johnson had won, that victory wasn't so clear. Mc-Carthy had won most of the delegates to the Democratic national convention and they were pledged to vote for the Minnesota Senator until they were released by the candidate, according to N.H. election laws. For Johnson, it was a defeat.

President Johnson may have been called "Snake Oil Lyndon" by Loeb and he may have been called a lot of other things by a lot of other people, but he was never called a stupid politician. On March 31, 1968, he went on nationwide television to explain to the American public the situation in Vietnam. Towards the end of his speech, totally unexpected, he said:

> "I have concluded that I should not permit the Presidency to become involved in the partisan divisions that are developing in this political year . . . I do not believe that I should devote an hour of my time to any personal partisan causes or to any duties other than the awesome duties of this office . . . Accordingly, I shall not seek and will not accept the nomination of my party for another term as your President."

Anyone who cared enough to analyze the New Hampshire primary knew that it had knocked LBJ right out of the box. William Loeb was one of these and he said:

> ". . . It is quite obvious that the President, just as he has surrendered to Ho Chi Minh on a national basis, has surrendered to Bobby Kennedy on a political basis. Anybody who thinks that Bobby Kennedy can now be blocked from receiving the nomination is simply dreaming . . .
> "THEREFORE, WHAT THE NATION IS FACED WITH IS THE DESPERATE NEED TO RALLY ALL RESPONSIBLE INDIVIDUALS, WHETHER THEY BE DEMOCRATS OR REPUBLICANS, BEHIND THE PRESIDENTIAL CANDIDACY OF RICHARD NIXON."

Former Attorney General Robert F. Kennedy had received only 606 write-in votes in the New Hampshire primary which he had purposely stayed out of. He had instituted the government's case against Hoffa. However, his campaign was moving forward on other fronts in other states.

In New York and on Long Island, lawyers for the late Mrs. Katharine W. D. Loeb had been busy gathering evidence and depositions to prepare for a court fight over the publisher's mother's will and in April, 1968, the case was ready for trial. On the day the Surrogate was to set a date for the trial, Loeb's attorneys arrived in the Mineola courthouse and informed the court they were unable to prove a *prima facie* case and asked for leave to withdraw the objections of their client. On July 3, 1968, an order was entered admitting the will to probate with Atty. Alexander C. Dick and The Chase Manhattan Bank as executors. Certain lawyers' fees were paid at that time. As matters proceeded in the settlement of the million-dollar estate, the executors became faced with an unexpected and much more serious situation, for on June 27, 1968, attorneys of the firm of Royall, Koegel, Rogers and Wells, in behalf of their client, William Loeb, in a separate action had sued the executors of Mrs. Loeb's estate for 75% of the net estate and introduced the following document upon which Loeb based his suit for breach of contract:

"AGREEMENT, dated this 27th day of June, 1941, by and between KATHARINE W. D. LOEB AND WILLIAM LOEB, JR., both residing in the Town of Oyster Bay, County of Nassau, State of New York.
"WITNESSETH:
"(1) In consideration of the agreements hereinafter made by William Loeb, Jr., Katharine W. D. Loeb agrees to give, devise and bequeath by Will to William Loeb, Jr., at least seventy-five per cent (75%) in value of her net estate at the time of her death or to otherwise provide for the transfer to him upon her death.
"(2) William Loeb, Jr., in the event of his receiving by gift, devise, bequeath or any other means selected by said Katharine W. D. Loeb at least seventy-five per cent (75%) in value of her net estate upon her death, agrees to pay to each of the sisters-in-law of said Katharine W. D. Loeb, to

wit, to Louisa Loeb Neudorf, Amelia Olive Loeb, and Lillian May Loeb, and to Helen M. Gilroy, sister of said Katharine W. D. Loeb, annuities at the rate of One thousand two hundred dollars ($1200.) per annum each, in equal monthly instalments commencing with the death of said Katharine W. D. Loeb and to continue during their respective lives.

"(3) It is the intention of the parties to this agreement that the agreements hereinabove made by William Loeb, Jr., shall be enforcible by action at law or other means commenced or taken by an Executor of the estate of said Katharine W. D. Loeb as her successor, or by the respective third party beneficiaries, to wit, Louisa Loeb Neudorf, Amelia Olive Loeb, Lillian May Loeb, and Helen M. Gilroy.

"(4) This agreement shall not be assignable or transferable by any party hereto in any manner.

"IN WITNESS WHEREOF, the parties hereto have executed this agreement as of the day and year first above set forth.

"Katharine W. D. Loeb   (LS)

"William Loeb            (LS)

This opened a whole new bag of worms for the executors of Mrs. Loeb's estate and it began a court battle which would last until 1971. The Chase Manhattan Bank and Attorney Dick again retained Attorney Handelman and they opposed the claim by William Loeb. The affidavit of Attorney Dick tells this part of the story:

"The agreement set forth (above) was mysterious on its face, and grew more so on investigation. Being unwitnessed and unacknowledged, its very existence was open to question but for a single entry in the diary that decedent kept faithfully until a few days before her death. On Saturday, June 28, 1941, she wrote: 'Took my will, agreement with Bill, &c. to O.B. (Oyster Bay) Trust Co. box.' Two days later she went to Vermont for the summer. Later that year she furnished Bill with money to buy the St. Albans Messenger. The purchase was consummated on or about October 24th. Bill was represented by Mr. Lauson Stone, who drew the agreement. (Mr. Stone is now a partner in Royall, Koegel and Wells.) In the following year Bill acquired a substantial interest in the nearby

Burlington News. His mother provided $106,000 for his buying into these two Vermont newspapers.

"From the face of the agreement, it can be deduced that Mrs. Loeb's object was to make sure that *if* she left her estate or a major part thereof to Bill he would pay to her sister and three sisters-in-law annuities of $100 per month each. Mr. Lauson Stone indicated in his testimony that this was her prime concern, and in fact the only object of the agreement. Bill testified that he took his executed copy of the agreement to Oyster Bay and promptly forgot all about it. Later, all his papers at Oyster Bay were sent to him in New Hampshire. He put them aside without examining them. Over twenty years later, in the early sixties, his new wife was going through the papers and found the agreement. He did not tell his mother of the find, nor did Mr. Stone whom he forthwith consulted.

"As far as can be ascertained, Mrs. Loeb never mentioned the agreement to anyone. Certainly not to her financial advisors, both of whom are living, nor to her lawyers affiant and Mr. Meleney. Her failure in this latter respect indicates that the agreement was not in existence, since Mr. Meleney, during the litigation he conducted for her in 1951 and 1952 explored her financial transactions with her son from his purchase of the St. Albans Messenger in 1941, through the loan of $250,000 in 1946 and on down into 1952 when her son refused to deliver the securities originally deposited with his mother to secure the 1946 loan. This close scrutiny was taken up by affiant and continued through the next several years when controversy with her son about Mrs. Loeb's income taxes waxed bitter. In the voluminous files of affiant's and Mr. Meleney's firm are many letters from Mrs. Loeb, and quite a number from her son to her. To these were added after Mrs. Loeb's death numerous letters and memoranda and documents from her desk and storage boxes. Her habit was to keep important documents carefully. There was no copy of the agreement in her files, and no mention of it in her papers."

The wheels of justice turned slowly on Loeb's claim of damages against his mother's estate, and the persons who were suffering most of all were his ex-wife and his own daughter, Mrs. Eleanore McAllister and Miss Katharine Penelope Loeb, who were being given some income by the

executors. They still operated the horse breeding and training farm in Amenia, and Penelope was attending Vassar.
But the going for them was rough.

Mr. Stone disqualified himself and the court's ruling on
this claim was slow. Loeb's claim in its final form included
an 18-page series of interrogatories. Answers required a
complete review of all documents, including Mrs. Loeb's
diaries from 1932 through 1966, as well as all of her personal correspondence. Other depositions were made at the
convenience of numerous prominent, and very busy, lawyers and persons coming from a distance.

The fight over Loeb's claim dragged on and on.

Meanwhile, in early 1968, the veracity of Loeb's Manchester newspapers had undergone another test and the
newspapers failed the examination, i.e., by their own admission the newspapers had been a little less than careful
with the truth. The Union Leader Corporation settled out
of court a suit brought by two ladies from the town of
Derry, not far from Manchester, who had claimed that a
series of "investigative reporting" about conditions in their
town had libelled them. The apology by Loeb's newspapers came in the form of a four-column story on Page One
of the January 28 *N.H. Sunday News* and the reproduction
by engraving of Loeb's letter of apology to the ladies which
appeared in place of the editorial page cartoon on the
same date. It is also understood that a payment was made
in settlement of the litigation, including counsel fees.

# 23

Sen. Eugene McCarthy was generally recognized as the
winner of the 1968 New Hampshire Presidential primary,
but the Democratic national convention, held in Chicago,

nominated Sen. Hubert Humphrey of McCarthy's own
state as the Presidential standard-bearer, with Sen. Edmund
S. Muskie, of Maine, as his running mate. Former Vice
President Nixon, as could be expected, had pretty much
clear sailing through the Republican convention and chose
former Maryland Gov. Spiro T. Agnew for the Vice Presidency. This did not bode well for Humphrey and Muskie,
if the New Hampshire barometer held true. (It did.) William Loeb promptly dubbed the Democratic candidate
"Hubert Horatio Hornblower" and his running mate,
"Flip Flop Muskie." The man whom Loeb had called
"Tricky Dick" and "Keyhole Dick" was immediately trans-
formed into the greatest Republican ever (including Abra-
ham Lincoln) and at least part of this sanctity rubbed off
on Agnew.

And in the intramural affairs of state politics, House
Speaker Walter B. Peterson, of Peterborough, was warming up on the sidelines to get ready for the dash for the
governorship, quite obviously carrying the banner of the
G.O.P. Old Guard, and it looked like Peterson might have
a fairly easy time of it. There was no way Loeb could ever
back Wesley Powell again, most people figured, and he
really didn't have a viable candidate to go for the governorship at this stage of the game.

But there was that fellow who had led that fluke effort
for the Florida governor in the Presidential primary, that
fellow Thomson, from Orford, or was it "Thompson"?
Anybody who looked him up in the N.H. Manual for the
General Court would figure he spelled his name with a
"p" because that's the way the Secretary of State spelled
it in the official record of the 1964 Constitutional Convention, Thomson's only previous political outing in New
Hampshire.

But Loeb was up to something because it was Thomson
this and Thomson that for many months, until finally,
Loeb figured his man was ready to run. The question
which nagged most people was as much "Who is Thomson?", as it was "Where the hell is Orford?".

Well, come to find out, there is an Orford, a very beau-

tiful hamlet about halfway up the western border of New
Hampshire with Vermont, on the shore of the Connecticut
River, several miles above Hanover and Dartmouth Col-
lege. The population of the town was 790 when Mr. and
Mrs. Meldrim Thomson, Jr., moved there with their family.

Meldrim? Meldrim was a law book publisher. He owned
Equity Publishing Co., Inc., which published the N.H. Revised Statutes Annotated and Vermont Statutes Annotated, among other volumes, and he was a well-dressed
gentleman, obviously adequately financed, who also spoke
with a Southern drawl. Come to find out, he was from
Savannah, Ga., named Meldrim after his great-uncle, Peter
Meldrim, who had joined the Confederate Army at 16 and
later bought the house in Savannah from which General
Sherman ruled after his historic march to the sea. His
great-grandfather had been too ill to have been a member of
the Confederate Army, but he had equipped a rebel company which was called "Thomson's Raiders" and he became
mayor of Macon. Thomson ranked third in his graduating
class from the University of Georgia Law School. He is
best remembered by close associates as the lone Republican at the University of Georgia at that time, having been
converted to the G.O.P., as the story goes, by the influence
of President Hoover, whom he had met as a child. He is
also remembered as having been a student whose each day
was measured with a caliper.

Being a Republican was no asset in beginning a law
practice during the Depression in Georgia, so Thomson
went to work for a law book publishing firm in Brooklyn,
N.Y., and rose to be managing editor. After about 20 years,
he left, migrated to Orford and started Equity Publishing
Co., taking with him certain accounts of the Brooklyn
firm, including the printing of statutes for some Spanish-
speaking countries.

So Thomson, with unusually heavy support editorially
from Loeb's Manchester newspapers, entered the gubernatorial race and filed as a candidate with the Secretary of
State. His main opposition was obviously Peterson, who
also filed. Peterson was a political "Mr. Clean" if there

ever was one. He was originally from Nashua, had attended Nashua High School and Dartmouth College, had taught retarded children for a while after getting his college degree and then settled into the real estate business with his brother in Peterborough. He had married a Peterborough girl, Dorothy Donovan, and the couple had two children. He subsequently ran for the Legislature, from Peterborough, became a member of the town budget committee; after his election to the Legislature, he became floor leader and then Speaker for two terms.

Then one day, into the State House strode Wesley Powell and he told the Secretary of State he'd like his old job back as governor and he was going to give it another try in the Republican primary, and that made it a three-way race. The year 1968 was going to be a Republican year, it looked like, and Wesley Powell was never one to let a bandwagon pass by. But Powell's decision confused what had looked like a Peterson victory.

There were many theories advanced as to why Powell actually entered the race, all of which would lead one to believe that Powell had other motives than to serve another term as governor. Some said he was trying to hurt Peterson and the Old Guard and others said he was trying to hurt Thomson, not so much because he had any feelings about Thomson, but merely out of spite for William Loeb, who so strongly backed—some say he invented—the man from Orford.

Loeb praised Thomson to the skies and attached to every move of Peterson the "sales tax" label. New Hampshire was the only state without a sales or income tax and every effort to put a broad based tax through the Legislature had failed, and the broad base tax issue was a very unpopular cause in the state. McQuaid, in his *N.H. Sunday News* editorials, called Thomson a " 'new face' in state politics [who] had labored under the handicap of having in a short time to achieve an appropriate statewide degree of 'exposure.' " McQuaid also suggested to readers of the *Sunday News* that "asking a Republican to support Powell again for office would be like asking George Washing-

ton to give Benedict Arnold a second chance!" The "treason" McQuaid referred to, of course, was in not following
Loeb's order to appoint Doloris Bridges to the U.S. Senate.

Powell went after both Loeb and Thomson, and practically ignored Peterson. Loeb responded in a Page One
editorial of Sept. 3, 1968:

> "Thomson had introduced refreshingly new insights
> into issues relating to taxes, education, highways and econ-
> omy in government. Powell, on the other hand, has been
> strictly 'Wesley-One-Note.'
> ". . . The Powell technique is one born out of sheer
> desperation: Assault the Orford man's character. Portray
> him as an unfriendly neighbor . . ."

Loeb further charged Powell with "smear" tactics.

McQuaid in a last-gasp effort for Loeb's man Thomson,
called Thomson a "progressive conservative."

The 1968 Republican primary was thus emerging as a
major test of strength for Loeb and a test, further, for the
political pull of his newspapers. There were four other
names on the G.O.P. ballot for the governorship, but it
was a stretch of the imagination to consider some of these
people whose names were entered as being serious contenders.

The principal result, in alphabetical order:

| | |
|---|---|
| Walter Peterson, Peterborough, r | 29,262 |
| Wesley Powell, Hampton Falls, r | 26,498 |
| Meldrim Thomson, Jr., Orford, r | 25,275 |

This primary, if it showed nothing else, did demonstrate
that the longer people read the Loeb philosophy, the more
followers he attracted. In the last prior clear-cut show of
strength, the Democratic Presidential primary of 1960,
about 15% of the vote could be directly traced to Loeb
and his newspapers in that he backed the Chicago man,
Paul Fisher, who ran against John F. Kennedy, and Fisher
got a sizable vote for a virtually unknown quantity. In the
Peterson-Powell-Thomson showdown, Loeb showed that
he was strong and getting stronger. Peterson was known, a
native with a Nashua and Dartmouth background, with
the backing of the "establishment" of the G.O.P.; he got

34.2% of the vote. Powell had four years in the State House, during which time he had dispensed patronage judiciously, had reorganized the departments of state government and appointed numerous new commissioners and directors of departments, and he had been on the ballot so many times people couldn't count the times; they just expected he'd be running for something and he apparently could whip a campaign force into platoon formation on very short notice. Powell got 31% of the vote. Thomson had been a stranger to New Hampshire politics, a virtual unknown who talked with a Southern drawl, and got 29.5% of the vote. This, in itself, was impressive, but Thomson's total strength was his support by Loeb.

Peterson's foe in the general election would be a Manchester attorney, Emile J. Bussiere, of French-Canadian extraction, who had entered the Democratic primary at the last minute when it looked like the nomination would go to the better of two Irish-Americans, Manchester Atty. Henry P. Sullivan or State Banking Commissioner Vincent P. Dunn, a recent Massachusetts import who had been appointed by Governor King. Bussiere profited by the obvious split, besting Sullivan by 1,100 votes. (Sullivan led Dunn by 500.)

Loeb had backed a Democrat before, John King for a third term, and apparently Loeb found that he could live with himself; he had done a lot of things and found he could live with himself. Loeb despised the Old Guard of the G.O.P., and he despised Peterson as the faction's spokesman, even though he had never met him. This group had embarrassed him on every occasion, except for the two times Wesley Powell had been elected; the group apparently never wished to give Loeb star status in their ranks. So Loeb threw all the weight of his newspapers against Peterson and the G.O.P. and went all-out in his support of Bussiere. In New Hampshire, French-Canadian candidates for statewide major office have almost as bad a track record as Dartmouth College professors; Bussiere was a hard quantity to merchandise. He lost to Peterson by 14,000.

To most everyone in New Hampshire the Peterson victory meant that the "people had spoken," but to William Loeb, the election had an entirely different meaning; his newspapers had lost. His power among the people of New Hampshire had again been measured and, although Loeb's power was considerable, he did not have enough clout to put his men across. Many people could explain this by saying that Loeb chose some of the most difficult assignments for himself, but Loeb apparently didn't see it this way. He would still have Nixon to "kick around" because he had waltzed over the Humphrey-Muskie ticket, but in New Hampshire it was different. To William Loeb, this meant war. It meant war between Pride's Crossing, Mass., and Peterborough, N.H. It meant that Peterson had to be embarrassed. But how?

That question must have cost William Loeb many sleepless nights because Peterson was a hard man to knock. He was clean, reserved, gentle. Peterson had a strong following, more than Loeb had gauged, and Peterson had done his homework. Peterson was friendly by nature, and he became friendly with a lot of people in a lot of towns. He could talk basketball with people he had met on the campaign trail. Peterson could talk basketball if there was nothing else to talk about, because Peterson played basketball, he liked basketball and he read about basketball. As a matter of fact, Loeb's own newspapers gave more space to basketball than any other sport; the *Union Leader* always printed the summaries and individual scoring totals of every high school basketball game played in New Hampshire. Basketball teams from New Hampshire can't compete too well with teams from other states but they surely compete in New Hampshire. New Hampshire people love basketball and the people in the small towns go to all the local games. Basketball is big in New Hampshire, if only because a gymnasium is a warm place to go on a cold winter evening.

But beyond that, Peterson had a good record in the Legislature and in Peterborough. He had been an effective legislator, a good floor leader, and a good Speaker of the House. As a member of the town budget committee, he

had won a lot of supporters, and as members of the Peterborough community, the Petersons were held in high es-
teem. In the September primary, Peterson got 736 out of
the 1,068 votes cast for the field of seven so there wasn't
much question about the fact that he was popular with
his friends and neighbors.

During Peterson's first year in office and during the 1969
term of the Legislature, there was no outstanding single
issue with which Loeb could find fault. A new inheritance
tax had been passed and this was a poorly constructed
statute and the tax was easily dodged. Peterson conceived
and executed the idea of naming a Citizen's Task Force,
a group of 25 prominent Granite Staters from every walk
of life, who would meet periodically and take a look at the
problems facing the state's government. Loeb found some
grounds to criticize Peterson both on the issue of the inheritance tax and the Citizen's Task Force, but this was
simply criticism for the lack of anything else to criticize.
Besides, Peterson had been astute enough to have given
the Loeb faction plenty of voice on the task force. So all
Loeb could use to attack Peterson was the charge that he
was a "weak" governor, a "do-nothing."

Loeb thus used his big arsenal on Washington; on
President Nixon who was going through the growing pains
of the first year in office. Loeb could always find something
wrong in national and international affairs.

Loeb had a particular field day during the summer of
1969 because in July, Sen. Edward M. Kennedy (D-Mass.)
had been involved in the death of Mary Jo Kopechne on
Chappaquiddick Island off Martha's Vineyard. Loeb dispatched his best men to the Vineyard for weeks to investigate the death of the secretary. Loeb delighted in making
life unpleasant for the Kennedy family. Of course, Loeb
had had a bit of experience in matters such as the Chappaquiddick affair. The matter of Reginald H. J. Nash, who
had been found in Lake Champlain in 1943, is a case in
point.

The Chappaquiddick affair took the heat off Governor
Peterson.

But Loeb had one more "new" target for his personal vendettas—lawyers, judges and the New Hampshire Bar Association. On January 30, 1969, William Loeb had been invited by the membership of the New Hampshire Bar Association to be a panelist for a discussion of the subject, "Fair Trial—Free Press: Newspapermen vs. Lawyers?", at the mid-winter meeting of the association at Concord. Other panelists included Atty. F. Lee Bailey of Boston, Atty. Donald L. Conn of Boston, and Thomas Gerber, editor and assistant publisher of the *Concord Monitor*.

Lawyers had always represented a challenge to Loeb and the *Union Leader*'s policies, mainly because the lawyers were an educated, aware and alert group of people who would and did challenge Loeb on many, many points.

The panel discussion was being televised live that evening by WENH-TV, New Hampshire's educational television network, and when Loeb arrived just before the discussion was to begin, his wish was granted that he be the last man to deliver his opening remarks. (Loeb is last to arrive at most functions. Many people feel that this excuses Loeb from informal discussions with any others who might be present for a given program.)

The other three panelists, in their opening remarks, spoke about the effect of pre-trial publicity on the fairness of the actual trial in many cases, e.g., the "Boston Strangler" and other such well-publicized affairs. When it came Loeb's turn to speak, he addressed himself solely to the matter of how the Kennedy family had unfairly persecuted Jimmy Hoffa. It was, he seemed to be saying, because of the Kennedys, and no one else, that Hoffa was then serving time in the Federal penitentiary at Lewisburg, Penn. During a question-and-answer period that followed, Loeb was the target for most of the inquiries. Among the reasons for this was his insistence on digressing from the topic which had been announced. Three of the younger lawyers in attendance particularly nettled Loeb. Finally, Loeb stormed off the platform and strode to the back of the hall. He said to no one in particular on the way, but overheard by many in the aisle seats, that his newspapers would never publicize the events of the bar association again.

(Six years later, Loeb has made good on his word. There is only very scant mention of the bar association in the *Union Leader*. The names of attorneys who are involved in notable local trials have been also conspicuous by their absence.)

Conflicts with attorneys were nothing new for Loeb. He had run the gamut of New Hampshire law firms for his corporate endeavors and interests, but was never satisfied. By 1969, he was using a Massachusetts firm. In all fairness, it must be noted that William Loeb had more than a casual need for lawyers in his own personal life, never mind his business affairs.

In December of 1969, Meg Peterson, 15, and Andy Peterson, 13, made their first trip to Washington, D.C. But for Meg and Andy, it wouldn't be the usual trip that other kids take to the Capital. They were going for only one day and they knew before they left home they were going to meet and speak to the President of the United States. Meg was then a sophomore at Contoocook Valley Regional High School and Andy was a seventh grader at Peterborough Junior High School. The occasion for the trip to the District of Columbia was that the governors of the 50 states had been invited to a one-day meeting on drug abuse to be conducted by Art Linkletter, the television personality. Governor Peterson had told Meg and Andy they'd probably have their pictures taken with President and Mrs. Nixon, maybe even their daughters, because it was to be a family affair, sponsored by the President.

Drug abuse? Sure, Meg and Andy thought, they supposed it was a problem in the big cities—in Boston, in New York, in Philadelphia. No problem in Peterborough. Sure, there was pot. Who didn't have it? Had had it for years. Everybody at school knew who was using it and how to get hold of it, but Meg was in that gang of kids who had not tried smoking pot and was not about to use it. A

lot of the kids at school had the stuff; the kids—heck, the
teachers. Don't try to tell a kid who's got a marijuana
cigaret in his hand. Meg was with a group of students who
had seen a teacher light up a marijuana cigaret a few weeks
before.

The Peterson family went to Washington by commercial
flight with the governor's State Police aide, Sgt. Ernie
Loomis, and, after spending the night in the hotel and
having breakfast, went to the State Department auditorium
where the day's activities would be conducted. Meg and
Andy spied a few kids they had met at the fall governor's
conference in Colorado, but, after receiving programs and
after a brief moment in the foyer, proceeded into the auditorium.

There was a greeting by President Nixon who introduced Linkletter. Linkletter told the audience of how his
daughter had tried LSD and then committed suicide, and
how Dr. Timothy Leary was a "poisonous, evil man" for
promoting mind-expanding drugs. Linkletter was almost
reduced to tears when he told of how Diane, then 20, had
died two months before. He said that he had decided "to
speak out on the grief and outrage of drug taking," and
said that his daughter had the "handicap of carrying a
famous name" and that "such kids are prejudged."

"Children of prominent people often go out of their
way to prove 'they are part of the gang,' " Linkletter said.

There was a break in the program; there would be refreshments and coffee in the foyer. Peg and Andy mingled
with the children of the other governors. The wives chatted; the governors chatted. Governor Peterson had noticed
that there were newspaper people all around the lobby
with their ball point pens and pads at the ready; wire
service people and stringers, hopeful of getting the kids'
reaction to the drug problem and siphoning it to home-
town newspapers all over the country. Dorothy Peterson
saw the lady reporter talking to the group of kids Meg
was with, all just like Meg, bouncy, pretty kids.

Fifteen and sixteen is such a difficult age, Dorothy Peterson thought. They apparently were enjoying meeting and

talking with one another. After the intermission, as they were filing back into the auditorium, Dorothy Peterson asked Meg what the woman reporter had asked them.

Not much, Meg told her mother, just a lot of questions about dope and junk. No, Meg said she hadn't said anything the other kids hadn't said. Yes, the woman was nice. Gee, Mother, I only told her what every kid in school knows about pot and all that. Gee, Mother; after all, Mother. "But, Mom, you should have heard what Bridge Flanigan was telling that woman when her mother grabbed her."

The rest of the day was routine—lunch, then an afternoon session which was punctuated by photographs of each Republican governor and his family with President and Mrs. Nixon. Back to the hotel for the Petersons and Sergeant Loomis, to bed and up for a return flight to Boston, early the next day.

No sooner had the Petersons disembarked from the plane at Boston's Logan Airport than up rushed three reporters. The governor recognized them as being from the Boston Globe, the UPI and the AP, and he offered his usual, if reserved, greeting. There had been two other governors on the flight with their families and the reporters weren't paying any attention to them. By the time Governor Peterson was able to put himself at the disposal of the newsmen, they were asking Meg what she thought of the conference, and the governor motioned the reporters to proceed, saying, "Meg certainly has the right to express her views."

Meg stood close to her mother and one reporter asked her if she had ever used pot, and Meg gave a firm, "No." Then, as all three reporters appeared to speak at once, the 15-year-old-Meg said to her mother, "Help, Mom, save me before I say something wrong."

And, at this point, the governor stepped in and told the newsmen they had had a tiring flight and that the daughter's remarks indicated that there was still a need for education of young people on the problems connected with drugs and their use. He excused himself and his family, and headed to the refuge of the waiting car, attended by Sergeant Loomis. Loomis told the governor that he had spoken with the governor's legal counsel, Atty. Warren Rudman, who suggested that they return to Concord immediately, instead of going to Peterborough, as they had planned. After the car had cleared the downtown Boston traffic, the governor called Rudman on the car telephone and Rudman informed him there was a furore in that day's *Union Leader* about Meg and something she had said at the Washington conference.

Rudman wasn't kidding. The *Union Leader* had given the "super" treatment to a story on Page One of both morning and evening editions that same day, three columns wide in a Benday border.

The *Union Leader* story is quoted in full:

## Meg Peterson, Governor's Daughter, Thinks 'There Is Nothing Wrong With Smoking Pot'

WASHINGTON—UPI—"I don't think there is anything wrong with smoking pot myself," said Meg Peterson. The 15-year old daughter of New Hampshire Gov. and Mrs. Walter Peterson added she had some friends in Peterborough, N.H., who smoked it.

Her mother stood by with a quizzical look.

Meg was among children of the nation's governors attending an all-day conference on narcotics and dangerous drugs Wednesday at the invitation of President Nixon.

"I'm convinced already it's bad. They don't have to sell me," said Anne Whitcomb, 15, daughter of Gov. and Mrs. Edward Whitcomb of Indiana.

Both Meg and her 13-year old brother, Andy, an eighth grader, said the schools use "scare techniques" by having a state policeman come in to deliver drug lectures to the students.

Meg added that in her school a teacher brought in a lighted cigaret and those students who recognized it was marijuana instead of tobacco were hauled off to the principal's office.

She did not elaborate on what happend to them.

One unidentified governor's wife complained she didn't understand the words to "rock" songs in the movie shown at the conference. "But, mother," her daughter chided, "you don't listen."

Bridget Flanigan, 14, daughter of Mr. and Mrs. Peter Flanigan—he's a special assistant to the President—replied "uh" when asked if she had ever smoked marijuana. She was prevented from finishing by her mother who assured reporters, "There are problems in every school."

Rudman had told the State House press corps that Governor Peterson would meet with them on his arrival from Boston and Peterson did just that when he arrived at the Concord State House, the meeting attended by a representative of the *Union Leader.* The governor made a brief, unprepared statement that generally covered the day's activities in Washington, and he announced that HEW Secretary Robert Finch had told the New England governors, who usually cooperated on regional projects, that a New England drug treatment center was under consideration. Questioning was brief and cursory and the "formal" aspects of the meeting soon ended. Then there was small talk to the effect that the *Union Leader* had cut out all the quotes of the other children at the conference in the same story which was received on the teletypes at the state's other daily newspapers, and that the *Union Leader* had, in fact, emasculated the UPI transmission to feature the only thing which could even be "stretched" to appear damaging to Meg Peterson.

Peterson felt that his remarks at the State House had put to rest any further play the story might get and he and his family headed for Peterborough. Peterson felt relieved because no one in that group at the State House had any other reaction—including the regular *Union Leader* State House reporter, D. Frank O'Neil—than that the *Union Leader* editors in Manchester had chopped up the original UPI transmission for their own purposes. Peterson felt the issue was dead, and that it could have been worse, especially knowing Loeb. It could have been worse, but Peterson was convinced that Frank O'Neil would quote him from his State House remarks and that it would be a closed issue. The governor had a sixth sense when it came to the *Union Leader* and its publisher and he knew William Loeb was out for him.

Early the next morning, a Friday, Sergeant Loomis picked up the governor at his home in Peterborough and headed for Concord. As was their habit, they stopped to purchase the morning newspapers at a store in Antrim. Leaping out of Page One of the *Union Leader* was a five-column headline:

## "School Head Says Meg Lied"

During the remainder of the trip to Concord, Peterson read the rest of the newspaper's stories, many of which had to do with Meg Peterson.

The story by D. Frank O'Neil reported only on the governor's press conference on the afternoon previous, after his return from Washington. This was not surprising to Peterson. D. Frank O'Neil was a *Union Leader* reporter long before the days of the Loeb ownership; he retained the Knox integrity and told the story fairly accurately.

The story under the five-column headline, however, quoted the superintendent of schools in Peterborough as saying the story Meg Peterson had told of seeing a teacher with a lighted marijuana cigaret was "completely false" and the principal and assistant principal of Con-Val High were quoted as saying that the incident never occurred. Then, at great length, the *Union Leader* story quoted an anonymous "New Hampshire educator," nowhere identified, who also said the story was false and, in effect, said that Meg Peterson was a liar. Inside the newspaper, on the editorial page, the lead editorial was entitled, "Parents, Get Angry!" It exhorted parents to take a more active part in drug education in general. It also featured quotes from children at the Wednesday conference.

Peterson, on arriving at the State House, immediately asked Loomis to return to Peterborough and inquire of the school officials as to the source of the news stories. He telephoned Mrs. Peterson and advised her of the newspaper's stories and they agreed it would be best to bring Meg home from school for the day.

Each of the school officials denied having been interviewed, said that there had been a telephone call to the school the day previous from a man who identified himself as a *Union Leader* reporter—there had been no visits to the school—and that their remarks had been entirely out of context. None of the school officials had any idea who the "prominent New Hampshire educator" might be.

Governor Peterson, on receiving this information, composed an open letter to Publisher Loeb with the assistance of Attorney Rudman, his legal counsel, and Rudman, together with Sergeant Loomis, went to Manchester to the offices of the Union Leader Corporation with instructions to have it inserted in the Saturday editions of the *Union Leader* and the *Sunday News* of the day following as a Page One paid advertisement. Employes in the advertising department of the Union Leader Corporation balked at first viewing the letter, but reluctantly accepted it, together with the governor's personal check in the amount of $840.18.* Attorney Rudman informed them that if they refused to accept the ad or if it were not to appear in its present form, the governor was prepared to bring suit as a private citizen.

The letter from Governor Peterson to Publisher Loeb (which is reproduced in its entirety as Appendix B to this book) asked Loeb to "stop picking on my 15 year old daughter, who, after all, is only a young girl with many years of life ahead."

"Why not pick on someone your own size?" asked Peterson. At the bottom of the ad was a notation to the effect that it was an advertisement "paid for by Walter Peterson, Peterborough." It was written on the governor's official stationery.

Receipt of the governor's letter at the Amherst Street offices of the Union Leader Corporation really set the

* Governor Peterson was later billed for an additional $14.36, which he paid.

wheels in motion. Loeb himself had an appearance scheduled that evening, at Goffstown, not far from Manchester,
to address the New Boston chapter of the Daughters of the
American Revolution. In his address, Loeb spared no
blows and he converted the patriotic gathering into a political rally. At the close of the meeting there was distributed a printed sheet with instructions for teenagers to fill
out with their own opinions and return to the *Union
Leader* their own answers to the single question, "Do You
Think Governor Peterson Is a Good Parent?"

The results of the questionnaire were never published
in any form.

Page One of the Saturday editions of the *Union Leader*
not only contained the Governor's advertisement, but more
saturation bombing by Loeb and his staff—three Page One
stories in all. One was a rewrite and a rehash of everything
which had already been said in the original story which
quoted the school superintendent and others. In another,
Loeb covered 31 paragraphs in denying that he had anything to do with the coverage afforded the incident, although he was quoted as giving his staff high praise for the
handling of the stories on Meg Peterson. The third story
was about the advertisement itself, entitled, "Peterson Rips
Loeb."

The next day's edition of the *N.H. Sunday News* also
contained the advertisement on Page One and a four-
column headline:

### Loeb Asked Gov. Peterson's
### Apology on 'Distortion' Charge

The lead editorial, entitled, "Poor Pa, Poor Meg," stated
that instead of unleashing a "bitter attack on Bill Loeb"
Governor Peterson should have investigated the drug situation in his own and neighboring towns. The editorial
went on to say that the newspaper's editors had believed
the original story of how Meg Peterson had lied, in her
story about a teacher with a marijuana cigaret and that
Governor Peterson was wrong in venting his "blind fury"

at Loeb. In addition, it said President Nixon was wrong for calling for relaxation of drug laws. It concluded by saying that if Governor Peterson and President Nixon had provided stronger leadership, the "poor, hapless Milford girl, Mrs. Kasabian," wouldn't be involved in those California murders. (Linda Kasabian, from Milford, N.H., had turned state's evidence in the Sharon Tate murder case involving the Charles Manson community, at about the same time.)

Monday's editions of the *Union Leader* contained a three-column Page One story in which the newspaper's correspondents from other parts of the state had asked high school age children in their respective towns what they thought of the case. As could be expected, the *Union Leader* story contained only adverse comment, or at least the better part of it was adverse, towards Meg Peterson.

In 1975, Meg Peterson is working full time with emotionally disturbed children at the Anna Philbrick Center of the New Hampshire State Hospital. Had she not been such a fine student in her earlier years of high school, she would not have been able to graduate as scheduled. But, despite hospitalization in a private Massachusetts institution during most of her senior year, she was graduated as a member of her original class.

There can be no doubt that the amount of publicity and the viciousness of this attack on Meg—which, in effect, it was—had a disastrous consequence on the young lady's life; because, after all, what Meg Peterson had said in the first instance to the reporter in Washington was an innocuous remark. She says that it was a contributing factor to her illness.

Meg has been taking college equivalency examinations and is doing well. She says she is happy in her job now, but she realizes the importance of a college degree if she intends to continue as an educator.

# IV
## Why?

Burke said there were Three Estates
in Parliament; but, in the Reporters' gallery yonder there sat a
Fourth Estate more important than
they all.

—THOMAS CARLYLE

# 24

It was most evident from the results of the 1968 elections that there were indeed three factions of the Republican Party in New Hampshire—the Old Guard, the Powell Party and the Loeb Party—and that these latter two were only slightly less strong than the Old Guard, and, in effect, had killed each other off in the last primary. Loeb had but one viable candidate in his entire stable—Meldrim Thomson, Jr., of Orford. Having had a taste of the political flavor of the state, Thomson was eager to go out again. He filed as a candidate for the governorship in 1970 on the Republican ballot and Governor Peterson filed for reelection.

And Loeb adopted a new bit of strategy. It was obvious that if he had a Democratic candidate running, he might have had an added bit of insurance after the primary elections. Loeb had given backing to former Governor King and then Attorney Bussiere, and he found he could live with himself (which was one of the least tests of whether Loeb could live with himself), so he began one of his now-familiar campaigns, this time extolling the virtues of Roger J. Crowley, of Manchester, a retired Navy captain who had served as Commissioner of Aeronautics and was then appointed by Governor King to be Commissioner of Resources and Economic Development. Crowley had known Bernard J. McQuaid from their days at St. Anselm's in Manchester in the '30's when St. Anselm's was both a prep school and a college. Crowley had gone into Naval aviation at the outset of World War II and had served continuously since then, his last sea duty being as skipper of an aircraft carrier. He ultimately served a tour at the Pentagon before retiring and returning to his home in Manchester. McQuaid was a strong supporter of Crowley's appointment as Commissioner of Aeronautics, a relatively minor state job. (There were only three airports in the state which were being used for commercial passenger purposes and these by the same airline, Northeast.) McQuaid was also one of Crowley's strongest supporters for his appointment to the Department of Resources and Economic Development by Governor King. The *Union Leader* and the *N.H. Sunday News* began a major publicity push so that Crowley's name would become a household word in advance of the 1970 gubernatorial elections.

All the while, the coincidence of the aviation career of Bernard McQuaid's son escalated. He was graduated from Virginia Military Institute to become a Navy pilot while Captain Crowley was on duty with the Navy Department in Washington; when he left Naval aviation he became a Northeast Airlines co-pilot during the time Crowley headed the Department of Aeronautics in Concord.

But at any rate, it must have entered Loeb's head that now that the Republican Party was splintered, it might be fun to play with the Democrats for a while. So Crowley filed as a Democratic candidate for the governorship in 1970 with the full support of the Loeb newspapers. Charles F. Whittemore, of Pembroke, also filed. At the last minute, the publicity-conscious mayor of Nashua, Dennis J. Sullivan, filed; a Democrat, but one who usually had been identified with William Loeb, Sullivan was never averse to using his position as Nashua's chief executive to make a public statement in support of one of Loeb's pet causes. It was obvious that the role of Mayor Sullivan was, at best, that of "spoiler."

The *Union Leader* and the *Sunday News* punched hard for Crowley and Thomson during the primary and spared nothing in lashing out at Governor Peterson, mostly on the supposition that it was Peterson's intent to impose a sales tax upon the electorate. To most readers of the *Union Leader* the wonder occurred as to what Loeb would do if both his men won and faced each other in the General Election. But this did not occur. The score:

Republican:
    Walter Peterson, Peterborough r      43,667
    Meldrim Thomson, Jr., Orford, r      41,392
Democrat:
    Roger J. Crowley, Jr., Manchester, d    17,089
    Dennis J. Sullivan, Nashua, d        4,747
    Charles F. Whittemore, Pembroke, d    13,354

So, it looked like Crowley would have to carry the torch for the Loeb following, wearing Democratic spangles in the November election. And, frankly, it looked like Crowley had a more than even-money shot at it. Loeb had hung the "tax" label indelibly on Peterson and it was obvious that most of the 41,392 persons who voted for Thomson in the Republican primary were followers of Loeb and persons who relied on Loeb for backing of their own pet projects and pet candidates.

In addition, Wesley Powell, of Hampton Falls, had not been a candidate for major office in this primary, the first time anyone could remember, or cared to. It was generally assumed, when Powell finally came out publicly for Thomson, that he had made some sort of a deal with Loeb. Most observers were quick to point out that, knowing Powell, and Powell having already been governor, it was entirely possible that Powell and Loeb, who had been so open and vehement in criticism of each other, had decided that they would lick their wounds and get together: Powell would back Loeb's candidate, Thomson, for the governorship in 1970, and Loeb would, in turn, publicly state that Powell wasn't such a bad guy after all and back him for the U.S. Senate in 1972, providing Powell stayed out of the 1970 race. It is hard to imagine Loeb coming out in favor of anything Wesley Powell could be connected with after all the insults and slurs he had printed about the Hampton Falls lawyer in the past nine years. And it is even harder to imagine how Powell could accept any graciousness on the part of Loeb after what Loeb had printed about him and what Powell had said in his replies. But it was finally rationalized that these were two very unusual men, indeed, with some sort of special sense of values when it came to politics. And, during the primary, Loeb even went so far as to compliment Powell on endorsing Thomson.

But, in all probability, Senator Thomas McIntyre would be seeking reelection in 1972 and most observers felt that Loeb could endorse the devil himself in a campaign against McIntyre. Loeb, of course, was keeping McIntyre's name, or any news of McIntyre, pretty well blacked out of the *Union Leader*.

By now, it was everywhere obvious that not only was Loeb a man possessed of an undying ego, but that Powell and Thomson also possessed egos of unusual size. And then the unexpected—at least by William Loeb—happened. Meldrim Thomson, Jr., of Orford, bolted the Republican Party and filed to run as an American Party candidate in the November election. This was certainly a development upon which Loeb had never counted and it threw him for a loss. He had created Thomson and he obviously felt that Thomson owed him loyalty, although Loeb never seemed to manifest those same feelings of loyalty to anybody else.

There was no way that Thomson's candidacy in the American Party could do other than help Peterson. Any Thomson followers—or at least the overwhelming majority—had gotten to be Thomson followers because of alliance with Loeb. Thomson himself was a dead duck; there was no way he could win. Immediately after the primary, it looked like Crowley had a clear shot at the governorship. He was from a highly respected Manchester family, his father having been an alderman and leading civic official for years. Crowley had a fine record of service in the Navy and about the only publicity ever given the Commissioner of Aeronautics was the nice things the *Union Leader* and *Sunday News* said about Crowley. He was head of the Department of Resources and Economic Development for only a brief period, but during that span nothing went wrong.

Then, too, there were many Democrats who "smelled a rat" with Loeb being so strongly pro-Crowley from the very outset of the campaign. Surely, Loeb had backed Gov-

ernor King four years before, but he clearly had no place
else to go, with former Governor Hugh Gregg as King's
opponent. Then Loeb's backing of Bussiere was of the
same variety. Loeb certainly could not say anything nice
about Peterson, even though he was an obvious winner in
1968. By 1970, Loeb hated Peterson and he certainly made
no secret of it. As a matter of fact, it was a matter of
wonder how Loeb could work himself up to the point
where he could write so severe an indictment of a man
whom he scarcely knew, if he knew him at all.

It was obvious that Loeb had been at least slightly sorry
to see Thomson lose in the primary, but an incumbent is
always a tough man to dislodge, and Loeb knew it. But
Loeb, it was obvious, could put Thomson back to pasture
for two years and use him in 1972 when Peterson's first
two terms were expired.

Loeb was very angry when Thomson actually filed as an
American Party candidate. On Oct. 1, 1970, he wrote a
Page One editorial (which was continued inside so that it
covered four columns in all) in which he lectured Thomson and, in the course of this, managed to utter one of
the most confusing lessons in political science which has
ever been delivered, anywhere, at any time.

Entitled, "The Thomson Tragedy," Loeb's Page One
epic treatise stated that Peterson and his followers had
wrongly criticized Meldrim Thomson, Jr., of Orford, for
calling Thomson an "extremist" during the primary campaign and owed Thomson an apology:

> "Instead the Peterson forces, stupid and arrogant as they
> are, ground their political heels into the more than 40,000
> Republicans who voted for Thomson and into Thomson,
> himself. Instead of a full-fledged apology for the 'extremist'
> statements, which apology Peterson is alleged to have
> promised Thomson, he sent a mealy-mouthed letter which
> said NOTHING. Apparently the letter was the last straw
> —and Thomson took his ill-advised action.
>
> "Of course, Thomson was also at fault, in the sense that
> if you go into politics or into the newspaper business, you
> have to learn to take it as well as dish it out. Furthermore,

anybody with a really profound philosophy and spiritual confidence pays no attention when filth is thrown at him by mud-slinging politicians who are about gutter high in their own stature as individuals.

"As Harry Truman said a long time ago, 'If you can't stand the heat, get the hell out of the kitchen.'

"Thomson was thus revealed as a man who couldn't stand the heat. As a result, as Senator Cotton pointed out, Thomson threw away a SURE nomination as Republican gubernatorial standard bearer and almost certain election in 1972.

"Thomson asserts that he has taken his stand in order to defend his basic principles. Well, he could have defended his basic principles a great deal more effectively INSIDE the Republican Party, instead of attempting something which will turn out to be an exercise in complete futility.

"Meldrim Thomson also made another basic mistake which revealed a weakness in character: He made a great point during the campaign that Peterson would not pledge to support HIM if he won, whereas he, Thomson, was perfectly willing to pledge his support to Peterson. Even AFTER the primary he and former Governor Powell had a press conference in which they both pledged to support Peterson. Powell has done exactly as he promised, but Thomson apparently doesn't think that when a man gives his word it is necessary to keep it. This newspaper takes an entirely different view of that situation. A word that is given is a word that must be KEPT.

"Another weakness of Thomson, in addition to his inability to take it when the going really got hot and his inability to keep his word, is his inability to even use his head in the face of defeat."

Loeb continued his dissertation, but it must be remembered that both the *Union Leader* and *Sunday News* had already inalterably committed themselves in support of Crowley, the Democratic nominee:

"This writer, when he first heard of Thomson's decision, was utterly astonished that Thomson was contemplating running on the American Party ticket. He phoned Thomson and reminded him of the 1912 presidential (sic) campaign. At the Republican convention that year Theodore

Roosevelt, who again wanted to run for the presidency
(sic) of the United States, had the vote of the convention
literally stolen from him by the high-handed and biased
rulings of the chairman of the convention. The latter was
none other than Elihu Root, who had been Theodore
Roosevelt's secretary of state in his Cabinet.

"Infuriated by the unfairness of the whole procedure,
the former President was determined to run as an independent. This writer's father, a close political associate
and former secretary to Theodore Roosevelt, pled with
him NOT to run because, as he pointed out, it would be
an exercise in futility, that he could not win the presidency and that he would spoil his chances at that time—
just as Thomson has—which added up to a 100 per cent
chance that T. R. would be the party's unanimous choice
for the presidency in 1916.

"Theodore Roosevelt nevertheless insisted on running
as the candidate of the Progressive Party, known popu-
larly as the Bull Moose Party. But, popular as he was,
Theodore Roosevelt was not able to win the election and
the Democratic candidate, Woodrow Wilson, was elected
President of the United States. The Republican candidate,
William Howard Taft, carried only two states, Maine and
Vermont."

Before the end of his four-column diatribe, Loeb reaffirmed his endorsement of Crowley, the Democrat, but
who was obviously running in the silks of the Loeb Party:

". . . Crowley understands that the way to produce revenue for the State of New Hampshire is to bring in more
industry and more tourist trade. We will continue to support Roger Crowley.

"This newspaper suggests that there is no future for
New Hampshire in either the arrogant high tax, high
spending policies of the Peterson group or in the weakness of the Thomson party."

Members of the New Hampshire Democratic Party had
an immediate reaction to Loeb and his strong endorsement
of Crowley, the Democratic nominee. Meeting in convention at Manchester, the party rejected the platform brought
before the convention by the gubernatorial contender and

instead adopted a platform the planks of which were opposed to many of Crowley's campaign pledges which had
been voiced by Loeb, including a condemnation of President Nixon for his conduct of the war in Southeast Asia,
a plank to reform the state Constitution in order to permit
enactment of "progressive, non-proportional taxes" and
another which called for repeal of the state's abortion laws.
Crowley asked that the state committee name Attorney
Bussiere, the man Loeb endorsed in the last campaign for
governor, as state chairman, and the state convention instead named a Nashua man, Harry Makris. Another proposal, on the question of a moratorium on the construction
of nuclear power plants, Crowley's only supporter was
State Sen. Laurier Lamontagne, who was the most vocal
objector to the 1957 State Senate resolution censuring
Loeb. Lamontagne obviously was looking for some publicity because, by his own admission on the convention floor,
he had a tough reelection battle ahead.

So Crowley was a loser with his fellow Democrats all
around, but the Democrats were adopting a tack much
more anti-Loeb than anti-Crowley. But it was true that
once you started to play politics with William Loeb in the
state of New Hampshire you became a marked man.

The *Union Leader* and the *Sunday News* kept up their
assault on the consciousness of the New Hampshire voter
in behalf of Crowley, taking an occasional swipe at Thomson and very often a smash at Peterson. McQuaid contributed a full-page Crowley profile—with many errors and
distortions—in the *Sunday News*. Then Loeb sounded the
two-week warning on October 20 with the statement:

> "A vote for Thomson is a vote thrown away because
> Thomson cannot possibly win. . . . Crowley needs all the
> help from you that you can give him."

And on the same day as the two-week warning from
Loeb, Thomson was rapping the ski pass system in the
state before the Meredith chapter of the Daughters of the
American Revolution, really a slap at Crowley because
the state-owned ski areas were under Crowley's adminis-

tration in the Department of Resources and Economic Development. Thomson showed now that he had little political know-how. If there was ever a group within the state of New Hampshire which could be less vitally interested in ski passes than the Meredith chapter of the D.A.R., it would be hard to find.

Of course, the reading public was advised whenever Loeb could resurrect a contributing columnist who had anything kind to say about Jimmy Hoffa and this type of an editorial would preempt any intrastate campaign activity with Loeb and his Page One editorials.

As the one-week warning, Loeb reprinted on Page One of the *Union Leader* McQuaid's editorial from the previous *Sunday News*, entitled, "The Man You Said You Wanted."

McQuaid added one little fillip to his Sunday-before-Election-Day edition. He contained a Page One story with the headline:

### Problems in Peterborough
### 'Meg' Peterson Views
### On 'Pot' Haunt Town

The story went on to say that "Although statements made last August by Margaret 'Meg' Peterson, 16-year-old daughter of Gov. Walter Peterson, that she saw nothing wrong with smoking pot (marijuana), created a furore from coast to coast, it failed at the time to move this small community to action . . ." and would have the reader believe that Peterborough, N.H., had become the sin capital of the world and that it was all the fault of Governor Peterson and his daughter.

But the day came and the people made their choice:

| | |
|---|---|
| Walter Peterson, Peterborough, r | 102,298 |
| Roger J. Crowley, Jr., Manchester, d | 98,098 |
| Meldrim Thomson, Jr., Orford, a | 22,033 |

Loeb's reaction was obviously one of utter and complete frustration and disappointment, mixed with a touch of anger. For on the Thursday after the election he took the Page One pulpit with this allegory:

"STUPID PILOTS WILL BE AT THE HELM OF THE SHIP OF STATE IN CONCORD AND IT WILL TAKE THE EFFORTS OF ALL THE REST OF US TO KEEP THE NEW HAMPSHIRE SHIP OF STATE OFF THE ROCKS."

Loeb said that the voters had deserted Crowley, as if Crowley had any to begin with, and that it was the people of the city of Manchester who had defeated Crowley and re-elected Peterson by not showing up to vote.

On Saturday after election, Loeb's *Union Leader* had an eight-column streamer:

## NAMES OF NON-VOTERS TO BE LISTED

The lead story of the newspaper said that Loeb would be the first newspaper publisher in the country to list the names of every voter who had failed to exercise his franchise. He further pledged that he would do so after each subsequent election. Manchester had had a voter turnout of nearly 70 per cent in the election, which was far above the average. But Loeb figured that Manchester had cost his man Crowley the election. Other people had other ideas, chief among them that Loeb had planted the "kiss of death" on Crowley and that it was Loeb's general unpopularity which cost Crowley the election.

It took Loeb almost two weeks to list all the names of the voters who failed to come out on Election Day, as listed with the city clerk. And it also showed that the city clerk's list of voters was an out-dated and inaccurate list which had hundreds of names of people not qualified to vote, dead, moved away, and the like.

Loeb never did follow through on his promise to list non-voters after subsequent elections.

What should be remembered are William Loeb's words of Oct. 1, 1970:

". . . If you go into politics or into the newspaper business you have to learn to take it as well as dish it out . . ."

# 25

The Page One editorials extolling the virtues of James Riddle Hoffa had become familiar fare to readers of the *Union Leader*. Loeb constantly promulgated new reasons why the labor leader, who was serving time in a federal penitentiary for the felonies of jury-fixing and mail fraud, should be released, because after all, Loeb reasoned, Hoffa was given a "bum deal" in the first place. Loeb's editorials were almost without exception accompanied by a photo of Hoffa, some of which made Hoffa look so angelic that they seemed either the work of Fabian Bachrach or they were Hoffa's First Communion snapshots. William Loeb's editorials must have meant something to someone, and they must certainly have been mailed to Hoffa in prison, and others, but the impact was always minimal in New Hampshire. This was a crusade Loeb was carrying on for very private reasons.

Then on Page One of Feb. 15, 1971, Loeb showed what else he was doing for his jail-ridden friend: there was a three-column photo of an over-all view of what was described to be Lewisburg Federal Penitentiary and high in the sky above the prison was an airplane towing a message banner with the words, "FREE HOFFA NOW—WRITE PRES. NIXON." It turned out the plane was hired by a group which called itself "New England Friends of Jimmy Hoffa" which was actually William Loeb, and the pilot, Harley Mansfield, had been chartered from a small airfield on the North Shore of Massachusetts, not far from Pride's Crossing. The occasion was a combination Valentine-birthday greeting for Hoffa, but what effect correspondence from the inmates might have on the President of the United States is questionable.

It galled Loeb no end that Hoffa was incarcerated and maybe that was because while Hoffa was in prison, Loeb could get no more funds from the Teamsters' pension funds. It was also a curious sort of a power test for Loeb. He had bent every effort on behalf of Richard Nixon in

1960 and again in 1968. Yet since being elected, Nixon had showed no inclination to make any move regarding Hoffa.

And one of the things which galled Loeb most of all was that while Hoffa was in prison, Muhammad Ali (a/k/a Cassius Clay) deposed heavyweight boxing champion of the world, was walking around free as a "bumblebee," even though he had been found guilty of draft evasion, fined $10,000 and sentenced to five years imprisonment. Ali had claimed he was a minister of the Muslim faith and he refused induction on April 28, 1967, while then heavyweight champion. He was stripped of his title by the World Boxing Association and his license to practice his profession was revoked by the New York State Athletic Commission, but Ali was free pending his appeal to the U.S. Supreme Court.

Immediately after the grand jury indicted Ali in May, 1967, and the title was vacated, an eight-man tournament was staged to decide a champion, and the most widely recognized champion after this mess was somewhat cleared up was Joe Frazier, who knocked out Jimmy Ellis in February, 1970. Ali, who might rival William Loeb in the ego department, was incessant in his claim that he was still rightful champion of the world. And so, the promoters got together and Joe Frazier and Muhammed Ali would go at it for 15 rounds in Madison Square Garden on March 8, 1971, for all the marbles. It was to be the biggest gate in Madison Square Garden fight history and the biggest over-all revenue from a fight because the battle was being shown on closed-circuit television at selected locations throughout the world. One of these locations was the New Hampshire National Guard Armory in Manchester, N.H.

William Loeb, who delighted in national publicity of any kind, took to his Page One and stated that his newspapers would not help promote the fight which was only to glorify a draft dodger who would fight for dollars but not for his country. Loeb also had many unkind words to say about the Social and Cultural Committee of the Student Senate of St. Anselm's College, sponsor of the affair in Manchester. Further, he said, his newspapers would not carry any news of the fight or its outcome, a deliberate news blackout, prompted, Loeb said, out of pure patriotism.

Without mentioning the fight itself, stories about protests of the use of a state building for such purposes by veterans' organizations, and other editorials by Loeb, kept the Ali-Frazier Page One news in Manchester. (Actually the ticket sale at the State Armory for the closed-circuit telecast profited.) Governor Peterson was asked by the veterans' organizations to ban the use of the armory on patriotic grounds and Peterson said that his attorney general, Warren Rudman, his former legal counsel, informed him use of the armory was legal.

So Loeb took to Page One again and said the governor's decision was predictable:

> "After all, look at the record: First of all, we have Governor Peterson's daughter's remarks about marijuana—which the governor attacked us for reporting."

Loeb's boring harangue covered two columns and he closed by calling Peterson the "HIGH PRIEST OF PERMISSIVENESS."

Then Atty. Wesley Powell got into the act and said that Peterson's decision to allow use of the armory "put a dollar sign on patriotism and honor." Much news space was given during the week-end before the Monday night fight with statements from self-righteous veterans' organizations urging their members to picket the armory. Had it not been for a platoon of Manchester police, there might have been a battle outside the armory as well as on the screen inside when the night of the fight arrived.

After the record crowd had filled the Garden on March 8, they saw Joe Frazier do his best to actually make Ali 4-F, as he battered the former champion for most of the fifteen rounds. Frazier left the Garden that evening richer by $2.5 million and headed for a victory celebration at the Statler Hilton across Seventh Avenue. Ali left the Garden

that evening richer by $2.5 million and headed for Flower
Fifth Avenue Hospital for examination and X-rays for a
very painful hematoma of the right masseter muscle.

Joe Frazier was the undisputed heavyweight boxing
champion of the world. But in Manchester there were
telephoned bomb threats to the *Union Leader* offices, and
the City of Manchester had to underwrite added expense
in providing police and fire searches of the building.

In Mineola, L. I., final preparations were being made
for the trial involving William Loeb's claim that he was
entitled to 75 per cent of his mother's estate, a claim which
the executors of the estate and the attorneys for the principal heir, Loeb's own daughter, Katharine Penelope, con-
tended was, at best, questionable. The total of the principal amount of the monies involved and the increases
realized on the principal since the woman died in 1966
amounted to $971,540.49, the bulk of which would have
gone to Loeb's daughter had it not been for his contest of
the will.

I quote again from the affadavit of Attorney Alexander
C. Dick, one of Mrs. Katharine W. D. Loeb's attorneys
and one of the executors:

> "The case was ready for trial in April or May, 1971. A
> pretrial conference was held March 17 with Mr. Radigan
> of the Surrogate's legal staff. In attendance were Mr. Han-
> delman, Mr. Meleney and affiant for the Executors; Messrs.
> William Glendon and Joseph H. Spain of Royall, Koegel
> & Wells, for the claimant (Loeb), together with Mr. Ralph
> Warren Sullivan of Boston, claimant's personal attorney;
> and Mr. Peter B. Allsopp, attorney for the residuary bene-
> ficiaries. After a lengthy discussion of the issues and vari-
> ous documents, the Executors' attorney was asked if there
> was any disposition to settle the case. Mr. Handelman indi-
> cated that he would recommend payment of $50, 000. This
> was declined by claimant's attorneys with the statement
> that nothing less than $100,000 would be recommended to
> claimant. The hearing adjourned with the understanding
> that it would be reconvened on short notice if justified by
> any development of settlement talk. Otherwise the case

would be set for early trial. The hearing was reconvened on April 15th.

"In the interim there were extensive talks between counsel arising from a suggestion that if a more generous present payment were made to claimant, he might set up benefits for Penelope by a trust or in his will. Mr. Handelman and Mr. Meleney researched the legal questions involved in implementing the several formulae suggested. No satisfactory answers were found, and all parties met again with Mr. Radigan on April 15th. A long discussion ensued which went back to the simple payment of cash as the only practical method of settlement. This finally resulted in agreement to pay claimant $92,500 out of principal of the Estate with no interest, "in full settlement of all claims against the Estate, excepting his rights under the Will of the decedent as probated." This agreement was formalized in open court, and the sum named was paid by the Executors within the period of 30 days provided. Claimant's only right under the will is that of a fractional life income beneficiary contingent upon Penelope Loeb dying without issue before attaining the age of 30 years.

"Affiant, as suggested above, was reluctant to pay anything to claimant, feeling that his claim would be rejected by the Surrogate after trial. However, the residuary beneficiaries were weary of the struggle and anxious to have it terminated. The Executors decided that they should comply with the wishes of the parties in interest, especially with the knowledge that, even if defeated, claimant was financially able and certainly disposed to keep the estate open for further years by endless appeals, with resultant hardship and strain on his daughter, just turned 21, and her mother. They had received only one-fourth of the income from the Estate in view of the claim for seventy-five per cent of the net estate which would include income after decedent's death. The accumulated three-quarters of income over the period of 4½ years became immediately available to Penelope and her mother.

"It is important to note that the net cost of the settlement was substantially less than $92,500 by reason of the fact that income on that amount for 4½ years benefited Penelope and her mother. During the period of administration, the principal of the Estate yielded income at a rate better than 6%, or a total for the period of about 30%, or $27,750. That sum, subtracted from $92,500, leaves $64,450 (sic). With some allowance for income taxes, the actual cost of the settlement to Penelope and her mother was about $70,000 or less. It was an excellent settlement, and the beneficiaries were very happy about it. Had the claimant prevailed, he would have recovered from five to seven times $70,000."

William Loeb had had his fun—practically all of it at the expense, fiscal as well as emotional, of his own daughter, Katharine Penelope, and of his second wife, Mrs. Eleanore McAllister, who had dutifully sent him her pay check for so long a period while he was starting in the newspaper business in Vermont. Loeb had hired some of the most high-priced lawyers in New York, necessitating the hiring of some costly talent to defend against what proved to be an almost frivolous claim—it couldn't have had much merit if Loeb settled for less than 10 per cent of the value of the estate.

But lawyers come high, particularly the kind involved here, and when Penelope and her mother could call their souls their own, well over half of the bulk of the estate which had been theirs, theirs to live on and to provide Penelope with her education, went for legal fees. There were other costs of administration, as well as estate taxes, which further diminished the principal amount.

William Loeb has seen his former wife and his daughter on various occasions since that time, notably at horse shows where Mrs. McAllister and Penelope show their horses and Penelope rides, and at which Loeb's other daughter, Edith, by Nackey Scripps Gallowhur Loeb, performs as a rider. Mrs. McAllister relates one instance in September, 1973, when she was approached by the present Mrs. Loeb, who asked that she (Mrs. McAllister), out of deference to Loeb's second daughter, do what she could so that some of the facts of Loeb's life be kept from the public notice. The request by Nackey Scripps Gallowhur Loeb was greeted by Mrs. McAllister with a refusal to discuss the matter, but a message to instruct her husband to discuss these matters himself in the future. He did not, although Mrs. McAllister says she could see Nackey give him the message from a distance.

In 1975, Penelope Loeb says that she saw her father at a horse show in 1974. Penelope had suffered serious injury in a riding accident earlier that year which required the removal of a kidney and she was recuperating at the time of the horse show when she saw her father. Loeb knew of Penelope's misfortune. "He was 10 feet away and wouldn't turn his head to say hello," says Penelope Loeb.

# 26

William Loeb has never confined his criticism to the political institutions of the states in which his newspapers are published, nor has he ever confined his flow of venom to the internal affairs of this nation. Indeed, William Loeb has propounded ideas which would improve on any facet of life in the entire world at any given moment. But one primary target of Loeb's vituperation has always been the University of New Hampshire.

There is no solid reason which makes itself obvious why Loeb should have such manifest feelings about this institution. For that matter, there is no solid reasoning behind the majority of Loeb's diatribes. But there is this history of conflict. And the story is worth telling.

Loeb immediately recognized the heritage and importance of the McLane family in New Hampshire in his very first dealings in the state, the buying of the Union-Leader Publishing Co., Inc., from Mrs. Annie Reid Knox in 1946. Atty. John R. McLane, Sr., represented the Knox interests and John McLane Clark, a nephew, was attempting to purchase the publishing property. Mr. McLane's father had been governor in 1905 and in the post-war years the

McLane family interests were evident at the top level of the state's legal, banking and business circles. Mr. McLane was a trustee of Dartmouth College, of which nearly all the male members of the family were alumni, and the same could be said of St. Paul's School in Concord. The senior McLane's law firm, McLane, Davis & Carleton, of a Republican bent, was one of the largest and most prestigious in the state and had, in fact, represented Blair Clark when he sold to William Loeb the original *N.H. Sunday News.* The McLane firm was into everything worth being into.

Another Manchester law firm which was drawing the attention of William Loeb was that of Devine & Millimet. Maurice F. Devine, the patriarch of this organization, was one of the state's best-known personalities, active in Democratic politics, the American Legion, St. Joseph Cathedral parish and the Roman Catholic Diocese of Manchester, and Mr. Devine was also a trustee of the University of New Hampshire. Indeed, to say that Mr. Devine had been "active" is an understatement: his interest in veterans' affairs extended to his being one of the principal authors of the World War II G.I. Bill of Rights; he was also counsel to the diocese and the university. What may have focused additional attention of William Loeb to this particular legal empire was that Joseph A. Millimet had had the audacity to have run for the United States Senate in 1948. Millimet lost in the primary, but he had many unkind things to say about William Loeb's hero, Sen. Styles Bridges, who would have been Millimet's opponent.

In the days immediately following World War II, the elder scions of both the McLane family and the Devine family returned to Manchester, each to enter his father's firm, each with a talented, attractive wife. It was no time at all before these two ladies were leaders in many of the community's affairs which usually attract the attention and devotion of young women such as these, including the League of Women Voters. They became leaders of the organization and, as such, made numerous public utterances of the League's policies. This, in itself, was a challenge to Loeb who sought to dominate the body politic; anyone who would present a thoughtful arrangement of ideas was, and is, by definition, an opponent of William Loeb.

So it was not long before William Loeb began to take the League of Women Voters to task and it was not long before he began to single out Mrs. McLane and Mrs. Devine for particular criticism. Now, it has always been said that Macy's does talk to Gimbel's, and it is known that the elder Devine did talk to the elder McLane, and, apparently, it was Devine who would take the counter-offensive against the publisher, who in the late '40's was still considered by many to be the "new kid in town."

Mr. Devine did, in fact, write a letter to Mr. Loeb asking that the publisher be a "man" and please find some other target if he had to have a target; that the two women were just doing what came naturally and that they were wholly within their rights and what they believed to be their privilege, even duty. To which Mr. Loeb replied to Mr. Devine, "Don't you flex your legal muscles at me." The war was officially declared.

It was not long before Loeb was calling Dr. John Sloan Dickey, Dartmouth College president, "inept and incompetent," and charging in the *Union Leader* that "Communists" had infiltrated the faculty at UNH. Loeb said he knew this because he had himself infiltrated the Communist Party. Loeb began using one of the Communists' favorite tactics: he attacked the places where people are taught to think, and his ire, as always, knew no limits. (Harvard's James B. Conant was called, in the *Union Leader*, an "Educated Ignoramus.")

Some things are never a matter of public record, and there is, quite obviously, no way of putting a definite time on when certain decisions are made. But it had to be about this time that it became the fate of William Loeb never to be honored with an honorary degree. From anywhere.

Loeb continued to snipe at the affairs of Dartmouth College, but his efforts in this direction usually went for naught and, really, were largely unnoticed. Dartmouth, although a New Hampshire institution, has always had influence far beyond the state's borders and any interference by Loeb was easily dismissed. Besides, Dartmouth is privately endowed.

But with the University of New Hampshire, a land-grant institution which derived and derives revenue from the State of New Hampshire as appropriated by the state's Legislature, it became an entirely different matter. Loeb belted UNH at every opportunity, relentlessly, unremittingly, tediously. By 1951, he had the Legislature convinced that UNH was a part of the Politburo. The New Hampshire General Court squandered a lot of taxpayers' money by appointing an investigative committee which, after a thorough search, reported back to the Legislature that the commission had found little or no evidence of subversive activity. In 1956, the *Union Leader* led a crusade to prevent a Marxist from speaking on the campus; the university refused to back down and this led to the award of the Alexander Meiklejohn Award for Academic Freedom by the American Association of University Professors to the UNH president and the school's trustees. The *Union Leader,* and several politicians at the newspaper's behest, tried to stop the university from accepting the award in 1958.

If it wasn't one thing it was another with Loeb and the University of New Hampshire. Over the years, it would appear that it might be a toss-up who had more job security, the president of the University of New Hampshire or the manager of the Boston Red Sox.

Dr. Harold W. Stoke was president of UNH when Loeb arrived in New Hampshire. He was succeeded in 1948 by Dr. Arthur S. Adams. In 1950, Dr. Adams had had enough and he was succeeded by Dr. Robert F. Chandler. Dr. Chandler held office until 1954 when the then vice president of the university, Dr. Edward D. Eddy, was named interim executive officer and later acting president until he begged off and was succeeded in 1955 by Dr. Eldon L. Johnson. Dr. Johnson's term lasted until 1961 when he was replaced by Dr. John F. Reed, vice president, who became acting president. Executive Vice President Jere Chase took over in 1962. Dr. John W. McConnell assumed the presidency in 1963, succeeding Dr. Chase, and he held office until 1971.

It was getting to be an old story that the University of New Hampshire was looking for a president. And, in educational circles, the institution had already gotten a bad name and any number of otherwise worthy applicants were discouraged from applying for the job as president of the Durham school.

Loeb himself was enough to contend with for any president, but the University of New Hampshire had more problems, too. The state has consistently ranked 50th in per-capita support of higher education and this has been enough to discourage the attendance of many young people who were disqualified on economic grounds, because the tuition is among the highest in the nation for land-grant colleges. The University of New Hampshire is also the only state university in the United States which has as an ex-officio member of the board of trustees the governor of the state. In addition, the governor has 12 politically-oriented appointments to the board of trustees, as well as the commissioners of agriculture and education, also ex-officio members. At the present time, there is provision for a student trustee, also, to be named by the governor. The presidents of the university at Durham and of Keene State College and of Plymouth State College are also ex-officio trustees, and the remaining few, to complete a board of 24 members, are elected by alumni. Thus partisan politics enters the realm of the university.

The trustees of the university again began the search for a new president after Dr. McConnell resigned in February, 1971, and by spring of that year they had decided on, and named, Dr. Thomas N. Bonner, then vice president and provost of the University of Cincinnati, a semi-public institution which received some city and state aid. The announcement of Bonner's acceptance of the position was made on April 7, 1971.

At about this time, the political pot was already brewing in New Hampshire for the March, 1972, first-in-the-nation primary and Loeb was busy building the candidate who was then a complete stranger to the New Hampshire electorate, Mayor Sam Yorty, of Los Angeles, Calif. (Yorty would later be Loeb's candidate for the office of President of the United States. In fact, Loeb began Page One coverage of Yorty in mid-March and by early April the *Union Leader* was waxing ecstatic over the announcement that Mayor Yorty would be coming to Manchester on April 26.)

Loeb reacted quickly to the naming of Dr. Bonner as president of UNH, and, with politics already so heavy in the air, it was probably because, at one time, Bonner had served on the staff of Sen. George McGovern, (D-S.D.). (In fact, Bonner had run for Congress himself, from Nebraska.) Governor Peterson immediately lauded Bonner's appointment and, in print, welcomed him to the state, but on April 13, less than a week after the official appointment, the Loeb newspapers carried a reprint from another smaller state newspaper, *Foster's Daily Democrat,* the daily of the city of Dover, the closest to the university geographically, which painted a grim picture of the new president. The news story was largely dismissed because of the author, a man who had been known to have been an extreme conservative and one of former Governor Powell's most ardent supporters.

Loeb's frontal assault began in earnest on April 20, before Bonner had even entered the state to be administered his oath of office. Loeb had dispatched a reporter to Cincinnati and a three-part series began on Page One of the *Union Leader.* Anonymous persons, supposedly professors and deans at the University of Cincinnati, were quoted liberally, and some of Bonner's writings, always out of context, were also quoted. The stories would blame Bonner for every ill suffered at the University of Cincinnati (e.g., April 21, 1971, "Bonner Lacks a Firm Philosophy"), even the flat-out statement that Bonner had acted to heighten the hysteria among the students which was prevalent at the time of the killings of other students on the campus of the nearby Kent State College in Ohio. At one point, the reporter quoted a television show panelist in Cincinnati who had a low opinion of Bonner.

It was just about as low as journalism can go, but it was right there in black and white for all the world to see. The reporter who researched and wrote the series was largely unknown in New Hampshire, being relatively new to Loeb's reportorial staff. It was hard to debate his credentials. (At a later date and in another connection, it was disclosed by the reporter to the Attorney General of New Hampshire that he had been sentenced to, and had served part of, a one- to four-year sentence in the State Prison of Southern Michigan after having been convicted of larceny.)

Dr. Bonner admits that upon coming to New Hampshire in the spring of 1971, he expected to find William Loeb a "laughable Neanderthal" and the *Union Leader* a "throwback to the darkest days of yellow journalism," and he could not understand how such "a showcase of antique horrors" could have an effect on the minds of independent "Yankees."

Dr. Bonner, in 1974, described this experience:

"Such grotesque journalism, I learned, had been common since Loeb's coming to New Hampshire in 1946. But my worst jolt on arriving in the state was to find that a number of otherwise thoughtful people took it seriously, including a corps of politicians who habitually scavenge for issues in the *Union Leader*. Almost no one spoke out in my defense. Faculty members and students, awed by the fury of the attacks and lacking specific information, were largely silent. The burden of proof that I was innocent of the gross calumnies of my character and record had fallen on me.

"It was then I learned that New Hampshire was afraid. Instead of dismissing with a laugh Loeb and his key henchman, James J. Finnegan, Director of the Editorial Page, and B. J. McQuaid, Editor-in-Chief, if they are indeed as harmless as many say, or else fighting the spread of their influence, if they are as evil as others believe, most people in New Hampshire, in fact, do neither. Leading politicians, churchmen, professional leaders, University trustees alike condemn the newspaper's frightening influence on New Hampshire in private, but few try to organize and fight openly its oppressive weight on life in the Granite State . . ."

Then, having formally taken office, Dr. Bonner began a series of counter-offensives against Loeb and the *Union Leader* with speeches, press releases, and messages to alumni, hoping, naturally, to strike a sympathetic note and to explain what to Bonner had been baseless charges, distortions and innuendo, which Loeb had printed. But Thomas Bonner didn't understand William Loeb.

The *Union Leader* had a "Bonner" story just about every day. Loeb found fault with Bonner personally because the UNH president's house was being redecorated; that an automobile had been provided for Bonner's use; that tax funds were being misappropriated because the Bonner family pet (a cat) was transported with the family to Durham.

On Aug. 12, 1971, another series began, a six-part series, the *Union Leader* announced, on Page One, by the same reporter, all under a Cincinnati dateline. If the first series by this same reporter had been bad journalism, words fail to describe the new series. The first part was put together in a Page One eight-column layout with the headline:

## "Brought Beer, Liquor, All-Night Sex to University of Cincinnati Campus"

The University of Cincinnati was founded in 1819. It is doubtful that the student body of this august institution had abstained from beer, liquor and all-night sex until the advent of Thomas Bonner in 1963. But, the facts notwithstanding, William Loeb and his newspaper would have you believe this was so. All six parts of the series went on in the same vein until Bonner could take it no longer.

He publicly challenged the authenticity of the *Union Leader* series and began a barnstorming tour throughout the state, walking main streets, shaking hands with whomever he could find. But within a matter of days, it apparently became obvious to Bonner that he was fighting a losing battle and he asked Loeb to agree to an impartial review of the newspaper's series by Sigma Delta Chi, the national professional journalism fraternity. Loeb reacted by denouncing Sigma Delta Chi as a "biased and leftist organization." Loeb said he would stand by his series and his reporter. The reporter countered by saying that he would sue Bonner for calling his series "unethical."

Bonner received little public support for his stand and he could easily see that no one in New Hampshire was willing to go out on a limb to defend anyone else if it meant incurring the wrath of Loeb. Bonner agreed to a meeting with the *Union Leader* executives to "iron the matter out" and within a day or so a multi-column picture appeared on Page One of the newspaper, showing a group of executives and Bonner in the Union Leader Corp. conference room, all smiling. The news story would lead the reader to believe that Bonner had come looking for a truce with the organization which had operated so much in the public good to "expose" this liberal who had come to "masquerade" as an educator. Loeb was not present at this meeting.

Bonner writes of this meeting:

"My education proceeded. At a meeting in the Union Leader offices attended by virtually all of the newspaper's top officers, except Loeb, I explained in depth my criticisms of the paper and [the reporter's] stories but apologized for the specific references to [the reporter's] lack of professionalism. As I said to a full news conference that day, 'It was the wrong war at the wrong time in the wrong place with the wrong enemy.' Later that week I explained my apology by remarking that the reporter was 'only a poor slob doing a dirty job' and that my real quarrel was not with him but with Loeb. Again the dovecotes fluttered but it was clear that if I were to beat Loeb at his own game of communications it would not be in the pages of the *Manchester Union Leader.*"

". . . As I sat with his top executives and reporters in that first summer of 1971, the words that occurred to me

over and over again was Hannah Arendt's phrase, 'The
banality of evil.' Surrounded by these well-mannered and
friendly men—they might well have been a group of
Baptist clergymen—I realized that so commonplace, so
banal had become the monstrous evil they do daily to
hundreds of human beings that they regard it as of no
more moral consequence than studying a dinner menu or
driving to work each day."

Bonner was whipped. He had just started a big job, and
he was defeated. He had run the gamut of the attacks
mounted by the *Union Leader* and Loeb and he had come
out second best. But, clearly, he could not resign. He had
just begun the job. It was simply that Bonner had finally
understood the "ground rules" of being president of the
University of New Hampshire and he made up his mind
to proceed.

Dr. Bonner began his own communications network. He
instituted a weekly newsletter which was sent to some
7,500 leaders in the state, including many notable alumni,
and a series of brochures, which were mailed to 50,000
New Hampshire residents, explaining the university's position on certain questions. But the assault by Loeb and
his newspapers never ended. If it wasn't one thing it was
another.

Although few were willing to come forward in Bonner's
public defense, it must be noted that almost no one had
any facilities with which to defend him. The other daily
newspapers in the state had jumped into the battle and
had written in Bonner's behalf, but Loeb always dismissed
this as being from the "Pipsqueak Press." Silly as this is,
it had, and still has, an effect. Also, Loeb's newspapers
were prone to continue harping on a theme long after the
battle had died.

Such attacks, and particularly the attack on Dr. Bonner,
were absolutely nauseating to thousands of those in New
Hampshire, but at best, they had no way to counter the
offensive. Had they made any public orations, they knew
they would become Loeb's prime targets, and, in many
instances, they knew that was all Loeb wanted. This would,

in turn, harm other aspects of life in the state which Loeb the Bully would then attack.

On the other hand, those who would seek to enhance their position with Loeb used this as an opportunity to be vocal in the denunciation of Dr. Bonner. One such was U.S. Sen. Norris Cotton (R-N.H.), who delivered a lengthy oration on the floor of the U.S. Senate denouncing the trustees of the university, and in particular Gov. Walter Peterson, for the naming of Dr. Bonner. Cotton based his criticism almost entirely upon the fact that Bonner had, at one time, served as a staff member for Cotton's Senate colleague, Sen. George McGovern (D-S.D.). Cotton called Peterson a "back stabber" and said that McGovern was "an avowed candidate for President" who would soon be campaigning in New Hampshire.

Senator Cotton was beginning to show how old a man in his early seventies can be—Peterson had been Cotton's campaign manager.

# 27

The office of Roman Catholic bishop of Manchester is a unique repository of power in New Hampshire. As such, it had always been treated with deference and respect. The state of New Hampshire ranks second among the states of the Union which are one diocese in the percentage of Roman Catholics to the total population. Rhode Island— the Diocese of Providence—is the state which ranks highest in the nation in percentage of Catholic population (more than 60%). Massachusetts, Connecticut, New York and New Jersey follow, in that order. New Hampshire, with a Catholic population of more than 32%, ranks sixth among all states in the ratio of Roman Catholic population. Although the state of New Hampshire had been largely "Yankee" and Protestants from the small towns have always dominated affairs of the state Legislature, the Roman Catholic bishop of Manchester was rarely, if ever, drawn into controversy.

Most Rev. Matthew F. Brady, D.D., became the fifth bishop of Manchester in 1945, succeeding Most Rev. John B. Peterson, D.D., who had died in that office. Bishop Brady came to Manchester from the See of Burlington, Vt., where he first came to know William Loeb while Loeb was publisher of the *Burlington Daily News.* If there was one person in the State of New Hampshire who never got any of Loeb's guff it was Bishop Brady. He had early served notice on Loeb that he would stand for no interference. In the one instance when an official of the diocese of Burlington had become enmeshed in a conflict with Loeb—that in the affair of the organization of the Textile Workers Union of America at the American Woolen Co. mills—Bishop Brady had promptly relieved the vicar general of his duties and replaced him, obviously with strict orders not to engage in any contact whatever with Loeb or his newspapers.

By the time Loeb came to Manchester, Bishop Brady was already head of the Manchester diocese and, until the death of Bishop Brady in September, 1959, there was never evidence of any contact between the two men. But, similarly, there was never a word other than that of praise in the *Manchester Union Leader* about the affairs of the diocese. Bishop Brady was a big man physically, prone to taking evening strolls through any given neighborhood in the city. He was an amiable man, well beloved by persons of all faiths in the city and state. The accomplishments of Bishop Brady's building program are unparalleled in the history of the diocese. During the 14 years of Bishop Brady's tenure, 30 parishes, 47 churches, 16 schools, 29 rectories, 11 convents, 18 parish halls and gymnasiums, three homes for the aged and two summer camps for youngsters were constructed within the diocese.

Installed as sixth bishop of Manchester in March, 1960, was the Most Rev. Ernest J. Primeau, S.T.D., a former monsignor on the staff of the Archdiocese of Chicago, who was elevated to the episcopacy coincident with his being named head of the Manchester See. And it was very shortly after his arrival in Manchester that Bishop Primeau became a key figure in the Second Vatican Council, to be convened by Pope John XXIII in Rome in 1962 to assess the role of Christianity in the modern world. During this period, Bishop Primeau was in Rome quite often, thoroughly engrossed in the affairs of the Church from that level. It was also during this time that the Roman Catholic Church brought about the greatest changes in its recent history, revising many of the basic laws of the church, chief among which was the saying of Mass in the vernacular. A greater participation in the affairs of the church was given the laity at this time, and the spirit of ecumenism was advocated, led by Pope John himself, who invited members of the Russian Orthodox Church to the Vatican Council to observe. The new involvement went both ways, and members of the Catholic clergy became more involved in affairs of state than before.

It was several years after Bishop Primeau had begun his term as head of the Manchester diocese that William Loeb began to become vocal about the affairs of the Roman Catholic Church in his *Union Leader*. Just about the first such occasion which anyone remembers occurred when Rev. Msgr. Philip J. Kenney, a Manchester pastor, took part in the 1965 march of integrationists from Selma to Montgomery, Ala. At that time, Loeb publicly took Monsignor Kenney to task for his participation.

Monsignor Kenney was not a guy who would take this criticism lying down. He took to his pulpit and said that his personal business was not that of William Loeb, mainly because Loeb had enough to do running a newspaper. Monsignor Kenney also relieved himself of some of his sentiments in the parish bulletin of St. Catherine Church, in Manchester's North End, of which he was pastor. As a result, the Sunday masses at which it was expected that Monsignor Kenney would deliver the sermon became very well attended, indeed. Among the worshipers on these Sunday mornings was one James J. Finnegan, director of the editorial page of the *Union Leader,* who was not averse to providing Monsignor Kenney ammunition for his following Sunday morning sermon, usually no later than the Tuesday or Wednesday editions of the newspaper. The parish council of St. Catherine, located in an above-average income neighborhood in Manchester, sponsored seminars and discussion groups on such subjects as the need of a broad based tax in New Hampshire, and this rankled Finnegan and, in turn, Loeb. But there was no interference with the pastor by the Bishop of Manchester. A protest march—3,000 students paraded to show support for a moratorium on the Vietnamese war—was staged in Manchester and Monsignor Kenney was a participant and the *Union Leader* bore down pretty heavily on the cleric for this, also. But Monsignor Kenney always stuck to his guns. In the process, he became a well-known and respected man throughout the length and breadth of the state. Of course, there was also a large number of those who adopted the posture that Monsignor Kenney should "keep his nose to himself" but these sentiments were usually voiced by those who wished to be viewed favorably by Loeb.

In the mid-'60's, Bishop Primeau restructured the diocesan staff. He chose as Episcopal Vicar for Community Affairs the Rev. Msgr. Philip J. Kenney, who subsequently suffered sporadic barbs from the Loeb press, but Monsignor Kenney could always be counted upon for an answer. He was never at a loss for words. But the reverence of the office of Bishop of Manchester was not yet singled out as a Loeb target, and, in that, it must be said that Loeb knew what he was doing in not picking on the bishop, mainly because the bishop had a little clout himself. He had clout, that is, only if he wanted to use it.

During all of this, there had never been any correspondence between the bishop and Loeb. In fact, the two men met only once during Bishop Primeau's entire term as Bishop of Manchester, and that was a chance meeting at a conference of New England community leaders in Boston when the two men happened to bump into each other (literally) in an exhibition hall.

But any editorial suggestions for Monsignor Kenney were always carried on the editorial page of the *Union Leader*. It was generally understood by most persons that the editorial page, in this regard, was the province of James J. Finnegan, himself a Roman Catholic, and it can only be assumed that this was the Loeb strategy. The name of Bishop Primeau was seldom, if ever, even mentioned in all of the space the *Union Leader* devoted to these diatribes; the target was always Monsignor Kenney.

However, on Aug. 15, 1971, during a Sunday morning mass at St. Joseph Church in Dover, near Durham, Rev. Daniel St. Laurent delivered a sermon in which he generally denounced the *Union Leader* for the series the newspaper had carried on Dr. Thomas N. Bonner on the occasion of Bonner's appointment as president of the nearby university. Father St. Laurent's remarks had not been reported in any form in the *Union Leader*. And it was 10 days after the incident occurred (on Aug. 25, 1971, to be exact) that the *Union Leader* devoted an eight-column "skyline" atop Page One to the effect that Father St. Laurent's pastor had been interviewed by the newspaper and the pastor, Rev. Joseph Desmond, was quoted as saying, " 'It is unfair' for priests to use the pulpit to air their political-secular views before a 'captive audience.' " It was a typical *Union Leader* interview, twisted, distorted and far from straight news. One of the quotes attributed to Father Desmond was one in which he was alleged to have said, "I'm not another Phil Kenney, I don't like conflict. I have to take courage in hand . . . to speak on these things, I felt driven."

So, of course, the *Union Leader,* never a newspaper to duck a "conflict" when it could exert the upper hand, sought out Monsignor Kenney for his views on the matter. The monsignor issued a statement which was printed on Page One of August 25, in which he said he was flattered by Father Desmond's reference to him in the interview and that the interview itself was "another illustration of the polarization that makes communication difficult." He went on to say in about 200 words that the priests had his support in what they said, that the *Union Leader* had, in fact, sought to make political capital out of unfortunate news reporting. The statement concluded: "In the Catholic community, we have come a long way since the Vatican Council in giving a voice to the laity in the affairs of the Church."

But Monsignor Kenney knew—anyone who read the newspaper knew, in fact—that anything that Monsignor Kenney said would be the subject of an editorial the next day. Finnegan, who himself was devoid of newspaper experience before assuming his position of control at the Union Leader Corporation, was the biggest second-guesser in the business. He could pick apart anything anybody said. Sure as the next day was August 27, there was the editorial blasting Monsignor Kenney: "New Policy On 'Pulpit Politics?' " and, what ho! Monsignor Kenney rated a double-header that day: the first editorial was followed by another, "He Likes Conflict." In both articles, the editorial writer adopted the stance that the Monsignor was picking on the newspaper and that he was taking political pot shots at the newspaper "from an ecclesiastical privileged sanctuary." Even Monsignor Kenney wouldn't bother to stoop to this level and the matter was apparently at rest for a few days. Then, several days later, on September 1, Page One headlines stated that the bishop would have no statement on "charges of secular politics from the pulpit." Whether or not this posture by the bishop infuriated the editors, the story went on for seven more paragraphs, rehashing what everyone hoped was a dead issue, the last paragraph reading as follows:

"Whether Bishop Primeau's refusal to issue a statement amounts to tacit approval of pulpit politics was not made clear. If approval is granted, it will represent a sharp departure from the church's traditional policy of keeping politics from the pulpit."

The *Union Leader* was goading the bishop and refused to let the issue die. On Sept. 2, 1971, Bishop Primeau issued another statement to the *Union Leader*, a six paragraph statement outlining the responsibilities of certain of his staff. The *Union Leader* saw fit to preface the bishop's statement with 11 paragraphs and the headline: "Bishop Approves 'Pulpit Politics.' " The story in the *Union Leader* that day was under a byline and the reporter apparently reported on what he wished the bishop had said, or, at least, this is the only inference which could be drawn from reading it.

The lead paragraph read as follows:

> "A statement issued yesterday by the Most Rev. Ernest J. Primeau, STD, bishop of Manchester Diocese, clearly sets forth a new policy condoning secular politics from the pulpits of Catholic churches in New Hampshire."

> "The bishop's actual statement, in full, is as follows:

> "I am well aware of the positions taken by Msgr. Kenney in issues currently under discussion in New Hampshire.

> "I welcome the opportunity to clarify the areas of responsibility within our diocesan structure.

> "The Second Vatican Council emphasized the concept of shared responsibility. Accordingly, the diocese of Manchester has been restructured so that, as bishop, I share my authority not only with a vicar general but with three vicars episcopal.

> "The vicar for Christian Formation is largely concerned with education, liturgy and ecumenism.

> "The vicar for administration is responsible for finances and is, as chancellor, the bishop's attorney in the implementation of church law.

> "The vicar for community affairs, who supervises the Offices of Mission Affairs and Communications, is the diocesan spokesman in public issues which have a moral dimension. Monsignor Kenney holds this post. In this capacity, he has my confidence and support."

There is no bully in the world who would have gone to the extremes that the *Union Leader* went in this matter on Sept. 3, 1971, unless the bully figured he had the fight won. It was probably because the editorial writers had already composed their editorials, that the reporter so distorted Bishop Primeau's statement. At any rate, two editorials appeared on the very same day, Sept. 3, 1971, blasting

Most Rev. Ernest J. Primeau, STD, Bishop of Manchester. They were entitled, "Pulpit Politics Condoned" and "Keep Your Eye On THE ISSUE."

Even though the statement by Bishop Primeau on September 2 was the last utterance from the episcopal headquarters made on the matter, the *Union Leader* kept on belaboring the issue, each time including a photograph of Bishop Primeau with an editorial: on Sept. 18, 1971, entitled, "Bishop Primeau's Clarification," and on Sept. 27, 1971, entitled, "A Problem of Conscience."

The *Union Leader* certainly had the last word in this skirmish, as it always did, but, by no stretch of the imagination, could anyone see that Loeb had won the battle. The Most Rev. Ernest J. Primeau, S.T.D., Bishop of Manchester, had retained his posture and refused to stoop to the level of the newspaper. The bishop adhered to an announcement made by the chancery on September 27 that it would answer any and all inquiries from the *Union Leader* if and when they were received in writing.

# 28

If there was one person of whom it can be said that he did the most to attract attention to the New Hampshire Presidential primary, this person has to be William Loeb. The reason is obvious: this test of political power became the focus of national attention every four years, bringing inordinate notoriety to a publisher who had spent most of the years of his adult life trying to make himself into a "kingmaker." The *Manchester Union Leader,* as the state's largest newspaper, was quoted all across the nation, and abroad, during times of New Hampshire's primaries, by the countless newsmen who came to the Granite State to cover the political doings. These visiting newsmen never

had the time or the insight to question the ins and outs
of the *Union Leader*'s pronouncements, and they weren't
really concerned with the intrastate politics of New Hampshire. What these newsmen could see and understand,
especially those who had visited the state on assignment
during previous Presidential primaries—and those who
were visiting for the first time could take the word, and
usually did take the word, of those who had seen New
Hampshire politics before—was that William Loeb, if he
were not a factor to begin with, would make himself a
factor in any situation which would bring attention to
bear on Loeb.

Another thing which the visiting newsmen could recog-
nize was the fact that during each quadrennial visit to
New Hampshire it was everywhere apparent that William
Loeb was strong, and getting stronger. And, really, why
wouldn't he? He had had four years more to hammer at
the consciousness of the residents of New Hampshire. By
the time of the 1968 Presidential primary there had been
an entire generation, or part of one, grown up in New
Hampshire without having seen any newspaper which
could be compared exactly to the *Union Leader,* and by
1972 primary time, there would be that many more young
adults voting who were in the same boat.

It had been a foregone conclusion since the 1968 national elections that Sen. Edmund S. Muskie (D-Me.) would
be a candidate for the Presidency in 1972 and that, in the
New Hampshire first-in-the-nation primary, Muskie would
be a tough man to beat. To those who had been in a position to notice, 1972 could very well be the year when
Muskie could cash in on the investments of time and effort
he had made on behalf of the Young Democrats in New
Hampshire in the mid-50's when Muskie, the Democratic
governor and then senator from the solidly Republican
State of Maine, was an oddity and had given freely of his
time to New Hampshire to appear at fund-raisers. Another
consideration was that those Young Democrats of the mid-
'50's whom Muskie saw fit to assist were, by 1971, no
longer young people a few years out of college, but were

persons who were established in their family and community lives and, to a large degree, persons who could give of their time, money and energies to assist Muskie.

Muskie knew this, of course. It was the name of the game in big-time politics, and he carefully nurtured a New Hampshire organization by making sporadic appearances and through correspondence to his "regulars." (That isn't really hard to understand if you also understand that the only way to get to Maine is by going over or going around New Hampshire.) Therefore, it is no exaggeration to say that Edmund S. Muskie was the front-runner in the 1972 New Hampshire Presidential primary the day after the 1968 Presidential election was decided.

William Loeb's target had already been selected for him. He had to be against Muskie, there was no way on God's green earth that he could go for the Maine senator. And, even though Loeb was finding more and more fault with the administration of Richard M. Nixon, most persons figured that, ultimately, Loeb would be in the corner of the President when it came reelection time.

Loeb fired the first real salvo of the 1972 primary on March 18, 1971, with a Page One story which reported that Los Angeles Mayor Sam Yorty struck out at Muskie at his weekly news conference in Los Angeles, saying that Muskie was avoiding a visit to Vietnam and Southeast Asia, an "area on which he has presumed to speak with great authority." The news story had neither AP nor UPI attribution (which connoted the *Union Leader* had obtained it from "private" sources) and went on to announce that Mayor Yorty had written Senator Muskie a 22-page letter in February, 1971, challenging the senator's view on foreign affairs, "particularly the latter's proposal of a fixed deadline for the withdrawal of American forces from Southeast Asia."

Then, on April 26, Mayor Yorty himself came to Manchester and he was given the first-class job of heralding by Loeb, including a front-page feature story on the Los Angeles mayor four days prior to his visit. It began to appear during the late spring that whenever William Loeb was not attacking Dr. Thomas N. Bonner and the University of New Hampshire and Most Rev. Ernest J. Primeau, he was telling his readers what a great guy Sam Yorty was, whoever Sam Yorty was.

Still there was the overriding suspicion that, despite all of his criticism, Loeb would end up in Nixon's corner many months later, even as Loeb more and more frequently mentioned Yorty as a possible Presidential candidate.

Summer was coming in that year of 1971, as always, but this time it brought with it a new problem. The State of Florida, which depended on tourists even more than did New Hampshire, had announced that it had moved forward its primary date for Presidential candidates to coincide with that of the Granite State. As blind as they are to many other things when they want to be, the New Hampshire legislators immediately knew what this meant: that Florida would steal all of the thunder away from the New Hampshire Presidential primary. This would never do. The New Hampshire General Court, whose 424 members met for six months every two years, were clearing up last-minute details before adjournment, and the matter of the Presidential primary immediately took top priority.

A bill was immediately set in the works to push ahead the date of the New Hampshire Presidential primary. It was amazing how quickly this bit of legislation got the proper action. It was read to the body; a public hearing was set within hours. The chairman and his committee were wide-eyed as they heard how beneficial it was to the State of New Hampshire to have the first-in-the-nation primary. (To bring to focus exactly how the state derived revenue from this political circus, the Speaker of the House arrived as a witness himself to attest to the fact that "besides, newspapermen drink a lot.")

There was, however, a dissenter, a representative who had the reputation, if not the habit, of lighting his pipe every few minutes and then automatically objecting to whatever was before whatever body in which he was in attendance. He pointed out the complications involved;

that Primary Day was also Town Meeting Day, and also the day the state's school districts were geared to their annual reporting; he went on at length as to how many statutes were geared to Town Meeting Day.

At just about this point, the Speaker of the House was again recognized and he told the committee chairman and its members: "I don't know about you guys, but let me say this: New Hampshire will have the first primary every four years if we have to compete with the Rose Bowl, so do anything you want, but get this goddam bill back upstairs, we're waiting to vote on it."

"Ought to pass," was the committee recommendation, and pass it did on voice vote, second reading; acclamation, third reading. It was law when Peterson paused in the hallway on his way out of the governor's office to sign the measure, after the Senate had passed the bill in a matter of seconds. Some 273 laws and statutes had to be altered to accommodate the measure, but New Hampshire was to have the first primary and every one of the other 49 states were put on notice that if they thought they were ever going to get the first primary away from New Hampshire, they were merely spinning their legislative wheels.

On Aug. 6, 1971, President Nixon planned to visit Campobello Island which is just about as far "down east" as you can go, in Maine, halfway between the equator and the North Pole. And the President decided to stop en route at a Nashua, N.H., nursing home, an appropriate setting for a major statement on Medicare. It was widely known that William Loeb was greatly chagrined that Nixon had not seen fit to effect the release from Lewisburg Federal Penitentiary of James R. Hoffa, and it was assumed that this was Loeb's major beef with Nixon and that he was just making waves with any other issues he raised with the President's policies.

It was no secret to those close to the efforts in getting Hoffa released that Loeb had visited the White House socially, that he had had numerous conversations with administration officials on the subject of Hoffa's release from prison, and that one *Union Leader* reporter openly boasted to many that Loeb had even gone so far as to have telephoned Herb Klein, director of communications for Mr. Nixon, and informed Klein that if Nixon wanted any help in New Hampshire, the President had better help Hoffa. Helping Hoffa meant only one thing—getting Hoffa out of prison.

The White House had earlier announced the visit of President Nixon to Communist China, an announcement which "shocked" Loeb a few weeks earlier. And on that Aug. 6, 1971, when President Nixon landed in New Hampshire, he was afforded the most unusual welcome imaginable by Publisher William Loeb.

The *Manchester Union Leader* carried an eight-column streamer across Page One which blared:

### "Welcome to N.H., Mr. President"

But occupying three columns immediately under the headline was a cartoon depicting a gleeful Nixon, carrying an umbrella labelled "appeasement" rushing to embrace a huge Chinese figure with a Communist hammer and sickle emblazoned on his jacket, while the Statue of Liberty shielded her eyes so she couldn't witness the scene. And on the two columns next to the cartoon was a Page One Loeb editorial entitled:

### "A Sad Good-bye To an Old Friend"

Some welcome! It took William Loeb about three columns of news space to "say good-bye" to his "old friend." Loeb narrated all the support he had given Nixon in previous political outings in New Hampshire and he told how "the publisher and Mrs. Loeb are very fond of the President and Mrs. Nixon personally, and we thoroughly enjoyed our recent dinner at the White House." Loeb condescended to say that he and his wife "found the Nixons to be fine people whose personal conduct has set a splendid example of what an American family should be like."

But Loeb then went on to say in 13 long paragraphs that he knew more about dealing with the Chinese Communists than did either President Nixon or Dr. Kissinger, and that he considered President Nixon's proposed visit to China to be "immoral, indecent, insane and fraught with danger for the survival of the United States."

On and on, boring, very boring. Finally Loeb said:

"THIS NEWSPAPER AND ITS PUBLISHER THEREFORE REGRETFULLY ANNOUNCE THAT IF THE DEMOCRATS—OR ANY OTHER POLITICAL PARTY WITH A PROSPECT OF CAPTURING THE WHITE HOUSE—NOMINATE A PRESIDENTIAL CANDIDATE WHO IS DEDICATED TO THE RESTORATION OF OUR NATIONAL DEFENSES AND WHO IS PREPARED TO SUPPORT A FOREIGN POLICY DESIGNED TO PRESERVE THE SECURITY AND HONOR OF THE UNITED STATES, WE WILL SUPPORT THAT CANDIDATE AGAINST PRESIDENT NIXON IN THE 1972 ELECTIONS."

With the President of the United States on Loeb's home court, Loeb had clearly spelled it out for him. Those close enough to the behind-the-scenes dealings on the Hoffa release from prison knew it meant just one thing: Hoffa gets out of prison or Nixon would have one hell of a time in New Hampshire. One of the men who would most assuredly know exactly what Loeb intended was Ken W. Clawson, a reporter for the *Washington Post* who had been assigned to cover the hearings and meetings which had been held in conjunction with Hoffa's many attempts at parole, the most recent only a few months before.

And maybe Richard Milhous Nixon was taken in by Loeb's stern warning. Maybe it was one of the factors that went into Watergate, the scandal which would begin to unfold nearly a year later. Maybe the national press was fooled. (Those included in the President's press party couldn't have been treated to a better display of William Loeb flexing his editorial muscles.)*

* Apparently one segment of the national press which was taken in, at least in part, was *The New York Times,* which published in its Sunday magazine section on Dec. 12, 1971, a very long, very well re-

The "Sad Good-Bye" was certainly a grandstand play, but it didn't impress anybody with any amount of political savvy in New Hampshire. B. J. McQuaid had pointed out in 1968 that asking Republicans to vote for Wesley Powell was like "asking George Washington to give Benedict Arnold another chance." And in 1970, when Meldrim Thomson, Jr., had run on the American Party ticket for governor, Loeb himself had depicted the man as showing "weakness of character," unable "to take it when the going got really hot," and unable "to keep his word." Gov. Walter Peterson had hardly put his arm back at his side after taking the oath of office in January when Loeb was building up Meldrim Thomson, Jr., again. Since May, Wesley Powell had been a Page One figure whenever Loeb needed anyone to quote with an ugly blast at anyone. Since June 8, to be exact, Powell had rated eight-column "skylines" when Loeb figured the situation warranted.

The weekend following the Friday of Nixon's visit was that time of the summer when the Democrats of New Hampshire held one of the year's biggest bashes—the annual outing of the Hillsborough County Democratic Committee at a picnic grove just outside of Nashua, the state's second largest city. Hillsborough County, which also includes Manchester, accounts for 60% of the state's registered Democrats and the voting strength of the county itself is enough to sway the balance in any primary in the state. Among those on hand for this occasion, a sunny Sunday afternoon, were: Sen. Birch Bayh of Indiana, Sen. Henry M. Jackson of Washington, Sen. George McGovern of South Dakota, Sen. Thomas J. McIntyre of New Hampshire and Gov. Kenneth Curtis of Maine, representing Sen. Edmund S. Muskie.

When someone asked the whereabouts of Mayor Sam Yorty, Senator McGovern answered: "Yorty's got enough

---

searched article entitled, "Nixon's Too Left-Wing For William Loeb," by Bill Kovach, at that time New England correspondent for *The Times*. Kovach's article, which must have taken quite some time to research and prepare, was by all odds the best of the many presentations made of Loeb and his newspapers of the countless profiles which had been done on the man up to that time.

to do in Los Angeles." And this was met with uproarious laughter, mainly because the Democrats knew that if Yorty entered the Presidential race in New Hampshire, it was a foregone conclusion that he would be on the Loeb Party ticket. But McGovern's remark, quoted in the press, did nothing to endear the Dakotan to William Loeb. Loeb had levelled his blasts at Dr. Bonner at UNH largely because of Bonner's past association as a staff aide to McGovern, and it was not long before McGovern got the Page One editorial nickname of "Georgie Chutzpah."

For the next couple of months, Loeb's editorials assumed a regular pattern: rap Bonner and UNH, praise Yorty, rap Muskie, praise Powell, rap Peterson, praise Thomson, rap Nixon, praise Crowley, rap McGovern. The line-up for the Loeb Party was coming through pretty clear—Yorty for President as a Democrat, Thomson for governor as a Republican, Crowley for governor as a Democrat, and it was flat-out that Loeb would back Wesley Powell who had already announced that he was planning to run for the U.S. Senate against Thomas J. McIntyre, who would be going after his second full term in 1972. And, if William Loeb could back Wesley Powell for public office after what he had said about him for almost 10 years, it was clear that William Loeb could back Jesse James for Secretary of the Treasury. Either that or Loeb was *never* to be believed, absolutely never!

It was November before Yorty came to Manchester formally to announce for the Presidency. From the outset it was clear that Yorty's campaign was a very well-financed one, indeed. McGovern opened a Manchester headquarters in December and shortly thereafter, "Scoop" Jackson, whose New Hampshire effort really had never gotten off the ground, announced that he was not going to make a run for the White House in 1972. William Loeb grasped at this straw to tell his readers that it was his assumption that Jackson was acting in this manner because Jackson was afraid of the threat posed by the candidacy of Sam Yorty.

Meldrim Thomson, Jr., announced his candidacy for the governorship and Loeb praised the Orford man, saying that Thomson "could not be a hypocrite and lay aside his principles of economy, service and honesty in government." Loeb said Thomson was a Republican worth voting for. This shot of Loeb's missed the mark, also.

Loeb was never one to show the slightest deference to women in his editorial judgments. He had already done a pretty good job on Jacqueline Kennedy, Eleanor Roosevelt, Marilyn Monroe, and Meg Peterson. In December, 1971, he chose Mrs. Eleanor McGovern, the senator's wife, for his Page One subject because she, on a tour through the Union Leader Building, had mistaken a portrait of Daniel Webster for that of President McKinley. This was more than enough for Loeb to justify as reason why her husband could not possibly be a good President.

Senator Muskie arrived in Manchester in December and was introduced by Senator McIntyre to make it official that he would be a candidate in the March New Hampshire Presidential primary.

At 3:45 P.M. on Dec. 23, 1971, James Riddle Hoffa walked out of Lewisburg Federal Penitentiary, having been one of 253 persons to whom President Nixon had extended executive clemency at Christmastime. Hoffa had served four years, nine months and 16 days of an eight-year sentence for jury tampering and an additional five years for mail fraud. As a condition of his freedom, Hoffa accepted, and signed, an agreement that he would refrain from "direct or indirect management of any labor organization" until March 6, 1980.

William Loeb, on Page One of the December 24 *Union Leader,* said he was "delighted" by President Nixon's act. "He never should have been there in the first place." said Loeb. The news story said that Hoffa telephoned Loeb at his Pride's Crossing home less than an hour after he was released. "Mr. Hoffa expressed his gratitude to me . . . for the long years of support in the fight for justice," Loeb was quoted as having said.

During the Christmas school recess, two huge buses pulled up in front of a downtown Manchester hotel loaded with college kids from Indiana who had gotten a free ride to Manchester during vacation to work for the candidacy for the office of President of the United States of their own Sen. Vance Hartke. Senator Bayh had long since ceased to be even a consideration, having announced publicly he was withdrawing because of the illness of his wife.

On the morning after the arrival of the Indiana college students, a Hartke campaign aide was making the rounds of the hotel rooms where the students were quartered and he was holding reveille. When he came to one room, a male voice called from within, "Tell the senator we're not working today and thank him for the free honeymoon he's giving me and my wife." It turned out that two of the students included in the entourage had detoured to a JP's office on the way to the bus station in Indianapolis.

That morning Hartke made it official that he was a candidate, to the "thunderous" applause of the college kids (minus two). The field was growing, and it was not all on the Democratic side. Congressman Paul N. McCloskey, Jr., of California, had opened Concord headquarters and was touring the state most actively as a Republican candidate to challenge Nixon. He drew a broadside from Loeb because his program for ending the Vietnam conflict was almost identical to that of McGovern.

The 1972 Presidential primary filing period opened, and it developed that it had retained a little bit of the comedy from previous years when Pat Paulsen, a sad-faced comic from the Smothers Brothers television presentation, arrived and announced his candidacy. And blossoming around Manchester and certain other parts of the Granite State were oversized buttons saying, "Howdy Doody For President."

Sam Yorty made it official through some of his New Hampshire workers and they filed him at the State House, and Sam, himself, spoke to Concord on the telephone to the "Yortymobile," a huge camper with a rear speaking platform mounted thereon, which had become a familiar sight as it cruised through the New Hampshire hills blaring Sousa marches.

And William Loeb, on Jan. 7, 1972, announced a "White House plot" on Page One. Loeb said he had received a telephone call from an unidentified caller asking him to back the candidacy of Florida Governor Kirk, the man Meldrim Thomson, Jr., had backed for Vice President four years earlier.

But Loeb was also following one of his earlier themes, claiming that the government had itself been guilty of jury tampering when Hoffa was found guilty of jury tampering. Loeb's papers had run Page One copyrighted stories to this effect. On Jan. 11, 1972, the Justice Department announced that it had investigated thoroughly Loeb's claim and that the story was an utter fabrication. Loeb responded with a Page One editorial calling Nixon the "Great Devaluator," and in an editorial entitled "Heaven Help Us," he ridiculed Texas Sen. John Tower's claim that "what we need and desperately need is another four years of Richard Nixon."

Finally, the Loeb Party candidate for President as a Republican was unveiled. It was Congressman John Ashbrook, of Ohio, and the greatest reason that could be found in the Loeb press for voting for Ashbrook was that he, like that "great Democrat, Sam Yorty," favored no sales tax for the State of New Hampshire. On January 29, Loeb himself took to the campaign trail, an infrequent event in itself. He appeared at the Knights of Columbus Hall in Milford alongside Mayor Yorty. Two days later, Loeb featured a column by Holmes Alexander (gave it the eight-column treatment, in fact), which stated that "Muskie Is Domestic and Dangerous," giving as the principle reason to support this headline, "He sees only what is close buy (sic)." Loeb himself proclaimed over an editorial, naturally, on Page One:

### "McCloskey, Muskie— Spells Taxskie"

By February 1, the starting lineup was complete. On the Republican side, the candidates for President in New

Hampshire would be Ashbrook, McCloskey, Nixon and Paulsen, and for Vice President, Austin Burton, of Greenwich, Conn., the "Chief Burning Wood" of the 1968 campaign who sold psychedelic posters in New York's Greenwich Village.

On the Democratic side, there was Edward T. Coll, a Hartford, Conn., man who said he was most interested in the problems of prison reform and those of the inner city; Hartke, McGovern, Muskie and Yorty. Former Gov. Endicott Peabody of Massachusetts had been touring the state asking nomination for the Vice Presidency, stating that it had too long been the office held by the designated candidate of the Presidential nominee and that the Vice President should be a candidate of the people. He had drawn some Loeb fire, not for his Vice Presidential platform, or suggestion, but because Governor Peabody's mother had been in the march at Selma, Ala., with Monsignor Kenney.

In order not to disappoint the three major television networks which set up shop earlier than usual to televise the New Hampshire proceedings, Loeb treated them to a February 7 Page One editorial entitled, "Flip-Flop Muskie Is a Phony." And, almost as if to show the nation via the three television networks just how vitriolic he could be, on February 11 Loeb carried one of his Page One beauties which he entitled, " 'Surrender Now' News Media." This last piece of composition was as if it were the personification of the adage, "Give a man enough rope. . . ." McGovern's campaign had been almost identical to that of Sen. Eugene McCarthy four years earlier: college students going door-to-door with the message to end the war in Vietnam at all costs; the war was nothing more than an exercise in futility. But, as of February 11, the candidacy of McGovern began to carry real meaning, because William Loeb had grabbed for too much rope.

The thing that nettled Loeb to the authorship of that Page One editorial was an editorial which had appeared in the *Keene Evening Sentinel,* a very well-respected daily in Cheshire County, in the extreme southwestern part of the state, with a daily circulation of more than 11,000

copies The *Sentinel,* normally a Republican-flavored journal, had said:

> "New Hampshire's primary is thus very important to
> both men (Muskie as well as McGovern). It's a pity they
> couldn't have met in head-to-head competition, without
> the likes of Sam Yorty and his sponsor, Bill Loeb, clutter-
> ing up the landscape.'"

Loeb, in reply, was at his brashest:

> "Of course, the Keene Sentinel WOULD be in favor of
> somebody like McGovern, who wants to sabotage the war
> effort in Vietnam and throw away everything that 50,000
> American young men died to save, who wants to leave the
> Catholics and other freedom-loving people in South Viet-
> nam to be massacred by the Viet Cong and the North Viet-
> namese Communists.
>
> "Over the years, the Keene Sentinel has consistently at-
> tacked the FBI and almost every other patriotic institu-
> tion we can think of. It is in favor of a sales tax, an in-
> come tax, more taxes generally, and anything that follows
> the so-called 'liberal' line.
>
> "As a matter of fact, the son of the publisher of the
> Keene Evening Sentinel fled to Sweden, returned to this
> country—and the last we heard, was under arrest in an
> armed forces prison. So, what can you EXPECT except a
> bleeding-heart attitude and a running down of the United
> States?"

Loeb went on to chastise Muskie, McGovern, McCloskey
and Hartke, give limited support to Nixon "if you want
a modified run-and-strike policy," but most of all to exalt
Yorty and Ashbrook.

He concluded:

> "Unfortunately, the majority of the daily newspapers in
> New Hampshire are in the hands of left-wingers who pur-
> sue an anti-U.S. policy in international as well as domestic
> affairs. They want to spend our tax money without limit.
>
> "It's a great shame that thousands of New Hampshire
> readers are, in our opinion, misled every evening as they
> read the propaganda that is printed in the leftist news-
> papers."

On Saturday, February 12, the next day, the following two-column full-face statement appeared on Page One of the *Union Leader:*

## "Editorial Error Prompts Apology

"We apologize for a typographical error in yesterday's Page One editorial, ' "Surrender Now" News Media,' which our readers must have caught immediately.

"The fourth paragraph of the editorial referred to the son of the ASSISTANT publisher of the Keene Evening Sentinel fleeing to Sweden, returning to this country, and being held under arrest in an armed forces prison. Regrettably, the word "assistant" was unintentionally omitted.

"Since the incident we cited has been the subject of news reports in this and other newspapers, we are sure that our readers were not misled.

"Nevertheless, to eliminate even the possibility of a misunderstanding, we would like to make it clear that it was the son of the ASSISTANT publisher of the Keene Evening Sentinel who fled to Sweden.—EDITORS."

Loeb was right in stating in his apology that his readers were not misled. A vast number of people knew exactly to whom Loeb was referring. Loeb was, on the other hand, wrong in trying to think that anyone would buy his story that this was a "typographical error." Loeb was wrong, dead wrong.

The tale of Jimmy Zwicker, formerly of Keene, N.H., was well known, certainly best known to any of those who were of draft age or anyone else, for that matter, who wanted a "classic" case to hold up as one of unfairness of military service in Vietnam.

The tale of Jim Zwicker was so well known, in fact, that it had been granted almost one-quarter of Page One in *The New York Times* on Dec. 27, 1971, little more than a month previous, and more than a half-page on the inside page where the story was continued. The story had been written by the same Bill Kovach who had done the magazine story on Loeb. Kovach's story on Zwicker had been widely noted in New England, especially in view of the McGovern and the McCloskey campaigns in New Hampshire. Reprints of Kovach's story were up in campaign headquarters all over New Hampshire for everyone to read and understand.

Loeb's " 'Surrender Now' " job had appeared in the morning *Union Leader,* the statewide edition, first, as was always the case, and by afternoon, most New Hampshire dailies had taken to their own Page One to denounce the Manchester publisher. In the *Keene Evening Sentinel,* Publisher James Ewing signed a Page One editorial, a rare act indeed, in which he stated that Loeb had attacked the *Sentinel* in a "despicable" front-page editorial. Ewing said the *Sentinel* had not backed Senator McGovern, or anyone else in either party. He reprinted Loeb's questionable fourth paragraph and called it "a gutter-level statement, which is also inaccurate and incomplete." Ewing gave a brief run-down of the facts and concluded:

> "To attack the Keene Sentinel because of the actions of the son of its assistant publisher is contemptible.
> "To attack the young man without stating all the facts is even more contemptible."

And "contemptible" in this case is a mild word. It is difficult and most trying to attach superlatives to the slobbering outbursts of William Loeb—the man who wrote his wife that he intended to drink straight alcohol so that he himself would escape the World War II draft—but this story on Jimmy Zwicker has got to take the cake. *The Times'* story on Dec. 27, 1971, had been wholly accurate—as are the overwhelming majority of stories in *The New York Times*—but even in the intervening month and a half, the Jim Zwicker tale had almost reached its conclusion, so far so that its conclusion was foregone: That James K. Zwicker, 25, Navy hospital corpsman attached to a U.S. Marine unit in Vietnam, would receive an honorable discharge from the U.S. Armed Forces after a five-year period of despair and disillusionment.

His father, Kenneth F. Zwicker, is assistant publisher of

the Keene newspaper, a World War II combat veteran of
the Marine Corps wherein he served as a non-commissioned
officer, and a capable, learned and hard-working newspaperman. Zwicker's talents as a journalist are so esteemed,
in fact, that he has served as a lecturer in journalism at
the University of Massachusetts in Amherst, Mass.

Jim Zwicker was 18 when he was graduated from Keene
High School in 1965 and he was no more eager to go off
to fight a war in Vietnam than any other kid of that age
and that era. His father says that he was somewhat of a
loner with a rather artistic bent, a writer of poetry and
such, who opposed the war and perished the thought of
the draft. Young Zwicker, one of six children, knew from
long experience it would be fruitless to argue with his
father about avoiding military service, and he went off to
the University of America in Mexico City in the fall of
1965, returning home at Christmastime when he decided
that the university was not for him at that time. Shortly
thereafter, accepting the military service as something of
an inevitable destiny, he enlisted in the Navy and was sent
to boot camp at Great Lakes, Ill., and from there to Marine training at Camp Lejeune, N.C., where he was assigned to duty with that branch of the Navy Medical
Corps which ministers to Marines. He was then sent to
Camp Pendleton, Calif., where he stayed for one year, and,
in early February, 1968, his unit was sent to Danang,
South Vietnam. The elder Zwicker had been a member of
a group of U.S. newspapermen who had toured part of
southeast Asia in 1967.

Jim's outfit, the First Marine Division, took part in an
operation called Allen Brook in May of 1968 and Zwicker
went along. The Marines carried rifles, Zwicker, a corpsman, carried a first aid kit. The infantry company was
ambushed and the entire unit was practically wiped out.
Zwicker was one of a few survivors who were evacuated.
Zwicker himself had been hit in the face and leg by shrapnel and taken to Tripler General Hospital in Honolulu,
from where Zwicker wrote a letter home.

"It's plainly inhumane, senseless, valueless, pointless and
ridiculous seeing 18-year-old guys turned into chopped

unidentifiable meat," Zwicker wrote his father from the hospital.

"And the crying and the echo of confusion, the mortally wounded crying to be taken out of there, screaming and pleading for the bird to land, asking you when the choppers will get there and begging you to somehow make them land when you can't.

"And you, lying to them as they die, telling them the choppers are on their way when they're not; telling him he's going to make it and to hang on, when you know he isn't."

Then in June, 1968, the Zwickers received a telephone call from their son, still in the Honolulu hospital, telling them that the doctors had told him he was to be returned to duty, even though the shrapnel had not been removed from his nasal cavity, and that he would be returning to Vietnam in about three weeks. It was another three weeks before the Zwickers heard of their son again when, through a group of Keene college-age students, they inadvertently heard of the "Jimmy Freedom Fund," a money-raising effort which had begun among Jim's friends in Keene for the benefit of young Zwicker. Ken Zwicker pressed the youths and discovered that his son was at that time in Alaska and that he had gone AWOL from the hospital in Honolulu when his return to Vietnam became imminent.

Ken Zwicker spoke to his son by telephone and told him he would send him some money. He told his son that he had a big decision to make for himself. He could either go back to Hawaii with the money he was to receive, or he could go to Sweden; no one else could make the decision for him. The boy received the money and went to Sweden, where he drifted from job to job for about three years.

In the latter part of 1971, young Zwicker contacted his father, who informed his son that, while he could understand fully why the young man had done as he had done, he could not help him until he approached the solution to his problem by way of the avenue which Jim himself knew to exist. Zwicker told his son he would help him only after he turned himself in to the proper authorities.

So James Zwicker went to Stockholm and surrendered himself at the U.S. Embassy. The authorities there arranged for his flight to the United States and he was transferred to the Brooklyn, N.Y., Navy Yard where he was held in detention. After initial examination, Corpsman Zwicker was transferred to the U.S. Naval Hospital, St. Albans, L.I.

Ken Zwicker went from Keene to New York where he contacted the Naval authorities, who, Ken Zwicker says, were honestly and deeply concerned with the case, especially with the family's feelings. Ken Zwicker retained civilian counsel in New York and he conducted a cursory examination. At the hospital, meanwhile, Corpsman Zwicker was undergoing thorough physical and psychiatric examination, then was transferred to the U.S. Naval Hospital, Philadelphia, where it was determined he would undergo more thorough treatment and be allowed a complete rest and rehabilitation.

It was at this stage of the game that Loeb wrote his vicious and inaccurate blasts in Manchester on February 11.

In early spring, 1972, Corpsman Zwicker was put on indefinite sick leave from the Naval Hospital at Philadelphia and, within a very few months, he was given an honorable discharge from the U.S. Navy.

The February 11 editorial by Loeb which concerned the *Keene Evening Sentinel* says quite a bit about Loeb the man, his biases, his complexes, his hates. But, to a greater degree, it says something about Loeb the publisher—he doesn't do his homework!

# 29

The cast of characters in the 1972 New Hampshire Presidential primary was growing. Congressman Wilbur Mills (D-Ark.), who had made a speaking appearance in New

Hampshire during October was not himself a candidate
(officially, that is) but on the day after the filing period
closed in January, an elaborate Mills-for-President campaign headquarters was opened amid much fanfare in
Manchester. The grand opening was well-orchestrated,
complete with a campaign film, "The Congressman from
Kenset," narrated by Burgess Meredith, which showed
Mills touring his home state as well as in action in the
Nation's Capital. A healthy slate of delegate candidates
who would run as "favorable to Mills" was unveiled and
many of these were former supporters of Sen. Henry M.
Jackson in the very early days of the campaign. There was
no shortage of Mills-for-President campaign literature, buttons, posters, bumper strips, and the like—even Mills-for-
President coffee cups—all prepared in advance waiting for
the filing day to come and go so that Mills could be a
non-candidate. As such, Mills' strength would have to be
shown in a write-in effort because the Congressman's name
would not appear on the ballot, although the names of his
delegate candidates would. In charge of the Mills headquarters was a former Razorback tackle, Joseph Ward, of
the Ward School Bus family of Conway, Ark., who said
that Congressman Mills was "like a daddy to me." Soon appeared a tailor-made Ward school bus, complete with bar,
to make the campaigning less rigorous. The New Hampshire campaign was a deliberate effort to find out just how
strong Mills would be on the national ticket.

But the *dramatis personae* of the 1972 New Hampshire
Presidential primary was not confined to actual candidates.
(It rarely is in New Hampshire.) The state had been
alive with nationally-known personalities who could be
counted on to draw a crowd in their own right, but who
were appearing on behalf of a candidate. Most of these
in the Granite State for this primary were working on behalf of Senator McGovern and all of them were working,
and all of them were drawing crowds, and most of the
crowds were impressed with the articulateness of these
persons who had gained their fame in fields other than
politics: Shirley MacLaine, the motion picture and televi-

sion actress; Dennis Weaver, most widely known in New Hampshire as "Chester" on "Gunsmoke"; Ray Schoenke, the offensive tackle for the Washington Redskins; Valerie Kushner, a POW wife whose surgeon-husband was being held prisoner in Vietnam, and Jan Stennerud, place-kicking specialist for the Kansas City Chiefs, to name a few. These five were all campaigning for McGovern and some were often introduced by Pierre Salinger, press secretary to former President Kennedy, who himself had covered the campaign trails in New Hampshire some 12 years earlier.

Yorty's campaign was clearly going nowhere. The main battery in the Los Angeles mayor's arsenal was the *Union Leader*. Loeb had run nearly full-page features about how much St. Patrick and Ireland meant to Yorty, a tasteless and ill-disguised, even crude, attempt to sway the Irish vote. Another half-page feature of Yorty receiving the honors of the French city of Bordeaux was aimed at the French-Canadian population and this latter effort showed how little Loeb knew about the state's demography.

Many, many years before, the French-Canadian population of New Hampshire had been a most significant part of any election, particularly on the Democratic side of the ballot, usually in primaries. But this had long since ceased to be. The elder generation was all but gone, and with the passing of the parents and grandparents who had been brought to live with their sons and daughters in the United States, the habit of speaking French in the home and the school was dying out. Even on Manchester's West Side, in its day noted for the concentration of Canadian-Americans, the French flavor was vanishing. (La Caisse Populaire de Ste. Marie was now simply St. Mary's Bank.)

Another factor which had a profound effect on the disappearance of French as a spoken language was the smaller enrollment in Catholic schools. The church in New Hampshire was suffering the same pains that the Catholic church was suffering all across the nation. Vocations to the religious and clergy were diminishing and the number of small parish schools was getting smaller. The bishop of Manchester had been forced to close many of these smaller schools, faced by the necessity to pay lay faculty salaries because of the scarcity of religious who could bear the teaching duties.

Where formerly French-speaking persons consulted French-speaking lawyers and doctors and traded in stores where the clerks spoke French, this was no longer the case. The next generation of these families whose roots had originally been across the northern border of the United States rarely even visited in Canada anymore. They had grown apart from their relatives there and the elder family members had long since departed. Most Franco-American families had been in this country for two, three, and even four generations, and the goal of the younger set was an education, the same as any other group. Schools such as Philips Exeter, St. Paul's, and Holderness, were eagerly accepting these students, as were the University of New Hampshire and Ivy-clad Dartmouth.

The names of Manchester's parks tell something: there was Pulaski Park, Lafayette Park, Sheridan-Emmett Park and Bronstein Common, as wide a mix as anyone could imagine. Another barometer was the state's system of "vanity" license plates where a person might avail himself of a combination of five letters and digits of his choice for his automobile, instead of the numerical and county designations. "CANUK" and "KANUK" were taken, as well as "FROG" and "FROG1" up to "6"; there were autos in New Hampshire with the registration "IRISH", "MICK" and "HARP," and others bore the designations "HEBE," "SWEDE" and "POLKA," and there is someone tooling around the Granite State, no doubt a Spanish-speaking wag, with the license plate "KPASA."

The wearing of a red necktie to St. Joseph Boys High School on St. Patrick's Day at one time meant an automatic invitation to a donnybrook in Nutfield Lane with the guys in the green neckties at the close of classes; but those days were gone, but so was St. Joe's. And the racial identity of names on a ballot did not mean ethnic loyalty that much anymore. If a name on a ballot signified a Franco-American background, it meant to the voter that it was most likely that he was identified with a particular geographical section of the state and this was a factor with the voter more than his racial heritage.

Yorty's campaign was geared to ethnic backgrounds. He emphasized appearances at Franco-American "snowshoe" clubs much more than the other candidates—McGovern, Muskie, Hartke and Mills—and whenever Yorty had one of these appearances at a snowshoe club scheduled, he would be preceded by an advance man who would promptly announce to the bartender that the drinks would be taken care of.

But the more Yorty campaigned, the more it became obvious that the whole thing was someone's idea of a joke. Yorty had no chance of winning, at all, and the common speculation was mostly about how much he was spending per vote and where the money was coming from.

McGovern was clearly gaining strength all the time and Hartke was making some appearances, but the cross-section of voters in the Granite State weren't taking Hartke much more seriously than they were taking Yorty.

Mills himself announced a visit to the state and a speech before the Legislature. Loeb gave him banner headlines, saying that the purpose of Mills' visit was to advocate a sales or income tax to the General Court. When the day arrived, Mills proved Loeb was a poor prognosticator by speaking to the Legislature in the vein that he was not in favor of taxes and never had been.

On the morning of February 23, shortly after the opening of normal business hours, a news release was delivered from the Mills-for-President headquarters on Hanover Street to the Union Leader Building on Amherst Street, a block away, announcing, for immediate release, that Mills, the powerful chairman of the House Ways and Means Committee, was taking the House floor that very morning to call for an increase by 20 per cent in Social Security benefits effective by June of 1972 instead of the 5 per cent increase provided in a bill which had been steered through the House in 1971. This was a most significant news happening and shortly after the news release, which was typed on

Mills-for-President news release stationery, had been delivered to the Union Leader Building, the story was moved by the United Press International and Associated Press on their main teletype circuits (which, for the Northeast, originate in Boston). Evening newspapers in Boston and other cities carried eight-column headlines about the Mills' proposal that afternoon. On the following morning, the *New York Daily News* came into Manchester with a front-page headline on Mills' proposal. *The New York Times* also carried the story, as did the Boston dailies.

But soon after the news release had been hand-delivered to the *Manchester Union Leader* it was relegated to a waste basket. Not one line appeared about it in the evening edition of February 23. Late that afternoon, some members of the *Union Leader* staff were asked why the article had not found its way into print and the answer came back that it had been decided at the Union Leader Building that the Mills statement was nothing more than campaign oratory, even though it came in a formal speech on the floor of the U.S. Congress.

During the few days before Feb. 22, 1972, there had been a conference in Durham, N.H., of college and university newspaper editors from the northeastern section of the country. The featured speaker at the closing session of the conference on February 22 had been Herb Klein, director of communications for the President of the United States. He had in his company Ken W. Clawson, newly appointed to be Klein's successor. Clawson was formerly a reporter for the *Washington Post* and, in that connection, he had been very close to the scene during the machinations involved in trying to get Jimmy Hoffa paroled from the federal penitentiary.

Klein and Clawson left Durham on the night of February 22 and spent the night at the Sheraton Wayfarer Motel in Bedford, N.H., the closest suburb of Manchester on the southwest. The Sheraton Wayfarer is about a long par-7 from the Manchester Country Club, also in Bedford, the club which discontinued the membership of William Loeb some 20 years before. It was not at all unusual for Loeb to frequent the club these many years later at a company function, always held in the name of one of the other executives of the Union Leader Corp., many of whom were, and are, members.

On Feb. 23, 1972, Klein and Clawson were guests of the Union Leader Corp. at a small private luncheon held at the Manchester Country Club at noontime. Clawson recalls that Loeb and Klein talked to each other during the meal, while Clawson spoke with B. J. McQuaid and an unnamed person from the Union Leader Corp. Clawson says that as they were leaving the small dining room, Loeb told Klein that he had something going into the *Union Leader* "tomorrow morning" and that both Clawson and Klein would find it very interesting.

(This was not the first meeting of Klein and Union Leader executives. On July 30, 1971, Klein made a special trip from Washington to Manchester for a conference specially arranged with the executives and editors of the Union-Leader Corp. A three-column photograph of the group and a news story of similar size detailed the conference on Page One of the July 31, 1971 *Union Leader*. The *Union Leader* said the meeting was arranged at the request of Klein.)

As he discussed this matter in his oversized office of the Executive Office Building in Washington, D.C., some two years later, Clawson was vehement in stating that he had no idea of what Loeb meant in this remark. "I was just new here then and I didn't even have a key to the men's room," said Clawson.

He said that as he and Klein got to the front entrance of the Manchester Country Club, Loeb again said words to the effect that both Klein and Clawson would like the next day's edition of the *Union Leader* very much because of the fact that it would contain an item of great interest to them. And, again, Clawson spoke his "men's room key" line.

Clawson recalls that after they left the Manchester Country Club, Klein seemed to be in quite a hurry to depart from Manchester. He said he told Klein that snow was forecast for the area and that flying might be treacherous, but Klein persisted in making plans to depart as soon as he could. Clawson adds that, despite the fact that it did start to snow, the pair left in a private airplane from New Hampshire that evening and returned to Washington.

On the left-hand two columns of Page One in the Feb. 24, 1972 *Union Leader* there appeared a Loeb editorial. It was entitled:

## "Sen. Muskie Insults Franco-Americans"

and was totally confined to Page One. The complete text of the editorial reads:

"It is always surprising to this writer that people who ought to be smarter than that seem to think that they can get away with saying something derogatory in some other part of the nation and that it will never get back to the home-folks.

"If you never do anything else, be sure to look at the letter which we have reproduced exactly as it was received and which we run in place of our editorial cartoon today.

"IF PAUL MORRISON, THE AUTHOR OF THE LETTER, HADN'T TAKEN THE TROUBLE TO WRITE ABOUT HIS EXPERIENCE WITH SENATOR MUSKIE IN FLORIDA, NO ONE IN NEW HAMPSHIRE WOULD KNOW OF THE DEROGATORY REMARKS EMANATING FROM THE MUSKIE CAMP ABOUT THE FRANCO-AMERICANS IN NEW HAMPSHIRE AND MAINE—REMARKS WHICH THE SENATOR FOUND AMUSING.

"We must remember that this is the same Senator who had the gall to come to New Hampshire and say that the publisher of this newspaper didn't understand northern New England.

"However, this publisher DOES understand northern New England and he respects the people therein, especially the Franco-Americans who have done so much to develop and build up New Hampshire, Maine and other sections of New England.

"WE HAVE ALWAYS KNOWN THAT SENATOR MUSKIE WAS A HYPOCRITE, BUT WE NEVER EX-PECTED TO HAVE IT SO CLEARLY REVEALED AS IN THIS LETTER SENT TO US FROM FLORIDA.
"/s/ William Loeb, "Publisher"

In place of the editorial page cartoon, on Page 19, the following letter appeared, in what, at first glance, appeared to be a child's scrawl:

"Feb. 17, 1972
Deerfield Beach
Fla.

"Mr. Loeb—
Manchester Guardian
Manchester
New Hampshire

"Dear Mr. Loeb—
"I saw you on TV the other night and my friends father gets your newspaper. We went up to Ft. Lauderdale to meet Sen. Muskie—we were right beside him at Seed House, when one of the men asked him what did he know about blacks and the problems with them—he didn't have any in Maine—a man with the Senator said 'No—not blacks but we have CANNOCKS.

"What did he mean? We asked—Mr. Muskie laughed, and said come to New England and see. Could you write me the answer or print it in your paper—my friend gets it from you—. Thank you.

"Paul Morrison
"Deerfield Beach
"Fla. 33064"

(This letter is reproduced as Appendix C in this volume.)

The response in Manchester and New Hampshire was immediate. The response in Manchester and New Hampshire was also unanimous, or nearly so: that the letter was a fake. There were the usual Loeb defenders who maintained that the publisher was a just man and a great newspaperman, and these were, as always, those favor-seekers or those who owed whatever political success they enjoyed to the publisher and his newspapers.

Immediately there came a cry from the Yorty camp, denouncing Muskie for his "attack" on the Franco-American population, intimating that Sam Yorty was the best friend of all Franco-Americans and Yorty's campaign manager in New Hampshire would accept nothing less than a public apology and a confession of guilt from the senator for this outrage.

Hardly anyone, even the out-of-town newspapermen and radio and television reporters who were by this time in Manchester in great numbers, placed any validity in the child's letter which appeared in the *Union Leader*. No sooner had the letter appeared than many of these newsmen contacted their central offices with the news of the purported letter. Most major news media had men who were in Florida covering the primary election activity there, inasmuch as that state's primary was being held on the Tuesday after the New Hampshire primary. Some of these men were immediately dispatched to Deerfield Beach, Fla., where no trace of Paul Morrison could be found. Reports came back to Manchester before dark the same day. Reports also came back to Manchester from the reporters who had been assigned to cover Muskie on the day he toured Seed House, a drug rehabilitation center in Ft. Lauderdale, and none could remember any incident occurring which had been described in the letter.

The evening editions of the *Union Leader* of February 24 carried the same editorial and the same copy of the boy's "letter."

What very few of the newsmen knew at that time, and hardly any of the rest of the people of the United States knew, was that Muskie's staff in New Hampshire, and elsewhere, was riddled with the "dirty tricks" guys who were to become so well known during the Watergate hearings many months later. It had been obvious to most persons assigned to cover the primary that there had been lots of monkeyshines connected with the Muskie camp, but, at that time, there was not the slightest inkling that any of this could be traced, as it ultimately was traced, to the Committee to Reelect the President. There had been many midnight phone calls in Manchester, the caller identifying himself as being a member of the Harlem Muskie-for-President Committee in New York and proceeding to tell the person whom he obviously awoke what Muskie was doing for the people of Harlem. There had been other instances of "something wrong" in the Muskie organization; soliciting persons who had already contributed to the campaign, appointments made and missed with potential contributors. This was all talk which surrounded the Muskie effort in New Hampshire. It was hard to differentiate between "dirty tricks" and general ineptitude.

On the morning of Feb. 25, 1972, the editorial page of the *Union Leader* contained the following paragraph over three columns at the bottom of the page, under the headline, "Big Daddy's Jane":

"Guest editorial from the 27 Dec. 1971 issue of News-week:

\*    \*    \*

"The White House could be in for a drastic change of pace if Jane Muskie becomes First Lady. Campaigning in New Hampshire last week for 'Big Daddy,' as she jokingly referred to her husband, the Maine Democrat's 44-year old wife unleashed the kind of style that provided a field day for Women's Wear Daily reporter Kandy Stroud, who took down all the breezy quotes. 'Let's tell dirty jokes,' shouted Jane to the reporters and aides aboard her chartered bus. Also: 'Pass me my purse—I haven't had my morning cigarette yet.' She chewed gum, sighed that she couldn't wear a certain dress because someone else had 'the G. D. thing on' and owned up to a preference for two drinks before dinner creme de menthe afterward 'because the next day everything seems to work just right. But I can't mix booze and wine or I get a headache and have little dreams.' Spying Senator Ed's picture in a newspaper, his wife hooted: 'There he is. Isn't he cute?' "

During the latter part of that Friday afternoon, February 25, members of the Muskie staff in Manchester notified as many members of the "visiting" press as they could contact that Muskie, who was in Florida that day, would be

returning to Manchester overnight and would give a
speech in front of the Union Leader Building on Amherst
Street the next morning. Later that evening, mingling in-
formally at various press rooms set up in Manchester, these
aides were pointing out that Kennedy did the same thing
before his election in 1960. When it was pointed out to
the campaign aides that Kennedy had delivered his blast
at Loeb at about 7 P.M. in the evening on the day before
Election Day, not a full week before Presidential Primary
Day, the aides dismissed this by saying that they "knew"
that Muskie would let loose such a blast at Loeb that Loeb
wouldn't be able to answer the senator even though there
was a 10-day period remaining before the voting. It would
be an understatement to say that there was more than one
veteran reporter who asked another, "Do these guys know
anything about what they're doing?"

Senator Muskie left Florida that Friday evening and,
travelling most of the night, showered and shaved in Manchester in the morning. He and his party left a downtown
hotel about 8:30 A.M. and walked to the Union Leader
Building on Amherst Street where waited a large flatbed
truck, with a sound system. Some Muskie supporters carried signs proclaiming their support for the Maine senator.
Muskie and his cast of supporters, about 10 in all, used a
municipal trash container which had been donated by the
Richelieu Club, a Franco-American business and professional men's club, to mount the truck.

Muskie, with his coat collar turned up to protect himself against a driving snowstorm, told an audience of about
200 persons who had braved the elements that Loeb's remarks in the *Union Leader* had been false and he called
Loeb a "liar" for publishing a letter which was supposedly
from a boy whom he had met at Ft. Lauderdale. He introduced the executive director of the Ft. Lauderdale drug
treatment center, who had accompanied the senator to
Manchester, and he also denied the allegations. Muskie
again spoke and said that he had been close to Franco-
Americans all of his life, and he introduced members of
the Maine Legislature to prove his friendship. But the

whole show was like the maiden defending her virginity.

"This man doesn't walk, he crawls," said Muskie as he grasped the coat at the neck with one hand and pointed to the Union Leader Building with the other. Standing in the doorway of the Union Leader Building was James Finnegan, editorial page director for the newspapers. Muskie said, "It's a good thing for him that he's not standing alongside me right now. My wife is a good woman."

Muskie's face and head were covered with moisture from the driving snow and several times during the brief proceedings he brushed at his eyes, either to clear them of snow, or perhaps of actual tears. No one could actually say from watching the demonstration whether or not the senator cried. When he was finished speaking, and as others took the microphone to reaffirm their faith in Muskie, he stood in the background, still on the truck bed, with his head bowed. Several times he brushed his eyes with his coat sleeve, but again it was impossible to see if the senator actually did cry, as if it made a difference. (Apparently it did to some newspapers because the furore over whether Muskie actually cried went on for a couple of weeks in some journals, notably the *National Observer*.) The last person to be in a position to notice was Finnegan in the protected doorway.

The event was recorded by network television which carried film over the weekend. Loeb, of course, was immediately contacted and he said it was a clear indication that Muskie was not a man that Americans "would want to have his finger on the nuclear button."

"You'll notice," Loeb was quoted in the next day's *Sunday News*, "the senator never denied the authenticity of the letter. The senator knows the letter is authentic. I think the senator knows he made a terrible mistake down there and he's trying to cover up." As for Muskie's emotional response to the item that was critical of his wife. Loeb said the editorial was not his but was a reprint from *Newsweek* Magazine. "I can't recall we've said anything about Mrs. Muskie," he said.

Franco-Americans from all over New Hampshire and

Maine turned out the next morning, a Sunday, and accompanied Senator Muskie on a two-mile walk to mass at Ste. Marie's Church on Manchester's West Side. In the line of march there were six drum and bugle corps from "snowshoe" clubs in the two states, all in their marching uniforms.

On Wednesday, March 1, 1972, Loeb again took a shot at Muskie, who, in just four days, had showed a drop in informal polls. Loeb's title was:

### "Hysterical—And Deceptive"

and he used up two full columns of news space to state that his newspapers did not originate the article on Mrs. Muskie. And just in case anyone missed the first presentation of "Big Daddy's Jane" it was reproduced three columns wide on Page One on March 1 and again reproduced even larger four columns wide, on Page 24 on March 1.

Loeb said:

> "We consider it one of the duties of this newspaper to bring to the attention of our readers any and all facts relevant to anyone who is running for political office and those associated with them. In pursuing this policy, we reprinted this article from Newsweek.
>
> "Therefore, Mr. Muskie's quarrel on the matter of this editorial is not with this newspaper. It is with Newsweek magazine and with Women's Wear Daily, a Fairchild publication, which ran the story some weeks prior to Newsweek's article. But you didn't notice Mr. Muskie going down in front of the Newsweek Building or the Fairchild publication building in New York and putting on a weeping act or attacking THEM. You bet your life he wouldn't do that because he figures that Newsweek, which is owned by the Washington Post, and Women's Wear Daily are too big for him to tackle. . . .
>
> "THUS, IF EVER A MAN STOOD CONVICTED OF TELLING A BALDFACED LIE, THAT MAN IS SENATOR MUSKIE! . . .
>
> "Citizen after citizen had spoken up and said, 'Boy!

THAT'S not the man I want to have with his finger on the nuclear button!' "

The quotation from Newsweek which Loeb reproduced was on Page 27 of the Dec. 27, 1971 edition, two full months before. And one of the newsmen who marched at least part way towards the mass at Ste. Marie Church that Sunday morning was Benjamin C. Bradlee, executive editor of the *Washington Post* and former Washington bureau chief for *Newsweek*.

The newspapers contained Page One stories on Muskie right up until the voting day arrived. On Friday, March 4, Page One contained an engraving of a letter from a "Harold W. Eldredge" of Ft. Lauderdale who said he was the man who had asked the question of Senator Muskie on the day in question, a clear attempt by Loeb's staff to lend credibility to the first letter from "Paul Morrison."

The weather was fairly good, considering it was New Hampshire, on March 7, and a record turnout was recorded at the polling places throughout the state. Voters numbering 214,961 went to vote that day in the Granite State, the previous high for a Presidential primary having been recorded in 1968 when 168,792 persons voted. President Nixon and Senator Muskie were the big winners.

The vote:

### Republican
| | | |
|---|---|---|
| Nixon | 79,239 | or 67.22% |
| McCloskey | 23,190 | or 19.67% |
| Ashbrook | 11,362 | or 9.64% |

### Democratic
| | | |
|---|---|---|
| Muskie | 41,235 | or 46.46% |
| McGovern | 33,007 | or 37.19% |
| Yorty | 5,401 | or 6.08% |
| Mills (write-ins) | 3,563 | or 4.01% |
| Hartke | 2,417 | or 2.72% |

In delegate strength, President Nixon won every G.O.P. seat allotted New Hampshire at the national convention. Muskie won the majority of the Democratic delegate seats

at that party's convention, but McGovern's delegates won
a few key contests.

But it was all over for Senator Muskie. He didn't make
a good showing at all in the Florida primary a week hence
and soon the Maine senator had all but withdrawn his
candidacy.

Senator Muskie has been widely quoted since that February day and political columnists have viewed the incident from every possible angle. And the result always
comes out the same as Muskie himself admits: that he had
been poorly advised and that it was his overreaction, not
the attack by Loeb itself, that ended the senator's 1972 run
at the Presidency.

The *Boston Globe* was quite effusive in the news coverage of the event and, in an editorial page column a few
days later, made remarks about Loeb and certain of his
editors which Loeb considered excessive. He promptly
sued the Globe Newspaper Co., Inc., for $5 million, a suit
which has not yet come to hearing.

A few days after the primary voting as the last of the out-
of-town newsmen were readying to leave Manchester, a tally
was made of the actual persons who had been actively
involved in the search for "Paul Morrison" in Deerfield
Beach, Fla. It turned out that a total of 52 newsmen had
conducted individual searches for the boy. One reporter
had found the boy. The reporter worked for the *Manchester Union Leader*. He said, on returning to Manchester,
that Paul Morrison was a nice boy and that if he had asked
the boy for an affidavit or other proof that he had, in
fact, written the letter it would have been an inference to
the boy that he didn't believe that he was telling the truth,
so he didn't ask the boy for proof that he had written
the letter. The reporter, by the way, is the same Loeb
reporter who later told of his own four-year sentence in
the State Prison of Southern Michigan for larceny.

Loeb has obviously taken great pride in having been the
one who upset the Muskie apple-cart. Muskie had been
seen by most polls taken in New Hampshire prior to the

primary as being a 54% winner, and most observers concurred that anything less than 50% for Muskie was too little for a nationwide run for the highest office. They were right.

In referring to the incident in the three years following Feb. 25, 1972, William Loeb, almost without exception, prefers to state that it was his reprint from *Newsweek* that derailed the Muskie Express. He rarely, and then only when pressed, discusses the letter from "Paul Morrison." In like manner, Loeb treats his reprinting of the *Newsweek* item as having been a routine thing. He certainly does not say that he reprinted it once in normal fashion, and then had it photoengraved twice, once three columns wide and another four columns wide.

In September, 1972, Ken W. Clawson, while still waiting to be publicly named as successor to Herb Klein, who was still on the White House staff, visited the apartment of Marilyn Berger, a reporter on the staff of the *Washington Post,* and during that meeting in her apartment, Clawson boasted that he had been the author of the "Canuck" letter which appeared in the *Manchester Union Leader.* Ms. Berger immediately made the context of this conversation known to Executive Editor Bradlee, whose reply was, "Write it," which she did. The story appeared in the *Post* and was promptly denied by Clawson. Bradlee accommodated Clawson by printing his denial. Bradlee and Clawson came face-to-face at a cocktail party in Washington some months later and the confrontation degenerated into one of Washington's best remembered "cockfights," according to *New York* magazine.

A lengthy interview with Clawson was printed in *New York* in June, 1974, in which Clawson again denied any complicity in the authorship of the "Canuck" letter, saying, "I came to the White House on the seventh of February and the letter is dated the seventeenth. At that point I didn't even know where the men's room was. Besides, I was the man from the *Washington Post,* and no one had a great deal of confidence in me."

Mrs. Clawson, herself a reporter, was also interviewed

in the *New York* article. Says the author, Nora Ephron, "The only time she is distressed at all is when she is asked about the Canuck Letter. 'I asked my husband if he had written it,' she said, 'and he said no.' She hit her fist softly on a table. 'Darn it,' she said, 'It does kind of frustrate me. When he was supposed to be writing the Canuck Letter he had been at the White House two weeks. He was still learning where the men's room was.' "

I visited the Executive Office Building on May 7, 1974, to discuss the matter with Ken. W. Clawson, such visit having been arranged and set by appointment. Clawson had been told of the subject matter we would discuss. After having been cleared by the security guards, I was guided by a secretary to the office of Ken W. Clawson in the northeast corner of the building. On the way down the carpeted hallway, the secretary announced that she was not sure if Mr. Clawson had time to see me and asked if I would like to talk to a Mr. Holland (or Howland, the maneuvers which this particular secretary could make with the English tongue were somewhat of a marvel in themselves). The young lady was told that the matter to be discussed with Mr. Clawson was a matter of personal recollection and that a visit with Mr. Holland (or Howland) would be of no value. I was ushered into an oversized secretarial office to wait. Watergate was at its height at this point—in time—and I was given my choice between the *Washington Post* and *The New York Times* (both previously unread copies), a most obvious move to show that the "opposition" press was available in the White House. I accepted *The Times*.

While I was staring at the newspaper, a door opened and a man emerged, a short, dumpy man, wearing a light blue shirt adorned with a crimson monogram. The shirt was immediately recognizable as one which Brooks Brothers would not sell, the monogram being as large as a small town police chief's badge; a person who wears such a shirt does not hide the monogram by wearing a suit jacket. The man in the monogrammed shirt took a 10-yard survey of me and disappeared into a door on my left. He reappeared from a door on my right and did a quick criss-cross passing from my right to left and back, from left to right, disappearing through a door on the far side of the room. I did not lift my eyes from *The Times*. Within moments, without telephone or any other signal, the secretary-guide announced, "Mr. Clawson can see you now, but only for a very brief visit."

I entered the door through which the man in the monogrammed shirt had disappeared previously and found a greatly oversized office which boasted an oversized conference table which could accommodate at least a dozen, along one side of the room looking out on Pennsylvania Avenue; a pair of couches with a coffee table arrangement in another corner, not to mention a couple of armchairs; and in the other corner a huge mahogany desk, oversized, of course, behind which the man in the monogrammed shirt was leaning back in an oversized chair with his feet extended to the desk top. The man in the monogrammed shirt introduced himself as Ken W. Clawson.

Mr. Clawson chain-smoked oversized filter cigarettes, stopping occasionally to brush the ashes off the oversized monogram which emblazoned his blue shirt, and told me a nearly incredible narrative.

Mr. Clawson emphatically denied any complicity in the "Canuck" letter, emphasizing that he didn't even know where the men's room was when the incident occurred. He went on to call Marilyn Berger a liar, among other things, and when he said that Ben Bradlee was a liar, that epithet could even be gauged as an act of charity in comparison to some of the other terms Clawson used to describe his former executive editor.

Clawson described the meeting with Loeb in Manchester on Feb. 23, 1972, but said that, on that occasion, Loeb had treated him "like a little boy" and had directed most of his remarks to Klein. Clawson acted like it was news to him that there had been any connection between William Loeb and James R. Hoffa, even though it was known that Clawson had covered meetings involving the two men while a *Washington Post* reporter. "I was new here and apparently Loeb knew that I didn't even have a key to the men's room," said Clawson.

In a meeting which lasted slightly over 30 minutes, on May 7, 1974, Ken W. Clawson accomplished quite a bit. He set a new IC4A and Gillette World Series Record for contradicting himself. He made it eminently clear (and perfectly clear) why Richard M. Nixon was in the trouble that he was in when he surrounded himself with men such as this—Clawson was at this time the Director of Communications for the United States. He also led me to believe that after two years and three months, to the day, in the Executive Office Building Ken W. Clawson still didn't know where the men's room was, even if by this time he had the key.

The Mills proposal to increase Social Security benefits by 20% did become federal law, having been passed by both houses after its initial proposal on Feb. 23, 1972, by the Arkansas Congressman. This was the story the *Manchester Union Leader* refused to print.

# 30

Much was written and much was filmed on the 1972 New Hampshire first-in-the-nation primary. Besides the fact that the election drew a record turnout of voters, it was also obvious that it set a new record for coverage of the state's unique Town Meeting Day activities. And the coverage did not end after the ballots were counted. Columnists harked back to the event for months, especially as it became apparent that Sen. Edmund S. Muskie was no longer a factor in many state's primaries.

Jules Witcover, a staff reporter for the *Los Angeles*

*Times* at that time (he is in 1975 with the *Washington Post*) assessed the New Hampshire primary in the May/June 1972 *Columbia Journalism Review* in a lengthy article entitled, "William Loeb and the New Hampshire primary: a question of ethics." Witcover prefaced his 14-page documented summation of Loeb's antics during the primary by touching briefly on the treatment Loeb had given Dr. Thomas N. Bonner at the University of New Hampshire the year previous. Witcover quoted *Newsweek,* saying that "*Newsweek* described 'one of the most brutal newspaper assaults ever directed at a U.S. university official' " Loeb's series of articles on Bonner.

As to the 1972 New Hampshire primary itself, Witcover observed:

> "Loeb always has maintained, as do most publishers, that, in the best tradition of American journalism, he fights his battles in his editorial columns, reserving the news columns to tell readers what has been happening. The tradition, while noble, sometimes is compromised even in the best newspapers. In the Manchester *Union Leader,* the tradition is not compromised, it is shattered—and seldom more glaringly than during the presidential primaries."

Witcover should have stuck around; he would have seen a show he could really write about.

William Loeb apparently didn't think that his end of the deal he had made with the President was completed— either that or he was having some of the unique Loeb brand of "fun"—because Sen. George S. McGovern, the former professor from Mitchell, S.D., never did get, and likely will never again get, the pummelling he got in the *Manchester Union Leader* at the hands of William Loeb.

McGovern had no trouble in being nominated. In fact, one of the seconding speeches was given by Mrs. Valerie Kushner, the POW wife who had campaigned during the winter months in New Hampshire, she being a delegate to the convention herself. But Loeb's persistent attack on McGovern began shortly after the March primary and did not end until the day before Election Day, Monday, Nov.

6, 1972, when, tucked up over two columns right underneath the masthead on Page One, was the 24-point type headline:

## " 'Kiss My Ass'
## "Says Sen. McGovern"

Loeb's editorial went on to tell of McGovern's reaction to a taunting hippie in Michigan a full week earlier, an event which scarcely got any coverage in other newspapers on the day after it happened, most of them deleting whatever it was the senator told the taunting youth. It was not hard to imagine that Senator McGovern was a fatigued and distraught man, facing almost certain defeat at the polls, who really didn't need this kind of abuse by a hippie in Michigan. What was hard for the vast majority of New Hampshire parents to imagine was that an adult, educated, supposedly articulate newspaper publisher such as William Loeb, the man who always proclaimed the fact that he was such a church-going Baptist, would print this kind of a headline so prominently on Page One of a family newspaper which, if it was not home-delivered, was certainly available at every corner store where young people would certainly be able to quickly see what was written on Page One.

The battle was over at the time of the November 6 headline, though, and everybody knew it—which may have made it all the more reprehensible—and McGovern was almost assuredly going to lose. But the series of articles which most observers feel was the most unfair of all was that which Loeb carried in his newspapers during early July.

Loeb directed that a series of articles be run on Page One of his *Union Leader* to show that George McGovern, as pilot of a B-24 during World War II in Europe, was "yellow." Loeb began by reprinting certain campaign propaganda distributed by the John Birch Society—which was appropriately edited for *Union Leader* use—and then in early July, a *Union Leader* reporter* was dispatched to Wichita, Kans., to interview McGovern's co-pilot during the war. The results of this interview got three-column treatment in the *Union Leader:*

## "McGovern Called
## "A 'Dangerous Man' "

The Page One story went on to widely quote Ralph C. "Bill" Rounds of Wichita and the unavoidable conclusion to the article was that Rounds was never fond of McGovern, even during their service together as pilot and co-pilot of a bomber. Rounds immediately repudiated the story the next day and the UPI quoted Rounds as saying that he had tape-recorded the conversation with the reporter and that he had misquoted him all the way through. The *Union Leader* paid scant attention to Rounds' denial, but several other newspapers printed it in full.

What Loeb's reporter was trying to prove was that, while the pilot of the "Dakota Queen" McGovern had failed to carry out his orders and had landed his plane on an island in the Adriatic Sea, on a so-called "milk run." A "milk run" was the name widely given at the time to bombing missions on diversionary targets, runs where the planes had little chance of meeting enemy resistance. It was normal practice during the closing days of World War II to offer these assignments to pilots when they and their crew had already received orders to return stateside, the thinking being that it would be cruel to have these planes shot down with the end of their duty so close.

This attack by William Loeb is the one which George McGovern carries with him as being the cruelest of all. It is unlikely that the South Dakota senator will ever really forgive the Manchester publisher for this treatment.

After the accusation originally appeared in Loeb's news-

---

* In 1975, this reporter was referred to by the editor of a prominent Western New England newspaper: "He is the most consistent man I have ever met. In 30 years he has never once let the facts interfere with his telling a story."

paper, three crewmen who had served aboard the "Dakota Queen" came forth vehemently to deny the statement carried in Loeb's newspaper.

Isadore Seigel, of Omaha, Neb., a tail gunner on the "Dakota Queen," Bill Ashlock, of San Jose, Calif., waist gunner, and Bill McAfee, of Port Huron, Mich., turret gunner, all responded voluntarily to the charge. They were unanimous in giving this version:

When McGovern and his crew received their orders to proceed to stateside duty, the plane was scheduled for one more bombing mission. McGovern was given the option of a "milk run." He told his crew about the choice he had to make and they unanimously voted to go on the actual bombing mission, which they did.

Senator McGovern, on hearing of the charges in Loeb's newspaper, which also said that a letter of reprimand had become a part of McGovern's official service record, immediately called for the Defense Department to make public that part of his service record which applied to the case in point. The record states:

> "Throughout many combat missions against highly important and strategic enemy installations, (he) . . . demonstrated the highest order of professional skill, heroism, leadership and devotion to duty."

Ashlock, the waist gunner, gave this account, in the *Washington Post,* of the final flight of the "Dakota Queen":

> "It was a typical deal that you got a milk run on your last mission, one that wasn't dangerous, so you wouldn't get shot down on your last mission. McGovern could have gotten out of it, but he left it up to the crew. We voted to go.
>
> "I flew this last mission. We were over target. There was heavy flak. We suffered three hits and we didn't deviate from course. We dropped our bombs. We had our hydraulic line shot out and, when we returned to base, we had to hand-crank down the flaps. When McGovern landed the plane, he ordered the crew to release parachutes out the waist windows to act as a drogue and halt the ship. That was the only thing that stopped us."

During the time following the Presidential primary and the end of summer, William Loeb was merciless in his treatment of McGovern; he also went to work on Dr. Bonner and the university anytime he felt he had to stay in practice. Governor Peterson had called for a state sales tax during a special session of the Legislature held in the early months of the year and the legislators defeated the bill. Loeb worked the governor over anytime he wasn't occupied with McGovern and Bonner, especially when Peterson announced he'd run for a third term in early July. Loeb was not at all hesitant to mention, at any given time, how permissive Peterson was in his attitude towards drugs, and even to bring up the name of the governor's daughter.

But William Loeb had long since begun boosting Meldrim Thomson, Jr., of Orford. And there was plenty of reason to believe that there had, in fact, been a "deal" between Loeb and Wesley Powell for Powell to stay on the sidelines during the 1970 election. Powell announced that he would run for the U.S. Senate against Sen. Thomas J. McIntyre and the news space which Loeb was converting into campaign advertising for Wesley Powell would have blown the top right off Jules Witcover's head. Powell was getting eight-column spreads on Page One on top of the masthead at the rate of at least once a week.

And also bringing flowers for Loeb to sniff was Roger J. Crowley, who had announced that he would run for governor again on the Democratic ticket. Crowley would be opposed by the House minority leader, Robert Raiche, of Manchester, but Raiche would be an easy target for Loeb because he had sided with Governor Peterson on the sales tax bill.

Loeb was just about at the peak of his power. He had wrecked Muskie, there wasn't a prayer that McGovern could carry the state of New Hampshire for the electoral vote; Loeb had the obvious primary winner running for governor on the Democratic ticket; Congressman Louis Wyman and Congressman James Cleveland were shoo-ins to win reelection to the Congress, and Loeb was backing

both of these men. All that remained was to get Meldrim
Thomson past Walter Peterson in the Republican gubernatorial primary and the ticket of the Loeb Party would
be all set: with Thomson going against Crowley, Loeb
was a winner either way. Powell would have his hands
full with McIntyre, but Wyman and Cleveland would be
locks—you couldn't get a 2-to-1 bet on either of these races.

Loeb was so confident in early September that he even
had a little time to spend on other things. The attention
of William Loeb had been attracted to a cute, talented 21-
year old girl named Kathy Hebert, who was in Atlantic
City, N.J., competing in the Miss America Pageant as Miss
Vermont 1972. What attracted Loeb was the results of an
interview with the Miss Vermont at the Chalfonte-Haddon
Hall, headquarters for the Miss America Pageant, and
written by Ewart Rouse for the Associated Press. It said,
in part:

> " 'My dad calls me a kooky freak . . . I believe in astrol-
> ogy and my signs say I'm a schizophrenic. I sit here and
> watch the other girls and it's like watching television—in
> color. I can't believe I'm here.'
>
> "Miss Vermont, 21-year-old Kathy Hebert, one of the 50
> contestants in the Miss America 1973 Pageant, sounded
> lost Monday during registration at Chalfonte-Haddon
> Hall.
>
> " 'I can't believe it,' the contestant, who was dressed in
> a floral print long gown, kept saying to herself. 'This is
> not the real me. If I were to be my real self, I'd be here in
> hot socks, jeans, t-shirt, no bra and with my hair hanging
> loose and natural.
>
> " 'Were I to become Miss America, I'd change the whole
> concept of Miss America.
>
> "Miss Hebert, a hazel-eyed ash blonde, said she was
> aware that she wasn't the 'typical' Miss America contes-
> tant.
>
> " 'I'm anti-Nixon, I've demonstrated against the war, I
> support Jane Fonda, and believe in premarital sex,' she
> said without pause or prompting.
>
> "A senior at Pratt Institute in Brooklyn, N.Y., majoring

in fashion designing, Miss Hebert said she entered the competition solely for the scholarship reward . . .

"While studying designing, Miss Hebert said her first love was music. She described herself as a guitarist-folk singer who paid her school fees by singing in restaurants during the summer."

Loeb was incredulous apparently. But then there was a lot about Miss Vermont 1972 and about Vermont, in general, that William Loeb didn't know. Loeb had exiled himself from the state of Vermont, principally to his elaborate castle in Pride's Crossing, Mass., more than 20 years before (or just about the time that Kathy Hebert was born). An awful lot of things had changed in the state of Vermont besides Miss Kathy Hebert blossoming into a good-looking, talented lady. Apparently, in Loeb's eye, the domain was still in control of the hands of Ethan Allen and the Green Mountain Boys.

The views expressed by Kathy Hebert were in no way different from those heard by Burlingtonians all year long, in the summer from the college kids who were away at school and during the school year from the college kids who came to Burlington to school.

But, notwithstanding, William Loeb assumed the pulpit of Page One of the *Vermont Sunday News* on the next Sabbath morning and pronounced:

### "The Wrong Kind
### Of Miss Vermont"

Loeb told how his newspapers had sponsored the Miss Vermont Pageant for many years. He continued:

"This year's Miss Vermont, who was not sponsored by this newspaper, but by a new organization which is now running the contest, in the opinion of this newspaper, is an utter disgrace to the State of Vermont . . .

"In the opinion of this newspaper, such a person with such distorted views is the product of miseducation. It is a tragedy to see a young person with such twisted and distorted and confused upside down values.

"Certainly, such a person should not have been chosen as Miss Vermont.

"It does not speak well for the management of the present Miss Vermont Pageant. Perhaps they had better forget the whole thing and not have any more Miss Vermont Pageants, if they can't send to Atlantic City some of the fine types of girls the Vermont SUNDAY NEWS and the St. Albans Daily Messenger sent."

People in Vermont, particularly around Burlington, hadn't heard a blast from William Loeb, the bigtime publisher, on a subject of purely local interest for a long time. Indeed, William Loeb was remembered by only a percentage of the population. Those who remembered him, remembered bad things of him. They remembered mostly how he had fired the entire complement of printers at the *Burlington Daily News* and affected the lives of so many who had spent their entire careers as printers on that newspaper. Others remembered how, through his abuse and mismanagement, he had caused the *Burlington Daily News* to vanish from the face of the earth.

Those who didn't remember Loeb had been told, and stories about him become greatly magnified and distorted. It is even fair to say that a lot of stories going around about Loeb were untrue, but there was never a shortage of folklore about the bigtime publisher and his unorthodox personal life. The Kathy Hebert incident kindled the fire under every one of those stories.

But the blast at Kathy Hebert was one shot. Miss Hebert has never lacked for a job in the Burlington area since that time. Her name is usually up in lights on the marquee of one of the motels along Williston Road where she has been appearing in the cocktail lounges playing her guitar and singing her folk songs. And Kathy Hebert has never had to pay William Loeb an agent's fee.

Two days after William Loeb criticized Kathy Hebert it was Primary Day in New Hampshire. The results were largely as expected.

Crowley had little trouble winning the Democratic gubernatorial nomination from Minority Leader Raiche, 29,326-to-16,216, and Meldrim Thomson, Jr., of Orford, just squeezed by Governor Peterson. It was a third candidate, State Sen. James Koromilas, of Dover, a person few people figured had any business in the race, who made the difference.

The final score:

| | |
|---|---|
| James Koromilas, Dover, r | 3,975 |
| Walter Peterson, Peterborough, r | 41,252 |
| Meldrim Thomson, Jr., Orford, r | 43,611 |

In the U.S. Senate primary on the G.O.P. side, William Loeb's man, the "hard-headed, progressive and economy-oriented thinking" Wesley Powell, won out over two guys named "Joe" and the Speaker of the N.H. House, Marshall Cobleigh, of Nashua, with Powell getting almost the total vote of the other three candidates. Louis Wyman and James Cleveland won their respective nominations to run for Congress, and the Democratic primary contests for these two seats in the U.S. House proved only that neither nominee could win in November: in the First District, the former Republican officeholder, Chester E. Merrow, of Ossipee, who had switched parties in an attempt to get his old job back, and, in the Second District, Charles B. Officer, of Hanover, who had once given Cleveland a run for his money, but that was before Cleveland had a few terms in Washington and a fairly large patronage following.

Loeb apparently had the bases covered. The state's senior senator, Norris Cotton, of Lebanon, would have no choice but to campaign for Powell over McIntyre for the Senate and Thomson over Crowley for the governorship.

Then, just a couple of weeks after the primary, Concord Mayor Malcolm McLane, a partner in the top-shelf Concord law firm of Orr & Reno, filed as an independent candidate for the governorship. Just to mention the name "McLane" to William Loeb was to risk trouble, but here was the younger son of the Manchester dynasty with a solid threat to upset Loeb's plans. McLane, as everyone knew, would appeal not only to a large segment of the

Republican voters, especially those who had supported Peterson, but he would also attract a number of the more
liberal Democrats as well as the Loeb-haters of both parties, who clearly saw that either Thomson or Crowley
would be little more than Wesley Powell had been as governor—a "puppet" for William Loeb—until the "divorce"
over the matter of naming Mrs. Bridges to the U.S. Senate.

McLane was successful in raising quite a bit of money
in a short period of time and he was a most active candidate, but one whose activities and pronouncements were
largely blacked out by the *Union Leader*.

Then, with seven days left before the election, on Oct.
31, 1972, Bill Loeb withdrew his support from Crowley's
candidacy. In a Page One editorial, which ended up running more than four full columns of news space, entitled,

## "A Sad Conclusion"

Loeb had this to say about his "good friend":

> "Candidate Crowley's activities during this campaign re-
> mind us of a warning given this writer by a good friend
> and fine Democratic legislator several years ago. At the
> time of the warning, this newspaper was strongly support-
> ing Captain Crowley for governor of New Hampshire. The
> legislator, who himself came to us, said, 'Look, I am just
> as friendly with Roger Crowley as you are, I think he is a
> fine, wonderful person but I have had more experience
> with Roger Crowley than you have and I think I should
> tell you what that experience has been....'
>
> "The legislator went on to say, 'There isn't a nicer per-
> son in the State of New Hampshire than Roger Crowley
> but the difficulty is he doesn't have the force and drive and
> determination when it comes to a sticky and difficult situ-
> ation. And,' our friend went on to say, 'I thought you
> should know this because my estimate of conditions in the
> state of New Hampshire is that we need in Concord a
> governor who cannot be pushed around and cannot be
> intimidated by any special interests or any group, and who
> knows where he wants to go and will carry through on it.'
>
> "We thought at the time that perhaps this warning was

too harsh and too strong, but now, viewing Candidate Crowley's performance during the campaign we must sadly and regretfully come to the conclusion that the warning was correct.

"While Roger Crowley is the nicest person in the world, when it comes to wanting to be governor he is apt to go back and forth and weasel, looking for more votes and forgetting the principles for which he has always stood. . . ."

Loeb admitted that at the outset of the campaign (which, by the way, was before the emergence of Mayor McLane as a candidate), he had said that he would remain strictly neutral. Then he raised a totally false issue, one which was contrary to every campaign utterance which Crowley had ever made, an issue which even Crowley knew would make him anathema to the voting public:

> "WE BELIEVE THAT THE STATE WOULD BE IN SERIOUS DANGER OF HAVING A SALES OR INCOME TAX IF ROGER CROWLEY WERE TO BE ELECTED."

With Loeb's statement, in capital letters, Crowley was tagged. Then Loeb had this to say about the alternative to voting for Crowley, Meldrim Thomson, Jr., of Orford, the man who had bolted the Republican Party two years before and drew a total of 22,033 votes, as well as drawing the fire of Loeb for having a "weakness of character" and being a man who "doesn't think that when a man gives his word it is necessary to keep it," and with an "inability to even use his head":

> "In contrast, whatever his critics may say, Mel Thomson has never backed off on a single one of his principles or ideas on how to bring financial assistance to the taxpayers of the State of New Hampshire . . .
>
> "THEREFORE, WE MOST SERIOUSLY URGE OUR READERS TO VOTE FOR MEL THOMSON FOR GOVERNOR. HE IS THE BEST CHOICE TO BRING RELIEF TO THEIR POCKETBOOKS AND TO ASSURE A BRIGHT FUTURE FOR THE GRANITE STATE."

Two days later Loeb wrote a double-column editorial which began on Page One and was continued to occupy the entire news space on page 9 of the Nov. 2, 1972 editions, both morning and evening, of the *Union Leader*.

Apparently Loeb had, at this point, realized that he had not as yet contradicted all the unpleasant things he had said (before Hoffa's parole) about Richard M. Nixon, because it was very, very important for William Loeb to be on record as having supported the President. He printed a photograph complimentary to Mr. Nixon in the Page One portion of his page-long editorial and dwelt, in the first six paragraphs, on what Loeb might not have altogether agreed with about the Nixon Administration.

> "On the other hand, if you look at Mr. Nixon's opponent, Senator McGovern, his policies, both in national defense and for the development of our country are so horrendous and so absolutely irresponsible and wild that Mr. Nixon is the OBVIOUS AND ONLY CHOICE that any sensible voter can make."

Of his candidate for the U.S. Senate, Wesley Powell, the man who Loeb said in 1961 was "corrupted" and "arrogant," William Loeb had this to say on Nov. 2, 1972:

> "Former Governor Powell is not afraid to speak out; he is a firm believer in God and country and strong national defense and the right of citizens to bear arms. We believe that former Governor Powell, if elected to the United States Senate, will give New Hampshire the sort of representation that is very badly needed in the nation's capital. The world is full of go-along people and mush-mouthed and marshmallow-spined politicians, especially in Washington; we need instead someone there—such as Wesley Powell—who is not afraid to call a spade a spade and to stand firmly for his principles."

To Meldrim Thomson, Jr., of Orford, who bolted the party in the election previous and whom Loeb had once said "showed weakness of character," William Loeb offered the following citation:

"Candidate Thomson has not weasled or wiggled on any of his promises. This newspaper therefore urges all who are interested in protecting their pocketbooks and the state's financial position to vote for Mel Thomson, who will surely give the state a progressive administration but —as in the case of Governor Powell—one that will be within our income . . .

"The election of Wes Powell and Mel Thomson is terribly important. We need hardly point out that this nation and this state are in a state of crisis where strong men are needed at the helm, men who will not flinch at the hardest decisions, who know what they believe and who know what they think should be done—and who intend to do it.

"Mel Thomson and Wes Powell are such men, the sort of men Daniel Webster must have had in mind when he wrote that the symbol of the men of New Hampshire was the Great Stone Face.*

"We hope our readers will give their enthusiastic support to both former Governor Powell and Mel Thomson. Many New Hampshire citizens who do not read the Union Leader have not ever been informed as to what these gentlemen have been proposing. As detailed on the Editorial Page today in the editorial, 'No News for Powell and Thomson,' the left-wing newspapers of the state continue to blackout almost all news about either former Governor Powell or Mr. Thomson.

"THEREFORE, IT WOULD BE MOST HELPFUL IF READERS OF THE UNION LEADER WHO ARE SUPPORTERS OF MR. POWELL AND MR. THOMSON WOULD DO THEIR BEST NOT ONLY TO INFORM THEIR FRIENDS AND NEIGHBORS WHO MIGHT NOT BE READING THE UNION LEADER OF THE FACTS ABOUT THESE TWO FINE GENTLEMEN, BUT ALSO TO EXPLAIN TO THEM HOW THEY HAVE BEEN DECEIVED BY THE NEWSPAPERS THEY HAVE BEEN READING

"The news censorship carried out against these two candidates by the leftist newspapers in the State of New Hampshire is a disgrace and a blot on the Granite State's reputation for fair play in politics.

"So frightened are these left-wing journals of having

* Nathaniel Hawthorne was the author of "The Great Stone Face."

two strong men such as Mel Thomson and Wes Powell win that they will stop at nothing in order to mislead the voters about these two candidates. You can help Thomson and Powell by spreading the truth to which readers of these leftist newspapers are being denied access."

For the first time in the history of the State of New Hampshire, more than 300,000 voters turned out on Election Day—334,055, to be exact. Nixon waltzed over McGovern, 213,724-to-116,435. Both Louis Wyman and James Cleveland had a free lunch, Wyman winning the First District seat in Congress by nearly 3-to-1 and Cleveland by better than 2-to-1.

Thomas J. McIntyre, the Democrat from Laconia, was returned to the U.S. Senate for his second full term, showing nearly a 45,000-vote plurality over Wesley Powell: McIntrye, 184,495; Powell, 139,852.

McLane, the Manchester native who was mayor of Concord where he had spent most of his adult life, scored well in the counties where these two cities were located and he also did well in Grafton County, wherein is located his alma mater, Dartmouth, and the seacoast county of Rockingham. It was a matter of cocktail party, wake and wedding, and of curbstone gossip for the next many months as to what might have happened had not Malcolm McLane tossed his hat into the ring, but the final score showed Meldrim Thomson, Jr., of Orford, a winner:

| | |
|---|---|
| Meldrim Thomson, Jr., Orford, r | 133,702 |
| Roger J. Crowley, Manchester, d | 126,107 |
| Malcolm McLane, Concord, ind | 63,199 |

It was remembered by an awful lot of people in New Hampshire how much of a fuss Loeb had always made when his candidate or candidates had been defeated by a person who had not received a majority of the vote cast. It didn't bother Loeb one iota that his man, Meldrim Thomson, Jr., of Orford, was a winner with 41.4% of the vote cast. To quote Loeb:

"These people who supported Thomson and Powell are people who believe also in the eternal verities of religious faith, of patriotism, and decent morals, both public and private. They do not expect to see angels in human form running around the hills of the Granite State, but they do want to return to the fundamental moral decencies which have been so scoffed at by many of the so-called intellectuals. . . .

"It is the firm belief of this newspaper, based on what our reporters and editors have observed, that the organizations of Congressmen Wyman and Cleveland didn't lift a finger to help Governor Powell's election. If anything, they did just the opposite. Many people who call themselves Republicans in the State of New Hampshire are really that in name only. Actually, they are more interested in political privilege and profit than they are in any basic moral or political principles.

"However, it is not necessary to waste much time worrying about these individuals or recriminating against them. They will lose their influence and their importance as the Thomson administration demonstrates, as this newspaper believes it will, that the principles on which Thomson as well as Powell campaigned can become a reality and benefit everyone in the Granite State."

Bernard J. McQuaid, editor-in-chief of the Loeb newspapers, apparently felt he had a little explaining to do, inasmuch as his close ties with Crowley dating back many, many years had gotten the retired Navy captain into this squeeze. It is not a normal thing for McQuaid to sign his own editorials, but in one initialed, "B. J. McQ.," the editor-in-chief assumed the pulpit in the *Sunday News* of Nov. 12, 1972:

"Twice Crowley has been kept out of the State House by developments that neither he nor anyone could have foretold at the time he announced his candidacies. What he has demonstrated, nevertheless, is an enormous popularity with the voters of New Hampshire.

"He is a two-time loser but his voice will continue to be heard with respect on all the vital issues facing his native state.—B. J. McQ."

With a lot of friends like William Loeb and Bernard J. McQuaid, who needs enemies?

# V

# How?

The best use of a journal is to print the largest amount of important truth—truth which tends to make mankind wiser, and thus happier.

—HORACE GREELEY

# 31

It still was not what anyone would call daylight outside, but Ed Grimes had been on the job for about an hour at the State House, straightening this chair in its desk slot, emptying and wiping that ashtray, putting that other pile of day-old newspapers in with the rubbish, just as Ed Grimes had been doing for more than 10 years every business day. And this stranger walked up to him, warming his fist with blasts from his pursed lips, then pausing to turn down the collar of his overcoat and removing his earmuffs.

"Do you have the keys to the governor's office?" asked the man.

"Sure I do," said Ed Grimes, "but who wants them?"

"I'm Mel Thomson, the governor," said the stranger, who had reverted to puffing on his curled fingers; after all, it was nine below outside.

"That sounds pretty good," said Ed Grimes, "but you've got to prove it to me."

So, Meldrim Thomson, Jr., of Orford, unbuttoned his coat and produced a driver's license for Ed Grimes, who, in turn, escorted the governor to his second floor corner office, where the new governor went to work.

Meldrim Thomson, Jr., of Orford, had been inaugurated as the 88th governor (or "supreme executive magistrate" as the N.H. Constitution calls it) on January 4, the Thursday before, and William Loeb, in a Page One editorial which he chose to call "A Great Opportunity," had hailed Governor Thomson "like a fresh breeze from the summits of the White Mountains he loves to climb, . . . with no commitments to any special interests."

Loeb went on:

"To begin with, the governor has stated, and this newspaper knows he means it, that he is going to conduct his administration without any view towards the coming election in two years. He says that if the people like what he has accomplished, he will be reelected, and if they don't, that will be that. He says he will make no concessions to politics nor will he aim specifically for reelection. His sole purpose, he says, will be to do the best job he knows for the State of New Hampshire—and to do it now.

"WITH THAT TYPE OF DEDICATION AND THAT TYPE OF INTEGRITY, AND WITH THE SUPPORT OF THOSE THOUSANDS OF NEW HAMPSHIRE PEOPLE WHO UNDERSTAND THAT THE GRANITE STATE IS SOMETHING DIFFERENT FROM THE OTHER 49 STATES IN THE UNION, AND WHO WANT TO PRESERVE THIS UNIQUENESS, SO WE CAN SERVE AS AN EXAMPLE TO THE CONFUSED REST OF THE NATION—WITH THAT SORT OF OBJECTIVE, AND WITH THAT SORT OF SUPPORT, GOVERNOR THOMSON CANNOT AND WILL NOT FAIL!"

The *N.H. Sunday News* had offered the new "supreme executive magistrate" accolades for his inaugural address, calling it "one of the most hard-hitting and, at the same time, scholarly addresses ever heard in the General Court of New Hampshire."

"If the sovereign people continue to support him as their agent the gentleman from Orford will give this state the most memorable administration in modern history."

What most New Hampshire voters did not know at the time—although there were many who suspected it would happen—was that concurrent with the inauguration of Meldrim Thomson, Jr., of Orford, as governor, New Hampshire, in fact, got another ruler: William Loeb, of Pride's Crossing, Mass., and Reno, Nev. Whatever Governor Thomson said or did, he was lauded for it the next day in the *Union Leader,* not unusually in a Page One editorial signed by the publisher. If the occasion so demanded, Governor Thomson was provided eight columns of news space above the Page One masthead to say it himself. If Governor Thomson were challenged elsewhere in a statement of fact, a reporter from the staff of the *Union Leader* would "investigate" the facts of the matter and a "true" presentation of these facts would be disclosed in the earliest possible edition, always in concert with the governor's view. If the subject matter was not of "urgent" priority, the governor's views on a given matter would be shifted to the center of the editorial page of the newspaper, but whether the governor's dictum appeared on Page One or on the editorial page, a flattering picture of Gov. Meldrim Thomson, Jr., of Orford, always accompanied the text.

What no detractor could take away from Governor Thomson was that he was an inexhaustible worker, at his desk bright and early each day and visiting at meetings of every description in all parts of the state each evening. Although the *Union Leader* and Loeb had said that the governor didn't have a thought about seeking reelection, hardly an edition of the Manchester newspapers was published without at least two, sometimes many more, pictures of Thomson making an appearance with a group, not unusually at a location or with an organization which had never in its history had the honor of a gubernatorial visit before.

Governor Thomson was ubiquitous, and it soon became public knowledge that he had also been to some places where he had had no business in going; he had secretly sent his administrative assistant to search the state's tax records for information on many people who were not known to be Thomson's political allies, and Thomson himself had sped by state limousine to the New England Organized Crime Intelligence System in Wellesley, Mass., where he inquired for the files of certain New Hampshire residents, among them U.S. Sen. Thomas J. McIntrye (D-N.H.).

Governor Thomson had summarily dismissed all members of the Governor's Commission on Crime and Delinquency, including State Supreme Court Justice William Grimes, a nationally-noted authority on crime, and Atty. Gen. Warren Rudman. He replaced them all—at an annual salary of $18,900—with a retired Navy captain from

Manchester, his former political "foe," Roger J. Crowley. To the suprise of absolutely no one, the appointment received praise from William Loeb, publisher of the *Manchester Union Leader.*

Indeed, there was no move Thomson made which did not receive praise and editorial applause from Loeb. When Thomson cancelled an agreement with Maine over fishing boundaries between the two states—without consulting anyone—Loeb said he thought this was swell. When the State Supreme Court ruled that Thomson's search of the tax files had been illegal, and Thomson retorted that the court's ruling was "bad policy and bad law" and that he would continue to interpret the Constitution as he saw it, "not as understood by others," Loeb said that this was as it should be.

It was not until the next campaign of the fall of 1974 when it became public knowledge—largely due to the efforts of Rod Paul, the State House bureau chief of the *Concord Monitor*—that, during the period from January, 1973, until the fall of 1974, Governor Thomson called Publisher Loeb on the telephone hundreds of times, as many as nine times in one day, all at state expense, at Loeb's homes in Pride's Crossing or in Reno, Nev. On the days following the maximum recorded number of telephone calls, Thomson invariably made some policy statement, named an appointee, or otherwise took some significant action. And, without exception, this move by Governor Thomson was applauded in the very next edition of the *Union Leader,* usually by Loeb himself in a Page One editorial.

In sum, Loeb had in the State House in New Hampshire a governor he could "live with"—in Pride's Crossing, Mass., or Reno, Nev. He began to look to other fields of leadership for editorial fodder. During the month of March he found what he had apparently been looking for.

Rev. Dr. David B. Shirley, pastor of the Brookside Congregational Church in Manchester, located in one of the city's more affluent neighborhoods, with a membership to match the location, was apprehended one evening by a Manchester police officer as he entered his parked automobile. The policeman took Rev. Dr. Shirley to the police headquarters where he attempted to book him for driving while under the influence of intoxicating beverages. The lieutenant on duty immediately saw that this was a case of false arrest, that the minister was not intoxicated—didn't even appear intoxicated. He apologized profusely, and instructed that the clergyman be given a ride to his home.

Within a matter of hours, Atty. James V. Broderick, Jr., an associate justice of the Manchester District (misdemeanor) Court, was apprehended by New Hampshire State Police on a by-pass highway around Manchester and he was charged with DWI. Judge Broderick was returning to his home from the Manchester Country Club.

In the editions of March 20, 1973, William Loeb occupied the top half of two columns of news space on Page One of the *Union Leader,* and continued it to Page 12, where it occupied even more news space, with an editorial which he chose to title:

## "A Sad and Regrettable Situation"

"Two events that occurred recently, involving a prominent Manchester clergyman and a prominent Manchester lawyer and judge, saddened this newspaper very much indeed. Yet, it is necessary to comment on these two sad events because, if society is to hold together, it must be able to look with belief and confidence to members of its clergy and members of its judiciary. If the leaders of these two branches are to fail, then what can be expected of the rest of us?"

Loeb continued:

"Ministers and judges are not only looked up to by the rest of the population, but also they are given special privileges because of their positions. When they fail to live up to the high standards which are set for them, and which are the basis of their elevated positions, then this newspaper feels that there is nothing for them to do but resign from their positions because they have lost the confidence of the people in the community and, hence, their authority.

"It is perfectly possible for such men to make a success in other occupations or in other communities, but it does not seem possible to this newspaper that the leaders of our communities who set a bad example for young people should be continued in their exalted positions.

"It is the policy of this newspaper to express editorial opinion based upon principles, not personalities. We praise our opponents when they act prudently and we denounce our friends when they don't.

"The reason this newspaper is bringing up this unpleasant and unhappy subject is that we see the collapse of morals and moral standards at the root of so many difficulties in the United States today. This rot is not only going through our communities on the local and state scenes, but also on our national scene, and it bids fair to destroy us as a nation. There is nothing more imperative today than the return to a set of moral standards and a reasonable adherence thereto.

"Therefore, if those in our communities in the clergy and the judiciary who are supposed to maintain these standards depart from them in such a conspicuous fashion as in these two particular cases, then this newspaper feels they should not continue in their positions of leadership in the communities, because their continuance there will be destructive of the morals of the community, rather than improving them.

> "/s/ William Loeb
> "William Loeb, Publisher."

The case of Rev. Dr. Shirley never even reached the police blotter. No charges were ever made. In the case of Judge Broderick, the city prosecutor, Atty. James J. Barry, Jr., also counsel for the Union Leader Corporation, immediately withdrew. Broderick requested, and received, a jury trial, on the basis that whatever action a fellow jurist might take would be suspect. The jury trial was duly conducted and Broderick was exonerated of all charges.

The city of Manchester and the state of New Hampshire were buzzing with the harshness of Loeb's editorial. Moved to compassion, another minister, the Rev. Arnold D. Johnson, pastor of the Amherst Congregational Church, located in one of Manchester's suburbs, wrote what he considered to be a privileged letter to the publisher. William Loeb published the complete text of Rev. Mr. Johnson's letter, together with his own answer, in all editions of the *Union Leader* on April 4, 1973. They speak for themselves:

## "Suggests Alternative
## To Cleric's Resignation

"Addressed to William Loeb: It was with dismay and a sinking heart that I read the Union Leader March 20th editorial regarding the DWI charges against a clergyman and a judge in Manchester. Most disheartening was your feeling 'that there is nothing for them to do but resign their positions.' I hope you will rethink your position.

"You have equated the charges with guilt. So let it be. But even assuming the worst, the judgment and the sentence pronounced in the editorial are overly harsh.

"I've known many ministers, and have yet to meet one who claimed to be a saint. All acknowledge that they are sinners. If perfection were a requirement for ordination, then we would have few if any ministers, least of all this writer.

"Sin may not be excusable, but thank God it is forgivable. When Jesus said to those who would punish the woman taken in adultery, 'He that is without sin among you, let first cast a stone . . .' He found no takers. When He was asked how often a person is called up to forgive, He replied, 'Seventy times seven.'

"These falls from grace may seriously impair the function of those men in their dealings with people. It does not have to. In fact, the minister may be a better minister, and the judge a better judge, precisely because of these incidents. It depends upon the situation.

"In the case of the clergyman, a great deal is up to the members of the congregation. If they are willing to minister to him in his troubles as he has ministered to them in their troubles, then both minister and congregation

may grow in grace. Insisting upon his resignation would
be thwarting any possibility of God working his miracle
of healing.

"This letter is not written for publication, but to point
out to you that resignation is not the only alternative in
this situation. In all probability it is not even the best
one.

                    "ARNOLD D. JOHNSON
"Amherst"

                  .    .    .

"Reverend Arnold D. Johnson
The Congregational Church
Amherst, N. H. 03031

"Thank you for your letter of March 21. In line with
our policy of printing letters whether they agree with us
or not, it has been turned over to the editors for publication.

"I am sorry to see the attitude you express in your letter, but it is typical of many well-meaning people who let
their sense of mercy and charity erode the standards which
make orderly, peaceful and moral life possible.

"People with your attitude seem to be always so concerned with the wrong doer, so sympathetic to him, than
to the victims—the people who suffer from the wrong
doers' actions.

"As I have tried to explain before, I think highly of
Reverend David Shirley. He has been a guest at my home
for dinner. I have praised his sermons, many of them are
splendid. He handled the funeral service of our late beloved Tad Dearborn, chief of our Editorial Page, I am
entirely sympathetic with his problem.

"However, it is not the question before us. The question
before us is the maintenance of certain standards in our
communities, and if the leaders of the community, our
ministers and our judges, are to become so involved that it
appears they have violated these standards, then don't you
understand, the average citizen says, 'Why should I live up
to these standards? Why should I try to be moral?' Then
the whole tenuous, delicate fabric of society collapses.

"This is what you see all across the United States where

obscenity and filth flood bookstores and newsstands, where moral standards have collapsed and there is violence and force and selfishness and greed almost everywhere.

"All of this happens because nice, well-meaning people such as yourself, have turned values upside down by being more concerned over the wrong doer than his victims.

"I have news for you. The victims are getting a little bit disgusted with all of this. They have seen your theories tried and they have not worked and now we want no more of them.

"Thank you for writing.

"Very sincerely,
"WILLIAM LOEB
"President"*

Near the end of the same month, April 27, 1973, to be exact, Loeb was back on his normal track, defending Governor Thomson against all comers. On the day in question, Loeb devoted nearly four full columns of news space to his daily editorial, this one entitled, "Beneath the Surface." Following Governor Thomson's expedition to the New England Organized Crime Intelligence System, the governor himself had excused the prying into the files, or possible files, of his political enemies by saying that he was only doing it to "test the security measures" of the crime information center. Following this, Senate President David Nixon, House Speaker James O'Neil and Senator Robb Trowbridge announced that, if the security precautions were so lax, they would investigate to see if New Hampshire should contribute to the six-state venture. Loeb said this was dastardly, that these men were really launching "another attack on Governor Thomson." Loeb even called John Milne, the UPI reporter who uncovered the facts on Thomson's visit, an "activist" who was "consorting" and "planning attacks against Governor Thomson."

* Loeb almost always uses the title "President" in replies to letters to the editor. He is, of course, president—of the Union Leader Corp.

"THE WHOLE UPROAR RAISED BY THE CON-
CORD MONITOR AND OTHER LEFT WING NEWS-
PAPERS IS NOTHING MORE THAN A HYPOCRITI-
CAL HOLIER-THAN-THOU ATTEMPT TO AT-
TACK THE GOVERNOR. . . .

"THEREFORE, DESPITE THE APPARENT PIOUS
AND WORTHY OBJECTIVE OF THIS COMMITTEE,
THIS NEWSPAPER ASSERTS FRANKLY THAT WE
BELIEVE THE REAL PURPOSE OF THIS COMMIT-
TEE IS TO TRY TO DO ANOTHER HANGING JOB
ON GOVERNOR THOMSON AND SMEAR HIM. . . .

"NOW THIS IRRESPONSIBLE, AND APPAR-
ENTLY HATE-FILLED GROUP, IN THEIR AT-
TEMPT TO GET AT THE GOVERNOR AND HARM
HIM, HAS USED RECKLESS SMEARING AND PUB-
LICIZING OF NAMES OF THESE INNOCENT PEO-
PLE WITHOUT ANY REGARD TO THE HARM OR
DAMAGE THEY MAY DO THEM. THIS IS A SHAME-
FUL AND DISGUSTING PERFORMANCE ON THE
PART OF MEN WHO SHOULD KNOW BETTER,
BUT WHOSE BLIND INDIGNATION TOWARDS
GOVERNOR THOMSON HAS APPARENTLY MADE
THEM UNMINDFUL OF COMMON DECENCIES."

But across eight columns of the same edition of the
*Union Leader* that day, in a story "By Arthur C. Egan, Jr.
Copyright 1973, Union Leader Corp." the newspaper
claimed that an attorney named Murray Chotiner was the
White House fixer who "gave birth to the idea of the
political espionage" teams in the Watergate affair. Egan's
story called Chotiner a "White House staffer and a longtime friend of President Nixon," and a "master intriguer"
who received the "full cooperation of Atty. Gen. John N.
Mitchell." Egan's story further told of how Teamsters
Union President Frank Fitzsimmons had been the fund-
raiser and had exacted donations from Teamsters locals
to finance the entire Watergate affair.

If it was headlines William Loeb was seeking, then it
could be said that he was unsuccessful. The story by Egan
on Chotiner was patently libelous and, to the surprise of
no newspaperman, or any lawyer, for that matter, it was

repeated in no other newspaper. However, the hand-in-glove antics of Thomson and Loeb, by now an accepted way of life in the Granite State, were attracting national attention. Most people wondered if Loeb wasn't right when he said, "The Granite State is something different from the other 49 states."

On May 1, 1973, *The New York Times* had this to say:

"CONCORD, N. H., April 30—The politics of this lovely New England state, long a source of puzzlement and amusement to outsiders, has taken a bizarre new twist in recent weeks with a series of exposures and controversies that local wags have dubbed Watergate North.

"The uproar has centered on reports that the state's conservative new Governor, Meldrim Thomson, Jr., ordered an aide to examine confidential business profits tax records of the Governor's political enemies, in apparent violation of state law, and personally sought criminal intelligence data on a number of political and business figures in the state.

"The reports have precipitated a storm of charges and countercharges that have paralyzed much of the state's political machinery. Critics accuse the Governor of "police state tactics" and of carrying on a repressive political vendetta, His defenders call the attacks politically motivated attempts to embarrass him.

"The Governor's behavior has been Topic A at political clubhouses from Nashua to the Canadian border almost from the day the 60-year old Georgia-born lawyer, a Republican, took office on Jan. 4. In just 16 weeks, he has become involved in a border dispute with Maine, denounced the State Supreme Court, cancelled a racing agreement with Massachusetts and Rhode Island and accused the state of illegal wiretapping, in addition to investigating the tax and crime files . . .

"All of this has sparked bitter debate among politicians and in the press. The Governor whose Georgia drawl seems odd in this staunch Yankee territory, has been stoutly defended by the state's largest newspaper, the Manchester Union Leader, run by William Loeb, its extremely conservative publisher . . ."

Whether or not it was Thomson's natural bent to act
this way, or whether he was acting at the suggestion of
Loeb, is not known. But, at about this time, the governor
established a post office box address in Concord, to which
only he and his administrative assistant had the keys, to
which the public was invited to address complaints and
reports of any knowledge they had of criminal matters,
even anonymously, with the promise that the governor
would act on these reports. It was at about the same time
that the *Union Leader* began including in its regular daily
editions a coupon for readers to fill out with any information they might have on welfare "cheats" which could
be forwarded to the newspaper, even anonymously, with
the promise that the newspaper would make sure the information reached the "proper" authorities.

It also became public knowledge that Governor Thomson had exacted from certain state officials, both those
already in office and those whom he appointed, signed, un-
dated letters of resignation addressed to the governor
himself.

On the morning of June 9, 1973, in the *Union Leader*,
Governor Thomson was quoted as saying that he planned
to wait until after July 1, after the Legislature had ad-
journed, to take any action on state appointments, whether
to reappoint those already in office, or to replace them with
new appointees. Prompting this quotation was the matter
of Insurance Commissioner John Durkin, whose appointment by Gov. John King to a five-year term had expired
on June 9. Durkin had been making quite a name for
himself as a consumer advocate, and a long battle he had
been having with Blue Cross-Blue Shield was reaching a
climax.

The governor's statement that he would take no action
on any appointments was the last word uttered on the
matter until the following Wednesday morning, June 15,
when, during the regular weekly meeting of the Governor
and Council, Governor Thomson proposed the name of
Frank A. Whaland to succeed Durkin as insurance commissioner. At that precise moment, unbeknownst to the

councillors, a state trooper had been dispatched to Durkin's office with instructions to tell Commissioner Durkin to take whatever contents of his desk he wished to take with him and to leave the building.

The spotlight then shifted to one of William Loeb's pet hates, the campus of the University of New Hampshire at Durham, presided over by Dr. Thomas N. Bonner. A group of self-avowed homosexual students, the Gay Students Organization, had applied for space in the campus student center to hold a function and, after a bitter wrangle, the trustees voted to grant the request, with the observation that apparently the Gay Students Organization was a valid student organization. Governor Thomson, himself an ex-officio trustee, vowed to replace all the trustees on the board as their terms expired, and this was no hollow threat because, as aforesaid, the governor has 12 appointments, including a student trustee, to the 24-man board. Loeb immediately took up this cause and has continued a campaign against the GSO for two years, preferring to call the GSO "sodomites" for headline purposes in the *Union Leader*.

But that was not all that was happening at the Durham campus. The Roman Catholic Diocese of Manchester was planning to be host diocese to the 27th annual New England Congress of Religious Education for a three-day series of meetings to be held after the regular summer school sessions at the university ended, using the regular campus buildings and classrooms to accommodate the expected 6,000 to 8,000 from all over the country who were planning to attend. As the name of the Congress implies, the sponsors of the affair were the 11 Roman Catholic dioceses of the six New England states. The Congress was held annually at a different location on a rotating basis. Most Rev. Ernest J. Primeau, STD, bishop of Manchester, was nothing more than host bishop with one-eleventh of a say in the proceedings. When it was disclosed that Rev. Daniel

Berrigan would be one of the speakers at the affair, the *Union Leader* began an extraordinary attack on Bishop Primeau.

William Loeb, whether by design or not, it is impossible to say, never did use one of his own signed Page One editorials in the assault, but there can be no doubt that it was all done with his knowledge and approval. The editorials were, without exception, the lead editorials on the regular editorial page, none of them with the full-face type faces and capital letters which were the identifying mark of a William Loeb-authored editorial. This, of course, meant that the editorials were authored by James J. Finnegan, himself a Catholic. The editorials in the *Sunday News* were initialed by Bernard J. McQuaid, also of the Catholic faith.

The first editorial, on June 22, 1973, stated that the Diocese of Manchester was paying Berrigan a fee for appearing and that laymen should protest this appearance of this "jailbird." The options which the newspaper offered were to "react in anger and go out and buy up a year's supply of church-boycotted table grapes and iceberg lettuce, turn sullen and do nothing, or protest directly to Bishop Primeau."

The *Sunday News* of June 24 concluded the editorial entitled, "Bishop Host to Berrigan," with the following two paragraphs:

> "A colleague writes for the Union Leader editorial page a suggestion that the Catholic laity might wish to protest to Bishop Primeau his invitation to scum like the Berrigans, but this is a waste of time.
>
> "Bishop Primeau and his liberal clack have ignored the protests of millions of Catholics, who, to express their disapproval, have had to stop going to Mass and contributing to the financial support of the Roman Church.—B. J. McQ."

The June 29 editorial in the daily paper, "What Price Berrigan?", also exhorted the laymen to protest to the bishop, and this editorial, besides including a worn picture of Rev. Daniel Berrigan in "hippie" attire, also included a picture of Bishop Primeau in full episcopal vestments, including a mitre, dispensing Holy Water.

Then came eight columns at the top of Page One on July 3, written by Donn Tibbetts, another Catholic, stating that the protests to Berrigan's appearance were mounting. On July 18, also by Tibbetts (or Tibbets, as the *Union Leader* spelled the reporter's name on this occasion), a story stated that the protests might cause the Congress to be so poorly attended as to cause its financial failure.

### "Berrigan Forecast: Still Cloudy"

on July 19 said that the newspaper was not critical of the other 99 speakers on the program at the Congress, but only Berrigan. It also called for disclosure of the terms of the rental of the UNH facilities to the Diocese of Manchester, even though the newspaper knew that the Congress was the function of all 11 New England dioceses. The *Union Leader* said:

> "The whole sorry affair sounds as if it had been orchestrated by Gilbert and Sullivan!"

But the crowning blow of the entire *Union Leader* assault came in the form of a cartoon on the editorial page of all editions on July 20, 1973. With the caption, "Same Place For These, Bishop," it showed Bishop Primeau in his robes, obviously in his office, putting a golf ball, while a priest assistant struggled through the door heavily laden with what were labelled "Berrigan Protests." The waste basket was filled to overflowing with similar envelopes, and a caricature of the cartoonist in the lower right-hand corner said, "Well, that's how the laity views it folks!"

On its own merits, the cartoon was in the worst possible taste. But, according to diocesan officials, the cartoon also portrayed a lie. In the first place, Bishop Primeau was a severely troubled man because of this incident and his health noticeably failed during the two-month tirade. The actual protests which the bishop received were very few in number, with those opposed to Berrigan's appearance nearly equalled by those who wrote to express support and understanding of the bishop's position in the whole affair. Too, it was stressed by the diocesan officials, Bishop Primeau wrote a personal answer to every communication he received concerning the Berrigan affair and the Congress, whether the communication was favorable or not.

The Watergate Committee of the U.S. Senate was in high gear at about this time in Washington and some investigators had come to New Hampshire to trace the by-now famous "Canuck" letter which Loeb had published during Senator Muskie's campaign and to look into other "dirty tricks" which occured during the reelection of President Nixon. They also paused to take a look at some of the persons on the staff of Equity Publishing Co., Inc., owned by one Meldrim Thomson, Jr., of Orford, which published statutes for the State of New Hampshire, but also for Puerto Rico and Costa Rica, and employed many Spanish-speaking lawyers in this connection. The Watergate investigators made it public that they were interested in knowing if there was any connection between these people and the Spanish-speaking burglars who were actually involved in the Watergate break-in.

Governor Thomson and Publisher Loeb both issued loud statements to Sen. Sam Ervin, (D-N.C.), committee chairman, and other committee members, urging them to recall their investigators from New Hampshire, calling them the "Watergate Gestapo." (We have seen the term "gestapo" used in earlier pages.)

At one point, Sen. Lowell Weicker (R-Conn.) replied to a letter from Governor Thomson, saying, "I feel that you should know, Governor, that some nut has stolen some of your stationery and is writing crank letters."

The Manchester newspapers continued to have names for other persons, too, as it had had for well over two decades. But there had never been any which reached such depths of taste and so violated every rule of propriety as the editorial in the *Sunday News* of Sept. 2, 1973, entitled:

## "Kissinger the Kike?"

The editorial had no real theme, unless it could be "hate," and certainly there was no reason for it even being printed on this occasion: it was in the context of no event or public issue which was then pending that would have a bearing on the editorial. (It is reprinted in its entirety as Appendix D to this treatise.)

William Loeb, having flexed his muscles against a young teen-aged girl, Miss Vermont, the year before, apparently was just waiting for the Miss America Pageant of 1973 to open. In Atlantic City, Michelle Cote, Miss New Hampshire, was being sponsored by the Manchester newspapers. In filling out a routine questionnaire required of all contestants, Miss Cote stated that she believed that minority groups should have equal rights and William Loeb interpreted this to mean that she endorsed the UNH Gay Students Organization. A student at the New England Conservatory of Music in Boston, Miss Cote said she was studying there because there were no such institutions in her home state. William Loeb interpreted this to mean that she had said that New Hampshire's educational facilities were sub-standard. So it went.

The *Union Leader*'s Page One included a story encased in a black border of mourning on Sept. 7, 1973, entitled, "We Regret," which went on to say that the newspapers "sincerely regret any embarrassment suffered by the people of New Hampshire as a result of the unfortunate remarks made in Atlantic City by Michelle Cote." There followed a long story, continued to an inside page, which detailed how the girl's parents had been separated and that her mother had suffered a "nervous breakdown" and her sister "had followed her mother to the hospital." The story stated that the newspapers would publish no further promotional material on Miss Cote, but would follow through with their financial sponsorship of her as promised.

# 32

A year after the election of Meldrim Thomson, Jr., Thomson and William Loeb had things pretty much their own way. The muscle of the governor's office, combined with the punch of the state's only big newspaper, had converted many people to their way of thinking. Thomson had vetoed 29 bills passed by the bicameral Legislature after its adjournment, and, as a result, a special session of the Legislature during the normal off-year of 1974 was practically inevitable. Although Loeb's newspapers trumpeted that "Thomson had kept his promise, no new taxes," there were other problems, notably in state services and, more particularly, in matters relative to the New Hampshire State Hospital and the Laconia State School for retarded children. The hospital was in danger of losing accreditation and the school was nothing more than a place where these unfortunate children could receive room and board. But, it was a fact that there were no new taxes, and it was also a fact that tuition at the state university was fluctuating between being the highest, or next to highest, in the nation.

No, there were no new taxes.

William Loeb was showing power he had not had since the halcyon days of the Powell Administration before Senator Bridges' death. Indeed, Loeb may never have had such power before. The administration of most Manchester city departments were being run pretty much as the *Union Leader* wanted them run and the city administrators knew all too well what would happen to them in print if they failed to follow the Loeb party line. Loeb's editorials began to exhibit the imperious attitude of a person speaking to his subjects. On two occasions, all other sports news in the *Union Leader* had been preempted for long narratives —almost two full pages each—of a fishing trip and a hunting expedition that Loeb and his wife, Nackey, had taken. Loeb also, on two occasions, had used his daily Page

One editorial space to give skiing lessons to the readers. Nackey Scripps Gallowhur Loeb also began to write her own Page One editorials on days her husband wasn't using this prime news space.

And Loeb's schedule of personal appearances began to be stepped up. In New Hampshire he was appearing at more and more functions, usually at small groups in out-of-the-way places, certainly never again before an audience such as the N.H. Bar Association, where people had an opportunity to shoot back. And, he even went to Burlington, Vt., for a speech before the Kiwanis Club and it was the first appearance of the man who so resents being called an "absentee publisher" in that city in over 22 years. After the luncheon meeting, Loeb went to a reception for all staff members of the *Vermont Sunday News* and the *St. Albans Daily Messenger,* who, at the time, were operating out of a small suite of offices in a building over a theatre on Bank Street in downtown Burlington and a converted trolley barn on the northern outskirts of St. Albans.

During the reception, Loeb greeted the sports editor of the *Sunday News,* Jules Brulatour, with the statement, "You're new around here." It seems this didn't sit too well; Brulatour had just been named Vermont Sportswriter of the Year after his many years of labor on the Sunday sports section. Brulatour's column is now missing from the newspaper.

Loeb had other reasons to be concerned about the workings of his Vermont newspapers. William T. Montague, the son of Loeb's general manager for so many years, had resigned as general manager of the two newspapers. According to Montague, he had not received a raise from his $200-a-week salary since he took the job in 1961 and, besides, every suggestion he had made to put the Vermont newspapers on a paying basis had been vetoed by Loeb, in absentia.

In the annual report filed with the Vermont Secretary of State of the Vermont Publishing Corporation for the fiscal year ending Sept. 30, 1971, Montague had attested that the corporation, of a value of $131,535.00, had borrowed $5,330.00—from the Union Leader Corporation, says Montague. In the report dated Sept. 30, 1972, Montague attested that the Vermont Publishing Corp., of a value at that time of $200,222.00, had borrowed $553,060.00—again from the Union Leader, says Montague. When the report for Sept. 29, 1973 was ready, Montague quit his job, explaining that he had children of the age which would require educational investment, besides which he wasn't going to sign another one of those reports. All the report said was that Vermont Publishing Corp. of a value of $198,401.00, had borrowed $707,742.00—from the Union Leader Corporation, says Montague.

Loeb found someone to sign it, though, in the person of Clifton Noyes, the new clerk of the corporation and the new general manager of the Vermont newspapers. Noyes was the fellow whom Loeb had brought to Burlington in the early 1960's and had made editor at the age of 18. Noyes became general manager and editor, with a $25 raise tacked onto his $175 editor's salary.

Governor Thomson was all the while continuing to make his appearances throughout every corner of the Granite State, each one duly recorded in the *Union Leader*. The pace of two group pictures a day of the governor seldom slackened. Two of Thomson's continuing themes were his bias against environmentalists and his advocacy of an oil refinery in New Hampshire. At a news conference in April he said, "I would be willing to do anything I can to encourage the establishment of a refinery." And at an October dinner meeting he said, "We must drill in the mountains and drill in the valleys" to find oil in New Hampshire.

Quietly, beginning in early September, "real estate" men began making the rounds of shore front property in Portsmouth, Rye and Durham. By late fall options had been taken on over 3,000 acres of privately owned land. The "real estate" men had explained to the owners that they were seeking the land for clients who wanted a retirement retreat, or who wanted to establish a game sanctuary, and, in one case, for a man who wanted his own hunting preserve. The price in each individual case had gone up as neighbor had consulted neighbor about the offers they had received, and which some had accepted. The largest segment of land being sought by these men was at Durham Point, a secluded section of land on the shore of Great Bay between the university community of Durham and the small manufacturing town of Newmarket immediately to the south. But options had also been taken on parts of the Isles of Shoals, a small group of islands about 10 miles off the coast of Rye and Portsmouth, about which Capt. John Smith had first written in 1614.

In late November, 1973, the nation was in a state of alarm over its first real energy crisis; the use of gasoline and oil was being drastically curtailed everywhere. Meldrim Thomson, Jr., made quite a show of stating his rules for the use of state vehicles, urging all departments to use compact vehicles, even though he figured his use of his Lincoln Continental was in the best interests of the state because of "the amount of work I get done in the back seat."

On Nov. 26, 1973, a platoon of state troopers was dispatched from Concord to travel to all corners of the state to hand deliver invitations to a news conference in the State House the next day. In some cases, these troopers travelled at speeds of up to 100 miles per hour during this mission, according to AP and UPI reports at the time.

Governor Thomson announced at the State House the next day that Aristotle Onassis, the Greek shipping magnate, would establish on the shores of Durham Point a $600-million refinery under the auspices of his Olympic Oil Co. The plan set forth by the governor told of how Onassis' super tankers would offload their cargoes of oil at moorings within the Isles of Shoals and the oil would be pumped through an underwater pipeline to the mainland at Portsmouth and through another pipeline system which would run to Durham Point where the largest single-unit oil refinery ever built would be located.

Governor Thomson told of the jobs such a project would create, the tax revenue the state would receive and the greater availability of refined products to the people of New Hampshire. William Loeb lauded the project in his

*Union Leader* and called it "an opportunity to escape the fuel and gasoline shortage which is burdening the rest of the nation." "Our fuel problems would be over," said Loeb of the plans to build the refinery.

Such a reception to a Thomson statement was not, in itself, unusual. But then the whole plot began to unfold.

Onassis himself announced a visit to New Hampshire on December 19, and that day's Page One of the *Union Leader,* in addition to a multi-column story about Onassis' advent, contained Loeb's personal editorial salute, "WELCOME To the Two Big O's—Oil and Onassis!" "He is the nearest thing to Santa Claus that the State of New Hampshire will ever see," said William Loeb. The rest of the editorial was extremely defensive in tone, as if to rebut all the statements which had been offered by those who had voiced opposition to the establishment of a refinery after Governor Thomson's first announcement of the project almost three weeks before. Besides the environmentalists, these vocal opponents included the people who had given options on their land—often the property of their respective families for generations—and who claimed that the "real estate" men had offered the options under false pretenses; persons who owned beachfront property along New Hampshire's 18 miles of seacoast; townspeople of Durham who had lived there all their lives who faced the prospect of the quiet university town being converted into an oil capital, and others, many others.

Loeb, in his editorial that day, indirectly suggested that there had been many conversations and disclosures that had already been made to persons in preferred positions, which had not been made to the rank and file of the New Hampshire citizenry. The overall theme of the editorial clearly spelled out what Onassis had in mind: to offload the oil near the Isles of Shoals and pump it to the Durham Point location. Loeb specifically compared the proposed refinery with those in New Jersey and specifically compared the proposed offloading facilities to those in other seaports, such as Portland, Me. His long editorial was punctuated with certain paragraphs, all in capital letters, designed to dispel any adverse criticism of Onassis' plan:

"FIRST OF ALL, THE ISLES OF SHOALS WILL
NOT BE HARMED . . .

"THERE WILL BE NO CONTAMINATION OF
ANY OF THE WATERS OFF THE COAST OF HAMP-
TON BEACH, RYE BEACH OR IN THE GREAT
BAY . . .

"THERE WILL BE NO DEFACEMENT OF ANY OF
THE SCENERY OF THE GREAT BAY . . .

"THERE WILL BE NO EFFLUENT DUMPED
INTO GREAT BAY OR ANYWHERE ELSE. SO
THERE WILL NOT BE THE SLIGHTEST CON-
TAMINATION OF THE WATERS OR INTERFER-
ENCE WITH ANY OF THE MARINE LIFE . . .

"THE MODERN ONASSIS REFINERY, ON THE
OTHER HAND, WOULD BE LOCATED ON 5,000
ACRES OF LAND AND WOULD BE HARDLY NO-
TICEABLE BY THE INHABITANTS OF THE SEA-
COAST AREA, UNLESS THEY WERE TO FLY DI-
RECTLY OVER IT . . ."

Two full columns later Loeb concluded:

"It is a fact, of course, that Mr. Onassis is sympathetic
to the conservationists and ecological cause and understands completely the desire of all people across the entire
world to minimize pollution—while at the same time
achieving a maximum of industrialization on which the
prosperity of the world depends.

"Therefore, and again we emphasize that this is just in
the rumor stage, Mr. Onassis is said to be thinking about
establishing in Durham, in connection with the University
what would probably be the world's largest laboratory to
study anti-pollution and pollution-prevention methods.

"If this rumor turns out to be reality, then certainly it
would be hard to think of any community on the face of
the globe which would have been given such a magnificent
Christmas present in this year 1973 as the Town of Durham in the State of New Hampshire.

"So, therefore, we welcome 'Santa Claus' Onassis and his
oil!"

One can only assume that William Loeb had been privy
to a lot of information which had not already been told
other persons who were within the circulation range of

his newspapers. But, the Department of Chemistry at the University of New Hampshire had had for many long years a most healthy reputation, and those close to the university scene were at least a little heartened when Dr. Thomas N. Bonner announced that his school would be happy to cooperate in any studies in connection with the proposed refinery. The townspeople of Durham knew they were in good hands in this regard.

Still it was disturbing to read of what was obviously inside information on Onassis' plan, and immediately rumors sprang up of a Loeb-Onassis deal. At any rate, Loeb's newspaper exuded as much, if not more, enthusiasm in favor of the refinery as it had for even the most hotly contested political elections.

Onassis flew to Manchester early the next morning where he and his party transferred to a helicopter for a flight over the state's seacoast region. Following that, Governor and Mrs. Thomson hosted a luncheon at the governor's residence in East Concord. Assisting the Thomsons in receiving the guests were Mr. and Mrs. William Loeb. In the Onassis party were Constantine Gratsos, in charge of Olympic Refinery's New York office; Major Alexander P. de Seversky, the World War II flying ace, who was introduced by Onassis to Loeb (according to the *Union Leader*) as "a magician who can make smoke disappear," and Peter Booras, a Keene, N.H., businessman, who presumably had been Onassis' leg man within the state for the refinery project. De Seversky had designed a new type of precipitator to extract impurities from industrial waste.

Following the luncheon the group went to the convention center of a Manchester hotel where Onassis met the press, and a lot of the general public, for the first and only time during his visit. According to the *Union Leader*, among Onassis' remarks were the following:

> "I want to make it clear that I am not a Greek bearing presents. The last thing I would like to do is to impose an unpleasant investment onto the inhabitants of New Hampshire, bearing in mind that the inhabitants of

New Hampshire are part of the American aristocracy . . .
However, even aristocracy needs a kitchen. All this time,
for years now, your supplies were coming from very far
away, expensive restaurants. So if we can manage to produce a refinery clean as a clinic without any smell or
smoke, and if we can persuade and convince the experts
and the officials of the environment and ecology, I hope
we will be doing something good for everybody."

Some of the visiting press—the "visiting press" at a
Manchester event is meant to include anyone not from
the *Union Leader*—pressed Onassis for a bit of amplifica-
tion on how he proposed to construct a refinery "clean as
a clinic" and the like, but Governor Thomson stepped into
the breach on every occasion, usually in words such as he
used when he first jumped into the press dialogue:

> "The answer to that has already been given because I
> have assured the people of Durham there will be no im-
> position of anything in that way—if they are not smart
> enough to understand this could be of great advantage to
> them, there are many others that do want it."

Mrs. Thomas Dudley was at that news conference and
the *Union Leader* specified that she had not been invited.
Mrs. Dudley is the state representative to the N.H. General Court from the Town of Durham. She was asked her
reaction to Governor Thomson's statement that Onassis
was considering establishing an anti-pollution laboratory
at the university in connection with the refinery, and the
*Union Leader* reported it this way:

> "'. . . I can think of no other word to use than as a
> bribe.'
> "Mrs. Dudley, whose first name is also Dudley, claimed
> that 'they are simply telling us that they are Santa Claus
> and they are going to make things fine for us but not tell-
> ing us how.'
> "Asked for her principal objection to the refinery, Mrs.
> Dudley said, 'The way the land was acquired,' in that it
> was not made clear that a refinery was planned. But,
> pressed as to whether she were buying land for an enter-
> prise she might not reveal her exact plans so as to not

drive up the real estate price, she allowed, 'It's conceivable that I would not tell them what I was going to use the land for, I guess I'm not a businesswoman, but, I would not lie.' She insisted the project was 'too big and too close to Pease Air Force Base.' "

It was apparent that the *Union Leader* had never paid much attention to this member of the state's General Court, even though she had run for office once previously, and had been in office for almost a year, the first Democrat in recent history to be elected from the town of Durham. The *Union Leader* might have done well to have known a little more about Mrs. Thomas Dudley, because they would hear a lot more from her—and they would print a lot more about her—in the future.

It goes without saying that a lady whose given name is Dudley would have to have some guts to contemplate marrying a young lawyer whose surname was Dudley. She is a native of Durham and a graduate of the University of New Hampshire, where her father is a professor of English. Mrs. Dudley's mother is a direct descendant of Joseph Dudley, president of New England in 1686 and governor of Massachusetts and New Hampshire from 1723 to 1728. Her husband's father was a descendant of Thomas Dudley, appointed governor of the province by Charles I in 1646 and again by Charles II in 1651.

The *Union Leader* of December 21 took Mrs. Dudley to task for her "impertinent" remarks towards Onassis, and the newspaper included an editorial which, in effect, was an open letter of apology to Onassis for the attitude of the "visiting press" who had the audacity to question the Greek millionaire:

> "If Aristotle Onassis came away from his Wednesday evening press conference at the Sheraton-Wayfarer Inn in Bedford with the impression that the Fourth Estate in this area of the country is composed largely of jackasses, he was not far off the mark.
> "The boorish performance of news media representatives who crowded into the Covered Bridge Room was not only insulting to a man who was attempting to make himself available for a free and open discussion of the oil re-

finery he proposes to build at Durham Point but also it was a sad commentary on our profession.

"The general tumult created by news media representatives who apparently felt that they were the center of attraction—rather than this world-renowned businessman who could have bought the lot of them for what they are worth and turned a handsome profit by selling them for what they think they are worth—made it virtually impossible to hear the questions posed let alone Mr. Onassis' answers. The questions that were audible were so juvenile that we had to admire the gentleman from Greece for not simply shrugging his shoulders and walking out of the room in disgust.

"The result was that what could have been an informative news conference turned out to be a mercifully brief mob scene.

"Since those responsible for the discourteous performance are probably not bright enough to extend their apologies to Governor Thomson and his eminent guest, we'll do it for them."

The sides were chosen up. Mrs. Nancy Sandberg, another native of Durham who lived with her school-teacher husband, Malcolm, in her family's farm on Durham Point, organized a group known as Save Our Shores, which provided legal services, bumper stickers, a speaker's bureau and lobbying services for opponents to the establishment of the refinery. Olympic Refineries began an all-out lobbying effort, opening offices in Portsmouth and Concord. It engaged the highest-priced lobbyists in the state and started an advertising program, promising jobs, more tax income and, in guarded terms, more refinery products for the energy-conscious Granite Staters. Demogoguery was not uncommon on either side of the issue, best epitomized by a Page One editorial in the *Union Leader* headline:

### "Let The Stupid
### Yankee Bastards Freeze"

Christmas brought a natural hiatus to the refinery issue. It would not be until the special session of the Legislature in February that the matter could be resolved.

High on the front page of the Dec. 31, 1973 morning and evening editions of the *Union Leader* was a three-column panel enclosed in a border, and it contained a picture of Murray Chotiner. The text of the story is as follows:

"THE MANCHESTER UNION LEADER retracts the allegations contained in articles by reporter Arthur C. Egan, Jr., published in its April 27 and April 28, 1973 editions charging Attorney Murray M. Chotiner with having organized the Watergate incident and other related activities, with having obtained finances for them, with soliciting campaign contributions to achieve the parole of former teamster president James R. Hoffa, and with 'double-crossing' Mr. Hoffa.

"All such accusations against Mr. Chotiner are false.

"Whoever the individual responsible for Watergate may be, we now, after the public inquiries and our own extensive investigation, are satisfied it is not Mr. Chotiner.

"We regret the false impression conveyed by our articles and extend our sincere apology to Mr. Chotiner."

In fact, Chotiner had earlier brought suit against the *Union Leader*. The cash settlement to Chotiner was never made public, but it is known that it was considerable.

The next day, Jan. 1, 1974, Loeb began the New Year with a Page One job entitled:

## "Integrity and Truth Needed in 1974"

"Probably this nation needs more than anything else a renewed sense of integrity and truth, and 1974 would be a good year to start on a program for restoring these virtues to American life . . .

"There is a general atmosphere of distrust and a feeling that almost everyone lies when it serves his or her own purposes and ends.

"In other words, this nation has lost that sense of integrity and truthfulness on which trust and confidence depend . . .

"The entire future of our nation depends on the integrity of its people. If ever we lose all trust and confidence in the written and spoken words of our political, spiritual and educational leaders, we will have lost everything.

"THEREFORE, LET OUR ONE RESOLUTION ABOVE ALL OTHERS FOR 1974 BE A DETERMINATION TO RETURN TO INTEGRITY AND TRUTH."

The refinery issue overshadowed all others when the Legislature went into special session in February. Immediately, Rep. Dudley Dudley introduced House Bill 18, which reaffirmed the home rule concept of New Hampshire government. But, almost immediately, another bill, House Bill 34, was set into motion by Majority Leader George E. Roberts, Jr., that would establish a new state commission, the Energy Facility Evaluation Committee, which, with subsequent amendments to the basic bill, would give this body final say in establishment of a refinery facility, superseding any local ordinance or regulation, such establishment to be, of course, in the greater public good. Rep. Roberts was an ambitious Republican who had already taken his place on the ladder of succession; he is from the town of Gilmanton Iron Works, a town immortalized in Grace Metalious' novel which called that town "Peyton Place."

The first public hearing on Mrs. Dudley's HB 18 was so well attended that the session had to be moved twice to accommodate the turnout. At the morning sessions, held in Concord's American Legion auditorium, Mrs. Dudley herself was the first speaker, and she showed that in addition to being alert and attentive she was also articulate.

"Artistotle Onassis, Peter Booras, Governor Thomson and William Loeb want to build an oil refinery in New Hampshire," said Representative Dudley. "It would swallow up one fifth of the town for which it is presently proposed. It would cover four square miles. Not only one refinery is planned, but two, with a third one planned for the future. The proposed refiner's tank farm and truck-dispatching terminal will be located on the final approach to the main northwest-southeast runway of Pease Air Force

Base. If a plane ever crashed into that refinery, and there have been four crashes so far at Pease, the whole area for miles around would look as if it had been hit by an atomic bomb. I don't believe that any community faced with such a predicament should be asked to take that kind of risk against its own best judgment."

Hundreds of representatives of seacoast towns cheered on Representative Dudley. They carried signs and placards and wore a wide variety of buttons. One member of the Municipal and County Government Committee which was hearing the two sides of the conflict, edged his way off the stage and down the side of the hall. Asked where he was going, he replied: "I'm going upstairs to have a shot and a beer." Asked if he weren't interested in the matter on the floor, he replied "I'm going to vote with Loeb anyway."

The state's educational television network covered the proceedings from the University of New Hampshire Field House live that evening. There the townspeople were given the opportunity to question officials representing Olympic and to give their version of the results of the studies they had undertaken. Again, it was Representative Dudley who took the floor and she said:

> "Some one may argue—indeed the governor has argued —that we are in the midst of an emergency situation so grave as to require that we disregard one of the most sacred tenets of our New Hampshire form of government —that of home rule, of self-determination. . . . I intend to show you that an oil refinery [in Durham] would have a negligible effect on our supply of refined products."

And she did just that, giving proof that the energy crisis was just as bad in coastal New Jersey as it was in New Hampshire. She went further, offering testimony that the establishment of the refinery would alter the nature of the university town.

Town Meeting Day arrived and the persons in the seacoast towns made no secret of the majority sentiment. The Town of Rye voted 1,073-to-194 to rezone Lunging Island (that part of the Isles of Shoals which had been optioned by Olympic Refineries to accommodate the mooring facilities for tankers) to single-family use. The largest crowd in memory to attend a Durham Town Meeting voted 1,254-to-144 against the refinery.

There was some resentment heard from the state's cities to the effect that once again it was the town governments which controlled the state, and the *Union Leader* took full advantage of this avenue of argument. Olympic Refineries, itself, paid for the printing and distribution of a tabloid insert to all the state's newspapers—which caused some resentment in itself because it was unsigned—and finally the matter was to come to a vote in the Legislature. As happens so often in parliamentary procedure, the Roberts Bill, HB 34, would be the telltale proposition here. The Dudley Bill, a shoo-in by itself, would be superseded by the authority written into Roberts' measure. Representative Dudley took the floor of the House:

> "Make no mistake that the effect of this wording is to override the century-old tradition of home rule in the State of New Hampshire, that tradition which is the very bedrock of democracy in New Hampshire, that tradition which our Municipal and County Government committee has upheld in its recent deliberation; that tradition which town meetings from Colebrook to Seabrook are carrying forward this week, that tradition which, when challenged, calls the people of New Hampshire to its defense in 1974 as it did in 1776.
>
> "I want to urge you to vote no on this amendment and ask you to consider your vote on this matter as a positive one—a vote for your neighbors and friends, a vote for your town, a vote for your city—and most of all for the maintenance of home rule in our whole state from Coos* to the sea."

Rep. Dudley was only one of many speakers who wished to be heard on this occasion; others were Reps. Read, George B. Roberts, Jr., Greene, Chase, Sayer, Parr, Colburn, Twigg, Hanson, H. Gwendolyn Jones, Spirou,

* Coos County is the northern extremity of New Hampshire, bordering Canada.

Hammond, Benton, Curran, Taylor, Elmer L. Johnson, Gorman, Deoss, Currier, Altman, George I. Wiggins and Stevenson. The tension was building as the vote on HB 34 approached. No legislator was leaving his seat and the drama was playing to a full house in Representatives' Hall.

One who rose was Rep. Tony Smith (R-Hampton), a known supporter of Governor Thomson. He told his colleagues that he would like to read a telegram which had just moments before been received in the governor's office. The telegram, as Rep. Smith recited it, was as follows:

> "I can assure you that if New Hampshire had a refinery now, the price of fuel to your consumers could be less and the availability of supply to your people greater than at present. Signed, William E. Simon."

Simon was, of course, Federal energy chief, appointed in the emergency situation by President Nixon.

Rep. Mabel E. Richardson requested a roll call and Reps. Gordon, Metcalf, Sweeney, Lebel, Pryor and Curran seconded.

The refinery lost, 109-to-233.

In the wake of this crushing defeat Loeb editorialized:

> "The New Hampshire Legislature has just cast the stupidest vote of its career. It is a vote against progress in the State of New Hampshire.
>
> "It is a vote of utter and complete selfishness, disregarding the best interests of the United States which so desperately needs this new refinery . . .
>
> "The vote at Durham illustrates the intellectual and moral bankruptcy of that campus community.
>
> "The vote in the Legislature illustrates how stupid and narrow and selfish legislators can be . . .
>
> "After that vote in the Legislature, this newspaper suggests that perhaps the New Hampshire state motto should be changed from 'Live Free or Die' to 'WHAT'S IN IT FOR ME?!' "

It was weeks before Loeb recovered. As a matter of fact, it may be that he never has recovered fully. For more than a year afterwards Loeb still referred generically to those from the seacoast region, as "fools" who "coddled their clams and lobsters," nowhere taking into public account that a good number of people in the seacoast region are professional fishermen.

In retrospect, if there was a single person who could be singled out as leading the successful fight against the establishment of the refinery, it was Dudley Dudley, with a lot of off-stage help from Nancy Sandberg and others. And it was Mrs. Dudley's continued polarization of the issue of home rule which is generally regarded as being her most successful tactic. Her oratory was simple, yet effective. She made a good case and she won it.

The *N.H. Sunday News* rendered to Mrs. Dudley some sort of fame, by giving her the nickname of "Mrs. Fuddy Duddy." The *Union Leader* paid her the ultimate compliment by calling her "Deadly Dudley." And history will show that this new orator on the New Hampshire legislative scene derived her forensic talents honestly: her maiden name is Webster and she is, in fact, a direct descendant of "The Great Orator" himself, "Black Daniel" Webster.

There is a rumor going around New Hampshire that "Black Daniel" Webster once said words to the effect, "There is nothing so powerful as truth," or something like that!

In a Page One two-column story, the *Concord Monitor* disclosed on April 12, about a month after the historic roll call vote was taken in the N.H. General Court on home rule, that the telegram which had been rushed from Governor Thomson's office to the House floor and which had been read by Rep. Tony Smith, was a complete and utter fabrication. Rep. Kathryn Cushman (D-Canterbury) had smelled a rat in Smith's reading of the telegram and she had inquired of the Federal Energy Office as to its authenticity. In a letter dated April 2, 1974, John W. Weber, assistant administrator of the Federal Energy Office, said:

"This is in reference to your letter dated March 10, 1974, pertaining to a telegram allegedly sent on March 7, 1974, to Governor Thomson.

"A search of our files fails to disclose any information that the telegram you referred to was sent from this office."

Other probes were then begun and all supported the *Concord Monitor* story which said that Governor Thomson had sent a fabricated telegram to be read to the members of the Legislature.

The *Union Leader,* which had taken as its New Year's resolution the "renewed sense of integrity and truth," never printed a line about the *Monitor's* discovery.

Now does anyone remember what it was that "Black Daniel" Webster said?

# 33

History will forever show that there is at least some reason to believe that the editorials which appeared in the newspapers of William Loeb unfavorable to U.S. Sen. Edmund S. Muskie were put there for the purpose of affecting the Maine senator's showing in the ballot box, at least in part in return for the parole of a man who had been serving time for having been found guilty of tampering with the jury box and the mail box. Just about the only American institution which had not been touched by the *Union Leader,* to any nationally significant degree, at least, was the batter's box. But William Loeb had thoughts along these lines.

An organization known variously as the Union Leader Fund, Inc., or the Union Leader Charity Fund, Inc., has been the sponsor for a quarter of a century of a function known as the Union Leader Baseball Dinner. It is held at the N.H. State Armory in Manchester and has been known to attract over 2,000 fans for an evening with selected players, all of whom appear as speakers on the program and most of whom are paid a fee. No one is entirely sure who has ever received any of the grants made by the Union Leader Fund, Inc., or the Union Leader Charity Fund, Inc. But a formal complaint against the organization being a tax-deductable foundation, initiated in 1964 by the Concord Monitor Corp. on the grounds that the expenses of the corporation exceeded 90%, was never acted upon by the Collector of Internal Revenue in Portsmouth.

At any rate, one of the highlights of the 1974 Union Leader Baseball Dinner was to be the presentation of an award to the outstanding designated hitter in the American League during the 1973 season; the "designated hitter rule" had been in effect only one year and, at that, only in the American League. Apparently, the more they thought about it, the better the idea seemed to those who masterminded the Union Leader Baseball Dinner. So, the sports editor of the *Union Leader*, undaunted by the fact that all baseball awards, if they are named at all, are named after diamond greats, came up with the idea of the First Annual William Loeb Outstanding Designated Hitter Award, and a suitable monument to this occasion was purchased from a trophy dealer.

The *Union Leader* used eight columns over the Page One masthead on Dec. 6, 1973 to proclaim that Orlando Cepeda of the Boston Red Sox had been chosen to receive this award. And this really wasn't news because practically everyone in New Hampshire who is a fan is a Red Sox fan. Since Cepeda had had a pretty good year, it would have been treason in the eyes of these many fans to give the Loeb ODH Award to anyone else. Cepeda, however, was a close choice over Tony Oliva of the Minnesota Twins and Tommy Davis of the Baltimore Orioles, according to the newspaper.

The presentation of the Loeb ODH Award was to be one of the highlights of the program, at least according to the *Union Leader*. But when the day of the dinner, Jan. 23, 1974, arrived and the 2,000 people thronged the state armory for dinner with the ballplayers. Among those who didn't bother to attend was Orlando Cepeda.

Gov. Ronald Reagan of California was slated to speak at a Concord Republican meeting on Jan. 21, 1974, and William Loeb that morning greeted the California governor warmly, saying in his Page One editorial, "Those who hear and see him may be hearing and seeing the next President of the United States." However, a few days later, in a Page One editorial, "Second Thoughts on Reagan," Loeb said:

> "The governor's speech following the dinner was competent, but it was not in any way up to the quality of the impression that he gives to individuals in private conversation. . . .
>
> "Since the governor had been an actor and since he must have given a similar speech many times before and perhaps will give it many times in the future, he READ his speech—and didn't read it too well at that . . .
>
> "Unfortunately the Reagan performance the other evening came across flat and unemotional to the audience . . .
>
> "The leader who will save America at this time must have the same ability that Winston Churchill had. Such a leader must be able to inspire the United States into a firm determination to arise from its present confusion and to go on toward its manifest destiny.
>
> "Alas, on Monday evening, Governor Reagan, with all his charm, decency and right thinking, was not able to put that message across to the American people. He MUST learn to do this or he will not be President."

On Jan. 30, 1974, Most Rev. Ernest J. Primeau, STD, Bishop of Manchester, announced his resignation. It was known that the prelate had been in poor health, and his announcement included the statement that he would serve as apostolic administrator of the Diocese of Manchester until a successor could be named. Part of the bishop's statement read:

> "I have tried in my years in the diocese to serve honestly and to the very best of my ability. Given the human

condition I am sure that I have made mistakes but they were made in all good faith. If I have hurt anyone personally I here publicly apologize and beg forgiveness. I carry away no ill feeling toward anyone. That true happiness, peace and contentment may be the lot of all in New Hampshire shall be my continued prayer to God."

Bishop Primeau was hailed by all of the community leaders of the city and state, notably the Congressional delegation. There was no statement from the publisher of the *Union Leader* and conspicuous by its absence was any editorial mention of the bishop's resignation.

Bishop Primeau says that he met William Loeb only once during his 15 years in Manchester, that at the meeting of New England leaders in Boston referred to earlier, and then accidentally and briefly. Reflecting on the attacks he had suffered at the hands of the newspaper, Bishop Primeau in his charity will only say of William Loeb, "He didn't help me."

It was open season on public figures for William Loeb. On Jan. 20, 1974, he called for the impeachment of U.S. District Judge Huge Bownes of Laconia. (Judge Bownes had ruled in favor of the Gay Students Organization of the University of New Hampshire, in effect saying that if a person wishes to profess that he is a homosexual, that does not mean he loses his right to vote and other civil rights.)

On Feb. 6, 1974, Loeb, in a Page One editorial, called for Major Wheelock, director of the New Hampshire State Hospital, to resign. (Wheelock had been brought in to straighten out serious difficulties at the mental institution and he claimed interference by Governor Thomson in any plans he wished to implement.)

And on the same day, Loeb's newspaper called for the impeachment of U.S. Sen. Thomas J. McIntyre. The newspaper's editorial said that in 1964 Senator McIntyre had refused to make public a 1964 decision by the then Defense Secretary McNamara to close the Portsmouth Naval Shipyard, which decision was later rescinded and reversed.

On March 5, 1974, the *Union Leader* appeared with a
four-column Page One story on what most observers felt
was inevitable: "Bonner Resigns UNH Presidency" It
told of how Bonner was resigning to become president of
Union College, in Schenectady, N.Y.

Editorially the *Union Leader* paid the matter of Bonner's resignation little heed. Perhaps William Loeb figured
it was inevitable; as did anyone else in the state who had
followed Bonner's career from the moment of his being
named to the post. That the state's leading newspaper did
not choose to editorialize, pro or con, on the stepping
down of the 15th president of the institution, may have
been due, at least in part, to the fact that Loeb and his
*Union Leader* was in the midst of its losing battle for
Onassis' oil refinery.

But *The Chronicle of Higher Education,* a weekly
"trade" newspaper devoted to such matters, consigned
most of its first page and almost two full pages inside of its
April 15, 1974 edition to Bonner and the University of
New Hampshire:

### "Behind Bonner's Resignation at New Hampshire: 3 Years of Attack by Publisher William Loeb

"BY PHILIP M. BOFFEY

"DURHAM, N.H.

"Early last month, the University of New Hampshire's
president, Thomas N. Bonner, announced he was leaving
his post on June 30 to become president of Union College
in Schenectady, N.Y.

"His departure after only three years on the job caught
most observers by surprise. His letter of resignation gave
the usual reasons for leaving—pride in having accomplished his major objectives at U.N.H. and eagerness to
accept 'a new professional challenge' at Union, along with
undefined 'personal reasons,' an oblique reference to his
recent divorce.

"It was all true, as far as it went. But it did not reveal
the whole story. For Dr. Bonner is, to a large extent, the
most recent casualty in a bitter, decades-long battle be-

tween the state university and New Hampshire's largest
newspaper, the Manchester *Union Leader,* whose 68-year-
old publisher, William Loeb, is probably the most contro-
versial figure in U.S. journalism.

"For the past quarter century, Mr. Loeb and his editorial assistants have been flogging the university for allegedly coddling communists, undermining patriotism, dis-
seminating pornography, and squandering the taxpayers'
money, among other sins.

"The steady barrage of unfavorable publicity has, in the
opinion of university officials, eroded public confidence in
higher education.

"It is one factor, they say, that keeps New Hampshire
ranking 50th among the states in per-capita support of
higher education, and that keeps the percentage of New
Hampshire's youth attending college well below the national average. It was also a factor in causing at least one
former U.N.H. president to retreat from the state.

"This conflict between the newspaper and the university
is nothing new. But the *Union Leader*'s attack on Mr.
Bonner seemed extraordinarily vicious, even by the standards of New Hampshire's often-turbulent political dis-
course.

"Richard C. Plumer, university assistant for public affairs, who is a member of the state legislature and a longtime student of New Hampshire politics, told *The Chronicle*: 'I have never seen a more vehement attack on one
person. It was the most concentrated, brashest, most consistent and constant attack I've ever seen.'

"Nor is this viewpoint limited to thin-skinned university folk.

"*Foster's Daily Democrat,* a newspaper published in
Dover, N. H., commented that Mr. Bonner was the victim
of 'one of the most unending and malevolent hate campaigns ever witnessed in our or any other state.' Similarly
the Concord (N.H.) *Monitor* lamented that 'Bonner faced
a hate campaign that made the activities of the Ku Klux
Klan a choirboys' picnic by comparison.' "

*The Chronicle* used a full page to detail the history of
the running battle between the *Union Leader* and the
University of New Hampshire over a 26-year period. Then

they attempted to present the views of the newspaper management:

> "In an interview with *The Chronicle,* James J. Finnegan, director of the *Union Leader*'s editorial page, said the newspaper stands by the accuracy of its previous coverage, but he declined to offer any further comments on the paper's fight with Mr. Bonner.
> " 'We don't carry on vendettas,' he said. 'We wish him nothing but good fortune and good luck in his new job.' Mr. Loeb was out of the state and unavailable for comment."

And so the search started anew for yet another man to head the university system in New Hampshire. Bonner said that he had tried, time and again, to arrange a meeting with Loeb to work out any differences which might exist. He says that he felt that if he knew exactly how Loeb stood or what he wanted, he might find some meeting-ground on which he might get on with running the affairs of the university, rather than constantly defending himself from editorial attack. Bonner says that every effort to meet with Loeb failed, that Loeb spurned his every offer. After three years in Durham, Thomas N. Bonner departed without ever having met with, talked with, or having received a personal letter from William Loeb.

The one part of William Loeb's make-up which has not varied from his earliest days is his love of the limelight—headline hunting, if you will; a yearning to be recognized as the powerful man that he is. When the Public Broadcasting Service decided to devote one evening's segment of "Bill Moyers' Journal" to a visit to William Loeb and Nackey Scripps Gallowhur Loeb during the spring of 1974, the *Union Leader* gave the show plenty of billing, insuring a good audience where it counted the most. (It was Page One news with a four-column headline as early as Dec. 12, 1973.)

PBS devoted a half hour to the show on the evening of March 19, 1974, and William Loeb was less than happy with the results. Usually, Loeb is able to conduct himself with absolute control, and his television appearances are generally head-to-head interviews, in which Loeb excels. But Moyers' show was something different, it attempted to offer a little more of a profile of the man. The television columnist for the *Washington Post,* John Carmody, had this to say:

> "The word 'controversial' pales when applied to 'The Man Who Made Muskie Cry'* and the editorials he writes for his Manchester Union Leader.
>
> "Yet in this entertaining half hour (and despite Moyers' open intention to divorce himself from the devil and all his works), enough of the outlines of a consummate grouch, a man with a gun, a master of invective, and a not unattractive lord of the manor appears to suggest Bill Loeb may be more than the sum of his meaner parts . . .
>
> "What emerges is an almost-magnificent bully, packing a .38 calibre Walther to the luncheon table in his Massachusetts mansion, just daring some faster gun (or editorial writer, anyway) to ride in from Boston or Washington or somewhere to try him. Meanwhile, the drinks are on Bill Loeb.
>
> "Moyers carefully leads Loeb past many of his rhetorical victims and the overall effect is finally almost funny. Eugene McCarthy was a 'skunk.' 'Tricky Dicky' Nixon is a 'bungler.' But his enemies are 'vultures.' Sen. Edmund Muskie is 'Flip-Flop.' Dwight Eisenhower was 'the supreme faker' and the leadership of the John Birch Society is made up of 'some absolutely nutty conservatives. . .'
>
> "Moyers, of course, doesn't let Loeb off all that easy. Citing a Loeb editorial written at the time of the 1972 murder by fire of a white woman in Boston, Moyers evinces from the publisher his belief that 'Bill Shockley (the Stanford Nobel laureate in physics whose home grown genetic theory suggests blacks are genetically inferior) will some day be recognized as correct.'
>
> "This is the bottom line in Moyers' too-short picture of Loeb. But Loeb is the man whose paper blankets New Hampshire and who, every four years, has much to say in the nation's first presidential primary."

* This is the title the network gave to the presentation.

The editorial writers and at least one reporter for the *Union Leader* quickly sprang to their boss' defense and the newspaper was filled with protests, saying that the Moyers' show was a "phony" which "lashed out at Loeb as some kind of a right-wing racist." The complaint which continued through all of the *Union Leader's* stories and editorials—they continued until at least April 25—was that Moyers had reduced the show from an hour to a half-hour.

Or, as the *Sunday News* editorial of March 24, 1974 put it:

> "Moyers had without warning compressed his show to a half hour, instead of the full hour he had promised, so that little could be shown of the six days of interviewing the Moyers TV crew had done at Prides Crossing and inside the Union Leader plant here in Manchester."

In fact, the original *Union Leader* Page One story on the event on Dec. 12, 1973, had said:

> "Ewing, the youthful independent producer of the Journal television piece on Loeb, said the 30-minute program will be telecast 'in late February' on the 232-station PBS network."

Near the close of the show, Moyers' interview went as follows:

Moyers: "What would you like to be remembered for?"
Loeb: "Having made some of my readers think."

Sometime between the time of the taping and the showing, Loeb apparently had second thoughts of what he would like to be remembered for, because in a lengthy statement issued on the day after the show, Loeb lamented some deletions and said:

> ". . . They came back and turned the TV cameras and mikes on Mrs. Loeb and myself as we played an entire set of tennis.
>
> "Amusingly enough, Mrs. Loeb and I discovered we both were a pair of hams because while we never play top tennis, we played better than we have ever done before

and with shots we ordinarily would let go by, either high in the air or on a different part of the court, we got every one of them."

The Public Broadcasting System apparently felt the world and the nation were not quite prepared for tennis lessons by William and Nackey Loeb.

The readers of the *Union Leader,* even though they were denied the privilege of watching Loeb and his wife play tennis, did get some gladdening news during the Spring: Gov. Mike O'Callaghan of Nevada announced the appointment of William Loeb, of Reno, as a member of the Nevada State Council on the Arts, and it was duly reported in New Hampshire's largest newspaper, in part, as follows:

"Loeb, a native of Washington, D. C., and a graduate of Williams College, Mass., has been a newspaper publisher for the past 33 years, while living in Reno since 1952.

"He is active in skiing and trap shooting and is a director of the American Rifle Assn. Loeb is a member of the Prospectors Club in Reno. He is married to the former Nackey Scripps."

Clergy and laity from every parish in the Diocese of Manchester assembled in Manchester on the afternoon of June 2, 1974, for the Diocesan Holy Year Pilgrimage which included a blocks-long procession along Manchester's Pine St. to St. Joseph Cathedral followed by a concelebrated solemn pontifical mass by Most Rev. Ernest J. Primeau, STD, apostolic administrator of the Roman Catholic diocese. Thousands witnessed the colorful and solemn affair and the church itself was filled to overflowing for the mass. The principal reason for the large turnout was that Bishop Primeau had announced that this was to be his last public appearance in Manchester as head of the diocese and that he was leaving for Rome shortly on a new assignment. The homily of the mass was a moving farewell by the prelate, who invited everyone to a reception at St. Joseph School auditorium after the mass for re-

freshments and a personal good-bye to each person individually.

Although the Union Leader Building and St. Joseph
Cathedral are but three short blocks apart in downtown
Manchester, the newspaper did not send a reporter to
cover what was the biggest story of the year within the
Roman Catholic diocese. Instead, the *Union Leader,* in
all editions of the day following, included an account
written, with a byline, by a member of the newspaper's
Citizens Advisory Board, Lucille Kelley, part owner of a
Manchester advertising and public relations agency.

# 34

The jockeying for position during the political year 1974
had begun early in 1973, despite William Loebs' statement that reelection was the furthest thing from the mind
of Gov. Meldrim Thomson, Jr., of Orford. On many occasions Loeb had cited the "conspiracies" and the "forces"
which were seeking to downgrade the performance of the
governor and were seeking to undermine his effectiveness.
Of course, the man elected governor of New Hampshire in
November of 1974 would be a man with a special kind of
power. During the biennium which followed that election,
the governor would be in a position to name one Superior
Court justice, a new attorney general, six members to the
board of trustees of the University of New Hampshire,
three members of the State Board of Education, four
members of the Fish and Game Commission, six members
of the Health and Welfare Advisory Commission, a director of Mental Health, two members to the Commission for
Human Rights, and the commissioner of Public Works
and Highways, all offices whose holders' terms would ex-
pire during the next two years. In addition to this, the

governor of New Hampshire would be in a very special
position during the ritual of the first-in-the-nation Presidential primary which was scheduled for March 2, 1976. If
running for reelection was, in fact, not the foremost
thought in the mind of Meldrim Thomson, Jr., of Orford,
it is safe to say that it had a fairly high priority in the
mind of William Loeb.

The early focus, however, came to bear on the U.S.
Senate seat which had been held by the senior senator,
Norris Cotton, who was in his mid-70's and was not in the
best of health. With Cotton's ailing wife confined to a
convalescent home in Lebanon, the Senator had made no
secret of the fact that he was soon going to announce that
he would not seek reelection. The candidates were forming
lines to see who would take his place.

Wesley Powell was always ready for a try at a Senate
seat, and Loeb had, for months, kept Powell's name in
headlines with a pronouncement on this, an open letter on
that, a speech hither-and-yon on the other thing. When
Powell got the political itch—which, apparently, was
nearly always—he never had to look very far for a press
agent. But it wasn't going to be that easy for Wesley this
time because Louis Wyman, the Congressman from the
First District, was also taken up with the desire to be a
U.S. Senator, and these two began a "debate" in Loeb's
newspapers during mid-1973 as to who was more qualified.
It was no secret to anyone that they both couldn't run because if they did, former Gov. Walter Peterson, who lived
in the Second District, could take advantage of the big
split in the First District and walk away with the nomination, and a Republican running for the U.S. Senate in
New Hampshire has a tremendous edge. Then, too, if
Peterson didn't feel he wanted to run, there was always
Congressman James Cleveland of the Second District, and
with a Wyman-Powell contest, he also would be a shoo-in.

An early entry on the Democratic side was Prof.
Laurence I. Radway, of the Department of Political
Science at Dartmouth College, a noted national authority
on matters of defense budgets and himself a former mem-

ber of the New Hampshire Legislature and an assistant minority leader in the House. Dartmouth College professors, however, have compiled a terrible record in New Hampshire politics—even less successful than the Boston Braves, who did win one World Series, that in 1914. Radway needed a gimmick and he knew it better than anyone so he decided to walk the length and breadth of the Granite State to meet the voters. But it was also obvious that this was an attempt to enlighten the New Hampshire voters that a Dartmouth professor is, indeed, human, with two arms, two legs, one head. Radway knew that he needed the gimmick because waiting in the wings was the former Insurance Commissioner, John Durkin, of Manchester, and anyone who knew anything knew that an Irish Catholic Democrat from Manchester could beat a Dartmouth professor in any statewide primary for anything in New Hampshire.

In December, 1973, Interior Secretary Rogers Morton, Tennessee Sen. Howard Baker, Ohio Cong. John Rhodes, Ohio Sen. Robert Taft and South Carolina Sen. Strom Thurmond got together to hold a $100-a-head reception for Congressman Wyman at the Sheraton-Carleton Hotel in Washington. The invitations to the affair were followed by a letter from Congressman Rhodes in which he said:

> "Please take a moment now to reply to the invitation you received, if you haven't already done so. We need Lou in the Senate, and with your help, we can insure his election next year."

William Loeb got wind of this and, on Jan. 26, 1974, he entitled his Page One opus, "Lacking In Political Integrity," which he devoted to the subject of Cong. Louis Wyman. It concluded:

> "Personally, his performance leaves a bad taste in this newspaper's mouth. Why say you are NOT a candidate when in actuality you ARE? Legal technicalities aside, Wyman knows—and the people know—that he is now actively campaigning for the U.S. Senate.
> "It is bad enough, morally, to lie, but also it is POLITI-

CALLY STUPID when it is so easy to PROVE that someone is lying about his political intentions.

"THIS IS A PERFECT EXAMPLE OF WHY THIS
NEWSPAPER WILL NEVER SUPPORT CONGRESS-
MAN WYMAN FOR THE UNITED STATES SEN-
ATE.

"THIS NEWSPAPER THINKS THAT NEW HAMP-
SHIRE, AS WELL AS THE REST OF THE NATION,
HAS HAD ITS FILL OF GOOD LOOKING, PLEAS-
ANT MEN WHO ARE FACILE TALKERS BUT WHO
ARE LACKING IN POLITICAL INTEGRITY."

While the infighting went on for the Senate contest,
Loeb never for one moment took his eye off that governor's
chair; that was the one Loeb wanted and the one he was
going to keep for Meldrim Thomson, Jr. The President of
the N.H. Senate was looming as the most formidable intra-
party opponent for Thomson. Thomson couldn't have
been luckier if he had been born in a field of four-leaf
clovers, because the Senate President's name was Nixon—
David Lee Nixon, to be exact—a three-letter man at
Wesleyan University where he was captain of both football
and baseball, and a graduate of the University of Michigan
Law School. Senator Nixon had served in the Senate from
his home district of New Boston, a suburb of Manchester
where he conducted his law practice. Early on, Loeb hung
him with the tag "Devious Dave" and the name took hold
right away. In late 1973 and early 1974 people were beginning to believe almost anything about people whose
name was Nixon.

At one point in the early campaigning, Candidate Nixon
approached one of the natives in the upper reaches of the
Granite State and offered to shake hands with the man.

Nixon: "How do you do, sir, I'm running for governor
and I'd like to shake your hand."
Native: "Don't trust no politicians. What do you do for
a living?"
Nixon: "I'm a lawyer."
Native: "Don't trust no lawyers. What's your name?"
Nixon: "Forget it."

Senate Vice President Harry V. Spanos of Newport, a town not too far south of Dartmouth College, was an early entry on the Democratic side. He had been a more vocal critic of Thomson during the past legislative session than his colleague, Nixon, and Loeb right away hung him with the nickname, "Midnight Harry," which really had been a long-standing town nickname for the lawyer, stemming from a day when he was presiding officer of the town school committee and, during one late session, had legally ordered the clock stopped so that the pending business could be transacted with full debate on the day specified by law. Spanos, even though he was Harvard and Harvard Law, also had a obstacle in his path because the memories of Vice President Spiro Agnew, like Spanos, a Greek-American, were fresh in everyone's mind.

Another who was making noises like a candidate was Rep. Hugh Gallen, a freshman member of the General Court, who apparently had caught the bug as "chauffeur" for Senator Muskie during the 1972 Presidential primary. Gallen was owner of an automobile dealership in Littleton, a town about 10 miles north of the Old Man of the Mountains, and this was about the worst thing Gallen had going for him; no one knew him in Southern New Hampshire.

With Spanos and Gallen poised to split the North Country vote, the Democratic gubernatorial nomination was practically up for grabs by anyone from Hillsborough County (which comprised about 60% of the Democratic strength in the state and which included the cities of Manchester and Nashua). The pressure began to build up on a Nashua lawyer and banker, Richard W. Leonard, a former state senator and representative. Leonard had retired from the Senate two years before when his brother and sister-in-law had been fatally injured in an automobile accident. He had spent the intervening time conducting the law firm and bank, as well as reestablishing his brother's family of four children. The Leonard name was well known throughout the state, his father having been an executive councilor on two occasions. In addition, both his father and his late brother had been state amateur golf champions. (Tom, Jr. had won the championship an unprecedented eight times, winning the 1948 final against Richard himself.)

In March, Leonard wrote a letter to Loeb informing him that he was thinking of running and Loeb's reply, dated April 4, was short and sweet: "I've heard nice things about you, but I'm going to support Meldrim Thomson for reelection."

Notwithstanding, Leonard announced his candidacy and so did Gallen and Spanos. The New Hampshire Democrats, with an extremely unpopular Thomson as the most obvious opposition, were off and running and the party looked more like Coxey's Army than usual.

Wyman announced for Cotton's seat and it was not long thereafter that Durkin also announced. He was followed on the Democratic side by Nashua Mayor Dennis Sullivan and an electronics engineer, also from Brookline, named Carmen Chimento. Wyman got token opposition from a man named Leslie Babb, of Freedom, N.H., but Wesley Powell was apparently scared away by the lurking Peterson who was still a threat even after Cleveland announced for reelection to Congress from the Second District.

Executive Councillor John Bridges, son of the late senator, announced his candidacy to replace Wyman in Congress from the First District. David Banks, a Concord automobile dealer, followed Bridges' lead and announced for the contest. He was followed by the former G.O.P. State Chairman, David Gosselin, of Center Barnstead and a man named John H. O'Brien, of Raymond.

Two more Republicans jumped into the race for the governorship, but neither—Ralph Brewster of Pittsfield or Elmer Bussey, of Salem, who was running for the 12th time—could be considered serious contenders.

Loeb wasn't kidding in his letter to Leonard. Every day in the *Union Leader,* it was Thomson, Thomson and more Thomson. Louis Wyman wasn't getting as much publicity as Wesley Powell, even after he became a candidate, and it was just assumed that John Bridges would win the Con-

gressional race because the *Union Leader* had always
backed anyone with the Bridges name in earlier elections.
But again the Citizens Advisory Board of the *Union
Leader* came into the picture and on June 27, 1974, the
newspaper all but gave its imprimatur to the Banks' candidacy when it was announced that a member of the advisory board, Frank Wageman, a Manchester insurance
man, had been named as co-chairman of Banks campaign
committee and a picture and an editorial appeared in the
newspapers to mark the occasion.

The Citizens Advisory Board of the *Union Leader*
entered into the political spectrum on the Democratic
side, also. Leonard had decided to conduct a low-key
campaign during the primary. His thinking was that if he
could win this first test without too much effort, largely
with votes from Hillsborough County, he'd go all-out during the campaign. During the first stages of his primary
campaign he had been using a Manchester advertising and
public relations firm, Cohen-Kelley Associates, Inc., on a
temporary basis for special assignments. Disappointed with
the performance of this firm, especially in publicity surrounding a May fund-raising dinner in Nashua, Leonard
wanted the agency used no more and gave firm orders to
this effect. His fiscal agent, Manchester City Clerk Dick
Stanton, and a former State Senate colleague of Leonard's,
Manchester Atty. Elmer Bourque, kept up the pressure to
retain the Cohen-Kelley Associates, because it was conducted by Miss Lucille Kelley, a member of the *Union
Leader's* Citizens Advisory Board. According to Leonard,
Stanton and Bourque in early June signed a contract in
Leonard's name with Miss Kelley's agency, explaining to
Leonard that "you don't know the pressure that's on us in
Manchester."

About the two worst things that can be said about
Richard W. Leonard are: 1) He's a big nice guy who
never learned that "o" follows "n" in the alphabet, and 2)
He's not much of a politician, mainly because of #1. He
went along with the decision of Stanton and Bourque to
engage Miss Kelley's advertising agency until the primary

only, and spent as much time during the primary campaign in the agency's offices in Manchester as he did on the campaign trail. At one point, Miss Kelley arranged a meeting for Leonard with William Loeb at the offices of the Union Leader Corp. in Manchester, at which Mrs. Loeb was also present. Towards the end of the meeting, which, according to Leonard, was taken up mostly by Miss Kelley, Loeb told him that he had decided to back him in the Democratic primary and Loeb asked Leonard if there was anything the newspapers could do for him. It had been no secret that one of the things about the coverage by the *Union Leader* which had galled Leonard the most had been the use of a single-column engraving of Leonard which was, by all estimates, a terrible, and unflattering, likeness of the man. Leonard says that he replied to Loeb's offer with the statement that he would appreciate it if Loeb would instruct his editors to discontinue using the picture to which Leonard objected and substitute the one which Leonard's staff had submitted for campaign purposes. Leonard says that Loeb immediately approved of this request—Loeb said he would order the unflattering photo destroyed—and from that day on for the rest of the summer, when a picture of Leonard appeared in the *Union Leader,* it was the "approved" picture.

Leonard had promised during his campaign appearances and in his news releases to veto a sales or income tax, if elected, and, of course, so had Thomson. Nixon, even though he was a tireless campaigner, never did make this public oath, nor did Spanos nor Gallen, all of whom had records in the Legislature to indicate that they would be friendly to a broad-based tax. The *Union-Leader* had stepped up the rate of pictures of Governor Thomson to as many as four or five a day and they strongly backed him, while blasting Nixon from every angle.

Early in August, the *Union-Leader's* Page One editorial appeared endorsing the candidacy of Leonard in the Democratic primary. And the newspaper's backing of David Banks for the Congressional seat increased in tempo. Not much was said about Louis Wyman, who still only had Leslie Babb to contend with. Wesley Powell, it was apparent, had decided to sit this one out.

Then, on August 16, the *Union Leader,* in Loeb's Page One editorial entitled, "New Hampshire's Own Watergate," Wyman's part in arranging a meeting for the former counsel to the President, Herbert Kalmbach, and Atty. Maurice Stans with Dr. Ruth Farkas, who subsequently was named ambassador to Luxembourg, was narrated. The whole story had come out a year before during the hearings before the Watergate Committee and the House Judiciary Committee was reciting the same litany at the moment. Loeb said:

> "This newspaper feels it is time for Congressman Wyman to make a clean breast of the entire situation and not make the mistake President Nixon did of denying—and then having the truth dragged out little by little.
> "We don't need any 'Watergate' in New Hampshire!"

Loeb treated Wyman's involvement in the Farkas-Kalmbach-Stans meeting as the most horrible case imaginable of using a public office for personal political privilege. Wyman had been introduced to Dr. Farkas, whose family conducted Alexander's Department Stores in New York, through Benjamin Mates, a Manchester manufacturer whose firms had at one time been suppliers to the Alexander's Stores. Mates had been a personal friend of Wyman's for many years. But, at best, it was "old hat" and no number of these Loeb diatribes would get Leslie Babb by Louis Wyman in the G.O.P. Senatorial primary.

It was a cheap shot, at best. Louis Wyman had begun his political career as a staff aide to Senator Bridges in Washington and had returned to New Hampshire to become Attorney General on Jan. 15, 1953, an office he held until Dec. 16, 1960. An entry in the diary of Mrs. Katharine W. D. Loeb for Sept. 29, 1955, reports a visit from a man named "Wylie," who claimed to be Attorney General of New Hampshire, at her Oyster Bay, Long Island, home. On Oct. 1, 1955, she wrote a letter to her daughter-in-law, Mrs. Eleanore McAllister, in which the following appears:

"On Thursday, a very nice young man, 37 or 38, Louis Wylie, Jr., Atty. Gen. of New Hampshire, came to see me. And Bill certainly must have cried on his shoulder and lead him to believe untruths. Mr. Wylie admitted that he was entirely under a misapprehension, he understood that Bill had not been allowed to come to Oyster Bay, that there was no communication, etc. He said he felt that Bill should be in N.H. running the paper. I asked him why Bill could not come to N.H. & he said Bill could but that female could not because in N.H. she could be sued for alienation of affections & any property she possessed attached."

Mrs. Loeb was nearly 80 at the time of this letter and was hard of hearing, so it is understandable that she confused Wyman's name. It is not so easy to understand why Loeb hit Wyman so hard in 1974, nearly 19 years after Wyman had interceded for Loeb at a time when it was generally assumed that Loeb's mother's suit was the factor which kept Loeb in a constant state of hiding.

Perhaps it was that Louis Wyman knew too much.

Senate President Nixon's cause took an even further step backward during August with the resignation of his namesake, the President of the United States. But Nixon's campaign against Governor Thomson was falling short all around. Nixon had no way to strike back at the almost daily attacks of William Loeb, who, for all intents and purposes, had converted his *Union Leader* into a campaign newspaper for Meldrim Thomson, with an occasional boost for David Banks. Loeb ran one editorial endorsing Leonard, solely on the basis of his anti-tax posture. Loeb had also endorsed Radway over Durkin in the Democratic Senatorial race, but no one thought that Radway had a shot at Durkin from the outset; the first to admit this was the political scientist, Professor Radway.

As the Banks-Bridges battle heated up, enthusiasm in the Democratic contest for the First Congressional District seat also heated up. A young Manchester lawyer, Norman D'Amours, was opposed by a Bedford housewife, Sylvia Chaplain, and a Manchester legislator, Joseph Cote. Cote had been a woeful kind of parrot for Loeb during past sessions of the Legislature, taking the floor at every opportunity, usually to give extremely monotonous speeches—even shouting—on any cause favored by Loeb. Few took Cote's candidacy seriously, except to divert the Franco-American votes which would otherwise be going to D'Amours.

The outcome provided no surprises. Governor Thomson got 47,244 votes to 37,286 for Senate President Nixon, while Brewster and Bussey got peanuts.

On the Democratic side, Leonard never went out of his living room and won:

| | |
|---|---|
| Leonard | 16,503 |
| Spanos | 14,149 |
| Gallen | 13,030 |

It was a matter of wonderment—or a tribute to Loeb's newspaper—that Leslie Babb received 13,670 votes against Wyman's 66,749 for the G.O.P. Senatorial nomination.

For the Democratic nomination, John Durkin got 22,258 votes. His opponents, Professor Radway, Mayor Sullivan and Mr. Chimento, got a total of 22,261 votes, as follows:

| | |
|---|---|
| Radway | 14,646 |
| Sullivan | 6,330 |
| Chimento | 1,285 |
| Total | 22,261 |

David Banks won a surprisingly easy victory over his principal opponent, John Bridges, and again it must have been the power of the newspaper which did it for Banks, a largely unknown figure only a few months earlier. Gosselin and O'Brien might have had an effect on the Bridges vote, too:

| | |
|---|---|
| Banks | 15,876 |
| Bridges | 12,732 |
| Gosselin | 9,439 |
| O'Brien | 2,217 |

D'Amours ended up with a convincing win for the Democratic nomination:

| | |
|---|---|
| D'Amours | 12,036 |
| Chaplain | 7,998 |
| Cote | 4,140 |

Congressman Cleveland did have some opposition for his Second District seat in the person of a Peterborough author, Lawrence Kamarck, but Cleveland won, 35,682-to-5,844.

Mrs. Helen Bliss, a Quaker grandmother from New Ipswich, won the dubious honor of opposing Cleveland in the General Election by defeating Kenneth Scott, a Wilton attorney, 9,860-to-7,578 in the Democratic primary.

During all of the infighting of the primary campaign, it became obvious to Governor Thomson (and perhaps also to William Loeb) that one of the political bases had been left uncovered. Robert F. Bossie, a Manchester lawyer who was also a Democratic state senator, was a holdover as the Democratic member of the State Ballot Law Commission, a three-member panel comprised of the Attorney General and two other persons, one from each party, which by New Hampshire statute, is the court of last appeal in cases of disputed elections. Senator Bossie, certainly no follower either of William Loeb or Governor Thomson, had served on the Ballot Law Commission since Dec. 30, 1970 and his term had expired on July 1, 1974. The statutory limit of the term is: "Four years and until successor is appointed and qualified." The Secretary of State is clerk and recording officer of the panel.

Apparently, while it was not a matter of prime public attention, both Thomson and Loeb must have felt that it would never do to go into an election of a governor, two Congressmen and a Senator without all bases covered. Roger Crowley, the two-time Democratic gubernatorial nominee who was serving in the $23,400-a-year (by this time) job as head of the Governor's Crime Commission, was playing golf one August day at the Manchester Country Club. According to Crowley, he was called in off the golf course and was hastily administered the oath as Ballot Law Commissioner.

Meanwhile, the administration of Richard Milhous Nixon had been sinking fast, and by early August, the President resigned his office in disgrace. William Loeb, who had been one of Nixon's severest critics, had, during the last few weeks of Nixon's term in office, become one of his staunchest supporters, and, in this, he was followed by Gov. Meldrim Thomson, Jr., of Orford. It was one of the strange quirks of Loeb's psychological make-up which always compelled him to be with the unpopular side in a battle. It was only a few months before that he was calling Nixon every name in the book, and had relented at election time when Nixon was faced by McGovern only to say, "Hold your nose and vote for Nixon." But in early August, 1974, William Loeb was hanging out the crying towel for the guy he called "Tricky Dicky." And on the day after Nixon resigned and Gerald R. Ford took office, Loeb called his Page One sermon, "The Victory for Hate." Loeb blamed the whole thing on the "leading newspapers, news magazines and the television networks, controlled by ultra-leftists and liberals" which "has resulted in the destruction of an American President."

"... As is well known, this newspaper broke with Mr. Nixon over what we regard as his foolish and dangerous policy of trying to appease the Chinese and Russian Communists. We have also considered him incredibly stupid in a number of things, especially his selection of key personnel, the sort of people who got him into Watergate.

"HOWEVER, THE PUNISHMENT METED OUT TO MR. NIXON IS ALL OUT OF PROPORTION TO HIS ALLEGED WRONGDOINGS ...

"Americans, themselves interested in fair play and justice, are going to wonder whether there will be such a thing as justice and fair play in the hands of the communications industry, crazed with power, and a Democratic apparatus that has no more interest in justice for its opponents than a Communist or a Nazi tribunal would have for its dissenters.

"MR. NIXON MAY HAVE BEEN NO PRIZE, BUT THOSE WHO DESTROYED HIM AND MORTALLY WOUNDED THE NATION IN THE PROCESS ARE A GREAT DEAL WORSE!

"This newspaper's deepest sympathies especially go out to Mrs. Nixon, Julie Eisenhower and Tricia Cox, who behaved like a loyal and gallant wife and daughters during a most trying and horrible ordeal."

Loeb's anguish over Nixon's leaving the White House was certainly not prompted by the fact that Loeb "wouldn't have Nixon to pick on anymore." Loeb had already taken care of that. The Vice President of the United States, Gerald R. Ford, had been the guest speaker at a Republican State Committee dinner at the State Armory in Manchester on May 31, just a little more than two months before. The banner headline in the *Manchester Union Leader* announced:

## "FORD ARRIVES TODAY"

But, William Loeb's Page One editorial was less than cordial:

### "Is This a Ford
### We Should Buy?"

Even though at that stage of the game it appeared inevitable that Ford would accede to the Presidency, Loeb made it clear that no incumbent President would have his support, because Loeb had this to say:

"To date, the picture of Vice President Ford that emerges is one of a pleasant, agreeable gentleman, a man who is presumably honest and means well but who has very little strength of character—and not a very high degree of intelligence.

"That sort of man is NOT the type of leader that this messed-up nation so desperately needs today!

"TO PUT IT BLUNTLY AND PERHAPS A BIT HARSHLY, BUT WE THINK ACCURATELY, JERRY IS A JERK AND WE CAN'T STAND ANY MORE JERKS IN THE WHITE HOUSE IF WE ARE TO SURVIVE AS A FREE NATION."

One week to the day later, Loeb gave Vice President Ford another blast. In a Page One diatribe entitled, "THIS FORD: The Closer You Look, The Worse It Appears," Loeb quoted from Women's Wear Daily, which had reprinted Comedian Mort Sahl's lines about the Vice President, which were anything but complimentary. Loeb's editorial also quoted WWD as saying that Mrs. Ford regularly used tranquilizers because of pain she suffered from a back injury.

"We would ask our readers whether these two items, viewed together, inspire them with any great confidence in a would-be president who has been described in this fashion by a former president, or a 'First Lady' whose responsibilities weigh so heavily on her that she had to take three Valium pills a day. She is hardly a woman who could handle the obligations and the stress and strain of the White House very satisfactorily.

"This newspaper is sorry about the Fords' problems, but our first obligation is to the United States, not to any individual or any political party. Candor and frankness compel us to point out, as we did previously, that Mr. Ford is NOT the man we need right now in the White House."

The House Judiciary Committee was bearing down on Nixon during July and his resignation, or impeachment, appeared imminent. The *Union Leader* and *Sunday News* continuously blamed the news media for the whole thing and said that "Rodino's Rabblerousers" were overly harsh on Nixon. Said the *N.H. Sunday News* of July 28:

"They are, for the most part, worse than Sam 'Senator Claghorn' Ervin's bunch. Only one speech during the House Judiciary Committee's opening impeachment hearing Wednesday was worth listening to and that was delivered by New Jersey Republican Charles Sandman ...

"Aside from Sandman's speech the most memorable episode of Wednesday evening was the 'bomb threat' which drove spectators and House members alike from the hearing room in a panic. The threat turned out to be a hoax, more's the pity."

Neither the *Union Leader* nor *Sunday News* expressed any editorial approval of President Ford as he took office in early August. There was no special editorial wishing the new President well in any form. Instead, the newspapers began beating the drum for the appointment of Barry Goldwater as Vice President.

In the excitement which followed the change of Presidents, Michael Ford, the 24-year old son of the President, a student at the Gordon-Cornwell Theological Seminary in Wenham, Mass., not far from the residence of William Loeb, made a statement that he would like to see Richard Nixon speak out and explain fully his role in Watergate. William Loeb, on Aug. 13, 1974, devoted his Page One editorial to the question, "Is Michael Ford Speaking for Dad?" and he said:

"Apparently, no one had broken the news yet to Michael Ford that Presidents' sons should be seen but not heard ...

"Let us hope, for the sake of possible future congregations, that young Mr. Ford will read those passages of the Bible which deal with mercy and charity."

Just eight days later, Aug. 21, 1974, Nelson A. Rockefeller was named Vice President of the United States. Loeb's editorial on Page One that day was complete with a cartoon drawing of two lemons, one labelled "Ford" and the other "Rockefeller," with the headline: "Lemon Plus Lemon Equals Bitter Lemon." It was beautiful—beautiful if you've got a strong stomach:

"As predicted by this newspaper many, many months ago, the sinister, shadowy figure behind the whole attack on Nixon has finally surfaced and what you have now is a Rockefeller administration with a ventriloquist's dummy taking orders as President.

"THE LEFT-WING-DOMINATED COMMUNICA-

TIONS INDUSTRY AND ITS SOCIALIST AND COM-
MUNIST ALLIES FROM COAST TO COAST HAVE
NOW ACHIEVED WHAT WAS THOUGHT TO BE
IMPOSSIBLE. THEY HAVE OVERTURNED THE
DEMOCRATIC ELECTORAL PROCESS OF THE
UNITED STATES!

"They got rid of a man who was overwhelmingly elected
by the citizens in a free presidential election. They got rid
of him by taking advantage of his lack of skill in defending himself and by building an unfortunate incident into
a national crime and brainwashing the electorate through
the left-wing press, radio and TV . . .

"NO AMERICAN MAN OR WOMAN WALKS SAFE
TODAY WITH SUCH UNFETTERED MONEY
POWER IN THE CONTROL OF THE WHITE
HOUSE!

"Rockefeller's errand boy, Ford, has already taken a
stand on amnesty for draft dodgers that is completely opposite to what most Americans believe.

"Rockefeller's Number 2 errand boy, Henry Kissinger,
has sold out Greece to the Turks and has been indirectly
responsible for the murder of the American ambassador
there . . .

"The American people have, by their own votes, some-
times placed some undesirable people in office, BUT
NEVER IN THE HISTORY OF THE REPUBLIC
HAVE WE HAD SUCH 'LEMONS' IN THE WHITE
HOUSE—AND THEY ARE THERE, NOT BECAUSE
THE PEOPLE ELECTED THEM, BUT BECAUSE OF
A SINISTER CONSPIRACY BY CERTAIN POWER-
FUL GROUPS IN THIS COUNTRY WHICH VIO-
LATED THE U.S. ELECTORAL PROCESS AND
PLACED THE NATION IN THE MOST SERIOUS
DANGER IT HAS EVER FACED IN ITS HISTORY.

"It will take TREMENDOUS effort to overthrow this
Rockefeller tyranny, but overthrow it we must, so we can
start our third century in the United States as a free nation—and not as a Rockefeller corporation!"

It wasn't over yet, however, not by a long shot. On Aug.
29, 1974, Loeb again went after President Ford, and this
time, the headline told the whole story of a very long and
very tiresome editorial. The headline:

## "Jerry IS a Jerk!"

Yet the long, hot summer of 1974 was not without its time for fun. The comic relief came on July 11, 1974 when Publisher William Loeb relinquished hold on the daily Page One editorial in favor of his wife, Mrs. Nackey Scripps Gallowhur Loeb. Mrs. Loeb's lesson for the day was entitled, "Betrayed," and it told about her great-aunt, Ellen Browning Scripps, the founder of Scripps College, which Mrs. Loeb had once attended. The reason for Mrs. Loeb's Page One editorial was that it had come to her attention that at some colleges the boys and the girls were sharing dormitory facilities and, most probably, this was also true at Scripps College. Mrs. Loeb was horrified! She punctuated her editorial much in the style of her husband, full of capital letters and full-face type and exclamation points. She spoke of "basic rights and wrongs" and "moral looseness" and "lack of judgment" and ended:

> "It looks as if college leadership has lost the will to lead. In refusing to make moral judgments, and in giving in to irresponsible demands, they have most definitely betrayed the dream Ellen Browning Scripps had, and have done damage to the students who now accept living with boys as that 'new life' they were promised.
>
> "As a great niece of Ellen B. Scripps, and as a former student of Scripps College, I am DOUBLY bitter over that betrayal.
>
> "/s/ Nackey Scripps Loeb<br>"Nackey Scripps Loeb."

In her entire editorial, Mrs. Loeb never once mentioned the Windsor County Court in Woodstock, Vt., and she never mentioned the letter from Loeb of May 20, 1949, in which he described their trysts and nowhere did she mention her apartment on University Heights near the campus of the University of Vermont in Burlington where William Loeb was an overnight guest. And she didn't mention that both she and Loeb were both married to other persons when all this was going on. She didn't even mention that they both had left children at home with their respective spouses during this period.

But there were many, many people who read her editorial in the July 11 editions of the *Manchester Union Leader* who did.

# 35

When Leonard had had the meeting with Loeb, arranged by Miss Kelley, at the offices of the Union Leader Corp. in July, Loeb had said that he would take the photograph which was unbecoming to Leonard out of the files, that the newspapers would not use that picture any more. Leonard had won the Democratic primary without lifting a finger and he would face Governor Thomson, to no one's surprise. Thomson's victory over Nixon had been relatively easy, and, really, so had Leonard's win over his two opponents, even though Leonard failed to take any district located more than 25 miles from his home city. Gallen and Spanos cut each other up all over the state and Leonard got by with a 2,500-vote margin.

The late endorsement of Loeb's newspapers might have been of some help to Leonard, but it came with about three weeks to go before Primary Day. Then, too, Loeb's endorsement has been the kiss of death to more than one Democrat. But Leonard didn't have far to look before he knew what treatment he was going to receive from Loeb in the general election when he came up against Gov. Meldrim Thomson, Jr., of Orford. Across eight columns of all editions of the *Union Leader* on the Thursday after the primary was a story headlined, "Hot Contests for Major Offices Seen." Adumbrative of Loeb's feelings about the election and the treatment Leonard could expect was the selection of photographs accompanying the story: to the left a flattering photograph of Governor Thomson, to the right the picture of Leonard which Loeb had promised him would be taken out of the files and destroyed.

And Leonard had another problem which, as he knew
better than anyone else, could probably prove to be more
of a drawback in the end than any harmful publicity, nasty
editorials or gutter invective that Loeb could throw at
him (which, of course, he did). It isn't very often that the
Democratic nominee for governor in New Hampshire is a
bank president and the head of one of the state's larger law
firms; as a matter of fact, it is almost never. Leonard was
obviously a wealthy man with a reputation of being the
nicest guy in the world, which attracted to the Leonard
campaign every political hanger-on and play-for-pay type
that the budget would stand. But the budget wouldn't
stand much. In the post-Watergate scheme of things, campaign expenditures were a subject of close scrutiny everywhere, and New Hampshire was no exception. A state law
limited the expenditure a candidate could make to 15
cents per qualified voter, so with 447,044 qualified voters
eligible, gubernatorial candidates could spend a limit of
$67,056.60. For a Democrat, a healthy chunk of that would
have to be reserved for newspaper space at the close of
the election, and the bulk of this, of course, would go to
Loeb's *Union Leader,* if for no other reason than to answer with paid advertisements the campaign propaganda
which Loeb would be publishing free for Gov. Meldrim
Thomson, Jr.

Leonard was somewhat relieved, however, that his campaign in the General Election would not be conducted
with the services of Miss Lucille Kelley, because his contract—or the contract which Stanton and Bourque had
signed for him—had expired with the primary election.

Loeb had a Page One editorial on that Thursday, as he
did every day, and in it he generally lauded the voters'
choices, with the notable exception of John Durkin and
Cong. Louis Wyman, the choices of their respective parties for the U.S. Senate. Loeb said:

". . . In the Senate race, on the Democratic side, John
Durkin unfortunately defeated Laurence Radway by a
very substantial margin. This is tragic because Larry Radway obviously was the much more qualified candidate . . .

"Of course, on the Republican side, the overwhelming

winner was Louis Wyman. On the other hand, when an absolute unknown, such as Leslie Babb, his opponent, can collect 13,480 votes, it should tell Wyman that a great many people are not satisfied with his explanation of the Farkas situation or his identification with the general atmosphere of Watergate in Washington.

"THE PEOPLE OF NEW HAMPSHIRE ARE NOW FACED WITH A VERY MISERABLE CHOICE BE-TWEEN WYMAN, ON THE ONE HAND, AND DURKIN, ON THE OTHER. THIS SHOULD NOT HAPPEN TO ANY STATE, LET ALONE THE GREAT GRANITE STATE BUT, IF THE VOTERS AREN'T MORE CAREFUL IN THE PRIMARIES, THIS IS WHAT HAPPENS TO THEM."

It was less than a week later that William Loeb had some further words on the upcoming Durkin-Wyman election choice, for on Sept. 20, his Page One editorial, "The Wyman and N.H. Tragedy," said, in part:

"The tragic scandal that is now surrounding Congressman Wyman because of his involvement in the Farkas case and the unfortunate way in which the congressman has handled this situation have placed the Republican Party and the State of New Hampshire as a whole in a most embarrassing and serious position ...

"For the seat in the United States Senate now held by Senator Cotton, and in the past held by Senator Styles Bridges,* to be filled by a man of Durkin's obvious shortcomings and inadequacies would REALLY be to disgrace the State of New Hampshire and violate the memory of the great men who have sat at that desk in the Senate!

"IT WOULD SEEM, THEREFORE, THAT IN THE INTERESTS OF THE REPUBLICAN PARTY AND THE STATE OF NEW HAMPSHIRE IT WOULD BE THE REALISTIC—AS WELL AS THE GENEROUS—GESTURE ON THE PART OF CONGRESSMAN WY-MAN TO WITHDRAW, AND THAT ANOTHER CANDIDATE BE SELECTED BY THE REPUBLICAN

---

* Loeb was in error. Maurice J. Murphy succeeded Styles Bridges, and Murphy was succeeded by Thomas J. McIntyre at the next regular election.

PARTY TO RUN, AS PROVIDED BY NEW HAMP-
SHIRE LAW, IN HIS STEAD . . .

"We hope that, under the circumstances, therefore, the
congressman will accept this bitter, unpalatable—but
nevertheless very real—fact and act accordingly, in the
best interests of the Republican Party and of the State of
New Hampshire."

Wyman was quick to answer Loeb. Loeb printed the
reply. Wyman said he figured "the next thing that will
be recommended for me will be to commit suicide. . . . I
am confident the voters will give me their support and
their vote on November 5 even if it drives Mr. Loeb up
a wall." Wyman said he'd hold a press conference to shed
more light on the Farkas affair. At the conference he distributed copies of a letter from Special Prosecutor Leon
Jaworski absolving Wyman of any criminal involvement in
Watergate. Immediately after the close of the brief question-and-answer period which followed Wyman's statement
and disclosure of the Jaworski letter, Wyman was apparently so confident of the voters' support that he flew to
Washington with Congressman Cleveland. That was just
about the last thing anyone saw of Louie, except for weekends, until about a week before Election Day.

For his part, Durkin adhered to his basic campaign
strategy; he repeated and repeated Wyman's part in the
Farkas affair, with heavy emphasis on the word "Watergate" and he broadly accused Wyman of being the "tool"
of big business in Washington all during his Congressional
terms. Durkin relied heavily on radio advertising and a
clever set of radio commercials was frequently heard on
almost every New Hampshire station. (The most memorable was supposedly behind-the-back talk at a cocktail
party, tying Wyman into the "big business" hosts.) Durkin,
immediately after the primary, began to amass a large campaign organization of volunteers, and Durkin himself
worked hard, appearing at as many functions as could be
squeezed into any day.

The specter of losing his pipeline to power in state government, which would be the case if Meldrim Thomson

were to be defeated, was a tremendous goad to Loeb. Beginning on the morning of September 21, the day of the state Democratic convention, and continuing until Election Day, Richard W. Leonard was the favorite target of William Loeb.

Leonard got it from every angle:

### *Dissension Hits Democrats*
### Lucille Kelley Out of Leonard Campaign

was the double-barrel headline fired at Leonard on the day the convention was to open and the story went on to tell how Miss Kelley had been disillusioned with the way the campaign had been going and long ago had decided she didn't want any more of Leonard. Even though the services of Miss Kelley had been retained for Leonard on a temporary basis, and then only reluctantly, the newspaper called it a "sudden and unexpected switch," which Leonard knew and Miss Kelley knew was an outright lie.

On September 26, Loeb's Page One editorial was called, "We Were Fooled, Don't You Be Fooled!" It showed the unflattering picture of Leonard and went on to explain that because certain persons were endorsing Leonard, it meant that Leonard was in favor of a broad-based tax and was lying in his campaign oratory. The fact was never explained that some of the persons who were endorsing Leonard were doing so because they had been fired by Thomson or, in some cases, had been the victims of Thomson's unauthorized tax search. Another story told of how Leonard's bank, the Colonial Trust Company, of Nashua, appeared to be in default on a sewer bond which had been posted for the City of Nashua, or so the story made it appear. (It was not.)

To anyone's knowledge, Attorney Leonard had never said "no" to anyone who wished to have Leonard defend him in court, and many of these persons bobbed up as volunteers on Leonard's campaign staff in many towns in the state. The *Union Leader* ran a story about the "ex-convicts" who were working on Leonard's campaign.

Leonard countered with a detailed presentation of the telephone calls which Governor Thomson had made to Loeb at Pride's Crossing, Mass., at Reno, Nevada, and at the Union Leader Corp., as well as the calls Thomson had made to Olympic Refineries. But, no full accounting of these calls was ever printed in the *Union Leader*. Having been the subject of so many surveys after the Yorty campaign in 1972, which all showed a disproportionate number of column inches given to the candidate of the newspaper's choice, the editors were careful during Leonard's campaign to print a lot of Leonard news releases and the candidate's daily schedule, so that in the number of inches devoted to Leonard, the *Union Leader* did fairly well. But the inches never told the story of the content of the articles nor of their position in the newspaper.

Loeb had always prided himself on printing every letter to the editor which the newspaper received. The *Union Leader* does print a lot of these letters, page after page of them. It provides the newspaper with an exceptionally high readership feature and it costs nothing to collect the material. But, during the Leonard campaign, there were many instances of persons who wrote letters to the editor of the *Union Leader* in favor of Leonard's candidacy and these letters were not printed. In at least one instance the writer of a letter did have his letter printed, and he received a personally dictated letter from William Loeb on Union Leader Corp. stationery, which was not printed, and which read as follows:

"Dear Mr. Sawtelle:
"We will publish your letter but I can see you are a died-in-the-wool Democrat with no interest in reality. Thomson is one of the finest governors New Hampshire has ever had. You seem to want to put some free spending fellows in there. Then you will come crying to me.
"Take Leonard. He's a nice fellow but he hasn't had any experience in state government. And don't forget, Leonard is the lawyer who represented those gangsters from Rhode Island who killed that Nashua man. They were sentenced to be hanged until the Supreme Court did

away with the death penalty. Leonard will say that every man is entitled to a defense, but every lawyer can choose his clients, too.

"Here at the paper we don't pay any attention to the party but support the best man, which is something you are not doing.

"Very sincerely,
"/s/ William Loeb
"William Loeb
"President"

The errors in fact in Loeb's letter are palpable. Leonard was the court-appointed defense counsel for two Rhode Island men who killed another Rhode Island man in Nashua in 1959. Leonard had had several terms in the General Court as a representative and a senator. Thomson's prior experience in government before becoming governor had been on a regional school board.

The complaint mail Loeb was receiving must have been heavy because he reprinted a couple of letters which were written for the purpose of questioning the propriety of the Thomson-Loeb telephone calls. One reader asked, "I would like to know when you were elected lieutenant governor." And Loeb shot back that he was sorry not to have answered the letter sooner but "frankly, I was up in New Brunswick goose shooting." Loeb said it was a "nasty letter" and he said that he and Governor Thomson "have been friends for years, and we have gone mountain climbing together. We have many personal things to talk over, such as family matters and friends." Another reader read Loeb's reply in the *Union Leader* to the first letter writer and he wrote Loeb to say, talk about your mutual friends all you want, but not on the State of New Hampshire telephone with the taxpayer picking up the tab. Loeb's reply was:

"Your nasty letter has been turned over to the editors for publication. You continue to want to beat this issue which obviously was not very important. . . . Frankly, I have other things to do . . .

"What amazes me is the venom which you anti-Thomson people display. It's certainly revealing as to their character or lack of it.

"Thank you for writing.

> "Very sincerely,
> "William Loeb,
> "President."

The major offensive of the Thomson campaign came in the form of what were called "hot dots." The so-called "hot dots" were small circular pieces of adhesive plastic, with a reflective fluorescent coating on the exposed side which school children could affix to their clothing or bicycles, or whatever, which would reflect the headlights of oncoming automobiles. Every school child in the state received a small packet of "hot dots" in class with a brochure which carried the governor's picture and a message to write a letter to the governor's office if a child wanted more. Many children were inspired to write the governor's office and when these received a personal letter back from the governor enclosing some "hot dots" more and more school children wrote Thomson letters. They were all individually answered. The mail was so heavy in the State House that secretaries were taken from their regular jobs to be added to the governor's staff to handle the correspondence. In practically all cases, the school-aged youngster had never received a personal letter from a governor before, if the child had ever received a letter at all.

But the hooker of the whole project was that the Department of Safety had executed the "hot dots" campaign with Federal money as part of a highway safety program. A small group of lawyers, all Republicans, noticing this, immediately brought this to the attention of the attorney general, claiming that this was using Federal funds for campaign purposes, but Atty. Gen. Warren Rudman paid the claim little heed and ruled that it was a legitimate safety program. The biggest batch of "hot dots" mail was prepared by the governor's office to be mailed on the Friday before Election Day so that it would arrive in the thousands of homes on the day before Election Day.

Loeb, in the meantime, had been hitting Leonard with the ring post, and Leonard had no way of answering back. He could spend no more money for ads. The newspaper never printed one of Leonard's direct replies to Loeb's acid editorials, and, with practically every story they ran about Leonard, they used the unflattering photograph. The rate of pictures of Governor Thomson appearing in the *Union Leader* was stepped up. Thomson was always smiling, always with a group. And Thomson had eight columns across either Page One or the back page, or the center of the editorial page, anytime he wanted it—all, of course, as news at no charge to the governor's campaign fund.

Leonard was catching on all around the state, despite Loeb's assaults, and he was picking up the backing of practically every other daily newspaper in the state. The trouble spot, then, would be the city of Manchester itself, always, or almost always, a Democratic stronghold. Here people only had Loeb's word to take for anything. Manchester residents, if they wanted a morning newspaper, either read Loeb's newspaper or a Boston or New York newspaper. In the evening, there was no alternative to the *Union Leader*.

When Loeb was not blasting Leonard and praising Thomson, he was praising Banks, the Republican candidate for Congress in the First District. Cleveland, running in the Second District, was about as sure a bet as the next high tide. It began to look like the D'Amours-Banks race was pretty much a toss-up, but no one can ever say William Loeb wasn't doing everything he could to insure a win for the Republican Banks. The Wyman-Durkin contest wasn't getting much of a play in the *Union Leader*, except for further stories of Wyman's connection with Dr. Farkas. Then William Loeb, under the title, "Durkin Versus Wyman," made the following pronouncement:

> "This newspaper has made no secret of the fact that we believe that for either candidate Durkin or candidate Wyman to take the seat in the United States Senate once held by Daniel Webster, Styles Bridges and Norris Cotton will be a disgraceful affair."

Loeb was off to a "good" start, mainly because Daniel Webster represented Massachusetts in the Congress for all but his first term, but Loeb went on:

"Certainly, neither Durkin nor Wyman could by any stretch of the imagination be considered outstanding.
"WE HAVE NO INTENTION IN THIS CASE OF SUPPORTING EITHER OF THESE TWO MEN. OUR CONSCIENCE WOULD CERTAINLY NOT BE CLEAR IF WE DID!"

The news value here, of course, was that Loeb said he had a conscience. In fact neither man may have wanted Loeb's support. They just wanted him to shut up. But that is never Loeb's style:

"Durkin is extremely unqualified for the position.
"He is a very clever politician.
"He has been riding the wave of consumerism in this country, which consists of telling the voters that, if elected, a candidate will go to Washington—or to the State House or wherever—and will place the consumer's interest first, last and always . . .
" 'Consumerism' as a political stance is one great fraud. But it is being successfully used by some politicians, such as Durkin . . .
". . . Congressman Wyman has served in the U.S. Congress for several years and, as such, has not done badly by the First District. In more routine and ordinary days, if Congressman Wyman were to go to the U.S. Senate, it would do no great harm.
"But at a time when we need every outstanding man we can find in that world's most exclusive gentleman's club, as it has been called, Mr. Wyman is hardly the quality of individual we want and need there! . . .
"We cannot, therefore honestly say that EITHER of these candidates is worth supporting . . .
"Voting for Wyman or Durkin is not a happy necessity!"

The sidewalk odds on Wyman, however, were running fairly high. A Republican has to be a prohibitive favorite in a head-to-head race for any statewide office in New Hampshire. But, to the consternation of Durkin more than Wyman, Carmen Chimento, the third party in the Demo-

cratic primary, filed at the last moment as a candidate for
the U.S. Senate on the American Party ticket. This apparently sealed Durkin's doom. As a matter of fact, Louie
Wyman, who hadn't made many campaign appearances up
until then, obviously figured that, with Chimento in the
race, he was in, and Wyman was hardly to be seen at all.

Norman D'Amours' campaign financing had just about
hit rock bottom by the end of October. Campaign aides
were wondering how they were going to get through the
last week until the election. Banks was beginning a small
surge in whatever polls had been conducted; on the one
hand, because the *Union Leader* ran the biggest poll itself,
and, on the other hand, because Loeb's harping in the
Banks' cause was having a noticeable effect. Then, on the
morning of October 30, William Loeb unknowingly caused
the election of Norman D'Amours to the U.S. Congress.
Loeb had two editorials that day, one entitled, "A Plea To
The Franco-Americans," and the other entitled, *"Un Appel
À Tous Les Franco-Américains."* The two two-column editorials ran side-by-side down Page One and were continued
at length on an inside page. The French language editorial carried a notation that it had been translated by
Mrs. Herve Tancrede, "Mr. Loeb's secretary."

By the time the sun went down that evening, D'Amours
had over $3,000 in instant campaign donations and his
telephones were ringing like there was a general alarm
fire. Money was pouring in, in tens, twenties, and in big
numbers, too. And it was coming from people who had
no Canadian blood in them. The French community was
incensed and insulted, and they had many sympathizers.
This facet of Franco-American life had all but vanished
from the scene in Manchester and William Loeb, secure
in his castles in Pride's Crossing and Reno, never knew it.
Every radio station was immediately booked solid with
D'Amours commercials for the closing days of the campaign with the donations and the young lawyer received
the public endorsements of many persons who previously
had been reluctant to do so.

While Loeb was calling Leonard "stupid" and "absurd" and a "criminal lawyer" in his editorials, Leonard was upsetting many of his campaign workers for his failure to stick to a prepared text during his appearances. In practically all cases, Leonard would depart from the text when it came to the part in which Leonard would recite his family's background or his many personal achievements, and most particularly his own military record. Leonard had been a pilot in the Army Air Corps during World War II and had been recalled into the Air Force during the Korean Conflict, during which period he was shot down on a mission over enemy territory in Korea. Wounded, he made his way back to safety and was decorated for his achievement. Leonard remained in the Air Force Reserve after release from active duty and was recalled to active service again, this time during the Berlin build-up in the early 60's. Both Leonard's mother and father were New Hampshire natives. His father was the son of a Lancaster lumberjack. He matriculated at UNH and later at Dartmouth mainly because he knew what to do with a football or a baseball if it were in his hands, and there was no sin in earning a college education this way in those days any more than it is today.

Richard W. Leonard reneged anytime it came to mentioning his own achievements, or the political background of his well-known and eminently successful father, who had served on two occasions on the Executive Council. Leonard recited his own background in city and state government just once in a speech, then cursorily. To the sometimes angry criticism of his supporters, Leonard would say that to do so was not his style, that people would not vote for him because of his military record—or at least, he hoped they wouldn't—nor for his father's achievements.

Other forces which hurt Leonard financially were certain members of his campaign staff. Many of these were openly identified as having been the backbone of the 1972 Yorty campaign which still holds the New Hampshire record for squandering money, and many persons backed off from donating to Leonard's campaign for this reason.

On the Friday before election, a letter appeared in the *Union Leader,* addressed to the editors, in which the author said that the governorship was not between Leonard and Gov. Meldrim Thomson, Jr., but between Leonard and William Loeb. The letter read: "The story of Loeb's continuing misuse of his rights as a journalist is legendary and needs no elaboration from me in this letter." Its signer was Richard W. Leonard.

During the last weekend, Leonard concentrated on Manchester; it could be the only trouble spot, but no Republican had ever taken Manchester, although two had received substantial help in the state's largest city, notably Styles Bridges and Wesley Powell. Manchester, though, was where Loeb had been publishing the city's only newspaper for 28 years.

The early returns showed Leonard holding his own in heavy Republican Rockingham county along the seacoast and winning in Strafford County, wherein the proposed refinery would have been located. But results of the Manchester wards, using voting machines for the first time in a general election, began to filter in and it was all over for Leonard, incredibly so, in fact. Thomson not only took Manchester, he took every ward. The final score:

| | | |
|---|---|---|
| Thomson, r | 115,933 | 51.15% |
| Leonard, d | 110,591 | 48.79% |
| Scatter | 141 | |

Leonard had lost by 5,342 votes, but, more incredibly, he had lost the city of Manchester by 6,065. In other words, if Leonard had even held his own in Manchester he would have won.

Leonard's defeat was a bit harder to understand when the final returns showed that Louis Wyman had eked out a 355-vote victory over John Durkin, and Carmen Chimento had been the difference in a Durkin victory:

| | | |
|---|---|---|
| Wyman, r | 110,716 | 49.78% |
| Durkin, d | 110,361 | 49.62% |
| Chimento, a | 1,327 | .59% |

In the contest for the First Congressional District seat, Norman D'Amours coasted over David Banks:

> D'Amours, d          58,388
> Banks, r             53,610

But D'Amours' election was guaranteed by the Manchester vote, usually heavily Democratic and heavily Franco-American, D'Amours carrying the city by 8,354 votes.

The Second Congressional District was strictly "no contest" as usual:

> Cleveland, r         69,068
> Bliss, d             38,463

New Hampshire statutes specify that a candidate may demand a recount, and receive a recount, if the difference in the total vote cast is less than one per cent. John Durkin easily qualified for the recount, the difference between him and Louis Wyman being .16% of the total vote, and he announced that he would request a recount of the Secretary of State.

The case of Leonard was slightly different. The Manchester vote was hard to believe—it still is—but Leonard's choice was slightly different from Durkin's. If the difference in candidates is over one per cent of the total vote, the Revised Statutes Annotated say that a candidate may receive a recount if he presents 2,500 signatures and $500, or deposit a sum with the Secretary of State to guarantee payment of the expenses of the recount; then the ballots will be recounted. The voting machines in Manchester did show some discrepancies, most specifically in that the cumulative total of votes cast on a given machine did not tally with the number of votes cast in that election and the previous cumulative total on the machine. But Leonard took a look at the stubs in his checkbook and, remembering that somewhere someone had said, "You can't beat City Hall," and decided not to risk several thousand more dollars.

As it later developed, Leonard would learn that his decision not to send good money after bad was a wise move. Leonard, as did everyone, saw the legal heavy artillery of the state was coming out to take part in the recount; Atty. Joseph Millimet, of the Manchester firm of Devine, Millimet, Stahl and Branch, would be counsel for Durkin and Atty. Stanley Brown, of the Manchester firm of McLane, Graf, Greene and Brown, would appear with Wyman. Apparently feeling that such a position would make him privy to certain facts of the election just past, Atty. Richard W. Leonard, of the Nashua-based Leonard Professional Association, agreed to represent Carmen Chimento, the American Party candidate.

They're still calling the Nov. 3, 1974 edition of the *Vermont Sunday News* the " 'Peanut' Kennedy Memorial Edition." Clifton Noyes, the editor of that newspaper whom William Loeb had installed some 13 years before at age 18, and who had matured to the point where he was general manager in addition to being editor, filled the Sunday paper with pure campaign propaganda designed to defeat incumbent Gov. Thomas P. Salmon who was being challenged by Republican House Speaker Walter (Peanut) Kennedy, who had his name printed on the Vermont ballot just that way. Noyes' Page One editorial was well over three columns long, topped by a four-column cartoon sketched by the regular cartoonist of the *Manchester Union Leader*. As far as the U.S. Senate race in Vermont was concerned, an effort to capture the seat being vacated by the retiring Sen. George Aiken, was clearly a case of "editor see, editor do." Noyes said he could not "in conscience" endorse either Chittenden County State's Attorney Patrick Leahy or Cong. Richard W. Mallary, but Noyes confessed that he leaned a little towards Mallary.

Governor Salmon began a second term in January of 1975 and Patrick Leahy became the first Democrat that Vermont had elected to the U.S. Senate since before the Civil War.

During the campaign of 1974, there was a death in the family of William Loeb, which few persons noticed or even knew about. The fact that so few knew about it was most probably because the death was barely reported in Loeb's Manchester newspapers.

The *Connecticut Sunday Herald* ceased publication in October. Loeb's Sunday circulation in Connecticut was down to about half of the 32,000 it enjoyed when he took it over. The man who so resents being referred to as an "absentee publisher" never went to the South Norwalk offices for the wake, but informed the employes on the Sunday Page One. As a matter of fact, the man who so resents being referred to as an "absentee publisher" never visited the South Norwalk offices at any time in his life. The fact that the newspaper had stayed alive as long as it did was only because of huge amounts of intravenous financial feeding from Manchester.

It was glaringly obvious from the moment of his first telephone call to Don Rogers during the brief days of the strike newspaper, *The Herald,* that the foremost reason for which William Loeb wanted the *Connecticut Sunday Herald* was so that he could, in the event of another New York newspaper strike, flood the New York metropolitan market with the editorial voice of William Loeb. The *Sunday Herald* died before another New York newspaper strike occurred.

# 36

William Loeb was exultant about the reelection of Gov. Meldrim Thomson, Jr., even though it was by only slightly more than two per cent of the vote cast. Just two days after the election, Loeb's *Union Leader* contained a Page One editorial entitled:

## "A Most Significant Victory"

which said:

> "Governor Thomson's strong victory over his Democratic opponent, criminal lawyer Richard Leonard, will attract a great deal of attention from political commentators across the nation because the governor now becomes the only Republican governor in New England and one of the few Republican leaders who succeeded in stemming the Democratic tide . . .
>
> "The governor, after this victory, should loom large on the Republican national scene, perhaps he will even be the vice presidential choice for the Republican ticket in 1976. THIS NEWSPAPER CAN'T THINK OF A BETTER MAN FOR THAT SPOT.
>
> "Of course, the governor's victory can also be attributed in part to the incredibly inept campaign put on by his almost absurd opponent, who pitched his campaign around three of the biggest non-issues this newspaper can think of."

Loeb said that Leonard was wrong to call Thomson a "dictator," that the "hot dot" campaign was not politically motivated and that there was nothing wrong with the governor calling Loeb any time he felt like it.

The same November 7 edition of the *Union Leader* was headlined:

## BALLOTS GUARDED
### City's Machines Locked

The newspaper's lead story told that the Manchester voting machines, many of which had shown discrepancies in the number of votes cast, had been sealed and padlocked at the direction of the Secretary of State, Robert L. Stark, who had been notified by Atty. Millimet, for Durkin, that a recount request would be forthcoming. On the next day, Durkin made it official in requesting the recount and, even though the unofficial tally had shown that his total vote was only .16% lower than that of his principal opponent, Durkin was required by Mr. Stark to pay the $500 recount fee.

A day later, Loeb lamented certain aspects of the election three days earlier:

"... The fact that many people voted for Richard Leonard against Governor Thomson is really shocking. It makes us wonder if our constitutional republic can really survive such irresponsible exercises of the franchise ...

"In the case of David Banks, we had an unfortunate rejection of a highly qualified and successful businessman with extensive experience in Washington in favor of a young man whose campaign rhetoric was mostly based on the claim that evil big business is causing inflation ..."

In the *N.H. Sunday News* of the weekend following the election, Thomson's "national role" was again extolled:

"The victory of Gov. Meldrim Thomson, Jr., was one of the few bright spots on a desolate national scene for the GOP ...

"As a result his national stature as a Republican leader is greatly enhanced and he has been represented by the media from coast to coast as a man who deserves to be closely watched in the future.

"The voters of Democratic Manchester deserve special credit for giving him a plurality which made the cause of Nashua's Richard Leonard hopeless, as Mr. Leonard promptly admitted, crediting support by the Loeb newspapers as the most important element in Thomson's success."

Seemingly, no one was treating Durkin's recount request with any special seriousness. The recount would be conducted by Secretary of State Stark, a direct descendant of Gen. John Stark, the Bunker Hill and Bennington hero, and everyone knew that Secretary of State Stark was a died-in-the-wool Republican. It was also no secret that Secretary of State Stark's son, Atty. Rodney L. Stark, was an attorney in the offices of Wyman & Bean, the Manchester law firm of which Louis Wyman was a founding partner. Furthermore, the office of Secretary of State in New Hampshire has always had a special type of sanctity attached to it. The Secretary of State is reappointed as a routine matter of business by each incoming legislature. There hasn't been a contest for the office in anyone's memory. Recounts conducted by Secretary of State Stark had always been handled by workers hired for that purpose under the direct personal supervision of Stark himself; this office was the repository of a special kind of trust, Stark having served continuously since the death of his predecessor, Harry E. Jackson, in 1957. And even though Wyman's margin over Durkin was a scant 355 votes, not too many serious thoughts were given to the idea that the margin might not stand up.

Governor Thomson lost no time after Election Day in setting his ship of state at flank speed. One of his first moves was to realign his legal staff. He nominated his counsel, 31-year-old Atty. Charles G. Douglas, III, for a vacancy on the Superior Court bench and the nomination was approved by the unanimously Republican five-man Council. To replace Douglas, Thomson named Atty. James J. Barry, Jr., of the Manchester and Boston firm of Malloy, Sullivan & Barry—the firm that is also counsel to the Union Leader Corporation.

The recount by the office of Secretary of State began on November 18 and proceeded in routine fashion, or so the readers of the *Manchester Union Leader* were lead to believe. As a matter of fact, there was not even one news item concerning the Senate recount in progress on Page One of the November 25 editions. On Page One on November 26 there was a "panel" to the effect that the *Union Leader*'s own tally showed that Wyman's recount margin was 156 votes, but on Page 14 of the same edition was a claim by Durkin that the gap had narrowed to 30 votes.

Then on November 27, Secretary of State Stark announced the official outcome of the recount:

| Durkin, d | 110,924 |
|-----------|---------|
| Wyman, r | 110,914 |
| Chimento, a | 1,513 |

The *Union Leader* account of November 28 said:

> "There is little doubt the final chapter in the spectacu-
> lar Wyman-Durkin battle will be written in the U.S. Sen-
> ate, the final arbiter by federal law . . .
> "The statewide recount uncovered a political pot of
> gold containing 947 additional Senate votes not recorded
> in the official election tally. Democrat Durkin captured
> 563, Wyman 198 and Chimento 186. That was the re-
> count in a nutshell."

Leonard, the defeated Democratic gubernatorial candidate, had his eyes opened a little bit as he followed the recount tally sheets acting as Chimento's attorney. Of the
120 voting machines used in the 12 heavily-Democratic
Manchester wards, Leonard registered a total vote higher
than Thomson on only four machines, two in Ward 3, and
one each in Wards 4 and 11. Leonard also knew, from long
years spent in courtrooms, that protest would be futile,
that nearly every judge in the land would say to him, "I
know what you're trying to tell me, but what have you got
for proof?"

Wyman immediately protested the result of the recount
by the Secretary of State to the State Ballot Law Commission, composed of Atty. Gen. Warren Rudman, a Republican, ex officio; Atty. Ronald L. Snow, of Concord, a Republican, and Roger J. Crowley, of Manchester, a Democrat.
And to this Durkin strongly counter-protested, citing that
Crowley's son, Thomas B. Crowley, a student at the University of Maryland, was a part-time employe of Congressman Wyman.

William Loeb came up with a solution to the whole
mess in his Page One editorial of December 5:

> ". . . THERE IS ONLY ONE FAIR SOLUTION AND
> THAT IS TO HAVE A SPECIAL ELECTION IM-
> MEDIATELY AND ALLOW THE VOTERS OF NEW
> HAMPSHIRE TO DECIDE WHICH MAN THEY
> WANT TO SEND TO WASHINGTON."

On December 6, Loeb left no doubt where he would
place his backing in the matter of the contested Senate seat

when, in his Page One editorial, he announced in head-lines:

## "Durkin Repudiates New Hampshire"

". . . Many folks in New Hampshire do not realize that Durkin employed in the original recount a professional expert who has been working for Democratic candidates for many years attempting to upset races where they have been defeated or where the Democratic races were very close against their opponents . . .

"This newspaper frankly believes that a more careful examination of the contested ballots and a few other aspects of the recount would show that Durkin was not the winner."

By December 9, Loeb had begun a cry which he would continue for a full seven months:

". . . THIS SITUATION SHOUTS FOR A NEW ELECTION . . ."

The Governor and Council decertified Durkin after having earlier certified Secretary of State Stark's count and issuing Durkin a certificate of election. Durkin asked the Federal court to issue an injunction against this procedure, but failed.

The State Ballot Law Commission set right to work on its own recount and it announced on December 23 that Wyman had actually been the victor by two votes:

| | |
|---|---|
| Wyman, r | 110,926 |
| Durkin, d | 110,924 |
| Chimento, a | 1,513 |

Durkin immediately cried "Foul!" On the day after Christmas, Loeb again echoed the cry for a new election:

"IN A SITUATION AS CONFUSED AS THIS, WITH AS MANY IRREGULARITIES AS HAVE SHOWN UP IN THIS ELECTION, IT IS PERFECTLY CLEAR THAT THERE IS ONLY ONE HONEST SO-LUTION FOR THE WHOLE UNPLEASANT AND

SORRY MESS AND THAT IS TO HOLD A NEW ELECTION."

A beneficent side of Louis Wyman suddenly emerged and he announced he would petition the N.H. Superior Court to call the election a tie. John Durkin said he would appeal the ruling of the Ballot Law Commission to the U.S. Senate, which, he claimed, could and would act under Article 1, Section 5, of the U.S. Constitution which states:

"Each House shall be the Judge of the Elections, Returns and Qualifications of its own Members, and a Majority of each shall constitute a Quorum to do Business."

The "beneficence" of Wyman and the "fairness" of Loeb may have been prompted by the fact that in New Hampshire Republican registrations have always far outnumbered those of Democrats. If the matter went to a new election, most observers felt, John Durkin, with Carmen Chimento in the race, would have about as much chance as Perkins Institute for the Blind against the Cincinnati Reds in Riverfront Stadium. But Durkin was more than a little bit incensed at the Ballot Law Commission for some of the "calls" it had made in its judgment of the ballots* and he felt that an impartial body, in this case the U.S. Senate, would repair these inequities.

Wyman and his attorneys proceeded to the Superior Court to request that the election be called a tie. Who was the justice assigned to the case? None other than the Honorable Justice Charles G. Douglas, III, the former legal counsel to Governor Thomson. Durkin again called "Foul," and two days later Justice Douglas stepped aside only after considerable public pressure had been brought to bear. Justice Martin Laughlin was assigned the case and he immediately disqualified himself on the grounds that he had been a classmate in law school of Durkin's brother. The case was then assigned to Justice Maurice Bois, the

---

* At a later date some of the ballots which the BLC had "called" for Wyman were reproduced in both the *Lebanon Valley News* and a Durham weekly called *Publick Occurrences*. On the evidence presented it did appear that Durkin had a legitimate complaint.

only other Thomson appointee to the Superior Court. Justice Bois fooled his would-be critics by immediately summoning counsel to chambers and outlining his plans; he then went to open court and asked all parties to the dispute to submit any questions in writing, for further submission to the N.H. Supreme Court.

The Supreme Court ruled that a two-vote margin was not a tie and that the court itself was powerless to act. And Durkin immediately appealed to the U.S. Senate, which had begun its session with 99 members. The Senate referred the matter to the Rules Committee.

Loeb kept up the hue and cry for a new election and he made no secret of the fact that the 60 Democrats who had been seated in the U.S. Senate would "steal" the election and award the disputed seat to Durkin. At Loeb's constant urging, Thomson proceeded within the Governor and Council and, later in the Legislature, to request the U.S. Senate to return the dispute to New Hampshire for a new election.

As the New Year arrived and the Legislature convened, Former Sen. Norris Cotton was unanimously elected to be chairman of the Republican State Committee. Alf Jacobson, a professor at Colby-Sawyer College in New London, was elected Senate President and George Roberts was named Speaker of the House, both of these Republicans.

Just a year before, it had been Thomson's announcement of an oil refinery in Durham which had had the entire state in an uproar, and shortly after 1975 began, Governor Thomson announced that the Parsons and Whittemore Corporation would establish a pulp mill along the Connecticut River, the western boundary of the state. Thomson also announced at a meeting of the Governor and Council that he had decided on a way to ease the nation's energy crisis and that was to construct windmills atop Mount Washington and Cannon Mountain in northern New Hampshire. (This plan has never been implemented.) Thomson was successful, however, in having half of the advertising account of the New Hampshire Sweepstakes Commission channeled through a Manchester agency, the head of which was Thomson's campaign chairman in Manchester. He also named as student trustee of the University of New Hampshire an undergraduate, from Rhode Island, who had been chairman of the Students for Thomson. And all of these moves by Governor Thomson were roundly applauded in the pages of the *Manchester Union Leader* by its publisher, William Loeb. Loeb kept up his cry for a new election at least once a week.

Governor Thomson was named chairman of an organization called the National Conservative Caucus and began to appear each weekend in a different part of the country as a keynote speaker of sorts for this group. In these appearances one theme which Governor Thomson always clung to was that he would, in no way, back the candidacy of Gerald R. Ford for reelection as President of the United States. Thomson said he would back former California Gov. Ronald Reagan as his first choice, and Alabama Gov. George Wallace as his second. Thomson said that if both of these men failed to run in the 1976 New Hampshire first-in-the-nation primary, he would run as a favorite son.

It was announced in the *Union Leader* that Governor Thomson had offered to Roger Crowley, the Democratic member of the Ballot Law Commission, the position as chairman of the New Hampshire Conservative Caucus. After several days lapse, Crowley publicly declined the job and it was duly promulgated in the *Union Leader*. He said he was too busy in his $23,400-a-year job as head of the Governor's Crime Commission, and didn't say a word about any possible conflict of ideology between being state chairman of the Conservative Caucus and being an appointed public representative of the Democratic party.

It was the turn of the State of New Hampshire to have its governor serve as chairman of the New England Governors' Conference, but the other five chief executives—four Democrats and one Independent—didn't want Thomson and Vermont Gov. Thomas Salmon was named to a second term to chair that group. When the body held a Spring meeting in New Brunswick, Thomson travelled to the affair in the Parsons and Whittemore airplane.

President Ford visited the state on April 18; he landed

in Manchester and stopped briefly in the downtown area to
shake a few hands; then he proceeded to Concord where he
addressed the Legislature. Loeb's *Union Leader* did not
honor the President with any more "Jerry IS a Jerk" headlines, but instead contained a full page of pictures, which
had appeared in a national magazine a year before, showing the President as a professional model on a skiing trip,
pictures which had been taken while he was then a law
student. A *Union Leader* reporter stationed himself outside the Press Room of the State House and personally
handed the President the opened newspaper as he made his
way to the legislative chambers.

President Ford spent a good deal of his time in New
Hampshire in the back seat of the Presidential limousine
with Governor Thomson and Former Senator Cotton. It
was a few days after the President's visit that Cotton announced he would step down as state Republican chairman.

One month to the day after Ford's visit, the members of
the Republican State Committee met at Concord for the
purpose of electing a new state chairman. Thomson had
hand-picked a Manchester businessman, Gerald Carmen,
and the only other candidate would be Senate President
Jacobson, obviously of the "Old Guard." The delegates,
244 strong, elected Carmen, 125-to-122. The next day the
*Concord Monitor* accused the governor of stuffing the ballot box. Thomson threatened libel action against the
newspaper, but withdrew his threat when the *Monitor* explained that the governor didn't actually stuff the ballot
box himself because he had left the meeting by the time
the vote was taken. The *Manchester Union Leader* criticized Thomson, but only with respect to insisting on having
his own man as state chairman. It made no mention whatsoever as to the method of the balloting.

Senate President Jacobson held a news conference the
next day and asked Carmen to step aside; Jacobson pointed
out that some delegates did not reside within the districts
they represented on the state committee, and that the results were not true. Carmen stood in the door of Jacobson's

office and heard every word. Carmen immediately called a
news conference at the offices of the Republican State Committee and began to outline his plans for a rejuvenation of
the state committee. When a reporter asked about Jacobson's charges, Carmen all but said, "Jacobson who?" and
went on to introduce his choice as the new treasurer of the
state Republican Party, David Banks, the defeated Congressional candidate.

And still Loeb kept hammering away in his newspaper
for a new election for the U.S. Senate seat. State Republican Chairman Carmen made a trip to Washington in early
summer to see what he could do to get the new election for
New Hampshire and, while he was in Washington, he publicly advised the President of the United States that he refrain from entering the New Hampshire primary in 1976.
"Anything that reduces the level of friction in our party,
I'd be for," said Chairman Carmen.

Governor Thomson was getting a bit of criticism from
Democratic leaders in New Hampshire for the amount of
money being expended for his personal staff. The Democrats claimed that Thomson's payroll had grown to $1,263,-
261, from the payroll of $280,717, for which the *Union
Leader* had criticized Former Governor Peterson. Topping
the list was Atty. Frederick D. Goode, the governor's administrative assistant, whose salary was listed at $25,937.
Next in line at $21,000 were James J. Barry, Sr., the father
of the governor's legal counsel, and Former House Speaker
Marshall Cobleigh. The *Union Leader* paid the story little
heed, printing the UPI version on a far inside page underneath a photograph of a different subject.
As if to answer the complaint of the Democrats, Governor Thomson nominated Goode for a vacancy as a trial
judge on the N.H. Superior Court, even though it was
Goode who had conducted what the N.H. Supreme Court
had called the "illegal search" of the records of the governor's political foes. What rankled most persons was the
fact that Goode is a patent attorney and had rarely, if ever,

engaged in courtroom litigation. But, even though two Council members dissented, three went along with Governor Thomson and Goode was named a judge. Loeb saluted the three Councilors in a Page One editorial and said that, "The fact that these three governor's councilors . . . refused to knuckle under to the abuse, pressure and cajolery which they received is a great tribute to the character of these gentlemen."

On that same day, Loeb's lead editorial on the inside editorial page was entitled:

## "The Wrong Speaker"

In it, Loeb said that the New England Association of Chiefs of Police, meeting at the Mt. Washington Hotel, should have investigated before they invited a Federal judge to address their meeting. He blasted the convention speaker from every angle and called the jurist, a member of the Second Circuit Court of Appeals, "one of the most unfortunate appointments that President Nixon made."

The jurist in question was Justice James L. Oakes, and, years before in private practice in Vermont, Oakes had represented Mrs. Eleanore McAllister in her claims of nonsupport against one William Loeb.

The Manchester city government was going along pretty much Loeb's way. A member of the Manchester Fire Department, Lt. George Fradette, had applied for advancement to the rank of captain and had been turned down. The *Manchester Union Leader* began to trumpet the Fradette cause and it later became public knowledge that Fradette's next door neighbor was James J. Finnegan, chief of the editorial page of the *Union Leader*. Atty. James J. Barry, Jr., counsel for the Union Leader Corp., represented Lieutenant Fradette and filed appeal proceedings in Fradette's behalf with the Superior Court, and the *Union Leader* carried the fireman's cause to the public in such an extreme manner that the newspaper began to become known as the *Fradette Gazette*, instead of the *Union Leader*. Fradette lost his appeal, but not before City Atty.

Clifford Ross resigned his job. Ross claimed he had been misquoted in nearly every instance by the newspaper but most bitterly complained of being harrassed by the newspaper's reporters. Ross was twice left unfamiliar telephone numbers while attending the wake of a member of his family at a Massachusetts funeral home. In both cases, when Ross returned the calls, he found them to be from *Union Leader* reporters. Lieutenant Fradette's case cost the City of Manchester over $27,000 for special legal counsel.

It was not long after that Mayor Sylvio Dupuis, in his second term as Manchester mayor, resigned to accept a position as chief administrative officer of the Catholic Medical Center in Manchester. Dr. Dupuis was succeeded by City Clerk Charles Stanton, who had been the fiscal agent for Richard W. Leonard during his gubernatorial campaign, and it had been Stanton and Former State Sen. Elmer Bourque, who had "set up" Leonard for Loeb's blast on the matter of his advertising agency. Shortly after Stanton was sworn in as mayor, Attorney Bourque was named Manchester city attorney at the annual salary of $30,000. This pretty much closed the circle for Loeb, who finally had someone friendly to him in every important city office or commission.

At about this time the Thomson administration named Lieutenant Fradette deputy state fire marshal.

Other New England states were advancing the idea of a regional Presidential primary, but New Hampshire was having none of this. In the final stages of the 1975 session of the General Court a New Hampshire law was passed giving the governor authority to advance the primary one week ahead of any other New England state which advanced its own Presidential primary. Backers of the regional primary constantly cited as its biggest advantage that it would save candidates time and expenses, but *U.S. News and World Report* said: "The real aim is to cut the clout of archconservative New Hampshire publisher William Loeb, whose newspaper—the State's largest—has for years exerted powerful influence on primary results."

Finally, House Majority Leader Thomas P. "Tip"

O'Neill, of Massachusetts, came right out and said it again in the *Boston Globe,* while endorsing legislation to advance the Massachusetts primary. To quote O'Neill: "Basically, why should you let a guy by the name of Loeb, who comes out of the age of McKinley, push his philosophy of the days of the high button shoe? He regulates the New Hampshire primary, and sends out the two leading candidates of each party."

Loeb was becoming almost frantic in his call for a new Senate election in New Hampshire. The matter had gone back to the floor of the Senate by Summer and the Senate Republicans conducted a filibuster which was successfully impeding the matter from ever coming to a vote. Other newspapers were echoing Loeb's cry, mainly on the grounds that it was simply a practical matter to return the contest to New Hampshire—it was tying up the Senate. The Wyman-Durkin dispute was the subject of an eight-column streamer nearly every day on Page One and, finally, with the August Senate recess imminent, John Durkin withdrew his appeal of the New Hampshire Ballot Law Commission ruling and the Senate declared the New Hampshire junior senator's seat vacant. Governor Thomson appointed Norris Cotton to collect a month's pay while the Senate was on a month's vacation.

The New Hampshire General Court had passed a law during its session that a new election for the disputed seat would be held within 45 days of the date the seat was declared vacant and Sept. 16 was set as the date for the special election.

If the Sept. 16 U.S. Senate election in New Hampshire is remembered for nothing else, it will be recalled as the dirtiest political campaign ever conducted in the Granite State.

*"Divide et impere,"* was the philosophy advanced by Niccolo Machiavelli, the ancient political theorist, and Loeb was putting this divide-and-rule idea into practice in his most obtrusive efforts to woo the Franco-American voters. The *Union Leader* carried a column written in French

at least once a week, authored by the wife of a prominent Manchester labor leader. Governor Thomson had directed the state highway commissioner to erect signs proclaiming *"Bienvenue Au New Hampshire"* on all major roads leading into the state, from Maine, Vermont and Massachusetts, as well as from Canada. And, as one of the first shots in the Wyman-Durkin campaign, Loeb began harping on a remark made by Sen. Claiborne Pell (D-R. I.), to the effect that the voter intent had not been clear in New Hampshire because of the large percentage of Franco-American population. Loeb gave this a *Union Leader* headline as follows:

## "Insulting N. H. Franco-Americans"

At some point during the Senate Rules Committee hearings on the Wyman-Durkin dispute, the inference was clearly drawn that Durkin questioned the integrity of the Ballot Law Commission. (At one juncture, Durkin referred to Roger Crowley as a "plain clothesman" for Loeb.) Counsel directly asked Durkin if he trusted the Ballot Law Commission (there are several versions of the actual dialogue), and Durkin is reported to have jocularly replied, "I wouldn't trust the Blessed Trinity." The headline:

## "Durkin Blasts Blessed Trinity"

appeared in the *Union Leader* and again appeared on Page One of a Wyman campaign tabloid newspaper.

On Jan. 26, 1974, William Loeb had stated in a *Union Leader* editorial: ". . . This newspaper will never support Congressman Louis Wyman for the United States Senate." But during July, August and September of 1975, William Loeb conducted a campaign of astonishing vigor backing Louis Wyman for the U.S. Senate seat. And the obvious reason for such devotion was elementary. For the first time in his publishing career, William Loeb did not have one friend among the Congressional delegations from either New Hampshire or Vermont.

Most moves which Loeb made were bad ones. He published picture after picture of Wyman together with Governor Thomson, the idea being to show party unity among the Republicans. But with every picture which was published enmity with Wyman heightened in the western portion of the state where the pulp mill issue had caused thousands of bumper stickers and T-shirts to appear bearing the slogan, "Kill Mel's Mill!"

Loeb harped on the theme that Durkin's supporters had insulted the Franco-Americans and New Hampshire persons of Canadian descent who hadn't been heard from in years openly endorsed Durkin. The "Blessed Trinity" slur angered very many Catholics who felt that if they were to take a course in Sacred Theology, neither William Loeb nor Louis Wyman would be the professor.

Several Democratic Presidential hopefuls had organized support groups in anticipation of the 1976 New Hampshire primary. Durkin declined all offers of help from the candidates themselves, all of whom directed their organizations to assist in the Durkin campaign. Durkin retained as his campaign manager a Nashua native, J. Joseph Grandmaison, who had successfully directed the 1972 McGovern campaign in New Hampshire and had been a winning campaign manager with Massachusetts Gov. Michael Dukakis in 1974. Loeb called Grandmaison a "carpetbagger" which didn't sit too well with anyone who realized that Loeb lived in Massachusetts and voted in Nevada. Nor did it make Loeb any more loved by the Franco-Americans when Loeb assailed one of their number.

Loeb's *Union Leader* was tireless in raising the "carpetbagger" issue, finally settling on Durkin himself, a Massachusetts native. He blamed Durkin for all of the troubles which he, Loeb, saw in the Commonwealth. This inevitably polarized the thousands and thousands of Massachusetts natives, most of whom are Democrats, who have come to live in the "Southern Tier" of New Hampshire, along the Massachusetts border.

Meanwhile, Louie Wyman went on the campaign trail. He was far from effective. For one thing he had Gov. Meldrim Thomson, Jr., with him a good deal of the time—or so the news photographs in the *Union Leader* would lead its readers to believe.

Then too, Wyman had the spectre of Watergate always with him. As a matter of fact, at one juncture in the campaign, Wyman had to take two days off to make another appearance before a grand jury in Washington which was still investigating the awarding of ambassadorships by the Nixon administration. Durkin made capital of this in his campaign publicity.

Grandmaison was spending most of his efforts in getting out the vote. Durkin's campaign fund was aided no small amount by contributions from organized labor. Loeb, who may just as well have been Wyman's campaign manager, particularly stressed labor's participation in the Durkin effort, even though Loeb had always maintained the public posture as labor's best friend—especially since it became public knowledge that he borrowed $2 million through Jimmy Hoffa. Durkin's radio advertising was again most effective and, with more adequate financing, was more widespread.

All the signs were there that Durkin was gaining momentum. But the fact remained that New Hampshire had always been a Republican stronghold. The Democrats feared that, come Election Day, the Republicans would pour out in their usual numbers in the small towns and the city folks would pay scant heed to the voting going on.

During the last week of the campaign, former California Governor Reagan visited Manchester to whoop it up for Wyman. He was introduced by Governor Thomson, and it appeared to most that all he did was whoop it up for the Conservatives. It didn't matter too much, though, because the house was largely "papered" and President Ford was due the very next day; he would conduct the longest motorcade in Presidential history, 138 miles in all, all across the "Southern Tier."

On the day of the Presidential visit, Loeb did not salute the Commander-in-Chief with any "Jerry IS a Jerk" headlines, nor did he contain any more denigrating photographs of Ford which had been taken nearly forty years before. On the morning of the Presidential visit, the *Manchester Union Leader,* in a signed Page One editorial, announced, and told at great length, that the Secret Service was incapable of protecting the President, that the Secret Service was an ineffective organization. Loeb further told his readers not to watch the President but to watch the people around them who might pull guns—as Squeaky Fromme had done just a few days earlier in California— and, in sum, Loeb all but invited every kook in North America to come to New Hampshire for target practice. On that day, the President of the United States wore a bulletproof vest!

Loeb's support of Wyman had reached depths to which perhaps no U.S. newspaper had ever sunk before. On August 21, 1975, there appeared in the *Union Leader* an unsigned letter to the editor, an engraving of which covered a quarter page, one of the most unusual items which has ever found its way into the home-delivered American press. (To reprint this once in this book is even too much, but for those interested it is contained as Appendix E.) The intent was to show the public that this was the type of supporter John Durkin had. After an unusual public outcry of protest, Loeb just wanted to show everyone who was running his newspaper, and he reprinted another, even worse, piece of garbage—again unsigned, naturally—covering another quarter page on September 10. (This letter will not find its way into this book.) The only noteworthy thing about the two letters is their resemblance to the "Canuck letter" which played such a part in the 1972 Muskie for President campaign.

The *N.H. Sunday News* rendered to Wyman the ultimate accolade on the weekend before the special election. The lead editorial was entitled:

### "Wyman—A Very Good Man"

and it said:

"Not in this century has New Hampshire been offered a U.S. Senatorial candidate worthier of its votes than

Louis C. Wyman. His record of five terms in the Congress is replete with examples of distinguished service to his neighbors, his state and the American nation. . . .

"By way of contrast, Mr. Wyman's Democratic opponent, former insurance commissioner John Durkin, was one of the wildest spending bureaucrats in Granite State history . . ."

Funny talk, many people thought, for a newspaper that "would never support Congressman Wyman for the United States Senate."

But if the *N.H. Sunday News* had any effect in swinging any voters into the Wyman column on that particular Sunday it was more than offset further down on the same editorial page. Sunday, Sept. 14, 1975, will be remembered a lot longer, not as the Sunday before the special N.H. Senate election, but as the day Pope Paul VI canonized the first native-born American, Elizabeth Ann Bayley Seton, to the level of sainthood in the hierarchy of the Roman Catholic Church. The associate publisher of the *N.H. Sunday News* and editor-in-chief of the *Union Leader,* Bernard John McQuaid, included a signed editorial of Page 34 of that edition in which he questioned the fact that Blessed Mother Seton was the founder of parochial school education in America. The editorial said:

"... However, we find no authorization for the claim she was 'the mother of parochial school education in America.' The Catholic Encyclopedia Dictionary says a school she tried to start in New York failed. She later founded a 'log cabin school' in Emmitsburg, Md. It is this institution which is bought by UPI as the 'first parochial school in this country.'

"'The founder of parochial Catholic school education in America,' we have been led to believe by the Catholic Encyclopedia and other sources, was Bishop Bernard John McQuaid of Rochester, N.Y., in the 1870's.—B. J. McQ."

The state of New Hampshire was blessed with beautiful weather for early fall on September 16 and the voter turnout was nothing short of astounding. The tradition of apathy towards special elections was shattered as 60 per cent of the registered voters made their way to the polling places, and, when the votes were counted, the result was also astounding:

| | | |
|---|---|---|
| Durkin, d | 140,778 | 53.6% |
| Wyman, r | 113,007 | 43.0% |
| Chimento, a | 8,787 | 3.4% |
| Scatter | 110 | |

Governor Thomson, chairman of the National Conservative Cauncus, appeared on the podium at Wyman headquarters immediately after Wyman had thanked his workers. The governor called for greater party unity among the New Hampshire Republicans. The very next day it was announced that Governor Thomson would be the keynote speaker at the convention of the American Independent Party at Reno, Nev., three nights hence. While in Reno, he would be the houseguest of William Loeb, publisher of the *Manchester Union Leader*.

It was a stunning victory for U.S. Sen. John A. Durkin, and it was the first time since the Democratic Party was founded that New Hampshire had two Democratic U.S. Senators. Durkin had captured all 13 N.H. cities and eight of the state's 10 counties.

For Wyman, the loss was blamed on a number of things. Many saw it as an affront to President Ford, others to Ronald Reagan, and still others to the Thomson-Loeb team. Many felt that Wyman's Watergate connection was to blame, and still others felt that Wyman's bombast after his close call in November, 1974, had had an effect. There were many, many more, however, who felt that the result was a warning to all present office holders that the American public was sick and tired of high prices, an energy crisis and other ills. And there were still other persons who felt that it was a slap at the United States Senate itself which had been unable to solve the minor dilemma of a disputed New Hampshire election when it was faced with the far more serious problems of the world.

# 37

Practically without exception, employes of the Union Leader Corporation, when asked, "What's with William Loeb?" will answer, "He's awfully good to his help." And this analysis, in very many respects, cannot be faulted. While the Consumer Price Index has risen 46.3 per cent over the past six years, the average wage of a Union Leader employe has risen about 66 per cent. The average wage of all categories of employment in Manchester covered by the N.H. Department of Employment Security is $7,659; the average income for a family of four in the Manchester area is $9,904.* The *Union Leader* pays copy editors and advertising salesmen $15,028; reporters and photographers, $14,508; stenographers, $9,802; janitors, $9,152; clerks and typists, $8,918. *Union Leader* employes, members of The Newspaper Guild, also receive hospitalization and health insurance for themselves and their families, wholly paid for by the corporation.

Loeb's public posture has always been that he has been pro-labor, but it is also a fact that, in Manchester at least, William Loeb has never had very much to say about it. (It has been told in earlier pages about how pro-labor Loeb was in his Burlington Publishing Co., Inc. His Vermont newspapers are still non-union.) The Union-Leader Publishing Co., Inc., was thoroughly unionized when William Loeb converted it to the Union Leader Corporation in 1946, and the plant has always been so strongly unionized that any effort to do away with the union structure has been, and still is, entirely out of the question; Loeb—better than most people—knows this. Since it has become public knowledge that Loeb is indebted to the Teamsters' Union pension fund, he never misses a chance to point out that he runs a union newspaper, e.g., letter to the editor of *Newsweek,* July 28, 1975, from William Loeb. But this has

* Source: *Sales Management* magazine annual survey.

not made life any easier for William Loeb. Labor contract negotiations are usually carried on by out-of-town negotiators who are hired for that purpose and they usually let it be known from the outset that the machinery is well-oiled and ready to produce news releases that the Union Leader is having contract troubles. This has been met, more obviously in recent years, by the management query, "Where do we sign?" No better example of this can be found, probably, than the request by The Newspaper Guild for the establishment of a Pension Plan Agreement as part of the Guild's contract for 1975. Loeb's much-heralded profit sharing has not paid any benefits to speak of for over a decade and the Guild asked, and the Union Leader Corp. agreed, to allot one dollar per man per shift in the first year, and two dollars per man per shift in the second year, to go towards a pension plan for Guild members.

In addition, Loeb has earned quite a reputation among his employes as a philanthropist in cases where a particularly distressed employe, or his family, is concerned. There are reports that Loeb has taken care of exceptional hospital or medical bills, and it is known that he has continued the full salary for some persons who had become disabled or ill while in his employ. And this most admirable trait is nothing new, either. It may be recalled that during his earliest days in St. Albans he extended himself to aid the employe with the vision problem.

Loeb demands absolute and consummate loyalty in return for his high wages. No one from the Union Leader Corporation holds, nor does the corporation itself hold, an active membership in any organization which even broaches the subject of journalistic ethics; e.g., the American Newspaper Publishers Association, the American Society of Newspaper Editors, the New England Society of Newspaper Editors, the Associated Press Managing Editors Association, the New England Daily Newspaper Association, or Sigma Delta Chi, the professional journalism society. And it is rare, very rare, indeed, that any employe of the Union Leader Corporation will publicly, or even privately, complain about Loeb's management. Nor will they be caught dead associating with persons who are thought to be on Loeb's list. In the fall of 1974 one employe of the *Union Leader* announced his intentions to run for public office against an incumbent who was of Loeb's stable. A closely guarded—very carefully worded—memorandum appeared on every Union Leader Corporation bulletin board to the effect that Loeb felt that enough employes were serving in public office.

This loyalty (or is it insecurity?) manifests itself most obviously, however, in what appears in the newspaper. The newspaper's writers adhere strictly, even imaginatively, to the Loeb line.

EXAMPLE: During the U.S. Senate deliberations of the disputed Wyman-Durkin election, the reporter assigned to cover these hearings was the man who was usually assigned as head of the State House bureau in Concord. It is widely known that Loeb is an archconservative Republican. The following appeared in a column, "Under the State House Dome," on July 13, 1975, in the *N.H. Sunday News:*

"... INTERESTING TO NOTE that Sen. George McGovern (D-S.D.) and his wife spent this weekend in New Hampshire. . . . In addition to McGovern, the Congressional all-star cast on our Friday night flight home included Senators Muskie and Hathaway of Maine, Congressman O'Neil [sic] (Mass.) and Jim Cleveland (N.H.). All but Cleveland were traveling first class on the taxpayers."

Of course, Cleveland was the only Republican.

EXAMPLE: Less than two weeks after Loeb's editorial in which he told of his vast newspaper experience, which editorial is quoted in full in the prologue to this volume, another *Union Leader* reporter described his own vast newspaper experience in a weekly column which he calls his "Notebook." The theme of the column was the hackneyed New York-is-a-great-place-to-visit idea, but he made sure to include in the column that, not once, but twice during his trip to New York he had gone to see the newspaper for which he once worked, the *New York Herald Tribune,* by the reporter's description, "one of the nation's best daily newspapers." He specified that he went to visit the former home of this newspaper on West 44th Street, again twice. It defies the imagination as to what this reporter was actually looking at because the Herald Tribune Building was between 40th and 41st, west of Seventh Avenue. The only thing along West 44th Street which even resembles a newspaper is the back of *The New York Times.*

No finer instance of how *Union Leader* editors and reporters follow the established Loeb line can be found than that which occurred during August, 1975, concerning Mrs. Betty Ford, wife of the President of the United States, to whose reelection Loeb had already said he was opposed.

Mrs. Ford appeared on the CBS network show, "Sixty Minutes," during which she discussed with Morley Safer the possibility of her daughter, Susan, 18, having an affair. The First Lady said she "wouldn't be surprised" if Susan told her she was actually having an affair, and the First Lady further said: "I think she's a perfectly normal human being like all young girls." She also said, referring to the fact that young people do, in fact, conduct premarital affairs, "After all, they're doing it." The television show was shown during the 9:30–10:30 time segment on Sunday evening, August 10. Loeb's morning *Union Leader* of August 11 featured the four-column Page One headline:

### *President's Wife Is Interviewed*
### Condones Premarital Sex

In the evening editions of the same day, a single-line Page One four-column headline read:

### "President's Wife Condones Premarital Sex"

This was right down Loeb's alley; he couldn't have done better himself. On Page One, Aug. 13, 1975, he had a Page One signed editorial entitled:

## "A Disgrace to the White House"

and it was complete with picture of Mrs. Ford. Loeb was absolutely horrified and said Mrs. Ford's remarks were "the best illustration of why the United States suffers from the moral confusion and misery that it does."

Susan Ford at this time was about to enter her freshman undergraduate year. And what had William Loeb done at this stage in his own life?

Record No. 172 of the Year 1926 of the Town of Petersburg, Rensselaer County, N.Y., shows that on May 29, 1926, William Loeb, Jr., successfully climaxed a romance he had been having with a Smith College instructor by going to that town and getting married. On his marriage certificate, William Loeb, Jr., falsified his age, adding two years, and he falsified his place of residence. His bride-to-be also falsified her age, subtracting some six years, and she also falsified her place of residence. The marriage was dissolved in Nassau County, New York, some five years later, when the then Mrs. Loeb brought and won a divorce libel in N.Y. Supreme Court. The only possible grounds for the award of a divorce in New York State until as late as the 1960's was that adultery on the part of the libelee could be proved beyond a reasonable doubt.

The tragedy of William Loeb is that he has never really been true to himself nor to his readers. His first pronouncement on becoming a publisher in Vermont in 1941 said:

"I consider a newspaper to be the servant of the community whose support it enjoys."

And upon assuming control of the *Union Leader* in November, 1946, Loeb told his readers:

"At this time, it is appropriate here to repeat the great words of Frank Knox and John A. Muehling, which have so long appeared in the masthead of this paper, and which so well express the principles for which the newspaper stands.

"'This paper will be the organ of no man, or set of

men. As an institution, it will belong to New Hampshire and will attempt, to the full extent of its power and ability, to serve solely the highest interests of the state.' "

It is true that, conducting general circulation newspapers in the manner and fashion in which he has, William Loeb has become a powerful man. He has made quite a few men and he has broken quite a few men. But he has shattered the body politic.

And it is safe and fair to say that in his career as a newspaper publisher, William Loeb has made a lot of friends and he has made a lot of enemies. He has lost a lot of friends, but he has never lost an enemy.

# Epilogue

To many persons, Manchester, N.H., may not appear to be one of those "alabaster cities" about which we are taught to sing at an early age; but there is little doubt that David Hume was correct when, in *Essays (1741–1742)*, he wrote: "Beauty in things exists in the mind which contemplates them."

Manchester is a fine city, lived in and loved by fine people. It has seen crisis come and seen crisis go; it was here long before the advent of William Loeb and it will be here long after he has gone. Manchester has taken all that Publisher Loeb can offer in the way of denial of the Constitutional right of the citizens, the abrogation of news. Those who have catered to his whims for their own personal betterment or aggrandizement will, quite naturally, miss him. The more knowledgeable, the more perceptive, the more deeply and truly concerned with the community's welfare—as if to "crown their good with brotherhood"—sincerely and reverently offer a prayer, a paraphrase of one of the quotations mentioned by one of the first reporters, a man named Luke: "Father, forgive him for he knows not what he does."

Newspapermen everywhere, except in Manchester, N.H. —and even a few in Manchester, N.H.—amend this prayer with the simple observation: "He knows not what he does because he doesn't know what in the hell he's doing."

The provincial assembly of Massachusetts said in a 1789 resolution: "The Liberty of the Press is a great Bulwark of the Liberty of the People; It is therefore the incumbent Duty of those who are constituted the Guardians of the People's Rights to defend and maintain it."

Daniel Webster, addressing the Festival of the Sons of New Hampshire in the Hall of the Fitchburg Railroad Company in Boston on Nov. 7, 1849, said: "In regard to the military character of her Revolutionary heroes, and her early statesmen, and in regard to every thing which was done, or ought to have been done, or was expected to be done, to bring New Hampshire honorably and respectably into the great circle of our Union, Gentlemen, I leave this all for abler tongues, fresher recollections, and more persuasive accents. I sit down myself, filled with profound veneration for the character of my native State, and acknowledging to her my own personal debt for her culture and nurture, and determined, so far as in me lies, to transmit the sense of that obligation to those who shall come after me."

# Appendix A

A glossary of some of the names, terms and phrases which have appeared in William Loeb's newspapers to describe public figures and institutions:

**Bella S. Abzug,** Congresswoman from New York: "A Prize Jerk," "The pot-bellied, porcine-featured Congresswoman."

**Dean Acheson,** U.S. Secretary of State: "Not much higher than Benedict Arnold."

**Sherman Adams,** governor of New Hampshire and Presidential assistant: "Shermy Wormy," "Ajax Adams," "Hatchet man," "Government by crony," "Like putting a freshman in the World's Series," "That prize political stupid bungler," "Vindictiveness known."

**George Aiken** and **Ralph Flanders,** U.S. Senators from Vermont: "Those disgraces to the State of Vermont."

**Warren Austin,** U.S. Senator from Vermont and U.S. ambassador to the United Nations: "A teacup mudslinger," "A fatuous representative of a fatuous policy."

**Perkins Bass,** Congressman from New Hampshire: "International-minded millionaire," "N.H.'s Shame," "Pontius Pilate," "A miserable sight to behold," "Personified idealism."

**Joseph R. Biden,** U.S. Senator from Delaware: "Stupid, conceited jackass."

**James C. Cleveland,** Congressman from New Hampshire: "An inveterate egghead and liberal."

**James B. Conant,** president of Harvard University: "An educated ignoramus."

**Norris Cotton,** U.S. Senator from New Hampshire: "Mass of second-rate double-talk."

**John Sloan Dickey,** president of Dartmouth College: "Inept and incompetent leadership."

**William O. Douglas,** U.S. Supreme Court justice: "Recklessness that demands censure and discipline."

**Dudley W. Dudley,** representative to the N.H. General Court: "Deadly Dudley," "Mrs. Fuddy Duddy," "Dum-Dum Dudley."

**John Foster Dulles,** U.S. Secretary of State: "Dulles, Duller, Dullest."

**Lane Dwinell,** governor of New Hampshire: "Dwindle Dwinell."

**Dwight D. Eisenhower,** President of the United States: "Dopey Dwight," "That stinking hypocrite," "Playboy President," "Fake Republican," "As much backbone and substance as a ribbon of toothpaste," "Fatuous—fat-headed," "A slick general on the political make."

**Sam Ervin,** U.S. Senator from North Carolina: "Senator Claghorn."

**Ralph Flanders,** U.S. Senator from Vermont: "All the sap isn't in the trees," "Fatuous Flanders."

**Betty B. Ford,** wife of the President of the United States: "A Disgrace to the White House," "Babblin' Betty."

**Gerald R. Ford,** President of the United States: "Jerry the Jerk," "Jerry IS a Jerk!"

**Gerald R. Ford** and **Nelson A. Rockefeller,** President and Vice President of the United States, respectively: "Lemon + Lemon = Bitter Lemon."

**J. William Fulbright,** U.S. Senator from Arkansas: "Fulbright the Despicable."

**Barry Goldwater,** U.S. Senator from Arizona: "A phony."

**William S. Green,** deputy attorney general of New Hampshire and chairman of the State Board of Education: "Buster Brown."

**Graham Greene,** British author: "A rump-sprung Catholic."

**Hugh Gregg,** governor of New Hampshire: "That brazen boy."

**Rt. Rev. Charles Hall,** bishop of the Episcopal Diocese of New Hampshire: "Needs self-searching."

**Learned Hand,** U.S. jurist: "Not learned, just bunk," "Peculiarly addle-headed."

**Seymour Hersh,** investigative reporter for *The New York Times:* "The ineffable ass."

**Oliver Wendell Holmes,** Chief Justice of the United States: "Preposterous old phony," "Old goat."

**Hubert Humphrey,** Vice President of the United States and U.S. Senator from Minnesota: "Hubert Horatio Hornblower."

**Henry M. Jackson,** U.S. Senator from Washington: "A boob."

**Lyndon B. Johnson,** President of the United States: "Snake Oil Lyndon."

**Jacqueline B. Kennedy,** wife of the President of the United States: "Unspeakable—uneatable."

**John F. Kennedy,** President of the United States: "Calamity Jack," "No. 1 Liar in the U.S.A."

**Robert F. Kennedy,** U.S. Senator from New York and Attorney General of the U.S.: "A copperhead."

**Rev. Msgr. Philip J. Kenney,** episcopal vicar for community affairs of the Roman Catholic Diocese of Manchester: "The trouble-making clergyman," "Regards the church as his personal plaything."

**John King,** governor of New Hampshire: "King John."

**Rev. Dr. Martin Luther King, Jr.,** civil rights leader: "A pious, pompous fraud."

**Henry M. Kissinger,** U.S. Secretary of State: "Kissinger the Kike?"

**James Langley,** publisher of the *Concord, N.H., Monitor:* "Old Sourpuss."

**Richard W. Leonard,** candidate for governor of New Hampshire: "Almost absurd," "Criminal lawyer."

**George C. Marshall,** U.S. Secretary of State: "Bungler Marshall," "Compared to Gen. George Marshall, Benedict Arnold was a piker."

**Thurgood Marshall,** U.S. Supreme Court justice: "Most unfortunate appointment."

**Eugene McCarthy,** U.S. Senator from Minnesota: "A charming non sequitur," "Skunk's skunk's skunk."

**George S. McGovern,** U.S. Senator from South Dakota: "Yellow," "Georgie Chutzpah."

**Thomas J. McIntyre,** U.S. Senator from New Hampshire: "Ballot Bagman," "Landryman," "Second Story Man," "Cheap political chisler."

**Malcolm McLane,** mayor of Concord, N.H., and candidate for governor of New Hampshire: "The Prince of Privilege."

**Susan N. McLane,** representative to the N.H. General Court: "Political opportunist."

**Robert McNamara,** U.S. Secretary of Defense: "Blubbering Bob."

**Krishna Menon,** Defense Minister of India: "True color—Red."

**Chester E. Merrow,** Congressman from New Hampshire: "Downright cowardly."

**Edmund S. Muskie,** U.S. Senator from Maine: "Flip-flop Muskie," "Moscow Muskie," "A phony."

**Maurice Murphy,** U.S. Senator from New Hampshire: "'Charlie McCarthy to (Gov. Wesley) Powell's 'Edgar Bergen.'"

**Jawaharlal Nehru,** Prime Minister of India: "Apostle of appeasement," "Cold-war middleman," "Enterprising opportunist."

**New Hampshire General Court Representatives:** "Same old bums."

**David L. Nixon,** N.H. State Senate president and candidate for governor of New Hampshire: "Devious Dave," "Mr. Clean Plays Dirty."

**Richard M. Nixon,** President of the United States: "Keyhole Dick," "Tricky Dicky," "The Great Devaluator."

**Jack Paar,** television master of ceremonies: "TV's Noisy Nuisance."

**Walter Peterson,** governor of New Hampshire: "High Priest of Permissiveness."

**Politicians:** "Vanished eloquence," "Politicians today are not only evil and corrupt, but cheap and banal; even the honest are dull."

**Wesley Powell,** governor of New Hampshire: "Wesley One-Note," "Too big for his britches," "Peculiar, vindictive, highly egotistical," "Dog in the Manger."

**Most Rev. Ernest J. Primeau,** bishop of the Roman Catholic Diocese of Manchester: "A throwback to a less enlightened era."

**Nelson A. Rockefeller,** Vice President of the United States: "Wife Swapper," "Home wrecker," "Kennedy's alter ego, errand boy and all-round flunky," "Nelse the Knife."

**George Romney,** governor of Michigan: "Chihuahua George."

**Leverett Saltonstall,** U.S. Senator from Massachusetts: "That fatuous ass."

**Margaret Chase Smith,** U.S. Senator from Maine: "Moscow Maggie," "State of Maine's liability."

**Harry V. Spanos,** N.H. State Senate vice president and candidate for governor of New Hampshire: "Midnight Harry."

**Harold Stassen,** governor of Minnesota: "Hand-out Harold," "Dunderhead," "Brother, how dumb can you get?"

**Adlai Stevenson,** governor of Illinois and U.S. ambassador to the United Nations: "Jigadier Brindle Stevenson," "Assinine."

**Achmed Sukarno,** President of the Republic of Indonesia: "No friend of ours," "Cheap little Asiatic leader."

**Charles W. Tobey,** U.S. Senator from New Hampshire: "Aging commissar of a Socialist New Hampshire," "Demagogue straddler," "How pious and how phony!"

**Harry S Truman,** President of the United States: "The little dictator," "Reign of ignorance," "General Incompetence," "The Maharaja of Washington."

**Al Ullman,** Chairman of the House Ways and Means Committee: "Another prize jerk."

**United Nations:** "Stupid as well as immoral," "Headquarters for spies and espionage agents," "The House That Hiss Built," "Defunct, futile organization," "Glorified debating society."

**U.S. Congress:** "This pack of jackals," "Stupid, treasonous cowards."

**U.S. House Judiciary Committee:** "Rodino's Rabblerousers."

**U.S. Secret Service:** "Keystone Cops."

**Robert W. Upton,** U.S. Senator from New Hampshire: "Too old."

**Barbara Walters,** co-host of the NBC-TV "Today" Show: "A shameless huckster," "A hussy."

**Tom Wicker,** associate editor of *The New York Times:* "Un-American."

**Peter Woodbury,** U.S. Circuit Court justice: "In favor of smut," "A judicial robe is an unlikely vestment for a war dance."

# Appendix B

As an aftermath of a Presidential conference on narcotics in December, 1969, the Manchester newspapers carried an unusual series of stories all directed at Miss Meg Peterson, 15, daughter of Gov. and Mrs. Walter Peterson. Miss Peterson had been interviewed at the Washington, D.C., conference, which was attended by the states' governors and their families. The letter which is reproduced on the following page appeared as a paid advertisement on Page One of the *Manchester Union Leader* of Dec. 6, 1969 and on Page One of the *New Hampshire Sunday News* of Dec. 7, 1969.

Massachusetts

There are just a
few more than 70 pupils in the grade school,
where they have instituted prayers under what

AN EDITORIAL                  Page 11

...... was man a ...,
curred

However in an appar-
effort to substantiate Govern.
Peterson's implication that the
Union Leader yesterday distorted his stand on the incident a...

**STATE OF NEW HAMPSHIRE**
· CONCORD 03301

WALTER PETERSON
GOVERNOR

December 5, 1969

Mr. William Loeb, Publisher
Manchester Union Leader
Manchester, New Hampshire

Dear Mr. Loeb:

I am writing you instead of one of your employees
because I know that no attack such as the one on my
daughter Meg that appeared in this morning's issue is
published in the Manchester Union Leader without your
knowledge and approval.

You will also note that I write you not only
as Governor of New Hampshire, but also as a private
citizen who is the father of two teenage children in
the public schools, and as a parent who is as seriously
concerned with the problems of youth as anyone could be.

Any thoughtful reader of your newspaper is aware of
your continued efforts to destroy me politically through
distorted news stories and vicious editorials. You and I
know, Mr. Loeb, that this campaign against me is caused
by your inability to force me to dance to your tune. I
respect your right to attack me and my programs to improve
the quality of life in New Hampshire. I shall leave it
to the people of New Hampshire to assess my performance.

I must object to your despicable tactic of attacking
my 15 year old daughter Meg as a means of getting at me.
This morning's story distorting the truth is a new low in
journalism, even for your newspaper. I am fair game, Mr.
Loeb, but I must ask you to stop picking on my 15 year old
daughter who, after all, is only a young girl with many
years of life ahead.

Why not pick on someone your own size.

Walter Peterson
Walter Peterson
Governor

(This space has been paid for by Walter Peterson, Peterborough)

# Appendix C

Reproduced on the following page is the now famous "Canuck letter" which appeared on Page 19, the first page of the second section, of the *Manchester Union Leader* of Feb. 24, 1972. The author of this letter has never been found.

Feb 17, 1972
Deerfield Beach
Fla.

MR Loeb—
MANCHESTER GUARDIAN
MANCHESTER
New Hampshire

Dear Mr Loeb — I saw you on TV The other
NIGHT and my friends father gets your
newspaper. We went to Ft. Lauderdale to meet
Sen Muskie — we were right beside him at
Seal house, when one of the men asked him
what did he know about blacks and the
problems with them — he didn't have any in
Maine — A MAN with the Senator said "No—
not blacks but we have CANNOCKS

What did he mean? We asked.
Mr Muskie laughed, and said
come to New England and see.
could you write me the
answer. OR print it in your
paper — my friend gets it from
you — Thank you.

PAUL MORRISON
DeerField Beach
Fla. 33064

# Appendix D

The lead editorial which appeared on Page 34 of the *New Hampshire Sunday News* of Sept. 2, 1973 is reproduced on the following page, together with the editorial page masthead for the newspaper, directly under which the editorial was published.

**UNION LEADER CORPORATION**

**WILLIAM LOEB**
President and Publisher

George E. Connell    B. J. McQuaid
General Manager    Editor-in-Chief

William J. Montague, Gen. Mgr. 1948-1960

---

**N. H. SUNDAY NEWS**

**B. J. McQUAID**
Associate Publisher

Joseph W. McQuaid
Sunday Editor

D. F. Ruemenapp
City Editor

Robert Ellis
Comptroller

Robert Lapointe, Circulation Director

---

Sawyer-Ferguson-Walker Co., Inc.
Publisher's Advertising Representatives

North American Newspaper Alliance
Member Audit Bureau of Circulation
Associated Press, UPI, NEA Service

Subscription rates: Single copy 50 cents. By
carrier or mail $25.00 per year in advance; 6
months, $13.00; 3 months, $7.00; monthly, $2.50.

Second Class Postage
Paid at Manchester, N. H.

Make checks payable to the
UNION LEADER CORPORATION
Box 780, Manchester, N. H. 03105
Telephone all departments: Manchester 668-4321

## Kissinger The Kike?

Henry Kissinger, once a darling of the leftists, is now the target of a bitter barrage from the liberal news media because of his acceptance of an appointment as Mr. Nixon's Secretary of State. All week the liberals were excoriating him as a deep-dyed villain. One of the commonest complaints against him was that he is not only a Jew, but speaks with a German-Jewish accent! This charge was leveled over an interlocking· cabal of TV networks and newspapers which are themselves owned and operated largely by Jews.

Typical was a piece by William V. Shannon, an editor of the N.Y. Times, which is owned by the Jew, Sulzberger. Shannon wrote that Kissinger has helped President Nixon to bring the United States down to its "present constitutional and moral crisis." Both Nixon and Kissinger, Shannon reported, are lacking "in ethical restraint . . . and innate respect for constitutional order."

Kissinger "covets power," he bugs reporters' phones, his former appointments secretary was deputy head of the White House "plumbers." On, on, infinitum.

Tuesday night Martin Agronsky, another Jew, picked up the Shannon column on his nightly news panel over the Public Broadcasting System —N.H. Channel 11. Agronsky quoted some of the most obnoxious allegations by Shannon. However the host of the panel was nonplussed. Both his panelists, though non-Jews, revealed themselves as long time and continuing friends and admirers of the Jew, Kissinger.

# Appendix E

Page 24 of the *Manchester Union Leader* of Aug. 21, 1975 was headlined, "Another Page of Your Letters." Occupying one-quarter of that page was the letter to the editor which is reproduced on the following page. Another letter, far more vulgar and containing language even more obscene, was published in the *Manchester Union Leader* of Sept. 11, 1975, in much the same fashion.

Lou

Why you fucking idiotic massachusetts bastard, who are you to tell us, who will do more for our state, just because Wyman is an by pierenced crook, does not mean that Durkin can't learn. Wyman has filled his pants with enough crooked money to last him the rest of his crooked life, let Durkin get some of it. also fuck you republican ass hole, have you got Hoffa on ice at your crooked Pride crossing home

this is not for publication

(As a rule we do not print unsigned letters but since this attacks only Publisher Loeb and he has given permission to run it, we are printing this letter as an example of Mr. Durkin's support—EDITORS.)

# Bibliography

BENSON, ALLAN L. *Daniel Webster*. New York: Cosmopolitan Book Corporation, 1929.

BISHOP, JOSEPH BUCKLIN. *Theodore Roosevelt and His Time*. New York: Charles Scribner's Sons, 1920 (2 volumes).

BLOOD, GRACE HOLBROOK. *Manchester on the Merrimack*. Manchester: Cummings, 1948.

BOWERS, CLAUDE G. *Beveridge and the Progressive Era*. New York: The Literary Guild, 1932.

BRADLEY, DAVID. *The Journal of a Johnny-come-lately*. Hanover: Dartmouth Press, 1957.

CONNECTICUT COLLEGE FOR WOMEN. *Koine*. New London: Connecticut College for Women, 1920.

FORSTER, ARNOLD, AND EPSTEIN, BENJAMIN R. *The Trouble-Makers*. Garden City: Doubleday & Co., Inc., 1952.

FRIEDMAN, LEE M. *Early American Jews*. Cambridge: Harvard University Press, 1934.

HAGEDORN, HERMANN. *The Roosevelt Family of Sagamore Hill*. New York: Macmillan, 1954.

HAGEDORN, HERMANN. *The Theodore Roosevelt Treasury*. New York: Putnam, 1957.

HARVARD UNIVERSITY. *Quinquennial Catalogue of the Law School of Harvard University*. Cambridge: The Law School, 1935.

HEALY, PAUL F. *Cissy*. Garden City: Doubleday & Co., Inc., 1966.

JAMES, RALPH C., AND JAMES, ESTELLE DINERSTEIN. *Hoffa and the Teamsters*. Princeton: D. Van Nostrand Co., Inc., 1965.

JENKS, LELAND HAMILTON. *Our Cuban Colony*. New York: Vanguard Press, 1928.

KOENIG, LOUIS W. *The Invisible Presidency*. New York: Rinehart & Co., Inc., 1960.

LEVINGER, RABBI LEE J. *The History of the Jews in the United*

*States.* Cincinnati: Union of American Hebrew Congregations, 2nd Revised Edition, 1935.

LORANT, STEFAN. *The Life and Times of Theodore Roosevelt.* Garden City: Doubleday & Co., Inc., 1959.

LYON, PETER. *Eisenhower, Portrait of the Hero.* Boston: Little, Brown & Co., 1974.

MORISON, ELTING E. *The Letters of Theodore Roosevelt.* Cambridge: Harvard University Press, 1951 (8 volumes).

ROOSEVELT, THEODORE. "The Battle of San Juan Hill." *The Roosevelt Book.* New York: Charles Scribner's Sons, 1904.

ROOSEVELT, THEODORE. *The Rough Riders.* New York: Charles Scribner's Sons.

ROOSEVELT, THEODORE, AND LODGE, HENRY CABOT. *Selections from the Correspondence of Theodore Roosevelt and Henry Cabot Lodge, 1884–1918.* New York: Charles Scribner's Sons, 1925 (2 volumes).

SHERIDAN, WALTER. *The Fall and Rise of Jimmy Hoffa.* New York: Saturday Review Press, 1972.

SORENSON, THEODORE C. *Kennedy.* New York: Harper & Row, 1965.

STATE OF NEW HAMPSHIRE. *Manual for the General Court.* Concord: N. H. Department of State, 1933, 1935, 1937, 1939, 1941, 1943, 1945, 1947, 1949, 1951, 1953, 1955, 1957, 1959, 1961, 1963, 1965, 1967, 1969, 1971, 1973, 1975.

SWANBERG, W. A. *Citizen Hearst.* New York: Charles Scribner's Sons, 1961.

THE HOTCHKISS SCHOOL. *Misch, Volume XXVIII.* Lakeville, Conn.: The Hotchkiss School, 1923.

THORP, L. ASHTON. *Manchester of Yesterday.* Manchester: Granite State Press, 1939.

VEBLEN, ERIC PAUL. *Newspaper impact in election campaigns: the case of two New England states.* Ann Arbor, Mich.: University Microfilms, 1969.

WALL ST. JOURNAL. *The Press.* New York: Dow Jones, 1972.

WEBSTER, DANIEL. *The Writings and Speeches of Daniel Webster, In Eighteen Volumes, National Edition.* Boston: Little, Brown & Co., 1903.

WHITE, THEODORE. *The Making of a President, 1960.* New York: Atheneum, 1961.

WHITE, THEODORE. *The Making of a President, 1964.* New York: Atheneum, 1965.

WHITE, THEODORE. *The Making of a President, 1968.* New York: Atheneum, 1969.

WHITE, THEODORE. *The Making of a President, 1972.* New York: Atheneum, 1973.

WILLIAMS COLLEGE. *The Gulielsmensian.* Williamstown, Mass.: Williams College, 1927.